POPULAR CULTURE

POPULAR CULTURE

Introductory Perspectives

Third Edition

MARCEL DANESI

ROWMAN & LITTLEFIELD
Lanham • Boulder • New York • London

Published by Rowman & Littlefield
A wholly owned subsidiary of The Rowman & Littlefield Publishing Group, Inc.
4501 Forbes Boulevard, Suite 200, Lanham, Maryland 20706
www.rowman.com

Unit A, Whitacre Mews, 26-34 Stannary Street, London SE11 4AB, United Kingdom

British Library Cataloguing in Publication Information Available

Library of Congress Cataloging-in-Publication Data

Danesi, Marcel, 1946-
  Popular culture : introductory perspectives / Marcel Danesi. — Third edition.
    pages cm
  Includes bibliographical references and index.
  ISBN 978-1-4422-4216-6 (cloth : alk. paper) — ISBN 978-1-4422-4217-3 (pbk. : alk. paper) — ISBN 978-1-4422-4218-0 (electronic) 1. Popular culture.
I. Title.
  HM621.D36 2015
  306—dc23

                                                                        2015000647

♾™ The paper used in this publication meets the minimum requirements of American National Standard for Information Sciences—Permanence of Paper for Printed Library Materials, ANSI/NISO Z39.48-1992.

Printed in the United States of America

CONTENTS

PREFACE

Popular forms of entertainment have always existed. In his *Historia*, Herodotus (circa 485–425 BCE) wrote about amusing spectacles and songs that he encountered as he traveled the ancient world, commenting that they seemed rather odd. Today, amusing spectacles and popular songs are everywhere. Together with various kinds of television programs, movies, YouTube videos, changing lifestyle trends, fads, and the like they make up what is called *popular culture*, a culture that is everywhere in modern urbanized societies, sustained by electronic media and digital platforms. How did it come about? What is it? Why do we hate to love it and love to hate it? What has happened to "high culture"? Is it hidden away in the libraries of academies and conservatories and staged for an exclusive group of people?

These are the kinds of questions that implicitly guided the writing of this book. In a world that is managed by those who hold the levers of media and digital power, it is little wonder that the study of the relations between the media and popular culture has been flourishing in several disciplines, including psychology, anthropology, sociology, and cultural studies. Many scholars seek to give ideological, political, or social explanations of the phenomenon. Some have attempted to explore the unconscious structures of the psyche that undergird the appeal and lure of pop culture. The purpose of this book is to look at the explosion of pop culture through the lens of history, focusing on the relationship between the media stages for the delivery of pop culture and the contents and forms of pop culture itself. Needless to say, the exploration is based on my own subjective interpretations. So, it is bound to leave gaps, venture into the speculative, and be somewhat selective. I have tried to cast as wide a net as possible, so as to offer the reader as complete a menu of ideas and analyses as is possible within two covers. And, of course, the study of pop culture is not a precise science, so treatments such as this one are themselves open to differing interpretations. I believe that the ultimate purpose of such a treatment is to open up debate. If I have done that, I will feel that the writing has been worthwhile.

I have tailored this book for the general reader, and especially for students taking beginning courses in cultural studies or in related fields such as semiotics, psychology, mythology, education, literary studies, sociology, cultural anthropology, communication studies, and media analysis. In all chapters, I have used a historical framework to introduce the subject matter, leading to various analytical perspectives. To facilitate its reading, I have avoided making constant references to the technical literature. The works that have informed my various commentaries, descriptions, and analyses are listed at the back. I have also used a simple writing style and have made absolutely no assumptions about any prior technical knowledge on the part of the reader. A convenient glossary of technical terms is also included at the back.

This is the third edition of the book. I had no idea when I wrote it for use in my own classes that it would be adopted by other instructors in universities across North America. I have revised it according to the many insightful comments made to me by my colleagues directly or through the publisher. The revision has been extensive in parts, taking into account the rise and dominance of the digital global village as a new context for the delivery of pop culture. The first three chapters introduce key theoretical and historical facts and ideas, including their expressions in print, radio, recordings, cinema, television, the Internet, and so on. Chapter 3 is completely new, dealing with the business of pop culture. Although I had avoided this topic in the past, preferring to focus on the content of the popular imagination, I now realize that the commercial part of pop culture intersects with its content and thus cannot be avoided. Identifying the distinguishing characteristics of pop culture necessarily involves understanding their association with commercial products, the business of changing technologies, and the marketplace changes that invariably affect the content and delivery of pop culture forms (and vice versa). The remaining chapters discuss the synergy between pop culture, mass communications technologies, and the mass media, along with the role of advertising in the rise and spread of pop culture. Of these, chapter 11 on digital culture is completely new. The last chapter then pulls together the various thematic threads weaved throughout the previous chapters, offering an overall assessment of the pop culture phenomenon. Finally, I have added an appendix of exercises and discussion topics that can be used optionally in any classroom environment or for personal reasons in order to increase the book's pedagogical usefulness.

I should mention from the very outset that I love many aspects of pop culture, no matter how crass they can sometimes be. It is liberating to know that entertainment can be as much a part of everyday life as anything else, including religious rituals and serious art (whatever that is). One does not preclude the other. On the other hand, I also feel that there must be a balance between entertainment and serious artistic engagement, between distraction and philosophical reflection. It is that balance that will be the target of my concluding remarks.

ACKNOWLEDGMENTS

I thank Leanne Silverman of Rowman & Littlefield for suggesting a third edition of the book and for all her patience during the rewriting phase. I must also thank the many students I have taught for their feedback and insights. I am particularly grateful to Stacy Costa, Vanessa Compagnone, Mariana Bockarova, and my grandchildren, Sarah and Alex De Sousa. Thanks!

1

WHAT IS POP CULTURE?

*The bosses of our mass media, press, radio, film and television, suc-
ceed in their aim of taking our minds off disaster.*

—Ernst Fischer (1899–1972)

In 1923, a landmark event occurred, changing American society radically. The event was a Broadway musical, *Running Wild*, which helped
turn a sexually suggestive dance called the Charleston into a craze for the
young (and the young at heart) throughout the nation. It was evidence
that America had started to yearn for a new, carefree, open, nontraditional
popular form of culture. This yearning was symbolized by a dance that
society's elders, politicians, and religious institutions condemned as vulgar
and crude. This was captured skillfully by the 2002 movie *Chicago* (based
on the 1975 Broadway musical).

But the condemnation could not stop its allure to common people
(especially young persons), as *Running Wild* had predicted. Burlesque and
vaudeville theaters, speakeasies (Prohibition-era night clubs), and dance
halls cropped up in the 1920s to satisfy America's desire to freely express
itself sexually in public. The 1920s came to be called, appropriately, the
Roaring Twenties. It was the decade when *pop culture*, as we now call it,
became a new type of recreational culture and a huge business. By the
1930s, it spread to all corners of American society and to other parts of the
world as well. It could not be curtailed, despite the severity of the legislative
measures taken, from Prohibition to censorship in various forms and guises.
It was then, and is now, unstoppable as a form of culture that appeals to our
corporeal selves, challenging moral stodginess and aesthetic pretentiousness,
while entertaining us with its earthiness. Because of its populist grassroots,

pop culture has been a primary driving force behind social, economic, and even political change since its appearance, simultaneously triggering an unprecedented society-wide, and worldwide, debate about the relation between art, entertainment, aesthetics, spectacle, and "true culture" that is still an ongoing one.

The purpose of this opening chapter is to trace the origins and evolutionary tendencies of pop culture, discussing its basic features, its close relation to the media and mass communications technologies, and how it can be decoded (or at the very least recognized as distinctive from other forms of culture). Along with the next two chapters, this chapter is designed to set the stage for discussing the expressive manifestations of pop culture through various media stages and platforms.

DEFINING POPULAR CULTURE

What is *pop culture*? The term is not as easy to define as it might seem at first blush. Let's start with a working definition of *culture*. Most anthropologists would define culture as a means of organizing and stabilizing communal life through specific beliefs, rituals, rites, performances, art forms, symbols, language, clothing, food, music, dance, and any other mode of human expressive, intellectual, and communicative behavior that is associated with a group of people at a particular period of time. In Western tradition, it is common to subdivide culture into *high* and *low*, according to historically based perceptions associated with aesthetic movements. High culture is considered to be a form of culture that purportedly has a more profound import on human life than does low culture, which is seen as simply recreational and perhaps even base. *Pop culture* alludes, on the other hand, to a form of culture that makes little, if any, such categorical distinctions. Its emergence in the 1920s was due, in large part, to unexpected affluence, which gave people in the mass, regardless of class or educational background, considerable buying power. Its spread was made possible by an ever-expanding and ever-reinforcing media-technology-business partnership. Since then, it has played a pivotal role in the overall evolution of American society (and virtually every other modern society). This is why cultural historians now tend to designate historically significant periods of social change in the modern era with terms such as the *hippie era*, the *disco era*, the *punk era*, the *hip-hop era*, and so on—all of which are references to major musical trends within pop culture. These designations stand beside political and technological characterizations such as the *Kennedy era*, the

Nixon era, the *Bush era*, the *Obama era*, the *television era*, the *Facebook era*, the *text-messaging era*, and the like.

Culture

The term *culture* requires further commentary. Essentially, it is a system of symbolic and expressive structures that a particular group of people has developed to enhance solidarity, understanding, and transmission of knowledge. The American anthropologist Franz Boas (1858–1942) claimed that culture shapes how people perceive reality. Known as *cultural relativism*, his theory was espoused by several of his students at Columbia University in the 1920s and 1930s. Edward Sapir (1884–1939) sought to determine the extent to which the language of a culture shaped the thought patterns of its users. Margaret Mead (1901–1978) wanted to unravel how cultural child-rearing practices influenced the behavior and temperament of individuals. And Ruth Benedict (1887–1948) argued that every culture developed its canons of morality and lifestyle that largely influenced how individuals viewed themselves and the world. By the time children can talk, Benedict suggested, they have become creatures of their culture—its habits are their habits, its beliefs are their beliefs, its challenges are their challenges.

The Polish-born British anthropologist Bronislaw Malinowski (1884–1942) contended that cultures originated to provide creative strategies for solving physical and moral problems that all humans face, no matter how divergent they might seem. Each strategy is an interpretation of reality. The British anthropologist Alfred Radcliffe-Brown (1881–1955) showed, for instance, that even an emotional response like weeping constitutes a culturally influenced behavior. Among the Andaman Islanders in the east Bay of Bengal he found that weeping was not primarily an expression of joy or sorrow, but rather a response to social situations characterizing such events as peacemaking, marriage, and the reunion of long-separated intimates. Weeping was, therefore, partly spontaneous, partly learned. In weeping together, the people renewed their ties of solidarity.

Pop Culture

In the history of human cultures, pop culture stands out as atypical, since it is not tied to any particular folk or artistic traditions. In fact, it often rejects, ignores, or adapts these traditions. Pop culture has always been highly appealing for this very reason, since it arises from new trends and needs, constantly renewing itself. It can be produced at any time by anyone, not just by an elite class of artists and cognoscenti. It is thus populist, unpredictable, and ephemeral, reflecting the ever-changing tastes of one generation after another. As American composer Stephen Sondheim has aptly quipped: "How many people feel strongly about Gilbert and Sullivan today compared to those who felt strongly in 1890?" (cited in the *International Herald Tribune* Paris, 20 June 1989). To some critics, this implies that pop culture is a commodity culture, producing trends that have the same kind of market value as do manufactured commodities, satisfying momentary and fleeting whims. The French semiotician Roland Barthes (1915–1980) saw the American and European form of popular culture that had spread broadly in the 1940s and 1950s as a "bastard form of mass culture" beset by "humiliated repetition" and thus by "new books, new programs, new films, news items, but always the same meaning" (Barthes 1975: 24).

There is little doubt that pop culture trends, like commodities, have fleeting value. But it is also true that it provides a space for creativity to be expressed by virtually anyone. It is a mirror of human needs. It is both cathartic and empowering, allowing common people to laugh at themselves, to gain recreation through music, dance, stories, and other forms of expression. Before the advent of pop culture, people sought entertainment through carnivalesque forms of entertainment, which typically existed alongside religious feasts. Pop culture is basically an outlet for recreation, designed to appeal to our fun-loving side. Admittedly, most of pop culture is a commodity culture. And this is why it is short lived and era specific. But within the commodity mix there has always been the artistic wheat that rises above the chaff. The question of whether or not pop culture works are "true works of true art" is a moot one. A work of art is something that people want to pass on to subsequent generations because they sense in it something of value. And, in fact, various works in the areas of jazz and blues are now classified as art by musical historians because they strike a resounding chord within people to this day. They are studied in conservatories alongside classical music.

The Analogy of Pop Art

The term *popular culture* may go back considerably in time, as some historians suggest. But it came to the forefront after the *pop art* (popular art) movement that took shape in the late 1950s, principally in the United States and Great Britain. Many of the works of those artists were satirical or playful, in contrast to what they considered to be unnecessarily abstruse artistic forms, and emphasized the role of everyday commercial life in common people's experience. They thus validated the experiences of common people living in a modern urban society. Pop artists represented scenes and objects from within mass consumerist culture, sometimes with actual consumer products (soup cans, comic books, detergents, and the like) as props in their sculptures. The movement began as a reaction against expressionism, an art movement of the 1940s and 1950s that emphasized forms in themselves rather than the realistic representation of external reality. Art critics and academics loved expressionism; common people ignored it. Pop artists sought, instead, to depict the reality that the latter experienced on an everyday basis—a reality characterized by fast-food items, comic-strip frames, celebrities, and the like. They put on *happenings*, improvised spectacles or performances of their art works for anyone, not just art gallery patrons. The unnamed leader of the pop art movement was the American artist Andy Warhol (1928–1987), whose paintings and silk-screen prints emblematized the whole movement, as did his famous (some would say infamous) portrait of a Campbell's soup can, painted in 1964.

Pop artists abandoned individual, titled paintings in favor of series of works depicting the same object over and over, mirroring the manufacturing process of replicated objects. Warhol carried the idea a step further by adopting the technique of silk-screening, turning out hundreds of identical prints of Coca-Cola bottles and other familiar commodities, including identical three-dimensional Brillo boxes.

Pop art engaged the masses, not just art critics. But was it art, as the critics asked? The pop art movement saw commercial culture as typical of the modern world and thus sought to express its forms and structures in sculptures and paintings. Ironic reflection was the basis of such art. Will generations two hundred years from now see it as art or as a snapshot of an era? This question can be raised but clearly not answered. And in some ways the same question applies to all of pop culture.

Levels of Culture

As discussed briefly, the terms *high* and *low* have been used constantly in the pop art and pop culture debate. *High* implies art and culture considered to have a superior value, socially, aesthetically, and historically; *low* implies culture considered to have an inferior value. *Low* is often applied to pop culture generally, along with terms such as *kitschy, slapstick, campy, escapist, exploitive, obscene, raunchy, vulgar,* and the like. Many of these are applicable to various forms and manifestations of pop art and pop culture generally. However, that same culture has produced works such as the

Beatles' *Sergeant Pepper's Lonely Hearts Club Band* (1967) album and Milos Forman's Hollywood adaptation of Peter Shaffer's *Amadeus* (1984). These merit the epithet of "high art," even though they emerge in a pop culture context. Because of this mix of "high" and "low," pop culture has itself been instrumental in blurring, if not obliterating, the distinction between levels of culture, historically associated with class structure. Already in the Romantic nineteenth century, artists saw folk culture as the only true form of culture, especially since they associated high culture with the artificial demands made of artists by the Church and the aristocracy in previous eras.

As O'Brien and Szeman (2004: 7) aptly point out, pop culture is popular because it consists of "what the people make, or do, for themselves." This includes material forms (magazines, videos, bestselling novels, fads), artistic and narrative forms (music, movies, TV programs), and recreational activities such as shopping for fun, going to sports events, and so on. It seems to offer a balance between serious and recreational forms of culture. As writer Milan Kundera (1984: 234) has perceptively observed, pop culture is something that appeals to us instinctively because "no matter how much we scorn it, kitsch is an integral part of the human condition."

The categories of *high* and *low* have not disappeared. Paradoxically, they exist within pop culture itself. We all share a sense of an implicit *culture hierarchy* (which is intuitive rather than formal or theoretical). People evaluate popular movies, novels, music, TV programs, Internet sites, and so on instinctively in terms of this hierarchy:

Table 1.1.   Levels of Pop Culture

Level	Examples Perceived to Occur at Each Level
High	*Time* magazine, Chanel perfumes, *Frontline* (PBS), *Psychology Today* magazine, the Discovery Channel, *New York Times* (newspaper), National Public Radio, *Huffington Post* (online news and blog site)
Mid	daily newspapers, best-selling novels such as the Harry Potter ones, various genres of jazz, classic rock, *American Idol*, TLC programs
Low	tabloids, Howard Stern, infomercials, the Kardashians (television), erotic movies, movies such as the *Hangover* series, *Maury* and similar afternoon programs

The encompassing of three levels (high, mid, and low), and the constant crisscrossing that occurs among the levels (some crime dramas such as *Criminal Minds* cross over from the mid to the high), are attendant tendencies within pop culture. Some are even designed on purpose to crisscross the levels. Any episode of *The Simpsons* TV show might contain references to writers and philosophers locatable at the top echelon of traditional high culture, as well as references to ephemeral trends, such as blockbuster movies. This admixture of styles and forms is what defines contemporary pop culture.

A movie such as *Amadeus* is appealing to masses of people as pure entertainment at the same time that it is acclaimed by critics as a cinematic masterpiece. It has a storyline that people can follow and understand easily, a soundtrack that moves audiences poignantly, and a visual power that grabs their attention and maintains it throughout the narrative. On the other hand, dance fads such as the Twist, adventure hero comics, wrestling matches, programs such as *ET* (*Entertainment Tonight*), seem to have little more than a pure recreational function. Pop culture makes little or no distinction between art and recreation, distraction and engagement. Such is the paradox of pop culture.

Types of Culture

Culture manifests itself, basically, through conceptual, material, performative, and aesthetic channels. The conceptual channel includes the language (or languages) spoken by members of that culture, its linguistic traditions and rituals (sayings, proverbs, and so on), its symbols (use of color, for instance, to designate certain ideas), its transmission practices (from oral instruction to formal educational structures), among other things. Conceptual culture is, to put it more concretely, "mind culture." Material culture consists of the artifacts, structural forms, (for example, architectural styles), cuisine, and other material forms that characterize a culture. It is "external culture," which can be seen, touched, tasted, and so on. Performative culture includes the rites, rituals, music, and various other activities that are performed for various functions. Some anthropologists would include communicative rituals as part of performative culture, since they involve ritualistic forms of contact ("Hi, how's it going?") and dialogue (ordering meals at a restaurant). Finally, aesthetic culture consists of the arts and creative texts (stories, poems, and so on) that are created by members or groups in a culture.

Pop culture transforms these dimensions regularly. It thus develops its own language or languages (often called slangs or colloquial speech). It has its own material forms (fads such as Hula Hoops and trendy digital devices). It is highly performative, developing its own musical styles, comic and satirical texts, and above all else celebrities and icons that emblematize performative trends. It has its own aesthetic canons, even though this might not be apparent. Musical forms such as jazz and the blues are examples of this.

The Blending with Youth Culture

The term *youth culture* surfaces constantly in discussions of pop culture. The main reason for this is that the makers and initial adopters of popular trends have tended to be young people. Already in the 1920s, it was young people who were the producers and practitioners of popular trends such as the Charleston and jazz music. Although the older generations initially saw these as immoral or vulgar, they eventually caught on more broadly, gaining emotional appeal and entertainment value over time. This seems to be a pattern within pop culture—trends enacted and performed by young people eventually make their way into the mainstream culture. This constitutes a cycle—as some trends from youth culture become generalized, new trends are created by subsequent generations of young people which, in turn, become mainstream, and so on.

Perhaps the main reasons for this transference is, of course, that young people become old, but do not discard the trends of their youth as they age. Rather, they carry them over into adulthood. Thus trends once considered to appeal to youthful fancy eventually become elements of cultural nostalgia. To this day there is a constant dynamic between youth culture and more general forms of pop culture in modern society. Needless to say, this cycle is tied to the requirements of the marketplace. This topic will be taken up in the third chapter. Suffice it to say here that, in the history of modern urban societies, especially the American one, youth and pop culture have always formed a perfect blend.

ORIGINS AND SPREAD

Tracing the origins and spread of contemporary pop culture is not easy, since diverse forms of folk and recreational culture have existed since time immemorial. In a way, pop culture has always existed. But modern-day pop culture is different, because it does not come from historical traditions directly. Rather, it transforms them and then generates many of its own new forms. Moreover, folk cultures are restricted to place and remain stable over time; pop culture is not restricted to any social system or place, and it certainly is not stable, constantly inventing and recycling trends. Pop culture would not have become so widespread without the mass communications technologies and the mass media. These are its channels of transmission and as they change so do the forms of pop culture.

In a sense, pop culture is a modern-day experiment. It arose in America, where the marketplace has always espoused an entrepreneurial DIY ("do-it-yourself") spirit. Communities exist in America to this day that reject pop culture. Other pop cultures (European, Asian, and so forth) are derivatives (and sometimes reactions to) American pop culture. Its hegemony in the global village, however, is attenuating and morphing in various ways. So, new forms of pop culture do not always originate from America, but from other countries. The channel through which this takes place is the Internet. We will return to this topic in the last two chapters.

POP CULTURE HIGHLIGHTS

1821: The *Saturday Evening Post* is launched, becoming one of the first magazines to appeal directly to masses of people.

1833: The *New York Sun* is published as a "penny press" newspaper, costing only one cent.

1836: *Godey's Lady's Book* is launched, becoming a highly popular women's magazine, creating a "women's print culture."

1860s: The *New York Morning* has a circulation of 80,000, highlighting the fact that newspapers had become an integral part of mass culture. The "dime novel" becomes popular in the same decade, literally costing ten cents, to be read for entertainment and easily discarded.

1887: Emile Berliner develops the gramophone, leading to the use of cheap mass-produced records to disseminate emerging forms of popular music

1894: Thomas Edison opens up the first nickelodeon parlors with coin-operated projectors. These are the first movie theaters.

1895: William Randolph Hearst uses sensationalistic techniques for his newspapers, establishing yellow journalism. The Lumière brothers show the first short films in Paris.

1896: Thomas Edison invents the Vitascope, which is capable of large-screen projection.

1900: Muckraking (seeking out and publicizing the misdemeanors of prominent people) becomes highly popular in magazine publishing.

1903: Edwin S. Porter's *The Great Train Robbery*, an early western, gains popularity, indicating that the era of movie culture is just around the corner.

1906–1910: Reginald Fessenden makes the first radio broadcast from the Metropolitan Opera House in New York City.

(continued)

POP CULTURE HIGHLIGHTS (*continued*)

1910s: Silent films become popular, and the first movie celebrities are born.

1916: David Sarnoff, the commercial manager of American Marconi, writes a famous memo, now known as *The Radio Box Memo*, in which he proposes to make radio a "household utility." Frank Conrad founds KDKA in Pittsburgh as the first radio station in 1916. The station's broadcast of the 1920 presidential election results on November 2, 1920, is generally considered to constitute the beginning of true radio broadcasting.

1920s: The Big Five studios (Paramount, MGM, Warner Brothers, Twentieth Century Fox, RKO) and the Little Three studios (Columbia, Universal, United Artists) are established.

1922: *Reader's Digest* is launched. The first uses of radio for commercial purposes begin with the airing of commercials on station WEAF. This causes an uproar, as people challenge the use of the airwaves for commercial purposes.

1926: NBC is created by RCA, and radio becomes a mass medium for news, entertainment, and the discussion of public issues.

1927: With the advent of soundtrack technology the first "talkie" movie, *The Jazz Singer* (1927), makes movies even more popular. Philo T. Farnsworth transmits the first television picture.

1933: FM radio is developed.

1936: The first television service debuts in Britain.

1939: Robert de Graaf introduces Pocket Books, making all kinds of literature cheaply available to large masses of people.

1947: Radio starts to lose audiences to television.

1948: 33 1/3 records are introduced by Columbia Records and 45 rpm records are introduced by RCA Victor, making records more and more available and popular.

1950s: Television becomes a dominant medium, as previous radio genres and celebrities make the move over to TV. Radio becomes more and more specialized as a medium for news and music.

1955: The *Village Voice* is launched as the first underground newspaper in Greenwich Village. Top 40 radio becomes popular, indicating that radio is becoming more and more a marketing arm of the recording industry. Rock and roll defines youth culture in the mid-1950s.

1960s: Rock music is linked with social protest, spearheading the counterculture movement.

1967: Rock and roll gets its own magazine with the launching of *Rolling Stone*.

1968: *60 Minutes* starts broadcasting, showcasing the power of television to influence public opinion.

1971: Borders opens its first store in Ann Arbor. Chain bookstores and superstores start springing up across America shortly thereafter.

1972: The first video game, Pong, is introduced.

1974: *People* magazine starts publication.

(*continued*)

POP CULTURE HIGHLIGHTS (continued)

1976: VCRs are introduced, creating a new rental and purchase industry for movies. *Star Wars* initiates a new era of big-budget blockbusters.

1978: Cellular phone service begins. Nicholas Negroponte of MIT introduces the term *convergence* to describe the multiple uses of media as part of mass communications.

1980: Ohio's *Columbus Dispatch* is the first newspaper to go online. CNN premieres as a twenty-four-hour cable news network.

1981: Music Television (MTV) debuts.

1982: *USA Today* is launched. Compact discs are introduced.

1989: Tim Berners-Lee develops concepts and techniques that a few years later lead to the establishment of the World Wide Web. AOL (America Online) is formed, later becoming the first successful Internet service provider.

1991: The World Wide Web is launched.

1994: The direct broadcast satellite (DBS) industry debuts.

1995: Amazon.com is established. The first megaplex movie theater is built in Dallas, leading to a wave of megaplexes and a new cinema-going culture. *Toy Story* is the first completely computer-generated movie.

1997: DVDs make their debut, offering more storage space than VHS.

1998: The *Dallas Morning News* is the first newspaper to break a major story on its website instead of its front page. Increasing use of the Internet leads to the development of blogs, online chat groups, and the like, which take on many of the functions of rubrics in traditional newspapers.

2000s: Microsoft and Adobe start making online books (e-books) available. E-zines, e-toons, and other digital genres start proliferating. Movies converge with the Internet, where trailers are shown and where even full features can be seen. Specialty channels become the norm in the world of television.

2001: MP3 technology shakes up the music industry, as Internet users share music files on Napster. Instant messaging services appear.

2002: Satellite and web-based radio and TV programs emerge. File-sharing becomes highly popular.

2003: Apple Computer's iTunes music store makes its debut, making it possible to buy music on the Internet. VOD (video on demand) is introduced.

2005–2010: The Internet converges with previous media (radio, television, etc.) to produce online versions of all previous forms of media. It also becomes a source of new forms of communication, social interaction, and pop culture, with sites such as MySpace, Facebook, YouTube, and Twitter.

2010–ongoing: Digital platforms of all kinds become dominant media for the delivery of emerging new forms of pop culture. Nano-celebrities emerge (celebrities created on sites such as YouTube whose fame lasts for a very short span of time). The global digital village introduces popular forms of culture from across the world.

A useful way to trace the origin, institutionalization, and spread of pop culture is to identify those media-based events that can be tagged as critical in the history of popular culture.

The 1820s–1940s

The publication of popular magazines and cheap newspapers in the 1820s, coupled with the publication a little later of dime novels in the 1860s planted the seeds from which pop culture would eventually sprout. With the launch of *Reader's Digest* in 1922, the activity of reading as leisure started to be shaped by compression—the edited reduction of information into small, digested bits for quick consumption or rapid delivery (over electronic media).

Especially critical in the success of pop culture were the rise of movie theaters, which began as nickelodeons in 1894, found mostly in commercial neighborhoods, and which attracted sizable audiences because admission was only five cents and curiosity was high. Affordability and curiosity have always been critical factors in promulgating popular forms of culture. Nickelodeons took their cues from the dime novel and vaudeville genres, simply adapting them to the new medium. By the 1910s, the first movie celebrities appeared on the scene. In the 1920s, movies became part of mass entertainment culture the establishment and rise of the Big Five studios (Paramount, MGM, Warner Brothers, Twentieth Century Fox, RKO) and the Little Three studios (Columbia, Universal, United Artists).

Another major influence on the rise of pop culture was jazz, once strictly background music in the brothels of Kansas City and New Orleans. It started to spread and flourish as a mass musical art across the United States, because young people simply loved it. It was fun and it bespoke a new social order, in contrast to the stodgy one of the previous Victorian era that had beset America as well as England. By the end of the 1920s, spurred by the cheapness and availability of mass-produced records and the emergence of the radio as a promoter of popular music, jazz and its derivatives, such as swing music, came to define pop culture. Big band leaders like Glenn Miller became cultural icons. To this day, recordings of music from the jazz and swing eras sell in the millions, with updated versions played and sung by a new cadre of "retrospective" pop artists.

The 1950s–1960s

In the years subsequent to World War II, new forms of music, fads, and fashion trends seemed to be springing up on a daily basis. As in previous decades, the young people led the way at first. The transference pattern discussed above (from youth-to-mainstream culture) became a powerful one. In 1948, *Life* magazine ran a cover story underscoring the fact that for the first time in American history young people constituted a serious cultural force. The article also pointed out that due in part to the many extra jobs that were created by World War II the ever-expanding generation of teenagers had plenty of spending money in their pockets. It thus became Madison Avenue's avowed aspiration to get them to spend it on faddish clothing, blockbuster movies, and rock and roll records. In 1953, *The Wild One* starring Marlon Brando as a motorcycle gang leader, and in 1955, *Rebel without a Cause*, starring teen idol James Dean, made it obvious to one and all that the *Life* article was a prophetic one. Teenagers had become a distinct market category, with their own evolving culture based on rock and roll music. Elvis Presley became the "king" of teen culture. Television further spread this culture broadly, as programs such as *American Bandstand* and the *Adventures of Ozzie and Harriet* gained nationwide popularity. The latter program was, revealingly, the first sitcom to deal with the problems of raising teenaged children (two sons).

Rock and roll music went mainstream by the end of the decade. The DJ radio era also took off, further promoting youth trends broadly. Movies became more and more marketed to the youth demographic, as did magazines, such as *Seventeen* (which was actually launched in 1944).

By 1960, the media and the business worlds had forged a partnership to cater to the new form of culture. Increasingly, fads that arose in youth culture soon after spread across generations. The teenager had morphed into a "rebel without a cause," as the movie mentioned above suggested. Adults expected the rebellion to fade as the teenagers grew up. But in the 1960s, something truly unexpected happened. The next generation of teenagers became "rebels *with* a cause," questioning the basic values of the society in which they were reared. Known as *hippies*, they denounced the adult "establishment," through their new music, campus sit-ins, public protests, and alternative lifestyles, seeking inspiration from Eastern mystical traditions and spearheading a political clamor for radical social change. The rock concert became a happening (in the tradition of pop art happenings), often spurring audiences on to social activism. Drugs were consumed openly to induce or heighten the experience. Sexual activities were carried out openly, in obvious defiance of adult moralism. The new musical styles were ambitious structurally. By the end of the decade, rock operas, such as *Tommy* (1969) by the Who, were being considered as serious works by traditional music critics. The high-versus-low dichotomy of culture was becoming more and more meaningless.

Elvis Presley was the figurehead of youth culture in the 1950s. By the mid-1960s he had crossed over into a more "adult-acceptable" realm of culture with his tame movies and Las Vegas concerts. The new counterculture groups, on the other hand, challenged the status quo. The long hair of the rock musicians and their clothing styles influenced youth appearance and fashion everywhere. Youth culture had broadened considerably, setting the stage for subsequent eras of pop culture.

In the same decade, television became increasingly influential as a stage for the broader diffusion of popular trends. With the launch of documentary news programs, the trend of compressing information into digestible bits had become widespread on TV.

The 1970s–1990s

The counterculture movement did not last long. By the early 1970s it had receded from the social scene. The hippies had become less inclined to revolt, as they started to age and have children of their own; also, many of their goals (gender equality, racial equality, and so on) were being realized through legislation and the political sphere. New musical trends emerged, as did new lifestyles. The trend that worried adults the most was punk culture, which constituted the first true *subculture*—a culture that keeps itself separate from the mainstream, offering an alternative lifestyle to its members. The hippies did not form a subculture; they were part of a counterculture movement that aimed to reform the main culture. A subculture largely ignores the mainstream one, developing its own values and lifestyles.

One can argue that counterculture and punk rock are not part of the paradigms of pop culture—in fact, they went against the pop cultures of their era. This is essentially true. But it is also true that many of the forms of the music and lifestyle of these movements have morphed into more popular forms and gained a broad audience. This fits in with the transference view of pop culture as stemming from youth culture trends, no matter how transgressive or subversive they may have originally been.

The early form of punk subculture was deliberately violent and confrontational. Punk rock band members spat on their audiences, mutilated themselves with knives, damaged the props on stage and in the hall, shouted, burped, urinated, and bellowed at will to a basic pulsating beat, inciting their audiences to do likewise. They wore chains, dog collars, and army boots, and sported hairstyles that ranged from shaved heads to Mohawk cuts of every color imaginable. Punk was parody culture; confronting the hypocrisy of traditional moralism and the commercialism of society.

The punks were antibourgeois and anticapitalist in ways that, ironically, their hippie parents found shocking and offensive.

The punk subculture would recede from the scene by the end of the 1980s. Again, the punkers got older. It was an important movement nonetheless, leaving as a residue an intrinsic anti-hegemonic impulse within pop culture, and thus instilling within it once and for all the same kinds of social mockery functions of the ancient carnivals. Satire and mockery have always been elements of popular performances. The vulgar has always existed alongside the pure and the authoritative. Sitcoms like *South Park* and *Family Guy* play similar roles in current pop culture.

This function of pop culture could be seen also in bands such as Kiss. Each musician in the band portrayed a comic book character—a glamour boy, an alien from outer space, a kitty cat, and a sex-crazed Kabuki monster. Kiss's stage act included fire-eating, smoke-bombs, hydraulic lifts, and instrument-smashing. The *Rocky Horror Picture Show* was another manifestation of the same ironic-satirical inclination in pop culture. The movie became a cult phenomenon, as hordes of teenagers and young adults went to see it week after week, month after month, year after year. It was both a parody of 1950s rock culture and a glorification of "outside-the-mainstream" social personae (cross-dressers, sexual perverts, and so on), also promoted by musicians like Alice Cooper.

Disco culture, epitomized by the 1977 movie *Saturday Night Fever*, emerged at the same time as a throwback to the days of swing and ballroom dancing. Many teens rejected it with the expression "disco sucks!" seeing it as too superficial. But disco culture thrived nonetheless, because it was fun and sexy. The antagonism between punk and disco culture was captured superbly by Spike Lee in his 1999 movie *Summer of Sam*, which takes place in the summer of 1977 during the Son of Sam serial murders. Punk, with its angry anti-hegemonic subtext, and disco, with its contrasting goodtime dance lifestyle, define the characters in the movie and justify the choices they make. By the early 1980s, all these competing trends receded to the periphery, although snippets of the punk, cross-dressing, and disco lifestyles are being recycled even today in movie remakes, TV nostalgia programs, and Internet websites throughout the world.

Two performers in particular—Michael Jackson and Madonna—emerged to challenge traditional gender attitudes even more than had Kiss and the *Rocky Horror Picture Show*. Michael Jackson merged male and female personae in his stage performances. He also emphasized occultism in his video-album *Thriller* (1982), an unconscious trend within general pop culture (as can be seen in the popularity of vampire stories and fashions such as astrology and fortune-telling). Madonna's early songs satirized the view of females as objects of voyeurism. She adopted a Marilyn Monroe look and a "sex-kitten" peep show attitude as her performance trademarks, but at the same time took over the reins of the voyeuristic performance. As Madonna knew and showed, lookers who are themselves "looked at" become powerless. Her powerful female persona has become a staple of contemporary movies, music, and television. Women in pop culture, and society generally, no longer see themselves as receivers of attention; they set the tone in representations of all kinds today.

By the end of the 1980s, youth culture continued to fragment, as metal, mod, prep, goth, grunge, and other subcultures emerged. But one trend rose above them all to capture center stage—rap music and hip-hop lifestyle. The word *rap* was actually used as a music term for the first time in the mid-1970s to describe an eclectic mix of funk, soul, and hard rock played by disc jockeys in the dance halls of Harlem and the South Bronx. The more enthusiastic members of those audiences would improvise sing-song rhymes, exhorting other teens to dance and "get into it." These were called rapping sessions.

The first rap records were made in the 1970s, put out at first by small, independent record labels. In 1979, rapper Kurtis Blow signed with a major label. Sugarhill Gang recorded one of the first major rap hits, "Rapper's Delight," in the same year. In 1986, the rap group Run-D.M.C. and the rock group Aerosmith collaborated on "Walk This Way," creating a new trend in pop music and pop culture generally—a trend toward eclecticism and diversity. The rap movement generated great controversy, since it adopted a brassy, subversive approach to social issues and traditional romance. But this approach was not unlike the approaches of young people in previous decades, as we saw. It has always been an impulse within pop culture.

In the same era, television, radio, and other traditional media started converging with the Internet. By the end of the 1990s, the online platform started to become a dominant one, changing the evolutionary patterns within pop culture drastically, as we shall see later in this book.

The Twenty-First Century

As computer technology improved steadily after World War II, smaller and cheaper computers could be built for all kinds of purposes. By the 1970s, the manufacture of personal computers (PCs) for mass consumption could be realized cheaply. The first PCs were mainly word processors; that is, they simply made the production and storage of printed text signifi-

AN INTERNET AND WORLD WIDE WEB TIMELINE

1822: Charles Babbage develops a prototype of the modern computer.

1844: Telegraphy is invented, constituting a forerunner of data networks.

1876: The telephone is introduced, gradually becoming a personal commodity across the world.

1939: John Vincent Atanasoff of Iowa State University is credited with designing the true first modern computer, developing ideas from Babbage and others before him.

1946: ENIAC, the first general-purpose computer, is developed by J. Presper Eckert and John Mauchly, mainly for military purposes.

1951: Eckert and Mauchly introduce UNIVAC as the first civilian computer.

1962: The first communications satellite, the first digital phone networks, and the first pagers are introduced.

1964: The first local area network (LAN) is initiated to support nuclear weapons research.

1965: A highly usable computer language, BASIC, is developed.

1969: Arpanet, the first digital communication network, is established by the U.S. Department of Defense.

1971: Microprocessors are developed, leading shortly thereafter to PC technology.

1972: E-mail is developed on Arpanet.

1975: The first personal computer, Altair, is launched.

1977: The first fiber-optic network is created.

1978: Cellular phone service begins.

1980s: Hypertext is developed in the mid-1980s, constituting an idea leading eventually to the creation of the World Wide Web.

1984: Apple Macintosh is the first PC with graphics.

1989: Tim Berners-Lee introduces the World Wide Web.

1990: The first Internet search engine, Archie, is developed.

1991: The Internet opens to commercial uses; HTML is developed.

1993: The first point-and-click Web browser, Mosaic, is introduced.

1994: The first Internet cafés open; Jeff Bezos launches Amazon.com.

1995: The first online auction house, eBay, is launched.

1996: Google makes its debut.

2000: Cookies technology allows for information profiles to be created, enabling data-mining practices to burgeon.

2001: Instant messaging services appear.

mid-2000s–2010: The Internet converges with all previous media technologies (radio, television, and so on) to produce online versions of all media forms. It also becomes a source of new forms of communication and culture, with social media such as MySpace, Facebook, Twitter, and YouTube. Wi-Fi becomes widespread, making access to the Internet ubiquitous and available on all kinds of mobile devices, from phones to tablets.

2010–ongoing: New forms of pop culture and advertising emerge on the Internet. Nano-celebrities are created by social media such as YouTube. Some now claim that the pop culture experiment, as it evolved from the 1920s onward, may have come to an end, as the global village has become a major force in human relations. Does popularity now consist in the number of hits and "likes" on a site? This question and related ones will be discussed in subsequent chapters.

cantly easier and more sophisticated. In 1975, the first microcomputer was introduced. It had the power of many of the previous larger computers, but could fit onto a desktop. This feat was accomplished because of new miniaturization technologies, called nanotechnologies. The first commercial software appeared shortly thereafter in 1978.

At the same time that computers were becoming faster, more powerful, and smaller, networks were being developed for interconnecting them. In the 1960s, the Advanced Research Projects Agency (ARPA) of the U.S. Department of Defense, along with researchers working on military projects at research centers and universities across the country, developed a network called Arpanet for sharing data and mainframe computer processing time over specially equipped telephone lines and satellite links. Used at first for military purposes, it became the first functional major electronic mail network when the National Science Foundation connected universities and nonmilitary research sites to it. By 1981, a couple hundred computers were connected to Arpanet. The military then divided the network into two organizations—Arpanet and a purely military network. During the 1980s, the former was absorbed by NSFNET, a more advanced network developed by the National Science Foundation. It was that system that soon after became the basis for the Internet.

One of the main reasons for the slow growth of the Internet was its complexity. To access it, users had to learn an intricate series of programming commands. The breakthrough occurred in 1991 with the arrival of the World Wide Web, developed by Tim Berners-Lee (b. 1955), a British computer scientist at the European Center for Nuclear Research (CERN), facilitating use of the Internet considerably. The arrival of browsers in 1993 further eased use, bringing about an astronomical growth in traffic on the Internet. In the history of human communications, no other technology has made it possible for so many people to interact with each other, irrespective of the distance between them, on a rapid and even instantaneous basis. Moreover, because of the Internet, it is no longer accurate to talk about "competing" media. Advances in digital technologies and in telecommunications networks have led to a convergence of all communications systems into one overall system. This has led, in turn, to the emergence of new Internet-based businesses, lifestyles, careers, institutions, and so on. There is now a real (offline) culture and a hyperreal one (online culture), to use the terminological dichotomy introduced by the late French philosopher Jean Baudrillard (1983), with little distinction being made between the two in the conduct of everyday affairs.

The digitization of print media started in 1967. Today, newspapers are produced by means of digital technologies and are available mainly in online versions. The special effects created for the movie *Star Wars* in 1977 introduced digital technology into filmmaking. In home video technology, the DVD supplanted the VHS tape in the mid-1990s. And the DVD itself has been replaced by downloading and video-on-demand technologies. The compact disc (CD) started replacing vinyl records and audiocassette tapes already in the mid-1980s, shortly after its introduction in 1982. Further compression technologies, known as MP3 have now rendered the CD virtually obsolete, as people are more inclined to buy music through iTunes and Amazon.com than they are in traditional record stores, which have virtually disappeared. The Internet has also become a producer and stage for new music, making labels less and less important. Cable TV went digital in 1998, allowing broadcasters to increase their channel offerings. This technology was introduced primarily to meet competition from the Direct Broadcast Satellite (DBS) industry, which started producing digital multichannel programming for reception by home satellite dishes in 1995. High-Definition Television (HDTV) became commercially available in 1998. Digital Audio Broadcasting (DAB) is the corresponding technology in radio broadcasting to television's DBS system. Radio stations now use digital technology universally to create their programs.

Until the early 1990s, most information on the Internet consisted mainly of printed text. The introduction of the World Wide Web made it possible to include graphics, animation, video, and sound. Today, the World Wide Web contains all kinds of documents, databases, bulletin boards, and electronic publications in multimedia forms (print, audio-oral, visual). The plethora of information it enfolds, and the rapidity with which it can be accessed, have allowed the Internet to replace traditional institutions such as reference libraries and to largely eliminate paper versions of texts such as encyclopedias—Wikipedia, for instance, has become the standard reference source for virtually everyone, from students and academics to scientists and researchers. More to the point of the current discussion, the Internet has become a dominant platform for pop culture, showcasing music, movies, and so on, both new and old. And it has greatly augmented the "populist" dimension of popular culture, since people now post their own art, writings, music videos, movies, and other creative texts on websites, on blogs, social media, and the like. Traditional media and entertainment enterprises are now using the Internet alongside independent producers. The Internet has also become a highly effective medium of advertising, making it possible for all kinds of businesses and individuals the world over to communicate inexpensively with the entire globe.

Webcasting is converging with, and in some cases overtaking, previous forms of broadcasting. Webcasts have no fixed schedules and no targeted audiences. A producer can offer audio or video presentations to anyone who wants them. Real-time play became possible through a technology called *streaming*. Radio and television often stream their programs in real time so that people throughout the world may listen or watch over the Internet. Some media outlets have started creating programs specifically for the Internet, many of which are extended versions of broadcasts on traditional media. Popular online sites range from those offering constantly updated weather reports and global financial information, to sports scores and breaking news.

The Internet has also led to a redefinition of the roles of the author and the reader of a text. Online novels, for instance, allow for multiple plot twists to be built into a story. They also enable readers to observe the story unfold from the perspective of different characters. Readers may also change the story themselves to suit their interpretive fancies. The same kind of editing power is now applicable to all kinds of Internet documents, from web-based encyclopedias and dictionaries to online textbooks. Electronic documents can always be updated and thus always kept current and topical. As mentioned, the "populist" in pop culture is now taking on more and more of a literal meaning, as readers interact directly with authors, scholars, artists, and others in determining how they will ultimately be informed, engaged, or entertained.

The main lesson to be learned from studying the history of pop culture through its association with changes in media and mass communications technologies is that there is no turning back the clock once an innovation has been introduced that makes access to information and culture more rapid, cheap, efficient, and broad.

POP CULTURE, MATERIAL CULTURE, AND TECHNOLOGY

As the foregoing discussion has attempted to emphasize, the spread of pop culture has been brought about largely because new mass communications technologies allowed for its diffusion to huge audiences. The rise of music as a mass art, for instance, was made possible by the advent of recording and radio broadcasting technologies in the first decades of the twentieth century. Similarly, the spread and appeal of pop culture throughout the globe today is due to the Internet. As the late Canadian communications theorist Marshall McLuhan (1911–1980) often claimed, culture, social evolution, and technological innovation are so intertwined that we hardly ever realize their mutual influence.

The Jukebox

Throughout the history of pop culture, it seems that some objects typically come to symbolize some general aspect or era in this history. Two examples include the jukebox and the automobile.

Jukeboxes were invented in 1906. Originally found in juke joints, places where southern field workers went to dance and interact socially, they were adopted by diners and soda shops in the 1920s so that customers could enjoy the pop tunes of the era as they ate or drank. By 1941 there were nearly four hundred thousand jukeboxes in the United States.

The jukebox was an intrinsic part of the early rock culture of the 1950s, functioning as a magnet for teenagers to come together in cliques, right after the Seeburg Company produced the first jukeboxes in 1950 to play 45 rpm records. It was a fixture in soda shops, bowling alleys, and other teen "hangout joints." The 1970s television sitcom *Happy Days* illustrated this perfectly. After school, the adolescent characters of that program hung out at a diner that featured a jukebox, blurting out the rock tunes of the era. In the 1953 movie *The Wild One*, Marlon Brando delivered his now classic juvenile delinquent's retort to the question "What are you rebelling against?" by drumming his fingers on a jukebox and then saying "Whaddaya got?" A number of other 1950s movies and television programs also featured jukeboxes. The jukebox metaphor had become so ubiquitous in American youth culture that it was satirized in *Dirty Work* (1998).

The jukebox reveals that trends in black pop culture become appropriated and institutionalized in general culture. The term *juke* meant, originally, a brothel or cheap roadside eatery and dance hall. It was associated with African American communities as a place for members to unwind and congregate socially. The verb form, *to juke*, denoted "to dance" in African American slang.

Jukeboxes were already popular in the 1930s, as evidenced by the fact that *Billboard* magazine started devoting a section to them in 1934. In that same decade, jukeboxes became an arm of the record industry. Jukebox operators depended on the recommendations of magazines and the radio. In an extended sense, MP3 devices or the iPod are ersatz jukeboxes, with

The jukebox was a symbol of an era of pop culture (© ThinkStock)

shuffle functions that recall the jukebox indirectly. The Karaoke machine is certainly a contemporary descendant of the jukebox. However, the original jukebox, contained in a decorative cabinet in a popular public setting, was a unique object symbolizing a specific period of pop culture.

The Automobile

Like the jukebox, the automobile became more than a means of efficient transportation almost right after its invention. The number of passenger cars in the United States jumped from fewer than seven million in 1919 to about twenty-three million in 1929. Traffic started spreading throughout the nation's highways, creating a need for new kinds of businesses catering to an emerging automobile culture, including gas stations, roadside restaurants, and auto clubs.

The media soon picked up on the automobile's role as a symbol of cultural trends. Nicholas Ray, for example, showcased the automobile in his 1955 movie, *Rebel without a Cause*, in which a game of "car chicken" is particularly memorable. In that scene, two male suitors are seen vying to impress a girl through the car duel. Before the duel there is a ritualistic rubbing of the earth. Then the camera zooms in on James Dean, one of the two combatants, behind the wheel of his car, showing him with a cigarette dangling confidently from the side of his mouth; the camera then shifts to his competitor in his own car, self-assuredly slicking down his hair. Cars, hair, and cigarettes were, clearly, all part of phallic-based rituals and symbols in the youth culture of the era. The movie caught on throughout the teen universe, radiating with a sense of restlessness and alienation that could only be resolved metaphorically through the duel.

The car is everywhere in pop culture, from TV programs like the now defunct *Knight Rider* to movies such as the *Fast and Furious* series. It also appears as a partner (like the cowboy's horse in westerns) in the James Bond set of movies and in many other adventure flicks, such as the *Batman* movies (the Batmobile). The widespread fascination with cars is also manifest in the hobby of collecting model cars. There are television channels, websites, magazines, radio programs, and the like that cater to car nostalgia buffs.

Some car models have unique value in the history of pop culture. Two classic examples of this are the 1957 Cadillac Eldorado and the 1964 Ford Mustang. The former became a symbol of the American metaphorical quest for its own Eldorado in the late 1950s—the magical city of the New World, thought to be in the northern part of South America, fabled for its great wealth of gold and precious jewels. The name fit perfectly—in its convertible design, with its large tail fins and its expansive body, the Eldorado epitomized the large-car craze that showed the extent to which cars had become symbols of wealth and of prosperity. Although its showy features did little for the performance of the vehicle, consumers loved the look, turning the car into a spectacle of its own—something to be admired like a celebrity more than a means to get somewhere cheaply and efficiently.

A Cadillac Eldorado (courtesy of Hyman Ltd. Classic Cars)

The Mustang was associated, from the outset, with youth culture. More than one hundred thousand cars were sold during the first four months of 1964, when the Mustang was introduced, making it Ford's best early sales success since the Model T. The Mustang's design as a quasi-sports car, for the young (and young-at-heart), was indisputably a key to its success. Marketed as a low-priced, high-style car, the Mustang appealed instantly to a large segment of people, men and women equally. Its had elegant, narrow bumpers instead of the large ones common at the time and delicate grillwork that jutted out at the top and slanted back at the bottom, giving the car a forward-thrusting look. The car's visual appeal was increased by the air scoops on its sides, which cooled the rear brakes. The Mustang's hefty logo of a galloping horse adorned the grille. The name and car design matched perfectly: a mustang is a horse that, although small, is powerful. It is also a wild horse, symbolizing the same kind of wildness implicit in the 1923 musical *Running Wild* (mentioned above).

As part of what has come to be known as "muscle culture," the Mustang has been featured in television programs and films with tough-guy characters or fast-action plots since it came onto the scene, including *Bullitt* (1968), *Back to the Future II*, and the *Fast and Furious* movies, largely replac-

The Mustang (© ThinkStock)

ing real mustangs—that is, the horses of the early cowboy movies. Iconic movie cars like the Mustang abound in the history of pop culture. Below is a selection:

- *Chitty Chitty Bang Bang* (1968): Inspired by racing cars of the 1920s, the car in the movie features a round body that is wooden at the back and metal at the front. The car becomes itself part of the family like a pet (McMorran 2006). The love affair with the car in America is sentimentalized perfectly in this movie.
- *The Love Bug* (1968): This movie features, Herbie, a 1963 Volkswagen Beetle Ragtop Sedan and an implicit symbol of the hippie "love culture." It is, both in physical appearance and in symbolic value, a "love bug."
- *Batman* (1997): The Batmobile is a major protagonist in the Batman movies, with its black interior and exterior matching the gothic feel of the movies. Its gadgets are part of the archetypal helper's kit of tools, replacing guns, swords, and other such tools.
- *Dukes of Hazzard* (2005): Based on a popular television series of the 1980s, the car in this movie is emblematic of the confederacy motif in some areas of American pop culture, including its orange body

paint, a southern confederate battle flag on its roof, and a horn that plays the confederacy rally song "Dixie."

- *Twilight* (2009): The main vampire in the movie drives a Volvo when he saves his love interest, Bella, from being assaulted by a gang. The car is sleek, with two doors and a rounded roof. It features a manual control, which is used as a plot device when Bella accidentally touches Edward's skin, prompting her to discover his true identity. The car is, symbolically, the shining armor protecting the vampire knight.

- *Skyfall* (2012): The introduction of the Aston Martin DB5 in the James Bond films started with *Goldfinger* in 1964. In *Skyfall* there is a nostalgic revisitation of the iconic car. The Aston Martin has appeared in eleven of the twenty-three Bond films, as a helper with its hidden gadgets. When the DB5's machine guns opened fire in *Skyfall*, well after the Bond theme proclaimed its entrance, it was the first time they had appeared on screen since *Goldfinger*.

Convergence

The term *convergence* was introduced in the mid-1990s to describe the digitization process. It is now used to refer more generally to the integration and blending of media, technology, and cultural forms. It is a defining characteristic of mass communications and mass media today, uniting the globe into one huge system that Marshall McLuhan (1964) called the "global village." Overreliance on this system and computers generally has fostered a new form of mythological thinking. This became apparent on the threshold of the year 2000 when the "millennium bug" was thought to be a harbinger of doom. So reliant had people become on the computer that a simple technological problem—making sure that computers could read the *00* date as *2000* and not *1900* or some other date—was interpreted in apocalyptic terms. That fear was striking evidence that computers had acquired a meaning that far exceeded their original function as computing machines.

Everything from romance on websites to self-presentation and diary-keeping on social media, now illustrates the critical role of computer technology. The term *cyberspace* was coined by American writer William Gibson (b. 1948) in his 1984 science fiction novel *Neuromancer*, in which he described cyberspace as a place of "unthinkable complexity." Human lives are literally becoming unthinkably complex in that space, which Baudrillard (1983) called a hyperreal space, and which now appears to be more real than real space. Pop culture, too, has converged with the hyperreal, as social media sites become more and more dominant channels for showcasing popular entertainment.

Cyberspace now has its own communities and its own set of conventions for communicating and interacting. As Mikael Benedikt (1991: 1) has observed, in cyberspace "the tablet becomes a page becomes a screen becomes a world, a virtual world. Everywhere and nowhere, a place where nothing is forgotten yet everything changes." The advent of cyberspace has led to many reassessments of, and debates on, traditional notions of popularity, since what goes onto the screen is often accompanied by a "Like" option. The number of views on a YouTube site is now, in effect, a sui generis rating system.

The foregoing discussion may be somewhat overdrawn. Forms of artistic expression from independently produced movies and music videos on YouTube to webcasts of documentaries and comedy routines are still based on the same sorts of concepts and styles that have characterized pop culture since the Roaring Twenties. Pop culture perpetuates itself (and has always perpetuated itself) by adapting to the technologically changing media that deliver it to large masses of people. It remains to be seen, though, if it will persist or if the online platform will have morphed the very idea of popular culture so much that, perhaps, a completely new form of global culture will overtake the experiment that started in the 1920s and eventually bring it to an end. This will be discussed in the final chapter.

FEATURES OF POP CULTURE

At the turn of the twentieth century in America, sexually suggestive and ribald musicals started attracting American audiences in large numbers. A perfect example of this new craze was the *Ziegfeld Follies*, produced in 1907 by the American theatrical producer Florenz Ziegfeld (1867–1932). The spectacle became popular for its follies, sexy chorus girls, dazzling sets, and catchy tunes. The spectacle is both a specific genre and a metaphor for pop culture generally. In its origins, pop culture was all about entertainment on the stage through a pastiche of spectacle, music, dancing, and laughter.

Spectacle

Spectacles are everywhere in popular culture—musicals, blockbuster movies, the Super Bowl, rock concerts, and the like—all constitute spectacles of one kind or the other. Most historians trace pop culture's origins to a specific kind of theatrical spectacle that featured a wide variety of acts, called *vaudeville*. Vaudeville was popular from the 1880s to the early 1930s and produced many of the celebrities who gained success in other entertainment media, such as motion pictures and radio. Some vaudeville theaters featured more than twenty acts in a single bill, ranging from juggling, animal acts, comedy skits, recitations, songs, and magic shows, to burlesque performances by actresses. Vaudeville was an offshoot of circus culture, where the term *spectacle* had a specific meaning. It referred to the segment that opened and closed performances and included performers, animals, and floats. As the band played and the ringmaster sang, performers dressed in elaborate costumes walked around the circus tent or arena. The spectacle usually ended with a trick called a long mount, in which the elephants stood in a line with their front legs resting on each other's backs.

Through the efforts of wealthy producers and theater owners, who saw the promise of huge profits from spectacle performances, vaudeville became a highly organized nationwide big business with its own theater chains. In its heyday it was the most popular form of live entertainment for family audiences. The *variety show* eventually replaced *vaudeville*.

Popular music has always been an intrinsic feature of vaudeville. As mentioned earlier, one cannot overstate the role of jazz in the spread of pop culture. Jazz originated around 1900. Its roots lay in the musical traditions of African Americans. Most early jazz was played by small marching bands or solo pianists. In 1917 a group of New Orleans musicians called The Original Dixieland Jazz Band produced records that garnered nationwide attention for jazz. Two groups followed: in 1922 the New Orleans Rhythm Kings and in 1923 the Creole Jazz Band, led by cornetist King Oliver. The most influential musician at the time was King Oliver's second trumpeter, Louis Armstrong, who showed the power of jazz to move people emotionally and to entertain them at the same time. By the 1930s and early 1940s, jazz developed into swing, and also spawned a new and highly popular style known as bebop. Bebop's tempos were faster and its phrases longer and more complex than previous jazz styles.

The term *cool jazz* surfaced in 1948, when tenor saxophonist Stan Getz recorded a slow, romantic solo of Ralph Burns's composition "Early Autumn" with the Woody Herman band. The work profoundly influenced many younger musicians. In 1949, a group that included trumpeter Miles Davis recorded several new compositions in this style. The recordings emphasized a lagging beat, soft instrumental sounds, and unusual orchestrations that included the French horn and the tuba. The recordings, with Davis as leader, were later released as the *Birth of the Cool*.

The movie *Chicago* brought out the importance of jazz in the origins and spread of pop culture, encapsulated in its opening musical piece titled "All That Jazz," alluding not only to the music itself, but also metaphorically to the role of open sexual attitudes in pop culture. The main character, Roxie Hart, becomes an overnight sensation after murdering an unfaithful lover. People react against her at first because she is a burlesque star, associated with jazz and promiscuity—the two evils in society. For courtroom purposes, Roxie and her lawyer devised an acceptable persona for her—a pregnant and loving mother figure—emphasizing society's hypocrisy. Roxie is a free-thinking woman unbridled by the yoke of tradition, which saw women as wives and mothers. Her persona continues to reverberate in all areas of pop culture. In the videos "Like a Virgin" and "Material Girl," Madonna showcased the power of that persona.

The key era for the rise of pop culture was, as mentioned, the Roaring Twenties. The public consumption of alcohol, sexy clothing, jazz music, and socializing late at night became part of a new social mind-set. Before World War I, women had worn long hair, ankle-length dresses, and long cotton stockings. In the 1920s, they started wearing short, tight dresses and rolled their silk stockings down to their knees. They cut their hair in a boyish style called the bob and wore flashy cosmetics. They danced cheek-to-cheek with men. Like Roxie, they acted sexually in public. The era of pop culture had arrived. The literature, art, and music of the 1920s also reflected the nation's changing values. In his novel *Main Street* (1920), Sinclair Lewis attacked what he considered the dull lives and narrow-minded attitudes of people in a small town. Many American authors, including F. Scott Fitzgerald and Ernest Hemingway, analyzed the attitudes and experiences of the era's so-called "Lost Generation," which was actually the generation that changed society in the end. H. L. Mencken, in his witty magazine *The American Mercury*, ridiculed the antics of dimwitted politicians, prohibitionists, and staunch puritans.

Needless to say, pop culture has not been immune to sexism (or racism, for that matter). But the fact remains that pop culture, like no other previous form of culture, has allowed women and racial minorities to flaunt their talents publicly and to become artists in their own right. Jazz and the Charleston could never have become part of American history without pop culture. In this framework, pop culture is much more than entertainment and a money-making enterprise; it is a mirror and a source of change.

Collage, Bricolage, and Pastiche

Three French words, *collage, bricolage,* and *pastiche,* are often used to describe pop culture. *Collage* is a term taken from painting, describing a picture or design made by gluing pieces onto a canvas or another surface. By arranging them in a certain way, the artist can create strange or witty effects not possible with traditional painting techniques. Many pop culture spectacles, from early vaudeville to *The Simpsons,* are created by an analogous collage technique. Vaudeville consisted of a combination of acts, ranging from skits to acrobatic acts; *The Simpsons* sitcom cuts and pastes diverse elements from different levels of culture in the same episode, as mentioned earlier, to create a satirical collage.

The term *bricolage* emphasizes a unifying structure, not just a mixture of elements. It was first used in anthropology by Claude Lévi-Strauss (1962) to designate the style of many tribal rituals that mix various symbols and myths holistically in order to evoke magical feelings and a sense of communal harmony. The disparate elements become unified in the act of admixture itself. Bricolage has been used used to describe the power of subcultures among youth (Hebdige 1979).

Finally, in painting *pastiche* refers to an admixture of elements intended to imitate or satirize another work or style. Many aspects of pop culture display a pastiche pattern. A daily television newscast is a perfect example of this pattern. A typical newscast amalgamates news about crime and tragic events with those involving achievements of pop stars, creating a veritable pastiche of emotions and meanings. Indeed, the defining feature of all pop culture spectacles and texts may well be pastiche.

Nostalgia

Nostalgia is the sentimental attachment to trends from one's youth. Whether it is Elvis movies, Disney cartoons, Beatles albums, disco dancing, Barbie dolls, punk clothing, adventure comics, and so on, people react nostalgically to the trends and popular artifacts of their youth. The business of memorabilia is a profitable one indeed, as sales of items from the past, including Hula-Hoops, Coca-Cola classic bottles, and the like continue to make conspicuously obvious. People seem to maintain and cherish the trends of their youth well into their later years.

But this does not mean that pop culture is incapable of producing truly meritorious and lasting forms of art that transcend simple nostalgic value. Indeed, some of the modern world's most significant artistic products have come out of pop culture (as previously mentioned). The comic book art of Charles Schultz (1922–2000) is a case in point. His comic strip *Peanuts*, which debuted in 1950 as *Li'l Folks*, appealed—and continues to appeal—to all kinds of audiences, because of its intrinsic philosophical and poignant portrayals of the human condition. Through the strip Schultz dealt with some of the most profound questions of life, such as the nature of good and evil, in a way that was unique and aesthetically powerful.

Occultism

In the late 1960s and early 1970s, a serial killer known as the Zodiac used astrological signs in his messages to the media, becoming a dark and mysterious celebrity. Two movies have since dealt with the lure that the Zodiac held on people from that era. The first one was *Dirty Harry* (1971) in which a killer, named aptly Scorpio, is exterminated by Dirty Harry Callaghan, a hardnosed cop played by Clint Eastwood, thus allowing for a pseudo-cathartic effect to occur. The second movie is David Fincher's 2007 *Zodiac*, which taps into our intrinsic fear of the unknowable that the Zodiac evoked in his heyday. These movies illustrate the grip that the figure of the serial killer has on pop culture. They also bring out the fact that pop culture delves into occultism—a fact borne out not only by movie themes, but also by the popularity of horoscopes and doomsday documentaries on television.

Occult practices, from palm reading to magic shows, have always been a part of carnival sideshows and early vaudeville. And the most popular of all pop culture genres—the mystery or thriller narrative—is really a form of occult storytelling, where mystery and fear of the dark are evoked. Television shows such as *Supernatural* and *Lost*, gothic adventure heroes such as Batman, and many other spectacles cater explicitly to the occultism instinct as a form of cathartic entertainment.

Celebrity Culture

Another salient feature of pop culture is the fact that it produces most of our celebrities. This topic will be taken up in chapter 3. For the present purposes, it is sufficient to point out that it is an intrinsic component of pop culture. Like the heroes of ancient myths, the celebrities of pop culture are both exalted and condemned. Some become icons, especially after their deaths, venerated (at least for a time) like religious icons. Two well-known examples of this are Marilyn Monroe and Elvis Presley. Icons can come from all areas of pop culture—from sports (Babe Ruth, Mickey Mantle, Hank Aaron, Wilt Chamberlain, Michael Jordan, and so on) to science (Albert Einstein, Steve Jobs, and so on). Differentiating between celebrities and icons is part of the aim of pop culture studies.

Laughter

In any episode of *South Park*, one is bound to find a moral subtext—something in society, such as political correctness, that is raised to general awareness through comedy. As Arthur Asa Berger (2005: 38–39) aptly observes, "People crave humor and laughter, which explains why there are so many situation comedies on television and why film comedies have such widespread appeal." Humor is also a basic feature of many YouTube sites that highlight very funny things from the spectacle of everyday life. In some ways, the phenomenon of pop culture is an exercise in laughter and its psychological benefits. Although many aspects of this culture engage us in serious emotional ways, many others allow us to laugh and express ourselves cathartically. The ancient theatrical dichotomy between tragedy and comedy manifests itself in various forms in pop culture, suggesting that they are complementary aspects of the human psyche.

STUDYING POP CULTURE

Studying culture is the aim of disciplines such as anthropology and semiotics. Other disciplines, such as linguistics and musicology, focus on specific aspects or components of culture. The findings and insights garnered in these disciplines are, clearly, useful to the general study of pop culture. In fact, since their inception in the 1950s, pop culture studies have been characterized by *interdisciplinarity*—the adoption and integration of findings and ideas from various disciplines.

On one hand, the study of pop culture is fundamentally an exercise in unraveling the psychological reasons why such things as sports spectacles, Hula-Hoops, jukeboxes, celebrity chef recipes, movie stars, cars, songs, dances, television programs, clothing fashions, and the like gain popularity. On the other hand, the way that scholars study pop culture is akin to the approach taken by literary critics to the study of literary texts. Like literary critics, pop culture analysts identify and dissect the various *genres* that make up their subject and explore the nature of audiences for each genre.

Genres

The books, movies, television programs, and websites that are produced for mass consumption are categorized into various *genres*. The term, as pointed out, originated within literary criticism but was adopted by pop culture analysts from the outset.

Genres are identifiable by certain conventions, which audiences have come to recognize through regular exposure. A soap opera, for instance, is a serial drama, with stock characters involved in romantic entanglements; a talk show, on the other hand, involves an announcer who interviews people. Since each genre attracts a particular kind of audience, its programs are sponsored ordinarily by manufacturers who wish to target that audience. Indeed, the term *soap opera* comes from the fact that the genre was originally sponsored by detergent companies, and was designed to appeal to homemakers who stayed at home to do house chores, such as washing dishes and clothes.

Audiences

Audience is the term used to refer to the typical readers, spectators, listeners, viewers, and web navigators attracted to a certain genre. Most audiences are divisible into segments defined by specific sociological and psychographic characteristics. The contemporary specialty radio stations and television channels in particular have taken this aspect of broadcasting into account by providing programming that is aimed at audiences with specific kinds of interests. To describe this type of programming, the term *narrowcasting*, rather than *broadcasting*, is now used. Many audiences tend to perceive their favorite type of genre as consistent with their own life experiences; others may view the same genre more critically. For example, a nonreligious viewer of a televangelism program will tend to interpret it critically and skeptically, whereas an audience of faithful viewers will perceive it as relevant directly to their personal life experiences.

Pop Culture Study Today

As will be discussed in the next chapter, pop culture study now has its own set of theories and analytical frameworks. These provide insights that can be applied in part or in whole to a study of some pop culture trend or product. The appeal of interdisciplinary study is that it leaves the interpretation of a text or spectacle flexible and open. This openness to interpretation is the main reason why there is really no one overarching theory of pop culture.

Many pinpoint the work of Michigan State University's Russel B. Nye as pivotal in defining an autonomous pop culture field of study. Nye helped establish the Popular Culture Association in the late 1960s, which publishes *The Journal of Popular Culture*. Pop culture courses and entire programs are now found throughout the academic landscape. This has brought about a veritable explosion of scholarly interest in popular culture. The pages that follow will, hopefully, impart a sense of what such study now entails.

With the advent of digital technologies, it has never been easier for audiences around the world to access programs and information. The traditional, localized (nationalistic) audience has become a more global, intercultural audience. As a result, pop culture research is changing, since it is becoming more and more obvious that the forms of media culture to which audiences are exposed today will be determined not only by those living in a specific area of the world, but increasingly by people in different regions of the globe. For example, YouTube has virtually obliterated the distinction between target and global audiences, and between media producers and consumers.

Actually, the world of pop culture is fast becoming more and more a world of "entertainment marketing," as Lieberman and Esgate (2014) aptly observe. With over $2 trillion in yearly revenue, the entertainment industries have appropriated new platforms, media, and global markets in making pop culture a truly global phenomenon. Pop culture study today is a serious academic enterprise, encompassing views of mass communications, mass society, consumerism, technology, politics, economic trends, and even emerging neuroscientific hypotheses of why the brain seems to be wired for entertainment.

2

EXPLAINING POP CULTURE

There is no comparing the brutality and cynicism of today's pop culture with that of forty years ago: from High Noon *to* Robocop *is a long descent.*

—Charles Krauthammer (b. 1950)

Why is pop culture *popular?* Why do some people hate it or love to hate it? Does simulated television violence lead to real-life violence? Given its broad dissemination, and often controversial forms, explaining the reasons for the emergence and spread of pop culture has become a major focus of psychologists, anthropologists, and other social scientists almost since the turn of the twentieth century. The purpose of the present chapter is to look at the main theories of pop culture in outline form. These are useful only insofar as they allow us to develop complementary perspectives on the phenomenon pop culture. No one theory can provide an overarching answer to its raison d'être. The next chapter is an extension of this one, focusing more on the actual business of pop culture, that is, on its relation to mass consumerist culture.

COMMUNICATIONS MODELS

The importance that mass communications technologies have played in the birth, rise, and spread of pop culture cannot be stressed enough. Thus, one approach to pop culture is to look at the relationship between different communications technologies and the content they permit through different platforms. Known as communications or transmission models, these deal with the effects of differing media on pop culture. Of special interest is the work of Marshall McLuhan, which expands upon an early model called the *bull's-eye model*.

The Bull's-Eye Model

The American engineer Claude Shannon (1916–2001) devised a theory in the late 1940s designed to improve the efficiency of telecommunications systems. Known as the *bull's-eye model*, its usefulness for pop culture study lies in the fact that it identifies and names the main components of such systems, describing how they shape the transmission and reception of information. In bare outline form, the model consists of a *sender* targeting a *message* at a *receiver*.

Adapted to pop culture analysis, the sender can be an individual (a musician, for example), a business (such as an advertiser), or a performative source (such as a television program); the message is the content of the performance or text (a television program, for instance); and the receiver is anyone to whom the message is directed, especially the audience. Four other main components complete the model: channel, noise, redundancy, and feedback. The *channel* is the physical system carrying the transmitted signal. Words, for instance, can be transmitted through the air (in face-to-face communication) or through an electronic channel (for example, through the radio). *Noise* is any interference in the channel that distorts or partially effaces the message. In radio and telephone transmissions, it is equivalent to electronic static; in verbal communication, it can vary from any interfering exterior sound (physical noise) to the speaker's lapses of memory (psychological noise). Communication systems have built-in *redundancy* features that allow for messages to be understood even if noise is present. For instance, in human communication the high predictability of certain words in some utterances and the patterned repetition of phrases are redundant features of conversation that greatly increase the likelihood that a verbal message will be received successfully. Finally, *feedback* refers to the capability of a sender in a communication system of detecting signals or cues issuing back from the intended receiver, or from the system itself, so that the control of the communication system (or the contents of a message)

Figure 2.1.   The bull's-eye model

can be maintained, adapted, modified, or improved. Feedback in human communication includes the physical reactions observable in receivers (facial expressions, bodily movements) that indicate the effect that a message is having on them as it is being communicated. In television, it generally corresponds to ratings.

This model provides a minimal nomenclature for describing how performances or programs (and other events) take place, with feedback consisting of everything from audience reactions to a joke recited on stage to ratings on the popularity of a TV sitcom taken by professional statisticians. Noise is any interfering element in the effective reception of a performance or text, such as competition from another sitcom, poor timing of a punch line, and so forth.

The SMCR Model

The bull's-eye model was used as far back as 1954 by the American social theorist Wilbur Schramm (1907–1987), who added to it the concept of *encoder*, which converts the message into a form that can be transmitted through an appropriate channel; and the *decoder*, which reverses the process so that the message can be received and understood successfully. It is called the *Sender* (or *Source*)-*Message-Channel-Receiver* model, shortened to the SMCR model. It continues to be used in media and pop culture studies, because of its applicability to all types of performances and texts.

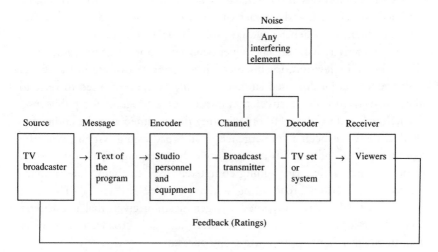

Figure 2.2. An SMCR model of a television broadcast

The SMCR model can, for instance, be used to describe the components of a television program, such as a sitcom. In this case: *source* = the broadcaster, *message* = the text of the sitcom, *encoder* = studio personnel and their equipment, *channel* = the actual broadcast transmitter or frequency band used, *decoder* = the television set or system (such as an Internet site) that has the capacity to decode the broadcast signal, *receiver* = the viewers or audience, *noise* = any interfering factor in the transmission or in the quality of the script, and *feedback* = the ratings garnered by the broadcast.

A further elaboration of this basic model was put forward by George Gerbner (1919–2005) in 1956. Encoding and decoding, according to Gerbner, involve knowledge of how a message refers to cultural forms, including relations between the sexes in, say, a sitcom, or the features that make a hero superhuman. He claimed that television and other popular media were "popular" because they recycled these forms and features in new ways. With Larry Gross (1976), Gerbner developed "cultivation theory," or the view that television viewing, over time, subtly entrenches a specific worldview. They found that those who spent more time watching television tended to have beliefs and values about reality that were consistent with those in the programs they watched. For example, they seemed to believe that the world was a much more dangerous and frightening place than it actually was, thus developing a greater sense of anxiety and mistrust of others. They called this phenomenon the "mean world syndrome." Television conveys a strong, implicit message about social relationships and power structures in society.

Communications models have often been criticized for not taking into account content and interactivity between senders and receivers. But without them, such debates would probably never have arisen in the first place. Interactivity has, actually, never been a component of traditional media (radio and television, for instance); it is now a fact of life in the digital universe as will be discussed later. *Broadcasting* is the term used to refer to the one-way (non-interactive) transmission of a program for public use. *Narrowcasting* refers instead to broadcasting that is aimed at niche audiences. Today, there has been a convergence of all broadcasting systems, whereby traditional forms of broadcasting are now either merging with Internet sites, which are interactive, or yielding completely over to them. The simultaneous use of various broadcasting systems is called *multicasting*. The term *broadcast network* today has gained a larger meaning given that it can refer to over-the-air radio or television broadcasting, cable broadcasting, satellite transmission, or some other form of broadcasting.

Broadcasting has brought the performances of comedians, actors, singers, musicians, and others to large numbers of people who would have had no access to them otherwise. The main lesson to be learned from studying the history of broadcasting is that there is no "turning back the clock." Once a new broadcasting technology is introduced that reaches broader audiences and is cheap, it will guide the future course of how people come to access and understand media products. Remarkably, this has not meant the elimination of previous systems and forms of broadcasting. The term now used to refer to the more general phenomenon of the blending of media, technology, and cultural forms is *convergence*.

Today *webcasting* has become a new and major source for the delivery of pop culture. A webcast uses streaming media to distribute content over the Internet. It can be live or on demand. The largest webcasters are, actually, the traditional radio and TV outlets that simulcast their content through streaming sites. Because webcasting is cheap and reaches all kinds of audiences, it has allowed independent media industries to arise and flourish. Also, streaming media are being coupled with social media sites such as YouTube, encouraging interactivity though live chats, online surveys, and the like. Again, this topic will be discussed in a later chapter.

Marshall McLuhan

The scholar most associated with linking mass communications technologies to pop culture was Marshall McLuhan, who claimed throughout his career that there existed an intrinsic synergy between the mass media and cultural forms. Each major period in history takes its character from the medium used most widely at the time. McLuhan called the period from 1700 to the mid-1900s the "Age of Print," and the "Gutenberg Galaxy"—after the invention of modern print technology by Johannes Gutenberg (c. 1395–1468)—because in those centuries cheap printed books were the chief means through which mass communications took place. The consequences of that event were felt throughout the world—the extensive gaining of print literacy encouraged individualism and the desire for nationalism. The "Electronic Age" converged with the Gutenberg Galaxy by the middle part of the twentieth century. Again, the consequences of that event have been monumental. Because electronic channels of communication increase the rapidity at which people can interact and because they make it possible to reach many people, the world has once again changed radically. Phones, radios, computers, cell phones, and mobile devices have influenced

---

MARSHALL MCLUHAN (1911–1980)

Marshall McLuhan was a professor at the University of Toronto. His theories on the relation between mass communications systems and culture caused widespread debate. McLuhan claimed that changes in communications technology affected our ways of thinking as well as our social institutions. He wrote several widely read books, including: *The Mechanical Bride* (1951), *The Gutenberg Galaxy* (1962), *Understanding Media* (1964), *The Medium Is the Massage* (1967), and *War and Peace in the Global Village* (with Q. Fiore, 1968).

---

the lives of everyone, even those who do not use them, leading to a new sense of community, as if we all lived in the same village, an electronic global village, as McLuhan called it.

McLuhan coined the phrase "the medium is the message," implying that a medium "shapes and controls the scale and form of human association and action" (McLuhan 1962: 9) and is therefore the message. He put forward four laws of media that have been applied extensively in the social sciences: amplification, obsolescence, reversal, and retrieval. A new technological invention will at first enhance some sensory, intellectual, or other faculty of the user. While one area is amplified, another is lessened or eventually rendered obsolete, until it is used to maximum capacity and must reverse its characteristics and is retrieved in another medium. An example given by McLuhan is that of print, which initially enhanced the concept of individualism, rendering group identity obsolete until it changed from a single printed text to mass production, whereby mutual reading allowed for the retrieval of group identity. These four laws can certainly be applied to the Internet, which has amplified all aspects of communication and information access, rendering traditional media obsolete, but has now converged with them in synergistic ways.

McLuhan saw the allure of pop culture as a symptom of what happens when philosophy and traditional ethics vanish from everyday intellectual life (Coupland 2010). His fear was that Big Brother, in the form of mass communications technologies, would take over the world and that people would acquiesce because it was convenient for them to do so—a theme that was explored in the 1997 James Bond movie titled *Tomorrow Never Dies*, where the evil villain, Elliott Carver, unlike the villains of previous Bond movies, seeks control over the world, not by means of brute force, but by gaining control of all mass communications media. The transparent message of that movie is that we live in a world that is being threatened more and more by those who hold the levers of media power.

Agenda Setting

One of the most relevant offshoots of communications models is agenda-setting theory, a term that refers to the fact that the mass media influence social opinion by virtue of the fact that they choose which stories, performers, events, and so on are worthy of attention. This emphasis often gets transferred to public and political agendas, called *salience transfer*.

Agenda-setting theory was introduced by Maxwell McCombs and Donald Shaw in 1972 in their study of the effects of media coverage on the 1968 American presidential campaign. The study found a correlation between the rate and extent of media coverage and people's opinions. As they put it: "Although the evidence that mass media deeply change attitudes in a campaign is far from conclusive, the evidence is much stronger that voters learn from the immense quantity of information available during each campaign" (McCombs and Shaw 1972: 176). In other words, events that are showcased on major media are felt to be more significant than those that are not. Televised events such as the John F. Kennedy and Lee Harvey Oswald assassinations, the O. J. Simpson trial, the death of Lady Diana, the Bill Clinton sex scandal, the 9/11 attacks, the Ebola crisis, and so on are perceived as portentous events. But the broadcasting rules have changed in the Internet Age; so agenda-setting theory needs to be revised. As Klaus Bruhn Jensen (2010: 136) puts it: "Compared with the relatively familiar terrain of national political issues, and with the delimited set of print and broadcast media that McCombs and Shaw (1972) selected from, digital media complicate the question of how public agendas are to be defined and understood, and how they may be set."

Overall, communications models of media suggest that changes in popular culture are connected to changes in mass communications technologies. Differences among broadcasting, narrowcasting, and webcasting, for instance, entail differences in the way content (performances, programs, and the like) are structured for delivery, thus affecting the content. The early communications models dealt with transmission platforms, whereby senders aimed their messages at receivers and feedback was garnered in a delayed fashion (through ratings systems such as Nielsen's); the current models deal instead with interactive digital platforms.

CRITICAL THEORIES

Pop culture—especially in its American and Western European versions—has been the target of many attacks and critiques from all kinds of intellectual and ideological angles. Such *critical theories*, as they can be called, look at the overall consequences that pop culture has brought about to contemporary societies, and at how these have affected the evolution of all forms of culture—conceptual, material, performative, and aesthetic (chapter 1).

Marxist Theories

Among the first to criticize pop culture as a negative force were the scholars belonging to the Frankfurt School, which included Theodor W. Adorno (1903–1969), Walter Benjamin (1892–1940), Max Horkheimer (1895–1973), Herbert Marcuse (1898–1979), Erich Fromm (1900–1980), and Leo Lowenthal (1900–1993). In one way or another, these scholars saw pop culture as a commodity culture, produced in the same way that material products are—made and sold in the marketplace. They thus saw capitalist societies as tying artistic forms to a "culture industry" obeying only the logic of marketplace economics. Adopting Italian Marxist Antonio Gramsci's (1891–1937) concept of *hegemony*, they claimed that the commodification of culture was controlled by those who held social-financial power. Gramsci used the term in reference to his belief that the dominant class in a society used instruments of persuasion, which varied from outright coercion (incarceration, the use of secret police, and threats) to gentler and more "managerial" tactics (education, religion, and control of the mass media), in order to gain conformity of thought among the masses. The concept of hegemony has found widespread use in current media studies and in some social sciences.

The Frankfurt School theorists were, overall, pessimistic about the possibility of genuine culture under modern capitalism, condemning most forms of popular culture as crude spectacles that pacified the masses because of their ephemeral entertainment value. Adorno and Horkheimer traced the source of this process to the Enlightenment and the secular scientific bias that developed from it—the view that science and technology could solve all human problems. Breaking somewhat from this mold was Mar-

---

THE FRANKFURT INSTITUTE FOR SOCIAL RESEARCH

The Institute was founded at the University of Frankfurt in 1922. It was the world's first Marxist school of social research. Its aim was to understand the ways in which human groups created meaning collectively under the impact of modern technology and capitalist economics.

cuse, who saw in some forms of youth culture (such as in hippie culture) a renaissance of Romantic idealism, and Benjamin, who put forward a "catharsis hypothesis," in which he claimed that the vulgar and violent aspects of pop culture allowed people to release pent-up energies and, thus, pacified them. The ideas of the Frankfurt School will be revisited in other parts of this book. Suffice it to say here that they reflected a basic Marxist critique of capitalist culture. Capitalist societies, they claimed, view culture as they do any economic process, as a commodity industry with monetary value.

Even before the advent of the Frankfurt School, British social critic Matthew Arnold (1822–1883) saw the mass culture that emerged after the Industrial Revolution and urbanization in the nineteenth century as crassly homogeneous, serving only the base instincts of human beings. Arnold argued that such vulgar forms of culture had crystallized from capitalist societies and were a threat to the progress of an enlightened human civilization. Arnold's attack was taken up by Frank R. Leavis (1895–1978) in the 1930s and 1940s. Leavis attacked American pop culture vitriolically, seeing in it evidence of the decline of civilization and a product of a bourgeois mentality.

Centre for Contemporary Cultural Studies

Marxist theory became highly influential in the 1970s after the widely read critiques of pop culture by British scholars at the Centre for Contemporary Cultural Studies in the University of Birmingham, which was founded in 1964. The scholars at the Centre took the commodification view of their Frankfurt predecessors researching its impact on contemporary societies and on the inequalities that, they claimed, it had brought forth. One of the goals of the Centre was political dissent, which is evident in the work of scholars like Raymond Williams, Dick Hebdige, Stuart Hall, and Angela McRobbie. Hebdige's widely cited book, *Subculture: The Meaning of Style*, which was originally published in 1979, has become a crucial point of reference in the study of youth culture generally. Angela McRobbie's work on the treatment of gender in pop culture has also become a major source of ideas in the field. The Centre's members were particularly concerned with depictions of otherness, from representations (or lack thereof) of different races to different sexual orientations. In *Policing the Crisis: Mugging, the State and Law and Order* (1978), Stuart Hall argued that the media's portrayal of crime is part of a game of social control, whereby crime statistics are manipulated in order to cause moral panic, which in turn induces the public to support repressive measures.

The members of the Centre incorporated insights from theoretical frameworks and fields such as semiotics, women's studies, sociology, and cultural anthropology. They examined specific facets of contemporary cultural representations in terms of the inequalities they produced and the misrepresentations they perpetrated by tacit agreement with those in power, as well as the ideological structures behind popular culture. Their views are now largely limited to traditional media forms and have been marginalized in the era of the Internet. But some of their ideas still persist and can be seen in various critical attacks on media culture today.

Propaganda Theory

The general thrust of Marxist models such as the Frankfurt and Birmingham ones influenced the development of propaganda theory in the United States, a framework associated primarily with Noam Chomsky (Herman and Chomsky 1988). Essentially, the theory maintains that those in power, such as the government of the day, influence how the media present news coverage for the simple reason that the power brokers control the funding and (in many cases) ownership of the media. As a consequence, the media tend to be nothing more than a propaganda arm of those in power or those who wield great financial clout. The mainstream media are set up to "manufacture consent." They do this by selecting the topics to be showcased, establishing the tone of the issues that are discussed, and filtering out any contradictory information. Contrary to the common belief that the press is adversarial to those in power, propaganda theorists have consistently argued that it unwittingly (or sometimes wittingly) supports them because it is dependent on them for subsistence. However, propaganda theorists have been severely criticized because they do not seem to accept the possibility that common people can tell the difference between truth and manipulation. Moreover, because of the Internet, the media moguls are increasingly being taken to task. If consent is really manufactured, why is there so much online critique against those in power?

Overall, propaganda theorists claim that pop culture and the mass media have formed an unconscious partnership. The end result is a vast media and pop culture industry that manufactures a view of the world that espouses an elemental form of patriotism and the essential benevolence of power brokers and the institutions that they head. Herman and Chomsky point out the presence of five filters to bolster their case. They call the first filter the ownership filter, implying that news information is filtered (behind the scenes) by the corporate conglomerates that control the flow of information. The second is the funding filter, whereby media outlets must abide by the wishes of those who fund them, including advertisers. The third is the sourcing filter, by which the government and major corporations are the ones who actually provide the news to be broadcast to the media outlets, filtering out, and even censoring, those not deemed supportive of their own views. The fourth filter is flak, which they define as any negative reaction to news items. The fifth filter is the "anti-communism" one, which is the view that any political ideology contrary to the American one is generally repressed or portrayed in negative terms.

Feminism and Post-Feminism

Another critical view of pop culture came from feminist studies starting in the 1970s and 1980s. By and large, they claimed that pop culture spectacles were degrading to women, and a source of influence in promoting violence against women.

Some of their critiques were well founded, given the effusion of images of women as "sexual cheerleaders" or "motherly homemakers" in many movies and television programs of the 1940s and 1950s. However, alongside such skewed masculinist representations of womanhood imprinted in such texts, there were others, such as *The Honeymooners* (broadcast from 1955–1956 on CBS), which portrayed women as independent and combative against the masculinist mold. Similarly, *I Love Lucy* (1951–1960 on CBS) featured a strong-willed, independent female who was completely in charge of her situation. Moreover, by viewing women's bodies in all kinds of popular spectacles and erotic movies only as a form of objectification and male voyeurism, the early feminists ignored the fact that this actually played a critical role in liberating women from seeing themselves constricted to the roles of housekeepers and mothers, as the movie *Chicago* has emphasized.

Perhaps no one has understood the ambiguity of the roles of gender in pop culture better than the American pop star Madonna. The subtext in Madonna's early performances was transparent—no man can ever dictate to her how to pose and act on the stage. Masculinity (in its patriarchal forms) can thus be subjugated to femininity in its sexual forms. Madonna's concerts were pure spectacle, blending "peep show" images with postures that were evocative of prayer. Using the power of her sexual persona she invited *spectare* (to look) from both male and female audiences. Her intermingling of performative modes was overpowering. Madonna turned the tide in feminist theory, inspiring the movement known as *post-feminism*. She did this by exposing the latent puritanism and suffocating white middle-class ideology of previous forms of American feminism, which were stuck in an "adolescent whining mode," as Camille Paglia (1992) argued. Madonna showed young women how to be fully female and sexual while exercising control over their bodies and their lives.

Post-feminist theory does not see the display of women's bodies on the stage of pop culture as exploitation, but rather as a transgressive form of dialogue (Phoca and Wright 1999). Eroticism is part of women's liberation. At its most extreme form, it has assailed sexual mores since the 1970s, after the pornographic *Deep Throat* premiered in 1972, a movie that was perceived not just as pornographic, but also as a serious threat to the political and social order. The reason for this was that women appeared to like it as much as men. The equality in reception truly upset those in political and moral power, who saw it as perhaps the greatest threat to their hegemony. As tasteless and offensive spectacle, pornography is often juxtaposed against more acceptable forms of female sexuality—namely, the romantic ones. But, as post-feminists argue, the notion that women's fantasy worlds are limited to Harlequin-type romance novels, movies, and songs is a distortion.

A sign that the tide turned in feminist theory is the fact that, as Francesca Twinn (2007: 19) reports, today pornography is viewed widely by women. As Debbie Nathan (2007) has pointed out, in some ways, the history of pornography overlaps with the history of pop culture. Walter Kendrick (1987) writes that in the ancient world, the term *pornography* referred to "writing about prostitutes," not to visual depictions of sexual activities. Ironically, it was during the sexually repressive Victorian era that, as Ken Gelder (2007: 23) puts it, pornography "became an underground cottage industry with its own traditions and its specialized audiences, able to retain at least some of its political edge and libelous force." In no way, does the forgoing discussion aim to diminish the detrimental effects that the porn industry wreaks on actors, and perhaps even on social mores. But the point is that it is part of the profane nature of pop culture and, like carnival sideshows, it is part of the act. All attempts to explain it clinically as aberrant behavior will not make it go away. Interestingly, despite what some critics claim (Hedges 2009), there has been a decline in visits to pornographic websites on the Internet, due, in all probability, to the fact that porn no longer has a deep hold on people living in a post–*Deep Throat* world, and because there are new and more participatory ways of seeking online sex. As Tancer (2008: 26) aptly writes: "Who needs porn when Facebook gives you the opportunity to hook up in the flesh?"

Today, feminism embraces critiques of all aspects of gender, including diverse sexual orientations and the redefinitions of masculinity, as evidenced by changing representations of men in such sitcoms as *Two and a Half Men* and *Big Bang Theory*. In the latter, the male geek emerges as a new masculine persona. The four main male characters are avid sci-fi, fantasy, comic book, and memorabilia fanatics. The show parodies both the geek male (and female) and romantic and sexual relations in general. It shows how the sitcoms have always mirrored social reality.

The Internet has also given rise to new forms of feminist theory. Some have suggested that the prevalence of digital technology is indicative of a veritable paradigm shift in how women are now positioned to exercise dominance in the world of cyberspace, given their supposed competencies in interpersonal communication. The most optimistic of these perspectives is called *cyberfeminism*, which claims that cyberspace is a space where traditional markers of gender, race, class, and age are all dissipating. While this is overly optimistic it does signal the fact that much has changed in the world today. There is no one critical theory that answers many of the questions that now arise. Regardless of which perspective(s) one may endorse, however, critical theories and practices have been crucial to the study of pop culture.

Postmodernism

The term *postmodernism* was coined by architects in the 1970s to characterize a new style that had emerged to challenge modernism, which by the mid-twentieth century had degenerated into barren and repetitive formulas (for example, box-like skyscrapers). Greater complexity and imagination, through a reinterpretation of traditional ornamental symbols and patterns, was called for by the new architects. Shortly after its introduction in architecture, the term postmodernism started to catch on more broadly, becoming a catchphrase in many areas of academia. Frederic Jameson, an early celebrated postmodernist critic, suggested that the end of modern liberal society came with the demise of true social protest in the 1960s. Since then, Jameson argues, a new crude pop culture has arisen that turns out to be nothing more than a late degenerative phase in the evolution of capitalism. Jameson (1991: 1–2) comments:

> Andy Warhol and pop art, but also photorealism, and beyond it, the "new expressionism"; the moment, in music, of John Cage, but also a synthesis of classical and "popular" styles found in composers like Phil Glass and Terry Riley, and also punk and new wave rock (the Beatles and the Stones now standing as the high-modernist movement of that

more recent and rapidly evolving tradition); in film, Godard, post-Godard, and experimental cinema and video, but also a whole new type of commercial film. Burroughs, Pynchon, or Ishmael Reed, on the one hand, and the French *nouveau roman* and its succession, on the other, along with alarming new kinds of literary criticism based on some new aesthetic of textuality.

Pop culture does not, in fact, make distinctions between popular and traditional forms of art. But pop culture is not chaotic, as Jameson implies. Jameson's statement is a clever condemnation of pop culture from a neo-Marxist view, but this view seems to ignore that pop culture is "hip" culture, not philosophical culture. It thrives in a capitalist society, because pop artists and their art must make it in the marketplace.

As postmodernist theory has been receding to the margins today, a derivative philosophy, called *post-humanism*, has come to the forefront. The term is used broadly to refer to an era in which humans no longer dominate the world but instead have merged with their machines and with animals to create a new world order that pits humans not at the center of the universe but as equal partners with other intelligences (artificial and animal). It is thus a philosophy in opposition to traditional humanism, or the view that humans are makers of their own world, not subject to external forces. In post-humanism, humans are just small organic particles in the overall scheme of things.

The question that all the above approaches raise is the following one: Who decides what is "good" culture and what is "tasteless" culture? The critiques put forward hide within them both an elitist subtext—only intellectuals (the theorists themselves) know what good culture is—and an ideological subtext—capitalism is a destructive form of social organization interested not in individuals, but in the bottom line. The masses are, thus, assumed to be zombies, unaware of the manipulation to which they are subjected on a daily basis through commodification. But, as many others have argued, capitalist-based pop culture has actually provided the means for common people to resist those in power, not be controlled by them, since the marketplace is open to anyone willing to take the risk to enter it and perform there, even politically (Artz and Murphy 2000).

PSYCHOLOGICAL AND SOCIOLOGICAL THEORIES

Does exposure to violent shows on television predispose us to be more violent and act out violent fantasies? Does exposure to inane sitcom humor corrupt true human dialogue? These are, clearly, important questions. Thus, it should come as little wonder to find that the investigation of the purported effects of pop culture on people has been a target of great interest to psychologists and sociologists.

The role of the media to affect people became evident early on, especially after the 1938 radio broadcast of a docudrama based on H. G. Wells's novel about interplanetary invasion, *War of the Worlds*. Many listeners believed that the broadcast was real, despite periodic announcements that it was merely a fictional dramatization. Hysteria resulted, with some people in the New Jersey area (where the invasion was reported as occurring) leaving their homes and phoning the local authorities in a panicked state of mind. The event became a topic of media attention and, a year later, led to the first psychological study on media effects. The research project was called the Cantril Study, after Hadley Cantril, who headed a team of researchers at Princeton University. The researchers wanted to find out why some believed the fake reports and others not. After interviewing 135 subjects, the team came to the conclusion that the key factor was critical thinking due to educational background—better-educated listeners were more likely to recognize the broadcast as a fake than less-educated ones. The study was criticized by psychologists and sociologists because it did not establish a true statistical correlation between the radio broadcast and the degree of reported panic. Moreover, the panic may have been caused by subsequent media stories that intentionally exaggerated the panic. No deaths or serious injuries were ever linked to the radio broadcast, and the streets were never crowded with hysterical citizens running around in panic as the media claimed. The reported panic may have itself been a media fiction.

Psychological Theories

The Cantril Study opened the door to a host of psychological studies aiming to determine the extent to which mass media content influences people. Many early studies claimed that media representations did not just mirror values and trends in society, but rather, shaped them and even generated them. Classified under the rubric of Hypodermic Needle Theory (HNT), the studies claimed that the media are capable of directly swaying minds with the same kind of effect that a hypodermic needle has in modifying bodily processes. Not everyone was convinced by the relevant findings. Contrasting research actually showed that audiences got out of media content the same views to which they were already inclined. For example, in an influential 1948 study, titled *The People's Choice*, American sociologist

One-Step Flow:

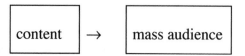

Two-Step Flow:

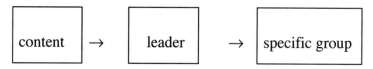

Figure 2.3.   Two-step flow theory

Paul Lazarsfeld (1901–1976) and a team of researchers found that the media had little ability to change people's minds about how they would vote in an election. People simply selected from newspapers or radio broadcasts only the views that fit in with their preconceptions and ignored the others. People perceive media content as interpretive communities—that is, as part of families, unions, neighborhoods, churches, and the like. In such communities, there are "opinion leaders" who mediate how the other members interpret content. In contrast to HNT, which viewed the spread of media content as a one-step flow reaching a homogeneous audience directly, Lazarsfeld saw it as a two-step flow. In the first step, the opinion leader takes in media content and interprets it; in the second step, this leader passes on the interpretation to group members.

Despite the improvements of the two-step model over the one-step model, it raises some questions. One is the identification of opinion leaders, which is usually carried out through the self-reports of the subjects interviewed, and could thus be incorrect. Another is that opinion leaders are not exposed randomly to any type of information, but to the kind that is related to areas in which they did indeed exert influence. In terms of the current methodology, these problems have been somewhat resolved. For example, social network analysis focuses on how individuals in society are connected and the connection creates a hierarchy of individuals, with leaders at the top.

Another critique is that, basically, the power of media to affect people directly psychologically cannot be underestimated, whether or not they belong to communities mediated by leaders. This was documented by a well-known media episode—the Kennedy-Nixon TV debate, which turned the 1960 election around in favor of Kennedy. People who heard the debate on radio maintained that Nixon had won it, coming across as the better candidate; those who saw it on television claimed the opposite. Nixon looked disheveled and worried; Kennedy looked confident and came across as a young, idealistic, and vibrant "president of the future."

Clearly, the study of audiences in media and pop culture is a central one. The field of Audience Research (AR) has confirmed many aspects of two-step theory. It has also shown that audiences negotiate the interpretation of a media text according to their backgrounds and life experiences, not passively. Known as reception theory, it posits moreover that interpretation is a variable phenomenon, not a static one as assumed by many early researchers. So, a sitcom like *Big Bang Theory* may be interpreted by some as part of how amorous relations are negotiated today, but by others as a sign of the breakdown of traditional courtship patterns. It all depends on subjective experiences, on educational background, and so on. With the advent of digital technologies, it has never been easier for audiences around the world to access programs. As a consequence, the traditional, localized (nationalistic) audience has become a more global, intercultural one. As a result, AR research is changing, since it is becoming more and more obvious that the forms of pop culture to which audiences are exposed today will be determined not only by those living in a specific area of the world, but increasingly by people in different regions of the globe.

As a consequence, traditional ideas about audiences have started to change. In effect, the Internet has obliterated many of the demographic and psychographic variables that affected reception in the past. Consequently, as culture theorist Ien Ang (1995) has argued, the goal of contemporary media and pop culture studies should be to understand the constituency of global audiences so that the structure of popular culture can be studied more realistically.

One psychological idea that continues to be relevant even in the context of contemporary research models is the catharsis hypothesis. The term *catharsis* was used by Aristotle to explain the effect that tragic dramas have on an audience, allowing for the release of pent-up emotions, and thus cleansing them. In pop culture studies, the same idea is used to claim that representations of violence and aggression have a preventive purging effect, since an involvement in fantasy violence provides a release from hostile impulses that otherwise might be enacted in real life.

Sociological Theories

In partnership with George Gerbner, Paul Lazarsfeld (mentioned above) initiated a series of sociological studies, showing that popular media representations had a conservative social function, not a disruptive one. The use of violence and the depiction of criminality on television crime programs did not induce more violence or criminality in society, because it had a preventive moral subtext to it—it warned people about the dangers of violence and crime. As already mentioned, Gerbner claimed that media representations "cultivate," not threaten, the status quo. The overrepresentation of violence in popular media is intended to reinforce respect for law and order, since the "bad guys" typically pay for their sins in the end. But this overrepresentation produced a heightened sense that the real world has become a de facto violent place.

In a series of related studies, a research team headed by Elihu Katz (Katz et al., 1973, 1974) found that audiences use the media for their own purposes and gratification. Known, in fact, as *uses and gratifications theory*, Katz maintained that media content does nothing to people; rather, people use the media for their own desires. This theory suggests, above all else, that television (and other popular media) are vehicles for escapism from the problems of everyday life. In this framework a distinction is maintained between gratifications obtained and gratifications sought. The former are those that people experience through the media; the latter are those that people expect to obtain from the media beforehand. When, say, a television program actually provides or even surpasses expectations, people tend to view it more habitually. Contrarily, people tend to seek out different media to provide the gratifications they are seeking. In the case of new media, such as video games, gratification can more easily be sought and gained given their interactive possibilities. Interactivity thus becomes crucial to the theory because it entails the notion of the active audience member who has control over the medium used. A series of recent studies have shown that instant messaging is used primarily for social entertainment purposes in addition to a means for contacting people.

An important sociological concept that has commonly been adopted by media scholars is that of alienation—a term coined by Marx to describe a sensed estrangement from other people, society, or work. Sociologists define alienation as a blocking or dissociation of a person's feelings. Some believe that alienation is produced by a shallow and depersonalized society. French social theorist Émile Durkheim (1858–1917) suggested that alienation stemmed from a loss of religious traditions. He used the term *anomie* to refer to the sense of alienation and purposelessness experienced by a person or a class as a result of a lack of moral standards and values (Durkheim 1912). The term is often used in the literature by those who believe that anomie makes some people more susceptible to the effects of mass media. Some media analysts also talk of "alienation effects," which are the effects produced by using alienating techniques such as unsettling lighting effects or bizarre soundtracks that force an audience to develop a critical attitude toward what they are exposed to.

Another sociologically oriented view to have arisen in the last few decades is that of Americanization, or the purported influence the United States has on the culture of other nations through the overrepresentation of its popular culture in the global mass media. The term has a negative connotation if the influence is imposed unwillingly; it has a positive one if the influence is sought voluntarily.

SEMIOTIC APPROACHES

Many scholars of pop culture today pinpoint the true advent of an independent discipline in the English translation of French semiotician Roland Barthes's book *Mythologies* in 1957. Barthes explained the appeal of

---

FOUNDERS OF SEMIOTICS

Ferdinand de Saussure (1857–1913): The Swiss philologist Ferdinand de Saussure is considered to be one of the founders of modern-day semiotics. He taught at the École des Hautes Études in Paris from 1881 to 1891 and then became a professor of Sanskrit and comparative grammar at the University of Geneva. After his death, two of his assistants collated the lecture notes of some of his students and published them in 1916 as a book (*Cours de linguistique générale*) that names Saussure as the author. A comprehensive model of semiotics (or semiology, as Saussure called it) is found in that book.

Charles S. Peirce (1839–1914): The American philosopher and mathematician Charles Peirce is another founder of modern-day semiotics. Peirce is also known for his philosophical system, later called pragmatism, which maintains that the significance of any theory or model lies in the practical effects of its application.

pop culture spectacles in terms of mythology theory, or the idea that the spectacles recycle ancient mythic themes in modern guises. Wrestling and blockbuster movies engage the masses, rather than the cognoscenti, because they tap into mythical meaning systems—good versus evil, hero versus villain, and so on. Everything from comic books to fashion shows have mass appeal because they emanate from within these mythologies.

Barthes used notions from semiotics to make his case. The five rudimentary semiotic notions that have become widespread in pop culture study today are: opposition, mythology, representation, code, and textuality.

Opposition implies that we do not perceive the meaning of something in an absolute way, but in differential ways. For example, if we were to think of *day*, its opposite, *night*, would invariably pop up in our mind. Indeed, we seem incapable of understanding *night* unless we oppose it to *day*, and vice versa. *Mythology* theory claims that popular texts, performances, and spectacles are linked to each other through a chain of mythic (ancient) oppositions, such as *good* versus *evil* and *male* versus *female*, that are recycled in new textual and performative ways. *Representation* refers to the view that any *text* or spectacle stands for something that is not immediately obvious in the text. The *text* defers to that "something else" instead of referring to it directly. It is based on social *codes*—systems of notions and beliefs that are channeled into representational structures and enacted in cultural ways.

Opposition Theory, Structuralism, and Post-Structuralism

The notion of opposition has proven itself to be a highly productive one in the study of pop culture, because it allows us to flesh out the hidden meanings built into characters, plots, performances, and so forth through a simple differential technique that shows the implicit meanings in them. As a simple example, consider the differences that are associated with the opposition of *white* versus *black* in Western culture. The color *white* is typically perceived as a symbol of *purity*, *innocence*, and so on, while its counterpart *black* usually symbolizes the opposite set of meanings, namely *impurity*, *corruption*, and the like. This opposition guides the construction of texts and spectacles in the form of symbols and details. In the early Hollywood western movies, for example, the cowboy heroes wore white hats and the villains black ones. This does not mean, however, that *black* is never associated with heroism. Reversing oppositions for effect is common. This is why the Zorro character of television and movie fame wears black, as did several Hollywood western heroes of the past (such as Lash Larue).

The French anthropologist Claude Lévi-Strauss (1978) claimed that binary oppositions (*night* versus *day*, *white* versus *black*) are built not only into narrative codes, but also into social systems. So, kinship systems invariably show oppositions between *father* and *mother* roles, versus subsidiary relations such as *sister* versus *brother*, *mother's sister* versus *mother's brother* and so on. These oppositions provide the social framework for kinship relations to cohere with each other systematically. As an analytical technique in pop culture studies, opposition also provides a template for understanding how spectacles and texts hold together. A perfect example is the six *Star Wars* movies, which started in 1977 and ended in 2005 under director and producer George Lucas. Elements of Greek dramatic style abound in the set. As in a Greek tragedy, the story began typically with a prologue, explaining the topic of the tragedy. The saga is also divided into individual episodes, released in a sequence that starts in *medias res* (in the middle of things) with the fourth episode being the first one put out, mirroring Homer's *Iliad*.

Significantly, the unifying theme of all the episodes is the universal opposition between evil (the tyrannical Empire) and good (the Rebel Alliance). Hero status in the set of movies cannot be attributed to one figure, but rather to a group who must work together for good to prevail. Luke Skywalker is one of them. Luke discovers that his father was a Jedi Knight, protecting the Old Republic. Luke is the last Jedi Knight who must fight against the dark side. But he has a tragic Freudian desire—he yearns for a father. In line with the Greek tradition of tragic irony, it is Darth Vader who turns out to be his father.

The other oppositions that constitute the unity of the overall text are essentially the same as those of the ancient stories: *young* versus *old* (Luke vs. Darth Vader), *rebels* versus *empire* (common folk vs. authority), and so on. As a modern morality tale, *Star Wars* simply renames it as a battle between the Jedi and Sith. Members of the Jedi Order have dedicated themselves for thousands of generations to mastering the knowledge and tranquility found in the benevolent light side of the force. They have pledged their lives to fight against evil, training to live an austere life, and using their skills to serve the Galactic Republic as guardians of justice and protectors of peace. They settle interplanetary disputes and defend the galaxy against aggression, thus earning universal respect. By using the Force, the Jedi can manipulate the minds of the weak-willed, move objects telekinetically, peer into the future, move around at enormous speeds, and survive death. After a devastating battle, the fallen Jedi are banished, settling in a far-flung planet (Korriban). The Sith want to conquer others, drawing their strength from the dark side of the Force, but are ultimately enslaved by it. After a savage battle thousands of years ago, all Sith were thought to have perished. But one survived who restructured the cult so that, at most, there could be only one master and an apprentice.

The use of opposition theory is part of an overarching approach to the study of meaning in human activities known as *structuralism*. Structuralism sees forms (words, texts, melodies, and so on) as resulting from oppositional relations within codes (language, narrative, music, and so on). For example, melodies are felt to be meaningful only if the combination of tones, rhythms, and harmonies is consistent with an established oppositional system of harmonic structure—major versus minor, tonic versus dominant, and so on. When putting together a simple sentence, we do not choose the words in a random fashion, but rather according to their differential and combinatory properties. The choice of the noun *friend* in the subject slot of a sentence such as *My friend is beautiful* fits our sentence structure because other nouns—*girl, man, woman,* and so on—could have been chosen instead. And the choice of any one of these for that sentence slot constrains the type and form of the verb that can be chosen and combined with it. Co-occurrence is a structural feature of all meaning-bearing systems.

The most severe attack on structuralism has revolved around the notion of *markedness* or the idea that in oppositions one of the two poles is more basic conceptually. In the *night*-versus-*day* opposition, it can easily be seen that the basic or "default" concept is *day*, because we perceive daytime as fundamental. This is called the *unmarked* concept, and *night* the *marked* one, because it is conceived as "absence of day," whereas *day* is not typically conceived as "absence of night." This analysis can be explained as having its source in human biology—we normally sleep at night and carry out conscious activities in the day. Now, the problem is deciding which pole is marked and unmarked in an opposition such as the *male*-versus-*female* one. The answer varies according to the society to which the opposition is applied, showing that some oppositions are universal and others are culture-specific. In patriarchal societies, the unmarked pole is *masculinity*; in matriarchal ones it is *femininity*.

This whole line of thought was dismissed by some scholars, notably Michel Foucault (1972) and Jacques Derrida (1976). Their critiques led to the movement known as *post-structuralism*. In post-structuralism, oppositions are attributed to the whims of the analyst, not as the result of some tendency present in the human brain (universal oppositions) or in a situation (culture-specific oppositions). Post-structuralism has largely receded to the margins in semiotics today. But it has left its mark on it by encouraging the use of *deconstruction* as a technique in textual analysis. The fundamental idea in deconstruction is that the meaning of a text cannot be determined in any absolute way through oppositions because it shifts according to who analyzes it, when it is analyzed, how it is analyzed, and so on. Moreover, every text has culture-specific worldviews built into it that are imprinted in the language used. These carry with them historically based biases and prejudices. The goal of deconstruction is to expose them. A text, therefore, has no unchanging, unified meaning, because the author's intentions cannot be identified. There are countless legitimate interpretations of a text that are beyond these intentions. Thus, the text deconstructs itself over time.

Mythology Theory

As mentioned, Barthes claimed that pop culture has great emotional allure because it is based on the recycling of unconscious mythic oppositions. In detective stories, for instance, the heroes and villains are modeled after ancient mythic heroes and their opponents. The heroes are honest, truthful, physically attractive, strong, and vulnerable; the villains are dishonest, cowardly, physically ugly, weak, and cunning. The hero is beaten up at some critical stage, but against all odds he or she survives to become a champion of justice. Because of the unconscious power of myth, it is no surprise to find that early Hollywood cowboy characters such as Roy Rogers, John Wayne, Hopalong Cassidy, and the Lone Ranger, became cultural icons, symbolizing virtue, heroism, and righteousness as did the ancient heroes. Although early Hollywood also showcased female characters as heroic, usually the women portrayed in them played a supporting role to the male hero. Hollywood has broken away from this male-centered mythology in recent times; but the tradition of the maverick male loner hero fighting for justice remains a central mythic image even in contemporary narratives.

The Superman character is a perfect example of the recycled mythic hero, possessing all the characteristics of his ancient predecessors but in modern guise—he comes from another world (the planet Krypton) in order to help humanity overcome its weaknesses; he has superhuman powers; but he has a tragic flaw (exposure to kryptonite takes away his power); and so forth. Sports events, too, are experienced mythically, with the opposition of *good* (the home team) vs. *evil* (the visiting team) guiding the whole event. The fanfare associated with preparing for the "big event," like the Superbowl of American football or the World Cup of soccer, has a ritualistic quality to it similar to the pomp and circumstance that ancient armies engaged in before going out to battle and war. Indeed, the whole spectacle is perceived to represent a battle of mythic proportions. The symbolism of the team's (army's) uniform, the valor and strength of the players (the heroic warriors), and the skill and tactics of the coach (the army general) has a powerful effect on the fans (the warring nations). As Barthes observed, this unconscious symbolism is the reason why spectacles are powerful. Like their ancient ancestors, modern-day people subconsciously need heroes to "make things right" in human affairs, at least in the world of fantasy.

In some ways, pop culture is pseudo-culture, if Barthes is correct. This view was taken up by another French scholar, Jean Baudrillard (1983) whose idea of the *simulacrum* has become a widely used and discussed one in pop culture studies. The 1999 movie *The Matrix* treated this theme in a brilliant way. The main protagonist of that movie, Neo, lives "on" and "through" the computer screen. The technical name of the computer screen is the *matrix*, describing the network of circuits on it. But the same word also means "womb" in Latin. The movie's transparent subtext is that, with the advent of the digital universe, new generations are now being born in two kinds of wombs—the biological and the technological. And the difference between the two has become indistinguishable.

Baudrillard maintained that the borderline between fiction and reality has utterly vanished, collapsing into a mind-set that he called the *simulacrum*. The content behind the screen is perceived as hyperreal, that is, as more real than real, as are all kinds of pop culture spectacles. Baudrillard used the example of Disney's Fantasyland and Magic Kingdom, which are copies of other fictional worlds. They are copies of copies and, yet, people appear to experience them as more real than real. They are "simulation machines" that reproduce past images to create a new environment for them. Eventually, as people engage constantly with the hyperreal, everything becomes simulation. This is why, according Baudrillard, people are easily duped by advertisers. It is instructive to note that the producers of *The Matrix* had approached Baudrillard to be a consultant for the movie. Apparently, he turned them down.

Representation

In 1997 a tragic event occurred that greatly affected people living primarily in Western societies—the death of Princess Diana at a young age. Her death was felt by many to be analogous to the deaths of legendary heroes. In other parts of the world, her death was felt differently. In some countries, it was ignored. In effect, her death was *represented* differently according to situation—as mythic tragedy or as simply a casualty. *Representa-*

tion is the process of depicting or recounting something in some specific fashion that requires special interpretation. The intent of the representer, the historical, cultural, and social contexts in which the representation is made, the purpose for which it is made, and what it is designed to depict all play a role in how it is interpreted and received by audiences.

As another example, consider the representation of fatherhood in television sitcoms. In the 1950s, the father was portrayed as someone who was all-knowing and in charge of his family. The sitcom that best represented this portrait of fatherhood was *Father Knows Best*. In the 1980s and 1990s sitcom *Married . . . with Children*, however, the representation changed drastically. The father was depicted as an ignoramus who had absolutely no control over his family. These different representations of fatherhood on American sitcoms reflected changing concepts of fatherhood in society. Consider how fathers are represented today in sitcoms such as *Family Guy* and *Two and a Half Men*. The former show revolves around the adventures of the Peter Griffin, his wife, Lois, and three children, Meg, their teenage daughter, Chris, their teenage son, and Stewie, their infant son. The family represents a deconstruction of the traditional American family. Meg is awkward and is constantly ridiculed; Chris is unintelligent and huge and thus a younger version of his father; and Stewie is a diabolical kid of ambiguous sexual orientation. The family dog, Brian, drinks martinis and engages in vapid conversation. The satire is powerful, deconstructing beliefs and notions surrounding the traditional family. The father is hardly an authority figure. He is, as the title of the sitcom puts it, a "family guy." In *Two and a Half Men* fatherhood becomes virtually irrelevant in a world where men and women tend to live apart through separation and divorce. The sitcom thus takes the deconstruction one step further—fathers are just custodians, serving no special role in a family or in society.

Among the first to consider the connection between representation and real life were the Greek philosophers Plato (c. 427–c. 347 BCE) and Aristotle (384–322 BCE). Aristotle considered representation as the primary means through which human beings came to perceive reality, identifying *mimesis* (imitation or simulation) as the most basic and natural form of representation. Nonetheless, Aristotle also warned that mimesis creates illusory worlds and, thus, can easily lead people astray. Plato believed that representations never really tell the truth but instead "mediate" it, creating nothing but illusions that lead us away from contemplating life as it really is. He argued that representations had to be monitored because they could foster antisocial reactions or encourage the imitation of evil things. Plato's argument has not disappeared from the social radar screen. It undergirds such practices as movie ratings and other restrictions on our freedom. These are modern society's "Platonic attempts" to restrict or modify representations so as to protect people (especially children).

Code Theory

In semiotics, representation is defined as a process that involves creating a *text* in a specific *context* according to a *code* or set of *codes*. To understand what this means, consider again the case of the fictional hero Superman, who was introduced in 1938 by *Action Comics*. What or who does Superman represent?

The answer is a pop culture version of an ancient mythic hero, such as Prometheus and Achilles. Like the ancient heroes, Superman is indestructible, morally upright, and devoted to saving humanity from itself. And, like many of the mythic heroes, he has a "tragic flaw"—exposure to kryptonite, a substance that is found on the planet where he was born, renders him devoid of his awesome powers.

Now, answering the question of why Superman (or any comic book action hero for that matter) appeals to modern-day audiences requires us to delve into the origin and history of the archetypal heroic figure. In myth and legend, a hero is an individual, often of divine ancestry, who is endowed with great courage and strength, celebrated for his bold exploits, and sent by the gods to Earth to play a helpful role in human affairs. Heroes embody lofty human ideals for all to admire—truth, honesty, justice, fairness, moral strength, and so on. Modern-day audiences understand the importance of a hero intuitively, as did the ancient ones. Rather than being sent by the gods to help humanity (something that would hardly be appropriate in a modern secular society), Superman came to Earth from a planet in another galaxy; he leads a double life, as hero and as Clark Kent, a mild-mannered reporter for a daily newspaper; he is adored by Lois Lane, a reporter for the same newspaper who suspects (from time to time) that Clark Kent may be Superman; and he wears a distinctive costume. His red cape suggests noble blood and his blue suit the hope he brings to humanity. Of course, the red and blue combination is also indicative of American patriotism—these are, after all, colors of the American flag. How Superman acts, how he behaves, how he looks, and what he does are connected to a *hero code*—a set of ideas, details, and so on that we associate with heroes. Each story in an issue of the comic or a television episode is a *text* derived from that code. We can expect to find our hero fighting some villain, flirting at some point with Lois Lane in the persona of Clark Kent, facing a crisis that he must resolve with his extraordinary powers, and so on. Finally, the meaning of the text is conditioned by *context*. The context is the situation in which the text is constructed or to which it refers. If read in its comic book format, a Superman text will be interpreted as an adventure story. However, if a satirist were to portray Superman in a movie, then the movie text would hardly be construed as an adventure story, but rather as a satire or parody of the Superman figure.

The concept of code was introduced by Saussure (1916: 31). For Saussure the code was a generic form of *langue* (the abstract knowledge of how signs such as words, grammatical structures, and their relations can be used and interpreted). The texts that it allows people to encode (construct) and decode (understand) was a form of *parole* (the concrete utilization of the code to represent something).

Textuality

Textuality is the term used in semiotics to refer to how texts are constructed and how they generate meanings. A basic classification of texts was introduced by Umberto Eco in 1979. He distinguished between *open* and *closed* texts. The latter is one that normally entails a singular or fairly limited range of interpretations. Most whodunit mystery stories are closed texts because one solution to a crime eventually surfaces, closing all other avenues of interpretation. An open work, on the other hand, allows readers to make up their own minds as to what it means. For instance, James Joyce's *Finnegans Wake* requires a reader who can make up his or her own mind as to its meaning, not a set solution or interpretation. Openness is, for Eco, the condition that leads to a free play of associations and, thus, to an aesthetic appreciation of a text.

The concept of *intertextuality* is also used in semiotics to refer to how texts are connected to other relevant texts by allusion, inference, implication, or suggestion. Extracting a meaning from John Bunyan's novel *Pilgrim's Progress* (1678, 1684) depends upon knowing the relevant Bible narrative and the theological concept of a journey from the City of Destruction to the Celestial City. James Joyce's novel *Ulysses*, which takes its title from Homer's *Ulysses* (*Odysseus* in Greek), connects the adventures of the main character, Leopold Bloom, to those of the Homeric Ulysses. Bloom, his wife Molly, and young Stephen Dedalus are the Joycean counterparts of Ulysses, his wife Penelope, and their son Telemachus. Bloom's one-day adventures in Dublin mirror the many wanderings Ulysses endures as he tries to return home to Ithaca after fighting in the Trojan War. Joyce's text is also replete with references to theological, mythological, astronomical, and linguistic texts.

The notion of intertextuality was introduced into semiotics by Roland Barthes, who saw a text as a collage of other texts reconfigured within it. For Barthes the text is, thus, a blend of unconscious quotations, without quotation marks.

In sum, semiotic theories of pop culture focus on two key notions: (1) texts are oppositional and (2) representations are part of a mythological system (which provides the codes for pop culture). In a way, the semiotics of pop culture is not an actual theory; it is a technique for fleshing out hidden meaning structures. As such, it is a very valuable tool, allowing the analyst to relate the meanings to any system of analysis he or she deems relevant.

TRANSGRESSION THEORIES

Many adults in the Roaring Twenties saw the clothing, lifestyle, and music adopted by young people as morally transgressive. Similarly, Elvis Presley's hip-swinging performances were seen initially by some as transgressing the boundaries of decency and decorum. Paradoxically, it is the act of transgression itself that enhances pop culture's appeal. From the short skirts donned by flappers to Madonna's open-mouth kissing of Britney Spears at the 2003 MTV Video Music Awards, Janet Jackson's subtle breast exposure during the 2004 Superbowl halftime show, and Miley Cyrus's simulated sex acts during the performance of "We Can't Stop," spectacles that intentionally cross the line of decency have always been part and parcel of pop culture.

Tattooing is a case in point. It is one of the most ancient forms of creative body decoration. Cave paintings date it to at least 8000 BCE. Almost every culture has practiced tattooing for various reasons. The adoption of tattooing as a rebellious fashion trend by young people started again in the Roaring Twenties, but began spreading more broadly in the 1960s and 1970s—an event captured by the Rolling Stones in their popular 1981 album *Tattoo You*. Since then, tattooing has evolved into a society-wide trend, having lost most, if not all, of its transgressive symbolism. It has become a cosmetic practice adopted by media icons and common people alike, crossing the boundaries of age, gender, and social class. There are now television programs devoted to the art of tattooing and the human stories behind those who seek tattoos.

Various popular forms of language and slang are similarly transgressive in the beginning. In the 1920s young people spelled *rats* as *Rhatz* and shortened *that's too bad* to *stoo bad*, fashioning a type of counter-language to the mainstream "correctness" in language. Similarly, counterculture youths in the 1960s spelled *tough* as *tuff*, *freaks* as *freeks*, and *America* as *Amerika*. Today, the same type of style is evident in the names assumed by rap artists. Sista Souljah's name, for example, suggests both *soldier* and *soul* at the same time that it alludes to Black English Vernacular pronunciation. Such spelling patterns bespeak an attitude that communicates the following implicit subtext: "I'll do it my way, not the way of proper speech." Such language, as will be discussed in a subsequent chapter, constitutes a transgressive code that is entertaining, generally containing an ironic or satirical element to it that invariably brings about a chuckle from those who use it. A phrase such as *stoo bad* or and expression such as *duh* is essentially a one- or two-line subtle joke.

Moral Panic Theory

Trends such as tattooing or new slang forms that gain popularity at first tend to be perceived as vulgar and a threat to the moral order. Transgressive trends tend, in a phrase, to be perceived with "moral panic," as Stan Cohen (1972) observed in his insightful study of mods and rockers. Whether it is a panicked reaction to Elvis's swinging pelvis on television in the mid-1950s or to the gross antics performed onstage by punk rockers or Miley Cyrus's sexual antics, many people typically react to them as signs of what is "wrong with the world." However, as the transgressive trends lose their impact, blending silently into the larger cultural mainstream or disappearing altogether, the moral panic subsides and even evanesces.

In 1952, the *I Love Lucy* program was forbidden to script the word *pregnant* when Lucille Ball (the main character of the sitcom) was truly pregnant; moreover, Lucy and Ricky Ricardo were scripted to sleep in separate beds. Such restrictions were common in early television to avoid creating moral panic. On his Ed Sullivan performance in 1956, Elvis Presley was shot from the waist up, to spare viewers from seeing his gyrating pelvis. But television soon after caught up to transgressive culture, co-opting it more and more. In 1964, the married couple Darrin and Samantha Stevens were seen sharing a double bed on *Bewitched*. In 1968, Rowan and Martin's *Laugh-In* challenged puritanical mores with its racy skits and double-entendres. In the early 1970s, *All in the Family* addressed taboo subjects such as race, menopause, homosexuality, and premarital sex for the first time on prime-time television. In 1976, the female leads in *Charlie's Angels* went braless for the first time in television history, and one year later the

Roots miniseries showed bare-breasted women portraying African life in the eighteenth century.

Throughout the 1980s and 1990s *Seinfeld* and *NYPD Blue* often made reference to previously taboo sexual topics (such as masturbation). In 2000, the winner on CBS's first *Survivor* series walked around naked (although CBS pixilated sensitive areas). And, as mentioned above, at the 2003 MTV Video Music Awards, Madonna open-mouth kissed Britney Spears; and a year later, Janet Jackson's breast was exposed by Justin Timberlake during the 2004 Superbowl halftime show. Today, all forms of transgression characterize television, the movies, and other media texts. Series such as *Desperate Housewives* that deal with the lure of infidelity hardly cause a stir. As Cohen had predicted, some of the things that once evoked moral panic are now simply part of the show, with only specific communities and groups (such as evangelical groups in the United States) seeing them as signs of moral decay, even though many churches now employ rock and rap bands to promote their messages. Indeed, evangelical forms of religion themselves have become part of the popular imagination, with their own television programs, televangelists, recording artists, and the like.

Carnival Theory

Why is transgression both so appealing and appalling at the same time? An insightful theory of pop culture, known as *carnival theory*, tackles this question directly. Inspired by the work of the Russian scholar Mikhail Bakhtin, the theory asserts that transgression is instinctual. By releasing rebellion and transgressive symbolism in a performative way, it actually validates social norms. Carnival theory thus explains why pop culture does not pose (and never has posed) any serious subversive challenge to the moral and ethical status quo. It is part of the comedic instinct that spurs us on to laugh at ourselves and at our most revered institutions. Many pop culture performers are modern-day carnival mockers who take it upon themselves to deride, confuse, and parody authority figures and symbols, bringing everything down to an earthy, crude level of theatrical performance. As the Greeks knew, we need comedy to balance tragedy, laughter to offset tears, and mischief to counteract propriety. The tragic performance is *cathartic*; the comedic one is *cathectic*, allowing for the release of libidinal forces within us. In this way a true balance between the sacred and the profane is maintained, guaranteeing continuity to the social order.

Carnival theory asserts that crude spectacles institute a vital dialogue among people. By pitting the sacred against the profane in a systematic

---

MIKHAIL BAKHTIN (1895–1975)

The Russian philosopher and literary theorist Mikhail Bakhtin claimed that pop culture has the same kinds of social functions as did the medieval carnivals. He also argued that the type of language used in carnivalesque situations did not merely function to exchange information, but rather, to create a *polyphonic* dialogue between performers and audiences. This is why at popular performances performers and audiences interact. Among his most important works are: *The Dialogic Imagination* (1981) and *Rabelais and His World* (1984).

---

gridlock, pop culture is an expression of this carnivalesque dialogue. The festivities associated with traditional carnivals are popular because they focus on the body, rather than on the spirit. At the time of carnival, everything authoritative, rigid, or serious is subverted, loosened, and mocked. Paradoxically, carnivals actually are the links between domains of life that are normally kept separate. Carnivals satirize the lofty words of poets, scholars, and churchmen, lawyers, politicians, and the like. But as they do, they actually validate them, although they introduce ideas for bringing about change in harmless, comedic ways.

Bakhtin introduced his theory around 1929. For Bakhtin, people attending a carnival do not merely feel part of an anonymous crowd. Rather, they feel part of a communal body, sharing a unique sense of time and space. Through costumes and masks, individuals take on a new identity and, as a consequence, renew themselves spiritually in the process. It is through this carnivalesque identity that the grotesque within humans can seek expression through overindulgent eating and laughter, and through unbridled sexuality. In such behaviors, people discover who they really are.

Some lifestyles are intrinsically carnivalesque. As a case in point consider the goth subculture that emerged in the late 1970s, but that now has diminished considerably in its size and appeal. The goths took their cues initially from Gothic novels, which revolved around mysterious and supernatural events intended to be frightening. The stories were called *Gothic* because most of them took place in gloomy, medieval castles built in the Gothic style of architecture, which included buildings with secret passageways, dungeons, and towers, all of which provided ideal settings for strange happenings. Most Gothic novels were set in Italy or Spain because those countries seemed remote and mysterious to English readers. In the 1800s, elements of the Gothic novel appeared in other forms of fiction. Novels such as *Frankenstein* (1818) by Mary Shelley and *Wuthering Heights* (1847) by Emily Bronte and other romances of the time were cut from the same narrative fabric of Gothic novels. The Gothic novel also influenced such American writers as Nathaniel Hawthorne, Herman Melville, and Edgar Allan Poe. In the 1900s, romantic adventure stories were also known as *Gothic*, but they were of a different narrative nature, placing more emphasis on love than on terror, although some critics would claim that they too were interlinked in the subtext.

The goth subculture came to prominence with punk performer Marilyn Manson, after he created widespread moral panic when his music was linked (erroneously) to the Columbine High School massacre. The influence of this subculture has, nevertheless, reached deeply into general American pop culture. It can be seen, for instance, in films such as *Edward Scissorhands* and *The Crow*, in Anne Rice's vampire novels, in bands such as Nine Inch Nails, and in the current fad of vampire romance novels, movies, and television programs. It can also be seen in cosmetic and clothing trends generally, with dark clothes and dark hair having become part of a generic fashion look. In effect, goth has become an unconscious pattern within general pop culture.

In a Bakhtinian sense, goth culture is carnival culture. The makeup is the mask that individuals wore at carnivals. Goths set themselves apart from the mainstream social order, at the same time that they have taken themes within it (Gothic literature) and reassembled them into a bricolage of new meanings. Engagement in the carnivalesque is, ultimately, a condemnation of the emptiness of consumerist society—its alter ego.

It is interesting to note that pop culture itself is its own academic critic, aware of the importance and role of transgression in human life. Consider, for example, Stanley Kubrick's cinematic masterpiece of 1971, *A Clockwork Orange*, as an example. The setting for the movie is Britain. A teenage thug, Alex De Large, engages routinely in criminal and sexual activities in a wanton and reckless fashion. Caught and imprisoned for murder, he volunteers to undergo an experimental shock treatment therapy that is supposed to brainwash him to become nauseated by his previous lifestyle. Mr. Alexander, one of Alex's victims, traps him with the aim of avenging himself. He hopes to drive Alex to commit suicide to the strains of Beethoven's ninth symphony. But the actions taken against Alex are condemned by the press as inhumane and, as a consequence, he is released and restored to health. The movie's portrayal of the senseless, aimless violence of which a teenager is capable has a transgressive subtext built into it. Alex is a goalless teen trapped in a weary, decaying environment. His only way out is through intimidation and crime. He is a ticking time bomb ready to explode at any instant. Alex has become this way because he has lost his ability to laugh at the social order and thus to help change it through laughter. Society needs to change, but violence and rage will hardly be effective as the vehicles for change.

Carnival theory is based on the notion that the human psyche is embedded in a basic opposition—the sacred versus the profane—and that both require expression or release through performance, ritual, and symbolism. Carnival theory is sustained by the fact that cultures tend to make a distinction between these two in their sets of rituals and in the distribution of their institutions. In many religious traditions, for instance, there are periods of fasting (in Catholicism, Lent) preceded by periods of indulgence in all kinds of carnal pleasures (the carnival period that precedes Lent). The transgressive antics of the latest pop musician, fashion model, movie star, or cult figure are perceived as carnivalesque. There is, however, a paradox to be noted. In contemporary pop culture, the line demarcating sacred and profane forms of expression is often blurry. Alongside nonsensical movies such as *Dude, Where's My Car?* or *Hangover* (and its sequels) one finds movies such as *Amadeus* and *Mystic River* that extol the spirit. Perhaps it is this ambiguity that gives pop culture its overall power and stability. This theme will be revisited in the final chapter.

Transgressive theories of pop culture focus on the subversive aspects of popular performances and texts. These challenge the status quo in representational form, rather than in strict political ways. So, ultimately, pop culture is an indirect agent of social change.

3

THE BUSINESS OF POP CULTURE

Only conservatives believe that subversion is still being carried on in the arts and that society is being shaken by it. Advanced art today is no longer a cause—it contains no moral imperative. There is no virtue in clinging to principles and standards, no vice in selling or in selling out.

—Harold Rosenberg (1906–1978)

Consider the following statistical fact (Lieberman and Esgate 2014: 3): the total revenue in 2012 from videos, magazines, television programs, and so forth exceeded $1 trillion. Clearly, the business of pop culture is a highly lucrative one and a significant cog in the American economy. The number of jobs and related businesses add up to a large segment of the world's global economy. With all the clutter in real and virtual space, there is now a fierce competition for the consumer's entertainment dollar. This also means that the shelf life of a trend, such as a popular song, will become shorter and shorter. Without doubt, pop culture is now part of a quick-turnover industry. Indeed, trends today truly come and go as marketers and media moguls now focus on selling an "experience."

We can add to this business scenario the fact that the new mass communications technologies are changing how pop culture content is delivered and received. The changes include the following: (1) free-of-charge access and illegal downloads are rising in number; (2) portability, or the ability to download a file on multiple platforms, is changing the nature of content distribution; (3) delayed viewing or listening is changing both the business and delivery of content. Moreover, global access to entertainment has created new kinds of consumers and celebrities. Thousands of magazines, radio and television programs, websites, and the like now deal routinely with new crazes and the lives of ever-changing celebrities.

So, in this chapter we will deal with the business of pop culture and the mania for fads and celebrities. Taking a look at the pop culture universe from this particular angle offers insights that complement the more theoretical ones discussed in the previous chapter.

THE MARKET FOR POP CULTURE

As discussed, the birth of pop culture in the 1920s came about from a partnership that it made with the mass media and the business world. Early radio broadcasting made songs selected for broadcasting popular, which brought an increase in sales of records and new performance possibilities for singers, often leading to celebrity status for them. Soon, record labels and radio broadcasters formed a tacit alliance to showcase new songs of selected artists. The same story can be told about radio stars, movie actors, sports figures, and even politicians. If they made it to radio, they became famous, and this allowed the business side of their activities to literally "sell" them to an increasingly large market of consumers.

Mega Companies

With the advent of television in the late 1940s this partnership expanded and became even more powerful as an economic force in society. And, although with the advent of the digital platform for pop culture the partnership has morphed, given the free-access possibility, it is still there and is still thriving in a global marketplace for pop culture content. Pop culture is now governed by so-called mega entertainment companies.

The movement from local to national and now international control can be charted across the domains of pop culture. For example, in the mid-1950s, rock and roll was at first performed and broadcast on local radio stations primarily in southern American cities such as Memphis and New Orleans. As it became popular, some of its early local celebrities, like Elvis Presley, made it to national television and eventually to the movie screen. From there rock and roll became a countrywide trend and craze, leading to new film genres, magazines, specialized radio programs, and the like. Today, any new song by a pop star jumps instantly onto the global stage through the digital platform, garnering new audiences. Quite simply, without mass media access, nothing would become of a new song, a new book, or anything else, whether or not it is worthy of attention. The exception to this pattern occurs when an indie self-presentation on, say, YouTube goes viral. This is, however, relatively rare, and when it does happen the mega company system intervenes to offer the "YouTube star" a means of insertion into the broader marketplace.

Reinvention

Unlike folk culture where the same performances are repeated ritualistically at regular intervals, nothing in pop culture can remain around for very long. And when something does remain, it tends to be updated for the new marketplace of ideas and taste. Take, as an example the Barbie doll. Since 1959, the doll has kept in step with changing conceptions of femininity. Through the years she has been an astronaut, athlete, ballerina, businesswoman, dancer, dentist, doctor, firefighter, paleontologist, police officer, lead singer of a rock band, and a Unicef volunteer (among other roles). Barbie has also been involved in a romantic relationship with the Ken doll, which appeared in 1961. They split up in 2006, a period when breakups among celebrities captured headlines throughout the pop culture world. She has had a variety of pets, cars, and companions, including African American and Hispanic dolls. In a phrase, the doll has remained a cultural icon through clever makeovers. Today, various books, apparel, cosmetics, and video games are branded Barbie goods, and Barbie has appeared in films such as *Toy Story 2* and *3*. She has even been immortalized by Andy Warhol, who made a painting of the doll in 1985. Moreover, like any celebrity, Barbie has been parodied within pop culture itself. *Saturday Night Live*, for example, has satirized the doll with pseudo-commercials.

This history of the Barbie doll is emblematic of the history of contemporary pop culture. Through reinvention it has retained its popularity. Some countries react to this situation negatively. Saudi Arabia, for example, has banned the sale of the Barbie doll, claiming that it does not conform to the ideals of Islam. Some Middle Eastern companies have actually produced alternatives to the Barbie doll that are more consistent with religious traditions. Such reactions show in microcosm that American pop culture also has a political presence in the global village and may even be behind some conflicts in the world today.

THE POP CULTURE INDUSTRY

As mentioned in the previous chapter, critics of pop culture see it as one huge commodity industry made possible by mass communications technologies and the media industries. The origin of the mass media is traced to the invention of the modern printing press by Johannes Gutenberg in Germany. Before that invention, the reproduction of texts was cumbersome and expensive because each was copied by hand. Gutenberg's invention allowed for the mass reproduction of texts. The novel became, soon after, the first true entertainment form of reading, leading to the birth and rise of popular print culture. It created the novelist as a celebrity. Of course, the success of books and other products could not really have occurred, and certainly not spread, without a mass society, as intellectuals such as the Frankfurt scholars claimed. They emphasized the challenges to art and religion that mass-produced cultural products (music, novels, and so on) presented, showing how they were highly uniform in content, obeying the laws of the marketplace, and thus destroying individuality and true artistic creativity. Although today's conception of the mass audience has changed dramatically, some of the critiques remain valid to this day.

Critiques

In his 1922 book, *Public Opinion*, the American journalist Walter Lippmann argued that the growth of mass media culture had a powerful and direct effect on people's minds and behavior. Although he did not use any empirical method to back up his argument, it is still difficult to find a counterargument to it. Lippmann saw the world of commodity culture as producing "pictures in our heads" (Lippmann 1922: 3), implying that the mass media shaped our worldview by providing us with images of things that we had not experienced before. In effect, the media control us.

Following up on Lippmann's coattails, in *Manufacturing Consent*, Herman and Chomsky (see previous chapter) argue that since the ownership of the mass media is concentrated in the hands of a few powerful and wealthy elites (the mega companies), agenda setting is largely controlled or at least influenced "from above," contrary to the grassroots origins of pop culture. Because media depend on advertisers for their revenues, they will focus on simplistic and lighthearted programming that supports a consumer mood in audiences. The experts used in news sources are likely to be members of the elite themselves, and if news stories contradict or dismiss the elite viewpoint, they use various forms of "flak" to keep the media in line. Ideologies are formulated in people's minds in terms of enemies or alliances that help justify the elite's political strategy, such as the threat of communism during the Cold War.

But things have changed since the Frankfurt School, Lippmann, and even Herman and Chomsky. In the current media landscape, audiences are highly fragmented because of the increase in media options, from radio to the Internet. In the world of TV, many channels are now available through cable, and as audiences move to the Internet there is no longer a uniform audience exposed to the same type of media content. A second trend is the shift from audiences as consumers to audiences as producers. Known as the *creative commons*—the sum of all original works produced—the new media have upset the traditional marketplace for pop culture consumption. Indeed, the cart has been so overturned that it may signal the end of pop culture as we have known it since the 1920s. YouTube, for example, has created a blur between consumers and producers of content as well as between experts and novices.

Populism

In a way, the creative commons movement emphasizes that pop culture has always been populist—that is, culture by the people for the people. Its appropriation by the business world was an inevitable one, but also a convenient one for artists and performers. And, as discussed schematically in the previous chapter, it started out as an implicitly subversive culture challenging the puritanical status quo that had solidified in the early part of the twentieth century. As some have claimed, pop culture has always been a site of resistance against dominant groups in society. This certainly was the case in the 1960s and early 1970s, when popular music was not only a money-making enterprise but also part of a political resistance movement against what the hippies called the "establishment." So, pop culture is an empowering culture, not an enslaving one. George Gershwin was clearly aware of this when he exalted jazz to the level of classical music art in works such as *Rhapsody in Blue* and the marvelous opera *Porgy and Bess*.

Certainly pop culture has become a kind of default culture, virtually obliterating the dichotomy between high and low culture. It is a highly intertextual culture, providing points of reference throughout the cultural landscape. Much of pop culture is self-referential, with many products (from television programs to bestselling books) creating one huge network of references to other popular products. The more salient example of the intertextual and self-referential textuality of pop culture is the *Simpsons* sitcom, which is a critical source of pop culture commentary, often referring to the crass commercialism of cultural products, parodying celebrities as ersatz gods and goddesses, and so on. In this sense, pop culture is a metaculture—a culture that comments on itself continuously.

All this suggests that pop culture may have brought an end to the traditional, book-oriented intellectual. It is not that intellectuals are no longer required by society, but simply that they now must share the limelight with the makers of pop culture themselves. This implies that the whole shape of academic discourse has changed and is continuing to change radically. There are those who desire a return to the past and "real" literature, philosophy, music, and art. The disappearance of what have been called the "grand narratives" and the appearance of "commodity narratives" that require little or no philosophical thought is a major strain of criticism leveled at pop culture. The deconstruction of authoritative voices and their replacement with pop voices, such as Bart on *The Simpsons*, is somewhat troubling. Still, there may be ways to wage revolt and create grand narratives in an age of mass media. Introducing gradual changes in products otherwise conforming to the requirements of a dominant ideology is definitely one way that this can be done. But, more importantly, using the new media forms as a means to do this, as Charles Schulz did (see chapter 2), is still a definite possibility.

FAD CULTURE

Proof that that pop culture and business have formed a partnership can be seen in the constant production of fads and crazes in society at large. In the mid-1950s Davy Crockett hats sold in the millions due to the popularity of the Davy Crockett TV episodes on the Disney program; in the first decades of the twenty-first century Xboxes became a craze, as did all kinds of digital gadgets. Lifestyle fashions derived from movies, hairstyles based on movie actor models, and on and on are now part of a veritable fad culture.

A fad is an object, a fashion style, a type of personality (or celebrity), or some event that becomes extremely popular relatively quickly, but loses popularity just as quickly. Some fads may come back if a subsequent generation finds out about them through media retrospectives. Fads and movies often go hand in hand. There is little doubt that the fad of taking karate as a physical pastime is due to the popularity of the Bruce Lee movies and, later,

---

AN ILLUSTRATIVE SELECTION OF FADS

1920s: doughboy lamps, flagpole sitting, crossword puzzles, flapper hats, the Charleston dance, jazz music, radio

1930s: goldfish swallowing, swing music, big bands, comic book magazines, hats for men

1940s: poodle skirts, bobby socks, Slinky, boogie-woogie, new dances based on swing music, top 40 hit parades

1950s: Hula-Hoops, beanies, rock and roll, coonskin caps, roller skating, sock hops, sideburns, ducktails, Pez dispensers, Polaroid cameras, droodles, phonebooth stuffing, cars with fins.

1960s: Dalekmania, drive-in theaters, lava lamps, troll dolls, Ford Mustangs, station wagons, pinball machines, peace signs, counterculture rock

1970s: bell-bottom pants, pet rocks, View-Master, Post-it Notes, small import cars, electronic calculators, disco music, punk music, mood rings

1980s: Cabbage Patch dolls, video game consoles, Rubik's Cubes, Smurf toys, Teenage Mutant Ninja Turtles, SUVs, skateboarding, Care Bears, Pac-Man, Dungeons & Dragons, jelly shoes

1990s: cell phones, PDAs, Barney dolls, Pokemon, pogs, spandex shorts, tamagotchi, Mighty Morphin Power Rangers, rap and hip-hop, Turbo chewing gum, Tickle Me Elmo, slap bracelets

2000s: iPods, digital mobile devices, Sudoku, Uggs, Rolie Polie Olie, YouTube, blogs, Facebook, Twitter, mixed martial arts, Crazy Frog, awareness bracelets, metrosexuals, Heely shoes

2010s: celebrity chefs, cupcakes, cronuts, Gangnam style, hipsters, yoga pants, flappy bird game, haul videos

---

of the series of Karate Kid movies. Fashion and hairstyle fads also generally come from the movies.

Toys

Perhaps in no other domain of consumerist culture can the emergence of fads be seen to occur more readily than in the "toy culture" aimed at children. A look at any listing of fads and crazes since the 1920s will invariably show a huge presence of toys on it.

Interestingly, toy fads often have generated mass hysteria, as the line-ups outside stores selling new video or electronic products today makes obvious. A case in point is the Cabbage Patch doll craze of 1983.

Scalpers offered the suddenly and unexplainably out-of-stock dolls (a marketing ploy?) for hundreds of dollars through classified ads. Adults fought each other to get one of the few remaining dolls left in stock. A *Newsweek* article of that year, titled "Oh, You Beautiful Dolls" offered the following depiction (cited in Berger 2005: 82):

> It was as if an army had been turned loose on the nation's shopping malls, braving the Ficus trees, sloshing through the fountains, searching for the legendary stockrooms said to be filled with thousands of the dough-faced, chinless, engagingly homely dolls that have become the Holy Grail of the 1983 Christmas shopping season: the Cabbage Patch Kids. Clerks were helpless before the onslaught.

It is instructive to note that the Cabbage Patch dolls came with "adoption papers." Each doll was given a name and a birth certificate. Thanks to computerized manufacturing, no two dolls were exactly alike. Parents did not buy a simple doll; they brought another "child" into the family. The fad certainly gave credence to mythology theory (discussed previously). In many societies, dolls have mythic-symbolic meanings. In the aboriginal Hopi culture of the United States, for instance, kachina dolls are given as sacred objects to children as part of fertility rites. In Christian traditions, dolls have been used to represent the Holy Family in the Nativity scene as part of Christmas observations. In Mexico, dolls representing Our Lady of Guadeloupe are ceremonially paraded every year. And in some cultures of the Caribbean, it is believed that one can cause physical or psychological damage to another person by doing something injurious to a doll constructed to resemble that person.

The commercialization of dolls can be traced to Germany in the early fifteenth century, when fashion dolls were created to model clothing for aristocratic German women. Shortly thereafter, manufacturers in England, France, Holland, and Italy also began to manufacture fashion dolls. The more ornate ones were often used by rulers and courtiers as gifts. By the seventeenth century, the dolls were given as playthings to children of all classes.

After the Industrial Revolution, dolls were manufactured in massive quantities as toys for little girls. Since the 1950s, the association of dolls with female childhood has been entrenched further by both the quantity of doll types produced and their promotion in the media, as we saw above with the Barbie doll.

Dolls have mythic power because they represent the human figure, and are thus perceived to possess a life force. Crazes such as the Cabbage

Patch doll one are evidence that this force is not limited to tribal or pre-modern cultures; it is recycled in the marketplace through advertising and media promotion.

The list of toys that have become fads is infinite. They define, in their own compact way, an era or period of pop culture. Many of the toys are de facto icons. Consider the list below as a case in point, which have all become collectibles:

- *Slinky* (1940s): a helical spring toy that can perform a number of moves and tricks, including going down a flight of stairs as it stretches and reforms itself step-by-step. It was a fad the instant it came out in the 1940s and still remains a staple of childhood toy culture.
- *Hula-Hoop* (1958): a hoop that is twirled around the waist or some other limb. The hoop was at first a craze among children, but it soon became a veritable pop culture fad for the mainstream market, remaining so to this day.
- *G. I. Joe* (1960s): perhaps the original action hero doll that continues to be popular among male children to this day. It has become an icon of American military power and an emblem of patriotism, above and beyond its toy value.

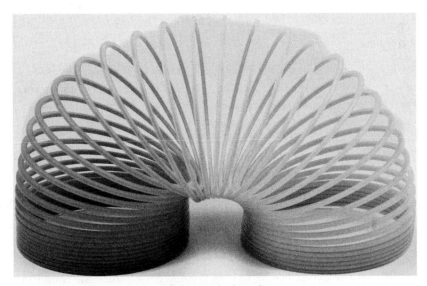

Slinky (© ThinkStock)

- *Hello Kitty* (1974): a catlike toy produced in Japan that became a fad throughout the world. It appeared as a logo on a coin purse first, gradually becoming a separate doll, remaining popular to this day.
- *Chia pets* (1977): terracotta figurines that produce chia sprouts, which grow within a couple of weeks resembling the toy's fur.
- *Beanie Baby* (1993): stuffed animal filled with plastic pellets ("beans") giving the toy a flexible feel and a real look.
- *Furby* (1998): electronic speaking robotic toy resembling a hamster or owl which became a "must-have" toy from 1998 to 2000. Its speaking functions have been translated into twenty-four languages.

Toy fads reveal the intertextuality of pop culture. This means simply that a fad is connected to other components of the same theme delivered in different media, such as television, radio, film, print, and so on. Take, for example, the action figure of Superman. This is, of course, a toy derived from Superman comics, movies, television programs and cartoons, and on and on. As another example, consider the Hula-Hoop. The Hoop spawned a 1958 song, "The Hula Hoop Song," sung by Georgia Gibbs, who also sang it on the Ed Sullivan television show in the same year. The *Hudsucker Proxy* (1994), by the Coen brothers, revolved entirely around the Hoop. Clearly, fads are part of the overall network of interconnected elements that make up pop culture, from the material part of the culture to the conceptual and performative.

Games

Games of all kinds, from crossword puzzles to Rubik's Cubes, Sudoku, and video games are as much a part of fad culture as are toys and other material objects. The first such fad was the jigsaw puzzle, which became so popular among both children and adults that in 1909 the Parker Brothers Company devoted an entire part of their factory to its production. The crossword puzzle became a craze in the 1920s, and millions of Rubik's Cubes were sold around the world in the early 1980s. In 1925, a Broadway play, called *Puzzles of 1925*, satirized the crossword craze in a hilarious way. The heart of the play featured a scene in a "Crossword Sanitarium," where people driven insane by their obsession over crossword puzzles were confined. Already in 1924, crosswords had grown into a national pastime. In that year the American publishing company Simon and Schuster printed the first-ever book compilations of such puzzles. Each book came equipped with a pencil and eraser and a penny postcard that buyers could mail to the publisher to request the answers. The first book alone sold nearly half a million copies. To take advantage of the spreading crossword mania, manufacturers soon began making jewelry, dresses, ties, and other accouterments with crossword designs on them. A song called "Crossword Mama, You Puzzle Me, but Papa's Gonna Figure You Out," hit the top of the charts in 1924. To this day, crossword magazines, books, and websites based on crosswords are a part of pop (recreational) culture as are newspapers, fashion magazines, and the like.

The same type of craze was generated by the Rubik's Cube in the 1980s and, more recently, by Sudoku. There are now hordes of websites that contain new Sudoku puzzles daily, information on how to solve them, general information on Sudoku championships, descriptions of different kinds and styles of Sudoku puzzles (there are board and three-dimensional versions, for example), and so on. All this bears witness to the fact that in pop culture games, toys, and various other kinds of mass-produced objects can easily become as popular as celebrities and pop icons, and are interconnected textually to other aspects of the business of pop culture. Sudoku, for example, has starred on television programs (*House*, *Numbers*); it was the main theme in the "Sudoku Song," composed by Weird Al Yankovich; and a main plot element in the novel *The Sudoku Murder: A Katie McDonald Mystery*, written by Shelley Freydont. It is, perhaps, this kind of connectivity to other areas of pop culture that gives sense to a fad, endowing it with what can be called "distributed meaning"—that is, with the same meaning distributed across media and thus across ages and classes of consumers.

Fashion

Fashion has always been a part of fad culture. Fashion shows are, in fact, popular spectacles in their own right, with all the pizzazz and glitz of any vaudevillian performance. And fashion is sensitive to changes in pop culture. In the 1920s, flappers were distinguished by the hat they wore, as well as the short dresses and stylish shoes. The flapper lifestyle was openly sexual. As Linda Scott (2005: 167) observes: "The flapper's dress was particularly well suited to her nightlife. Going without a corset left the girl free to move—and all the fringe, beads, and spangles shimmied with her." In the 1950s, young people imitated the clothing and hairstyles that characterized early rock and roll culture (with Elvis pompadour hairstyles for males, poodle skirts and pony tails for females). In the 1960s, the fashion trends came out of the hippie culture, epitomized by long hair for both males and females and the wearing of blue jeans for both, in a unisex fashion style.

Fashion for all classes of people began to appear in northern Europe and Italy with the rise of the bourgeois class in the late Middle Ages, although it was mainly aristocrats who had the time and the financial ability to indulge in fashion trends. One of the first true fashion trends emerged among young bourgeois Italian men during the Renaissance, who wore tights and short close-fitting jackets called doublets. Before the 1800s, however, many nations regulated fashion with laws that limited the amount of money people could spend on private luxuries. These laws were intended to maintain divisions among the classes. In some countries, only the ruling class could legally wear highly fashionable clothes. But the lure of fashion caused many people to break these laws.

Many fashion trends have come to symbolize a specific era. Take blue jeans and T-shirts. In the 1930s and 1940s, jeans were cheap and mass-produced blue-collar working clothes. As early as the mid-1950s, young people adopted blue jeans as part of a new dress code. By the 1960s and 1970s, they came to symbolize equality between the sexes and among social classes. By the 1980s, this meaning receded, as jeans (of any color) became a fashion statement. Blue jeans became much more expensive, much more exclusive, often personalized, and available at chic boutiques. Today, jeans are just jeans—comfortable clothing worn by people of all ages in informal settings.

White T-shirts constituted regulation underwear for the U.S. Navy in the early 1900s. By the 1920s and 1930s football players started donning them to prevent chafing from shoulder pads. But it was the 1951 movie *A Streetcar Named Desire* that featured Marlon Brando wearing a T-shirt in highly erotic scenes that finally catapulted the T-shirt into the realm of pop culture.

In the 1960s T-shirts became obligatory hippie dress. By the 1970s and 1980s T-shirts entered the fashion world with messages inscribed on them promoting social issues. Today, they may have lost their political and social connotations, but they emblematize the deconstruction of social difference—they are ageless, classless, and genderless.

Like all fads, fashion styles tell side stories of pop culture and of social evolution generally. Flapper hats defined the era of the Roaring Twenties, representing an emerging women's liberation movement; blue jeans worn by both males and females symbolized the beginnings of gender and class equality. Some fashions start out as transgressive, as for instance the punk dress code, but are soon appropriated by the mainstream to become part of a new fad culture. Wearing socially transgressive clothing demonstrates membership to a specific group. Subculture affiliation through dress codes exemplifies the potential of dress to express dissidence and social criticism. The *stilyagi*, or style hunters of Stalinist Russia, drew from their limited knowledge of American culture to cultivate the identities they were struggling to assume.

Food

Today among the most popular television programs are those dealing with food, featuring famous chefs. Even entire channels are devoted to food, promoting a faddish food culture. TV chefs are pop icons, as famous as music and cinema celebrities. There are now culinary trends, with restaurants having become locales of popular entertainment, as people go out to enjoy food and the whole ambiance of restaurant life in the same way that they would go to the theater, the movies, or a concert. In fact, the two events often coincide—going out to a restaurant followed by a concert is now a relatively common lifestyle practice. It is, in fact, a fad.

Food is a primary constituent of rituals, from feasts (weddings, bar mitzvahs) to simple social gatherings. The importance of food in this regard was noted by the Greek historian Herodotus, who spent a large part of his life traveling through Asia and the Middle East. In each society, a formal meal invariably involved some ritualistic practice or had some specific social meaning. Early civilizations developed rules for proper manners during formal meals. This notion has remained to this day. People behave and dress much differently in a high-class restaurant than they do at a McDonald's restaurant.

Food fads are harder to connect to general pop culture trends. In some ways, they are sui generis trends. A perfect example is the donut. How it emerged as a popular food item and how it is connected to other domains of pop culture is unclear. Similarly, it is uncertain how health food fads can be interconnected to other areas of pop culture. Food fads too are gauges of social changes and social emphases. The most interesting topic of all in this area is the rise of so-called junk food to the status of regular food, a process that best exemplifies how fads change society.

Hamburger is beef and, in Western society, beef has long been a common food, because cattle meat is seen as part of traditional meals. But whereas a beefsteak is part of the historical cuisine of most Western societies, hamburger is not. In the 1950s, hamburgers were hardly construed as standard options in this cuisine; they were seen as part of "junk food culture," aimed at young people by an ever-expanding fast-food industry. This situation has changed today. Hamburger is no longer considered to be "junk," but a food option for people of any age or class, even if it still harbors the meaning of "unhealthy food." Restaurants and various eateries now offer hamburgers as part of their regular fare. Thus, the cultural definition of hamburger has changed and the reason lies not in any scientific discovery related to any previously undetected nutritional benefits of this food item, but to shifts in society, largely supporting Barthes's (1957, 1981) critiques of consumerist cultures as antithetical to the continuity of historical cultures.

What we call junk food emerges in America as part of an ever-expanding consumerism. Some historical accounts of the hamburger, for instance, indicate that it was sold at fairs, amusement parks, and other recreational venues in the early part of the twentieth century. But why was hamburger, served on a bun and eaten in specific amusement locales, perceived as "junk," when, as discussed, beef has always been a part of American cuisine? The answer is, arguably, that it was decontextualized from traditional cuisine. The hamburger was produced commercially for a specific purpose—to be part of a recreational venue. Any food item can be reconceptualized in this way. Take fried chicken. As such, it is part of traditional southern American cuisine where it would hardly be classified as junk. But in the context of a Kentucky Fried Chicken fast-food outlet, it would fall, even today, under the rubric of junk food. Thus, junk food can be defined as commercially produced food with no connection to traditional cuisines. This would include not only fried chicken and hamburgers, but also candy bars, hot dogs, donuts, and the like.

The topic of junk food makes its way into various domains of pop culture. It can be seen on TV programs such as *Happy Days* and in various movies aimed at teenagers. In Woody Allen's 1973 movie *Sleeper*, a granola-eating geek, who desires junk food rather than granola foods, awakens in the future after falling asleep. In that world, he discovers that junk foods actually prolong life, rather than shorten it. His dreams have come true. Do we desire junk food because the modern consumerist world has influenced us to do so? Are we all secretly "sleepers" who ignore the health effects? The movie may hold the key to understanding the transformation of junk food into simply popular food. Once a food item makes it to the screen it virtually guarantees its popularity. As David Sax (2014) has shown, cupcakes were a bit player in a scene in the TV program *Sex and the City*, evolving to a starring role in cookbooks, blogs, and TV chef programs, morphing into a veritable fad.

Diners (the predecessors of junk food joints) generally started appearing in the 1920s. They were locales serving mainly young people: hot dogs, milkshakes, and other fast foods were the core of the menu. Adults would visit such diners only on occasion, perhaps to treat their children to an ever-growing set of trendy pop foods. By the 1950s, teenagers had their own burger and milkshake joints. However, very soon, junk food, promoted by effective advertising campaigns, became an indulgence sought by anyone of any age, from very young children to seniors. The compulsion to consume junk food has, consequently, became a fact of contemporary life.

Given the global village in which we live, junk food has even become a kind of international commodity that is not only the preferred food of young people, but of anyone. Junk food is, in a fundamental sense, a democratic food, carrying with it few constraints as to age, class, gender, and so on. The fact that it is available also in mainstream restaurants (not just diners or joints) corroborates this implicit principle of food equality. Reactions against junk food as part of American popular culture persist, but they are more reactions against global pressures to homogenize (Americanize) cultures than particular objections to hamburgers or hot dogs.

The "number one" hamburger joint of all time is, of course, McDonald's. The success of McDonald's in becoming a "family restaurant," rather than a simple joint is tied, of course, to changes in the economics of modern society. The need to have a two-person, working household led to radical changes in the traditional family structure in the late 1960s. Fewer and fewer North American families had the time to eat meals together within the household, let alone the energy to prepare elaborate dinners. The home, ironically, had become a place where very busy people tended to eat apart. Enter the fast-food eatery to the rescue—a place designed to bring the family together, at the same table, under the same roof. Compared to one hundred years ago, eating out has become a common fact of urban life.

Restaurant chains such as IHOP (International House of Pancakes), Applebee's, Chili's Grill & Bar, Pizza Hut, Kentucky Fried Chicken, Burger King, Wendy's, and Buffalo Wild Wings, to mention but a few, are considered casual dining chains, rather than fast-food joints. They have thus been renamed quick-service restaurants (QSRs), rather than fast-food places. The total revenue of QSRs is estimated to amount to over $200 billion. The notion of cuisine has been relegated to exclusive domains of food consumption (traditional meals at Thanksgiving, Christmas, and so on), whereas QSRs now have become intrinsic to the food economy and part of a veritable faddish food culture.

CELEBRITY CULTURE

Before the age of television and long before the age of the Internet, radio and movie performers, jazz musicians, big band orchestra leaders, among others became as recognizable and important to Americans as presidents and writers. From this, a "celebrity culture" crystallized that spread broadly, becoming an all-embracing one.

The topic of celebrity is a central one in pop culture studies. Celebrity culture and pop culture are really one and the same. Andy Warhol showed himself to be a perceptive observer of a society that had been conditioned by exposure to the media by stating that eventually everyone would be famous for fifteen minutes. Warhol also realized that a celebrity need not necessarily be a real person; it could also be a product or a fictional character (for example, a cartoon character or a comic book superhero). Warhol's most famous celebrity subjects included both commercial products, such as Campbell's soup cans and Coca-Cola bottles, and people such as Elvis Presley, Elizabeth Taylor, Mao Tse Tung, and Marilyn Monroe.

There is a difference between *fame* and *celebrity*. Scientists may be famous, but they are not necessarily celebrities, unless the interest of the general public and the mass media are piqued in tandem. A classic example is Albert Einstein, who was famous as a scientist, but who also became a celebrity through the attention paid by the media not only to his work, but also to his personal life. Like a movie star, Einstein has shown up in all corners of pop culture. Another intellectual who received similar attention was Sigmund Freud. But Einstein and Freud were exceptions. It is mass entertainment personalities, such as movie actors or pop music stars, who are most likely to become celebrities. That became obvious in the radio era, when a radio or movie celebrity became the object of interest of magazines, newspapers, and other media.

The first movie celebrities go back to the 1910s, when silent movie actors, such as Rudolph Valentino and Charlie Chaplin, became popular throughout society. It became obvious at that time that in order to jump from the screen into celebrity culture, other media were required. The tabloid newspaper, for example, helped create celebrities by focusing on the private lives of movie stars, musicians, and other performers. The radio then came forward to further enhance recognition of actors and others. By the middle part of the twentieth century, entire magazines were devoted to stories about celebrities. With the advent of television and now online media, celebrity culture has become even more widespread and an integral part of pop culture. Today, anyone from any walk of life can become a celebrity—a chef, a sex-hungry politician, a serial killer, a terrorist, and so on—as long as he or she gets airtime, so to speak, across the various popular media.

Celebrities who become extremely popular for various reasons are now called *icons*. The actress Marilyn Monroe (1926–1962) is an early example of an icon. Her great beauty made her a sex symbol. The magazines and newspapers were filled with stories about her love affairs and her various intrigues. But in spite of her success, Monroe had a tragic life, dying at the age of thirty-six from an overdose of sleeping pills. After her death, she became an icon, similar to religious icons, revered in the same way a martyr would have been revered in the past. Elvis Presley (1935–1977) is another example of a pop icon. Presley was one of the first American stars of rock music and perhaps the greatest in the genre. He gained popularity through records and the radio, with his songs constantly hitting the top of the charts. His voice and his particular style of musical performances became the standards of rock. His popularity continued after his death, rising to legendary status, because of his relatively early death at the age of forty-two. Movies about his life, reissues of his music, and academic treatises on his legacy continue to this day. His home in Graceland has become a shrine to his memory. Thousands of fans from around the world continue to make a pilgrimage to Graceland every year, especially on the anniversary of his death. As Chris Hedges (2009: 17) aptly puts it, celebrity culture has, in many ways, replaced religious culture in the contemporary world:

> We all have gods, Martin Luther said, it is just a question of which ones. And in American society our gods are celebrities. Religious belief and practice are commonly transferred to the adoration of celebrities.

Decoding Celebrity

The analogy between religious and pop culture icons is not purely analogical. It is intended to show the probable psychological raison d'être of celebrity culture. Originally, the word *icon* was used to refer to a painting considered sacred in the Eastern Orthodox Churches, created according to rules established by church authorities, which are intended to emphasize the heavenly glory of the holy subjects portrayed. Pop icons are similarly created according the rules of the media, the church of pop culture. If one is noticed by the media, then he or she may easily become an icon of pop culture,

The media's celebrity- and icon-making power can be called a *mythologizing effect*, because the celebrities that it creates are perceived as mythic figures, larger than life. Like any type of privileged space designed to impart attention and significance to someone, the media have the power to create mythic personages by simply containing them, suspended in a simulacrum between fantasy and reality. The radio was called appropriately a "magic box." Radio personages became infused with a mythic quality by virtue of the fact that they were heard from inside the magic box. The same effect is created by all media stages. This is why meeting a celebrity in the real world is exciting for many people. They are perceived as otherworldly figures who have stepped out of the magic box to meet with mere mortals, in the same way that a hero of mythic lore would come into the human world to interact among common people.

Early or tragic death often helps establish icon status. Monroe and Presley both died relatively young and under tragic circumstances. Similarly, James Dean, Bruce Lee, Tupac Shakur, and Kurt Cobain (to mention but a few) have achieved pop icon status through their premature tragic deaths. The assassination of John F. Kennedy turned the young president into a posthumous pop icon. But pop icon status can also be achieved through longevity. Examples are the Rolling Stones; Madonna; fictional characters such as Bugs Bunny, Superman, and Batman; and brand products such as Campbell's soup, Coca-Cola, and Pepsi.

Celebrities influence society broadly. Their appearance is imitated widely. During the 1920s, many young men wore their hair slicked down with oil in the manner of the movie star Rudolph Valentino. In the 1950s, many sported a crew cut, in which the hair was cut extremely short and combed upward to resemble a brush, in imitation of movie actors; while others sported a ducktail (with the hair long on the sides and swept back), in imitation of stars such as James Dean. During the 1960s, young men copied the haircuts of the Beatles, who wore long bangs that covered the forehead. The imitation of the clothing styles, speech mannerisms, and overall demeanor of rap stars in the 1990s was evident across the youth spectrum. A similar story can be told about female fashions and trends.

Each country has its own celebrity system, developed from its own history of film, radio, television, and so on. In Italy, for example, names such as Marcello Mastroianni, Sofia Loren, Renato Carosone, and Totò evoke the same kinds of mythic responses as do names such as Marlon Brando and Marilyn Monroe in America. A similar celebrity-based history

Table 3.1.   Celebrity Culture, Past and Present

1950s
Music: Elvis Presley, Jerry Lee Lewis, Buddy Holly, the Platters, Chuck Berry, Pat Boone, Little Richard, Johnny Cash, Ray Charles, Fats Domino, doo-wop
Cars: models with fins, the Edsel (fiasco)
People: Marilyn Monroe, Burt Lancaster, Humphrey Bogart, James Dean, Elvis Presley
Movies: *From Here to Eternity, House of Wax* in 3-D, *Rebel without a Cause, The Blackboard Jungle, Love Me Tender, Jailhouse Rock, Some Like It Hot, Bridge on the River Kwai, Rear Window*
Publishing: The first issue of *Playboy* (1953), with a nude calendar photograph of Marilyn Monroe, *L'il Folks* (later *Peanuts*), *The Old Man and the Sea* (Ernest Hemingway), *The Catcher in the Rye* (J. D. Salinger), *The Lord of the Flies* (William Golding), *Lolita* (Vladimir Nabokov), Agatha Christie's detective novels, various works of C. S. Lewis, J. R. R. Tolkien, Dr. Seuss, and Dr. Benjamin Spock
Television: *I Love Lucy, The Ed Sullivan Show, Jack Benny Show, The Lone Ranger, The Adventures of Ozzie and Harriet, Father Knows Best, George Burns and Gracie Allen Show, Leave It to Beaver,* quiz shows
Fads and Pastimes: the Hula-Hoop, roller skating, drive-in movies, eating at drive-ins, sock hops, sideburns, ducktails, poodle skirts, Pez dispensers, white buck shoes, Polaroid cameras, super glue
Sports and Sports Celebrities: Yankees win the World Series several times, Ted Williams, Hank Aaron, Willie Mays, Mickey Mantle, Joe Di Maggio, Gordie Howe
1960s
Music: the Beach Boys, Chubby Checker, the Beatles, the Rolling Stones, Bob Dylan, Jimi Hendrix, Led Zeppelin, Steppenwolf, the Who, Tom Jones, Engelbert Humperdinck, the Doors, Janis Joplin, Sonny and Cher, the Jackson Five, the Supremes, the Temptations, James Brown, Otis Redding, Aretha Franklin, Dolly Parton, Santana, Credence Clearwater Revival, limbo dancing, counterculture music generally, Woodstock (the festival)
Cars: the Corvette Stingray, the Ford Mustang, the El Dorado, the Chevy Impala, the Pontiac GTO, the Mercury Cougar, station wagons
People: counterculture rock groups, Jackie Kennedy, Bridget Bardot, John Lennon, Barbara Streisand, Jane Fonda, Sophia Loren, Diana Ross, Twiggy
Movies: *Lawrence of Arabia, To Kill a Mockingbird, Tom Jones, The Pink Panther, The Great Escape,* Elvis's musical movies
Publishing: *The Feminine Mystique* (Betty Friedan), *Vogue* magazine, *To Kill a Mockingbird* (Harper Lee), *Catch 22* (Joseph Heller), *Where the Wild Things Are* (Maurice Sendak), *Charlie and the Chocolate Factory* (Roald Dahl)
Television: *Bonanza, The Fugitive, Sixty Minutes, The Dick van Dyke Show, The Dean Martin Show, The Flintstones, Mission Impossible, The Mod Squad, The Jetsons, Gilligan's Island, Get Smart, The Newlywed Game, Sesame Street*
Fads and Pastimes: long hair and beards for men, pinball machines, peace signs, lava lamps, Easy-bake ovens
1970s
Music: punk rock, disco, Pink Floyd, Roberta Flack, Elton John, Black Sabbath, Marvin Gaye, Stevie Wonder, Billy Joel, ABBA, Bob Marley, Bruce Springsteen,

(continued)

Table 3.1. *(continued)*

Queen, the Sex Pistols, the Ramones, the Bee Gees, Donna Summer, Neil Diamond, K. C. and the Sunshine Band, Alice Cooper, Kiss, the Osmonds, the Carpenters, Chicago

Cars: small import cars, Volkswagen Beetle

People: Al Pacino, John Travolta, Jim Morrison, Farrah Fawcett Majors, Rock Hudson, Dustin Hoffman, Robert Redford, Robert De Niro, Al Pacino, Goldie Hawn, Mary Tyler Moore, Raquel Welch, Clint Eastwood

Movies: *American Graffiti, Last Tango in Paris, The Godfather, The Rocky Horror Picture Show, Grease, Saturday Night Fever, Star Wars, A Clockwork Orange, Rocky, Jaws*

Publishing: *The Joy of Sex* (Alex Comfort), *The Day of the Jackal* (Frederick Forsyth), *Jaws* (Peter Benchley), *Watership Down* (Richard Adams), *All the President's Men* (Carl Bernstein and Bob Woodward), *Playgirl* magazine

Television: *M*A*S*H*, All in the Family*, the *Muppet Show, Schoolhouse Rock, The Price Is Right, Happy Days, The Brady Bunch, Three's Company, Saturday Night Live, Dallas, The Jeffersons, Taxi, The Carol Burnett Show*

Fads and Pastimes: electronic calculators, pet rocks, Post-it Notes, View-Master, Lite-Brite

Sports and Sport Celebrities: jogging, John McEnroe, Muhammad Ali, Bobby Orr, Pete Rose, the Harlem Globetrotters

1980s

Music: Michael Jackson, Madonna, Wham, Duran Duran, The Police, U2, Billy Idol, Prince, Cyndi Lauper, Metallica, Guns N' Roses, AC/DC, Bananarama, Bon Jovi, Whitney Houston, New Kids on the Block, music videos, MTV

Cars: Hondas, Toyotas, first SUVs, the Camaro, the Firebird

People: Jennifer Beals, Julia Roberts, Sylvester Stallone, Tom Cruise, Don Johnson, Mr. T, Arnold Schwarzenegger, Michael J. Fox, Cindy Crawford, Tom Selleck, John Belushi, Bill Cosby

Movies: *Cujo, Raiders of the Lost Ark, Footloose, Fatal Attraction, Top Gun, Aliens, Blade Runner, Back to the Future, The Breakfast Club, Sixteen Candles, E. T., Tootsie, The Terminator, The Karate Kid*

Publishing: Stephen King's novels, Danielle Steele's novels, *Cosmos* (Carl Sagan), *Jane Fonda's Workout Book* (Jane Fonda), *Richard Simmons' Never-Say-Diet Cookbook* (Richard Simmons), *Lucky* (Jackie Collins), *The Frugal Gourmet Cooks with Wine* (Jeffrey L. Smith)

Television: *Dallas, Dynasty, Falcon Crest, Knots Landing, Married . . . with Children, The Simpsons, The Love Boat, The Cosby Show, Miami Vice, Cheers, Family Ties, Who's the Boss? Alf, The Wonder Years*

Fads and Pastimes: supermodels, Care Bears, Rubik's Cubes, Smurfs, Cabbage Patch dolls, Commodore 64, Nintendo, break dancing, Pac-Man, jazzercise, shoulder pads, leg warmers, skateboarding, Teenage Mutant Ninja Turtles, Dungeons and Dragons

Sports and Sports Celebrities: frisbees, working out, Carl Lewis, Kareem Abdul-Jabbar, Joe Montana, Bjorn Borg, Arnold Palmer, Magic Johnson, Michael Jordan, Hulk Hogan, Wayne Gretzsky

1990s

Music: rap, grunge, boy bands, new country (Shania Twain, Billy Ray Cyrus), dance (techno) music, Nirvana, Pearl Jam, MC Hammer, Britney Spears, Spice Girls, Backstreet Boys, New Kids on the Block, Mariah Carey, Ricky Martin, Janet

Jackson, Salt-N-Pepa, Jennifer Lopez, Eminem, Celine Dion, Puff Daddy, Snoop Dogg, Green Day

People: Will Smith, Johnny Depp, Adam Sandler, Luke Perry, Bill Gates, O. J. Simpson, Monica Lewinski, the Olson Twins, Steve Urkel, Leonardo Di Caprio, Pamela Anderson, Brad Pitt, Princess Diana

Movies: *Philadelphia, Schindler's List, Boyz 'n the Hood, Titanic, Jurassic Park, The Matrix, Forrest Gump, Toy Story, The Lion King, Seven, The Sixth Sense, Pulp Fiction, Silence of the Lambs*

Publishing: *Sex* (Madonna), *Bridget Jones's Diary* (Helen Fielding), the *Harry Potter* books (J. K. Rowling)

Television: *Beverly Hills 90210, Seinfeld, Friends, X-Files, Full House, Fresh Prince of Bel Air, Beavis and Butthead, Saved by the Bell, Law and Order, ER, Buffy the Vampire Slayer*

Fads and Pastimes: Internet surfing, Pokemon, pogs, power rangers, spandex shorts, tamagotchi, cell phones

Sport and Sports Celebrities: Mike Tyson, Mark McGwire, Sammy Sosa, Tiger Woods, Shaquille O'Neal, Derek Jeter, Tonya Harding and Nancy Kerrigan

2000s

Music: 50 Cent, Coldplay, Il Divo, Andrea Boccelli, Amy Winehouse, The Black Eyed Peas, Alicia Keys, Kanye West, Timbaland, Usher, Beyoncé, Lady Gaga, Ludacris, Jay-Z, Justin Bieber, DJs (such as Deadmau5 and Alesso), Bruno Mars, Adele, Katy Perry, Rihanna, Jay-Z

Cars: Hummer, Jaguar, German cars (BMW, Mercedes Benz, Audi), Smart car, the Escalade, Denali

People: Paris Hilton, Oprah Winfrey, William Hung, Susan Boyle, J.K. Rowling, Justin Timberlake, Tina Fey, Sarah Jessica Parker, Steve Jobs, Jon Stewart, Sarah Palin, Barack Obama, Hannah Montana, the Kardashians, Will Smith, Angelina Jolie, Cameron Diaz, Jennifer Lopez

Movies: *Matrix Reloaded, Avatar*, the *Harry Potter* movies, the *Lord of the Rings* movies, *The Dark Knight, Memento, Gladiator*, the *Kill Bill* movies, *No Country for Old Men, Slumdog Millionaire, V for Vendetta, Brokeback Mountain, Pirates of the Caribbean, Finding Nemo*

Publishing: The *Harry Potter* line of books (J.K. Rowling), *The Da Vinci Code* (Dan Brown), *Freakonomics* (Steven D. Levitt and Stephen J. Dubner), *The Girl with the Dragon Tattoo* (Stieg Larsson), *Eat, Pray, Love* (Elizabeth Gilbert), *Fifty Shades of Grey, The Hunger Games, Breaking Dawn, Twilight*

Television: CSI programs, reality programs, *The Kardashians, Ellen DeGeneres, Jersey Shore, The Sopranos, Dexter, Family Guy, 30 Rock, Mad Men, Lost, The Office, The Daily Show, Arrested Development, Two and a Half Men, 24, The Wire, American Idol, South Park, Glee, Gray's Anatomy, Desperate Housewives, Criminal Minds, Breaking Bad, House of Cards, House, The Big Bang Theory, Game of Thrones*

Fads and Pastimes: surfing the Internet, Facebook, Twitter, YouTube, mobile devices, blogs, iPods, skinny jeans, Wikis, metrosexuality, webkinz, speed dating, online dating, Sudoku, Uggs, Crocs, tablets, iPhones, emo, leggings

Sports and Sports Celebrities: Serena Williams, Tiger Woods, Michael Phelps, Lance Armstrong, Lebron James, Tom Brady, Kobe Bryant, Chuck Liddell, David Beckham, Brett Favre, Alex Rodriguez, the UFC and mixed martial arts generally, yoga, Roger Federer, Usain Bolt

of diverse pop cultures can be written for India, Germany, Japan, Spain, France—virtually any nation. In fact, in the Internet Age, the celebrity-making stage has become truly international. That same stage, however, canonizes saints and sinners indiscriminately. The exploits of "dark celebrities," such as serial killers and ruthless businessmen, are also part of celebrity culture. The names of Jeffrey Dahmer, Ted Bundy, the Zodiac killer, Son of Sam, and BTK are probably better known than those of the actors who portray them in movies and docudramas. Even academics can gain celebrity status if their ideas are showcased by the media. The blurring of the lines of who and what is considered newsworthy and eligible for celebrity status now includes the religious sphere. Evangelist preachers promote their version of Christianity in the same way pop stars promote their music. Celebrity preachers are in all media today. As Warhol suspected, "fifteen minutes of fame" is a symptom of the media world. Many celebrities are not famous for their accomplishments, but merely for having gained a place in the spotlight. For example, Paris Hilton or the Kardashians would not be celebrities without that place. Like some celebrities of the past, they are famous simply because fame is now a commodity.

But a paradox has emerged today, with celebrities of the past often outdoing present celebrities in gaining media and fan attention. Simon Reynolds (2010) calls this *retromania*, referring to a vague nostalgia felt by people about the icons and the fads of the past. The subtext is that today's trends are unoriginal and unexciting. The global Internet stage has fragmented the unity of the pop culture spectacle, leading to the acceptance of the past as the only future. Current artists like Lady Gaga are often accused of being clones of previous ones (in this case Madonna). But, then, repetition, imitation, and ritualistic performance have always been part of pop culture.

Celebrities created by the Internet are called cybercelebrities. More and more celebrity status is being gained through the online medium. YouTube in particular has become extremely influential in this domain. Becoming famous on YouTube often allows the cybercelebrity to cross over to other media. This across-media movement is one of the many manifestations of convergence—the phenomenon of media converging into one overarching system. To become a celebrity today, one must be showcased by all media, but especially (more and more) by the online one. Cybercelebrities are sometimes dubbed nano-celebrities because of the extremely short duration of their celebrity status. A perfect example was the South Korean musician Psy and his YouTube hit "Gangnam Style" (2012), which is now part of digital pop culture lore. If something goes viral, then nano-celebrity status is virtually guaranteed. The content of the event is called an Internet *meme*, since it spreads throughout cyberspace quickly and massively. A meme may be an image, a video, a hyperlink, a hashtag, a website, or even just a word or phrase. It spreads virally via social networks, blogs, and e-mail. Memes will be discussed in a later chapter.

A MODEL

The discussion of fads, celebrities, memes, and their connection to the business of pop culture leads to a model. As long as common people maintain an interest in pop culture events, the model will remain; otherwise it will disappear. So, the model would show how the popular imagination, which is built on mythic impulses, such as good versus evil, love versus hate, and on an engagement with the profane, much like the ancient spectacles that took place in amphitheaters, seeks expression through spectacle. Spectacle needs a stage; this can be physical, such as in vaudeville, or electronic— recordings, radio, television, and the Internet. Finally, as the popularity of someone or something rises, the marketplace steps in to coopt it and give it an economic value, thus turning it into a commodity. This does not, however, impugn the quality of the event or trend; it just puts a money figure on it. So, the model will show that pop culture is constituted as follows: (1) it is based on the popular imagination and thus on ancient and

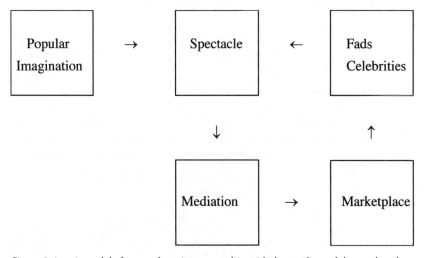

Figure 3.1.   A model of pop culture in partnership with the media and the marketplace

common themes (love, adventure, satire, and so on); (2) these themes take form through various spectacles, understood as performances or texts that have broad appeal; (3) the spectacles need a stage to showcase them, and this can be called *mediation* since in the case of pop culture the main stage has typically been the media; (4) the marketplace then steps in to promote the spectacles broadly through financial support and advertising; and (5) this whole process produces fads and celebrities.

The popular imagination found outlets for its expression well before the era of pop culture, of course. The ancient comedies, the commedia dell'arte, which will be discussed in due course, carnivals, and the like have always been its expressive channels. But they were exceptional events, localized and subsidiary to other kinds of spectacles and events. For the expressive form to gain a foothold more broadly, mediation (the mass media) has to be involved. The mediation process involves all available media, from print to electronic. This is when the marketplace steps in to provide the business aspects to the whole process. These in turn generate fads and celebrities. This whole cycle goes round and round to produce ever-changing fads, celebrities, and trends so that the marketplace can renew itself economically and remain sustainable.

Virtually anything within this process can become faddish and then double back on the popular imagination, thus reversing the process. The example of this is the automobile, which has a practical locomotive function but in the context of this process becomes in itself part of pop culture. The list below provides a case in point of how the automobile acquires meanings that cater to the imagination in a pop culture context:

The Rich Person's Toy

- Cars were initially rare, much too expensive for the everyday person. Rich people, therefore, displayed their wealth by purchasing an automobile.
- This meaning of the car persists in pop culture. Television host Jay Leno, for example, is known for having a massive collection of over eighty cars, including a 1928 Bugatti Type 37A, an 1832 Steam Engine, and various Lamborghinis and Corvettes. Leno would often speak and even showcase some of his automobiles on his show. He also has a website dedicated to his vehicles.

The Rebel Car

- As the automobile became increasingly cheaper and thus popular among the general population, it became associated with excitement, entertainment, individuality, and freedom—a fact that has not escaped the movies and television programs.

- The 1948 Ford, "Greased Lightning," in the movie *Grease* (1978) is an example of this; Danny and the T-Birds rebel against their school's "preppy" image, and race their car against Leo, the leader of the rival gang called the Scorpions.
- Rebel movies associated with cars abound. In these movies "drag racing" (where vehicles compete to be the first to cross a set finish line) constitutes a ritualistic scenario involving the meaning of the car as a rebel machine.

The Sidekick

- The car as a sidekick abounds in pop culture representations of all kinds. Batman's Batmobile (as mentioned briefly) is a prime example of the sidekick car. It has wing-shaped tailfins; it is covered in armor and is equipped with lasers, rockets, an on-board telephone, radar, dash monitor, computer, and police beacon, among other gadgets. It is capable of doing a quick 180-degree "bat-turn" due to the two rear-mounted parachutes. It is equipped with a smoke emitter and a nail spreader to discourage pursuit as well as a Batmobile Parachute Pickup Service Signal.
- Another example is Herbie, the Volkswagen Beetle featured in *The Love Bug* (1968), *Herbie Rides Again* (1974) *Herbie Goes to Monte Carlo* (1977), *Herbie Goes Bananas* (1980), *The Love Bug* (1997), and *Herbie: Fully Loaded* (2005). In the franchise, Herbie has a mind of its own and is capable of driving itself.
- Other sidekick cars have included The Scooby-Doo Mystery Machine van (a 1966 Chevrolet Sportvan), "General Lee" on *The Dukes of Hazzard* TV program, *Knight Rider's* Firebird Trans Am, *Starsky & Hutch's* Ford Gran Torino, and *Mad Max's* Ford Falcon Interceptor.

The Soccer Mom Car

- The minivan is the "soccer mom's" vehicle of choice, as a result of it being featured in movies and television programs with this meaning. Often portrayed as overburdened, but putting her family's interests ahead of her own, the soccer mom drives a minivan to emphasize this role.
- The phrase "hockey mom" was popularized by Republican vice presidential candidate, Sarah Palin, during her speech at the

Republican National Convention in 2008. Hockey moms are seen as more intense than soccer moms, in terms of the commitments and the intensity with which they become involved with their children. The vehicle associated with hockey moms is the pickup truck.

Art and Nostalgia

- Known as "cartists," some artists modify a vehicle to express themselves. During the 1960s, Janis Joplin had a Porsche 356 that was psychedelically painted and John Lennon had a paisley Rolls Royce.
- In 1975, racecar driver Herve Poulin began the BMW Art Car Project, where artists were invited to create a canvas on a car. Andy Warhol, Frank Stella Robert Rauschenberg, Roy Lichtenstein, and other pop artists participated in the project.
- TV shows where older cars are refurbished are very popular, tapping into both the car as art and its nostalgia function. As Parissien (2014) has observed, the nostalgia function of cars is called "retrofuturism," the effort to upgrade classic automobiles from the past, such as the Volkswagen Beetle and the Fiat 500.

A Vision of the Future

- Cars can also be seen as a vision into the future. A classic example of this is the DeLorean DMC-12, which starred as a time machine in the film *Back to the Future*, where Marty McFly is accidentally sent back in time from 1985 to 1955, and again, back into the future.
- In *Minority Report*, Lexus starred as a futuristic car in the year 2054, when a Lexus future vehicle would drive itself, take dinner orders verbally, and select music to match occupant moods. This resulted in the popularization of the Lexus in pop culture.

The same story could be told about virtually anything in pop culture today, suggesting that social evolution and pop culture move in tandem. Popular spectacles, objects, media forms, modern-day economics, the popular imagination, all converge to produce a synergy that is emotionally powerful. That synergy defines pop culture.

4

POPULAR PRINT CULTURE

There are only two or three human stories, and they go on repeating themselves as fiercely as if they had never happened before.

—Willa Cather (1873–1947)

Even in the Internet Age, reading printed books such as novels, "do-it-yourself" books, magazines, comic books, newspapers, and the like is still part of how we get information, skills, recreation, and enjoyment. Starting in the sixteenth century, when the printing press brought into existence the Gutenberg Galaxy, as McLuhan called it (see chapter 2), cheap mass-produced books became not only the primary means for propagating and storing knowledge and ideas, but also props in ensconcing "pleasure reading" into common people's repertory of recreational activities. The purpose of this chapter is to look at the role of print culture in the constitution and evolution of pop culture.

BOOKS

As early as 2700 BCE, the Egyptians used material made from stems of the papyrus plant that grows along the Nile River to make pages that they joined to each other. These were the first books. Shortly after the rise of papyrus books, libraries started sprouting up in the Middle East. One of the largest was built by the Greeks in Alexandria. By the second century CE public and private libraries had been established in many parts of the world, leading to an increase in the desire to gain literacy and, eventually, to the rise of modern universities in the late eleventh century.

With the spread of literacy came a concomitant need to organize the knowledge contained in books. This led, among other things, to the rise of the *encyclopedia* as a book of compiled knowledge. The oldest encyclopedia still in existence is the *Natural History* (79 CE) by Roman writer Pliny the Elder (23–79 CE). The modern type of encyclopedia was largely the

---

THE DEVELOPMENT OF BOOKS

2700 BCE: Papyrus made from plant reeds found along the Nile River is used to produce the first books.

350 CE: The *codex* book is produced by the Romans with parchment pages bound together.

600: Illuminated manuscripts featuring decorative designs on each page are created by scribes (primarily monks).

1453: Johannes Gutenberg turns a wine press into a printing machine, leading to the mass production of books.

1455: The Bible is the first mass-produced book published with the new print technology.

1602: The first lending library, the Bodley, is established.

1640: The first book published in the American colonies, *The Bay Psalm Book*, is printed in Boston.

1751: The first modern encyclopedia is produced by French scholars.

1790: The first U.S. copyright law is passed. Publishing houses start proliferating.

1846: The rotary press is invented in the United States.

1860s: The dime novel becomes a mass reading phenomenon.

1880s: Linotype and offset lithography lower the cost of book production.

1909: The Copyright Act is passed in the United States.

1939: Robert de Graaf introduces Pocket Books.

1960s: Computer-based typesetting begins.

1971: Borders opens its first store in Ann Arbor, Michigan. Chain bookstores and superstores start springing up across America shortly thereafter.

1980s: Desktop publishing gets under way.

1995: Amazon.com is established, turning its first profit in 2002.

1998: The Digital Millennium Copyright Term Extension Act is passed.

2000s: Microsoft and Adobe start making online books (e-books) and other print materials available. E-reader devices allow for instant downloading of books from websites. Online publishing of books starts proliferating, skipping (in some cases) paper printing. Publishers have both online and print versions of major books.

2010s–ongoing: Paper books decline considerably, evidenced by the fact that bookstores used more and more of their store space for other objects, including magazines, souvenirs, and the like, as well as integrating with coffee brands to serve drinks and light food in the stores. Tablets and other types of devices become more and more common as new media for books and e-publishing start dominating.

result of the Enlightenment movement in the eighteenth century, which entrenched the view that knowledge could be arranged logically according to key words, names, or special topics.

Origins and Spread

The Sumerians and Egyptians introduced many of the conventions that are still used today in book production, such as a cover page with a title and the author's name on it. Professional scribes, who either copied a text or set it down from dictation, were responsible for book reproduction. The ancient Greeks, and later the Romans, became aware of the book's potential, but the books they produced were prohibitively expensive and thus were owned chiefly by scholars, rulers, and a few wealthy individuals.

This pattern continued up until the early Middle Ages, when books were produced chiefly by clerics for other clerics and for rulers. They were written with a quill pen by monks working in the *scriptoria* (Latin for *writing rooms*) of monasteries, and either had wooden covers fastened with clasps or were bound in leather. Often they were adorned with gems. Books were artistic objects, commissioned by a very small percentage of the population who could afford them and who knew how to read. Books thus remained mainly the privilege of the few.

In the fifteenth century two developments occurred that broke this pattern. One was the advent of the cheap production of paper; the other was the invention (or more accurately, the development) of typesetting and the printing press. These technological advancements made it possible to manufacture books cheaply for a mass market. As a consequence, book production flourished. New genres emerged, as books were being written not only for religious or scientific purposes, but also more and more for public edification and for diversion.

By the time of the Industrial Revolution vast numbers of books could be published at a relatively low cost, as printing and paper technologies became highly efficient. The book had become an item of mass consumption. While other media challenged, and continue to challenge, the popularity of paper-produced books in the electronic age, they have shown a remarkable staying power. To this day, books remain primary tools for the preservation and dissemination of knowledge, as well as sources for creative expression.

But since the advent of the Internet, the paper book has started to decline. Two novels by Stephen King, *Riding the Bullet* and *The Plant* were published in 2000 on the Internet, rather than in traditional print paper format. Shortly thereafter, the e-book started changing the way we read, write, and sell books, as more and more authors started writing for Google than for a traditional publisher, or else had their books put out in both paper and electronic forms. Actually, the first e-books were put on CD-ROMS between 1985 and 1992. In 1992, Charles Stack's Book Stacks Unlimited began the practice of selling books online. By the late 1990s online publishing became a reality. In 2008, e-books became even available for use on mobile devices, as authors circumvented the usual process of submitting a manuscript to a publisher and simply put out their works in digital form. In the same year, Smashwords allowed anyone to publish his or her book online, making it available through sites such as Amazon and iBookstore. A lover of Shakespeare can now download all his works and read them in any sequence desired. Google's massive digitization project, which is transferring library collections to the online format, is making access to books efficient and widespread.

Still, people are social beings. Going to a bookstore seems to satisfy various social needs. Bookstores now provide a social environment for books, including the sale of coffee and various products, as mentioned. The bookstore and print books will likely continue to exist, at least in the immediate future, because of their social value.

Fiction

The popularity of fictional books, or novels, starting in the late 1400s, brought about a veritable revolution. For five centuries, the innumerable novels that have come down to us have been read by countless numbers of people for the pure enjoyment of it. Novels are stories for the sake of storytelling. They are evidence that the narrative instinct is universal. A *narrative* is a text that has been constructed to represent a sequence of events or actions that are felt to be logically connected to each other or causally intertwined in time and space. The sequence may be fact-based or fictional, or a combination of both. It is often difficult, if not impossible, to determine the boundary line between fact and fiction. Even in the recounting of life-stories, fiction is often intermingled with fact in order to give the stories more coherence and credibility. The psychologist Paul Ekman (1985) has called this the "Othello effect," defining it as convenient lying in order to emphasize truth. And, as American novelist E. L. Doctorow has aptly remarked, "There is no longer any such thing as fiction or nonfiction; there's only narrative" (cited by the *New York Times Review*, January 27, 1988).

Making sense of a narrative is not a straightforward process of determining the meanings of the individual words with which it is constructed and adding them together; rather, it involves interpreting the whole narrative at various levels. One level is the *subtext*. This is the main theme or intent of the narrative, which is not announced explicitly by the characters or narrator. It is implicit or becomes understood by the reader from cues within the main text. Some of these may come in the form of *intertexts*, which are allusions within the narrative text to other texts external to it. For example, the main text of the movie *Blade Runner* unfolds as a science fiction detective story, but its subtext is, arguably, a religious one—the search for a Creator and thus a meaning to life beyond mere physical existence. This interpretation is bolstered by the many intertextual cues to biblical and philosophical themes and symbols in the movie.

Narrative is decomposed traditionally into four main constituents—plot, character, setting, and narrator. The *plot* is basically what the narrative is all about; it is a series of events connected logically (chronologically or historically) to each other and perceived as mirroring real-life events. *Character* refers to the people or beings that are part of the story, either shaping it or being shaped by it. Each character stands for a personality type—the hero, the coward, the lover, the friend, and so on. The *setting* is the location where, and the time when, the story takes place. The *narrator* is the teller of the story. The narrator can be a character within the narrative or someone outside the text. Each type of narrator provides a different perspective on the story for the reader. The reader can thus feel a part of the narrative, looking at the action as if he or she were in it; or aloof from it, looking at the action as if from the outside.

Fiction did not emerge as such until the Middle Ages, although there is some evidence that it may have ancient roots. Papyri from the fourth Egyptian Dynasty indicate that King Cheops (2590–2567 BCE) delighted in hearing the fictional stories that his sons told him. The Greek statesman and general Aristides (c. 530–468 BCE), moreover, wrote a collection of what we would now call short stories about his hometown, Miletus, to celebrate the Greek victory over the Persians at Salamis. The *Golden Ass* of Apuleius (c. 125–200 CE) was a fictional narration providing social and moral commentary. But the tales of the ancient world were hardly perceived as fictional in the modern sense of that word, but rather as dramatic reenactments of historical-mythical events. Fiction became a standard narrative craft only after Giovanni Boccaccio (1313–1375) published *The Decameron* (1351–1353), a collection of one hundred fictional tales set against the gloomy backdrop of the Black Death, as the bubonic plague that swept through Europe in the fourteenth century was called. The *Decameron* is the first real example of fiction for entertainment. To escape an outbreak of the plague, ten friends decide to take refuge in a country villa outside Florence. There, they entertain one another over a period of ten days with a series of stories told and totally made up for the occasion by each member of the party in turn. Ever since, fictional narration has been a yardstick for exploring the human condition. As the Argentine writer Jorge Luis Borges (1899–1986) suggested in his *Ficciones* (1944, 1962), the mind is inherently designed to understand life as a narrative. Sigmund Freud (1856–1939) saw the conflicts recounted in mythic narratives as attempts to come to grips with unconscious psychic life. In the myth of Oedipus—the king who was abandoned at birth and unwittingly killed his father and then married his own mother—Freud discerned a narrative mirror for probing hidden sexual desires. Carl Jung (1875–1961) similarly saw narratives as windows into the collective unconscious—an area of the mind constituted by primordial images, which he termed archetypes, and which are imprinted in narrative forms across the world.

Archetype theory nicely explains why we find narratives so emotionally powerful and understandable across the world in the same way. Archetypes are unconscious symbols and forms that enable people to react to and comprehend situations in similar ways. Common archetypes like clowns, villains, and heroes, for example, are found throughout narratives and appear today in pop culture figures such as the Joker (a Batman foe), the Shadow (a crime-fighting hero of pulp fiction fame), and comic book adventure heroes (such as Superman and Spider-Man). Each archetype represents a different psychic need—the need for laughter, the need to confront fear, and the need to emphasize valor in human life.

The Renaissance commedia dell'arte (a type of comedy characterized by improvisation on a standard plot outline) was highly popular, arguably because its stock characters were archetypes—Harlequin, the clownish valet, the Doctor, who was a quack with fraudulent solutions to human problems, the licentious Pulcinella, who concocted schemes to satisfy his desires; and so on. Similar archetypes are found in fiction throughout time. The Sage archetype, who comments on a situation in which others have put themselves, can be seen in the character of Wilson on the TV sitcom *Home Improvement*; the Clown can be seen in the role of Cosmo Kramer on *Seinfeld*. These characters strike a responsive chord because they represent real people through verisimilitude. The main Jungian archetypes are: the Self; the Shadow, the archetype of fear; the Anima, the feminine sense in all of us; the Animus, the corresponding masculine sense; and the Persona, representing the face or role we present to the world. Other archetypes, such as the Trickster, the Hero, the Mentor, the Sage, and so on, are derivatives of these.

In a famous 1928 study, the Russian critic Vladimir Propp (1895–1970) recast archetype theory, showing how it can be mapped onto thematic elements in a story, such as a fairy tale. After an initial situation is described in the tale, a sequence of thirty-one functions unfold, and these can be mapped against seven major archetypal figures:

1. The *villain* who opposes the *hero*.
2. The *dispatcher* who identifies a crisis situation and sends the hero off on a quest to rectify it.
3. The *helper* who helps the hero in the quest.
4. The hero's *reward* or *prize*, such as the attainment of marriage.
5. The *donor*, who prepares the hero by giving him or her some magical object.
6. The actual *hero*.
7. The *false hero* who takes credit for the hero's actions and attempts to steal his or her reward.

To see how this can be applied to fiction today, consider the James Bond movies. Bond, of course, is the hero, and M is the dispatcher who sends him off to resolve a situation. Q is the donor, who prepares him with magical gadgets. There is always an evil villain who wishes to destroy Bond. Bond has various helpers, especially beautiful and physically powerful women. Bond's reward is both the satisfaction of having saved the world from evil and, in many of the stories, ending up with the female helper in romantic tryst. The almost regular way in which Propp's categories can be applied to narratives, especially popular ones, has opened it up to much criticism. Indeed, not all narratives have Proppian structure, but a lot of them do, especially those that seem to gain popularity. Other types of narrative may, of course, gain popularity, such as experimental ones and those that deal with the stream of consciousness (like the novels of James Joyce and Virginia Woolf). But by and large, the many genres of stories that inhabit the world of pop print culture tend to be in synch with Propp's analysis, revealing a likely universal structure to storytelling that is embedded in the psyche, much like Jung had suggested.

The Novel

There are various media, modes, channels, and devices for delivering popular narratives. But the one that may have started it all off is the *novel*.

Novels have been sources for many cultural practices over the centuries—children were (and still are) named after characters in novels; real places are named after places described in novels; and so on and so forth. Novels such as Fyodor Dostoyevsky's *Crime and Punishment* (1866) have been used as templates for evaluating human character or the nature of crime. It is amazing indeed to contemplate that a text that is essentially a lie has been used throughout its history to get at the truth, about people, life, and the universe.

As mentioned above, proto-fictional narratives were composed in the ancient world, and to these the term *novel* is sometimes applied retrospectively. But the novel did not emerge as an autonomous narrative genre until the Middle Ages. Many literary scholars regard the eleventh-century *Tale of Genji*, by the Japanese baroness Murasaki Shikibu (c. 978–1026), as the first true novel, since it depicts the amorous adventures of a fictional Prince Genji and the staid lives of his contemporaries through a narrative frame (plot, character, setting, and so on). The novel paints a charming and apparently accurate picture of Japanese court life in the Heian period. Among its chief features are the portraits of the women in Prince Genji's life. They are aristocrats, with many talents, especially in the arts of music, drawing, and poetry. As the work nears its conclusion, the tone becomes more mature and somber, colored by Buddhist insight into the fleeting joys of earthly existence.

Etymologists claim that the word *fiction* was first used around 1412 in the sense of "invention of the mind." It is not a far step from this coinage to the sense of "imaginative literature," first recorded in 1599. The first fictional works became popular with the rise of the long verse tale, the prose romance, and the Old French *fabliau* in the medieval period, culminating, as mentioned above, with Boccaccio's *Decameron*. In Spain during the sixteenth century, the novel gained great social importance with the picaresque genre, in which a hero is portrayed typically as a vagabond or a wanderer who passes through a series of exciting adventures. The most widely known example is the novel by Miguel de Cervantes Saavedra (1547–1616), *Don Quixote de la Mancha* (Part I, 1605, Part II, 1615), which is considered the first great novel of the Western world.

Novels gained enormous popularity in the eighteenth and nineteenth centuries, especially those satirizing contemporary life and morals. During that same era, the novel spawned its own genres, including the Gothic novel, which aimed to horrify readers through stories of bizarre supernatural happenings. The first Gothic novel was *The Castle of Otranto* (1764) by Horace Walpole (1717–1797). But perhaps the most well-known example of the genre is *Frankenstein* (1818) by Mary Wollstonecraft Shelley (1797–

1851). Another narrative genre of the period was the comedy of manners, which explored the hypocritical and spurious nature of social relations. The novels of Jane Austen (1775–1817) are probably the most important ones in this category. Throughout the nineteenth century, novelists were as popular and well known as media personalities are today. The French writer Marcel Proust (1871–1922), the German author Thomas Mann (1875–1955), English author Virginia Woolf (1882–1941), and Irish novelist James Joyce (1882–1941) were veritable icons to the reading public. To this day, novelists are held in high esteem and can become celebrities, as their novels are turned into movies. Writers such as Dan Brown, Jackie Collins, Stephen King, Stephenie Myers, and John Grisham are as part of contemporary celebrity culture as are pop musicians, movie stars, and television personalities.

Some novels become *bestsellers*, which is the equivalent in the print medium of the movie *blockbuster*. Bestellers include all kinds of books, from recipe books of famous chefs to self-help manuals. But novels still share a large segment of the bestseller domain. New novels by Stephen King, for example, tend to become bestsellers. The books that make it to prestigious lists, such as the *New York Times* list or Amazon.com's list, qualify as bestsellers, even though other books that do not make it to the lists may sell more copies. Today a book's popularity can also be determined by the chatter in social media it stirs up and by sites such as Goodreads, indicating a convergence of print with Internet culture.

Evaluations of the role the novel has played in social evolution have varied. Twentieth-century Marxist critics (chapter 2) saw fictional books as meaningful mainly when they showcased the social imbalances in capitalist societies or else dealt with the human condition. Freudian critics, on the other hand, believed that the value of novels lay in the insights they provided into the psyche. The conflicts, fantasies, and daydreams of fictional characters in novels are those of ordinary people, and thus can be read through a psychoanalytic lens. The French philosopher and writer Jean-Paul Sartre (1905–1980) saw narrative fiction as providing an "escape hatch" from inner psychic turmoil. Perhaps the most radical view of narrative ever to have been formulated comes from the pen of the late French philosopher Jacques Derrida (chapter 2), who challenged the traditional way of interpreting literary fiction as a mirror of life and as seeing the author of a work of fiction as the source of its meaning. The author's intentions in writing, Derrida claimed, cannot be unconditionally accepted, because the words in a text become entangled and deconstruct themselves in the process, producing meaningless garble.

Derrida was fixated with *logocentrism*, or the view that knowledge is constructed by linguistic categories. Words can stand on their own for virtually anything. Derrida's ideas were very popular among literary critics in the 1970s and 1980s. They have become less so since they apply mainly to writing practices in print culture, and not to new forms of narrative and writing in general.

To reiterate, the novel has always constituted a form of popular reading entertainment (for those with literacy skills). It is, arguably, the first true medium for the configuration and delivery of pop culture. The novel is a "portable narrative entertainment device" that anyone can enjoy at any time. Novels have been used to fulfill all kinds of interests, from the prurient to the highly intellectual. Moreover, as Bakhtin pointed out in his writings (chapter 2), novels are transgressive, because they portray social conditions and personages as fictitious, using verisimilitude as their ploy, and thus authors cannot be directly held responsible for libel or political treason, although they can be censored and even imprisoned on various charges.

The Pulps

By the era of the Roaring Twenties novels were being produced in bulk for mass consumption and entertainment, in response to the rise in popularity of pulp fiction, stories published in inexpensive fiction magazines in serial form. The first true pulp fiction magazine is considered to be Frank Munsey's *Argosy Magazine* of 1896. The word *pulp* refers to the fact that the magazines and derivative novels were produced with cheap paper made from wood pulp. In contrast, magazines produced with higher-quality paper were called *glossies* or *slicks*. The pulps were successors of the dime novels of the nineteenth century. They were popular because they revolved around the themes of great interest to people, such as crime, adventure, and sex, and they were written in a sensationalistic and lurid way. Fictional pulp detectives and crime fighters such as Doc Savage, the Shadow, and the Phantom Detective became household names, appealing to the archetypal instinct within people. Titles of the early pulp magazines included: *Dime Detective, Planet Stories, Startling Stories, Flying Aces, Amazing Stories, Black Mask, Spicy Detective, Horror Stories, Unknown and Weird Tales, Marvel Tales, Oriental Stories,* and *Thrilling Wonder Stories.* The popularity of these magazines was bolstered by their cover designs, which imitated the sensationalistic poster art used by circuses and vaudeville theaters to attract audiences, with scantily dressed "damsels in distress" or virile heroes involved in fisticuffs with villains. The pulps became the basis for the early movie serials, such as those made by Republic Pictures in the 1930s and 1940s. The serials kept audiences in suspense as an episode ended with the hero or heroine caught in some dangerous situation. The audience would eagerly come back the week after to find out how the cliffhanger situation would be resolved.

With rising paper costs and competition from other media, the pulps started losing market dominance by the late 1950s. The bankruptcy in 1957 of the American News Company, the main distributor of pulps, marked the end of an era. The influence of the pulps has not subsided however. The cliffhanger formula is still evident in the James Bond movies, the *Raiders of the Lost Ark* films, the *Mission Impossible* television and movie series, and other television series and motion pictures. But, more importantly, pulp genres—such as the detective and mystery story, science fiction, westerns, the sword and sorcery story, the horror tale, the romance tale, and many others—are now staples of pop culture fare in all media, from movies to comic books. Some of the fictional characters they created have become an enduring part of pop culture lore. These include: Buck Rogers, Fu Manchu, Hopalong Cassidy, Perry Mason, Nick Carter, Secret Agent X, Tarzan, The Shadow, and Zorro, to mention but a few. Pulp fiction, incredibly, engaged some of the greatest writers of the twentieth century, including Isaac Asimov, Ray Bradbury, Edgar Rice Burroughs, Arthur C. Clarke, Philip K. Dick, Zane Grey, Robert A. Heinlein, Frank Herbert, and Upton Sinclair. Current popular fiction writers such as Stephen King and Anne Rice are cut in the same tradition of the pulp fiction writers. So, while the original pulps may have disappeared, the pulp meme has obviously not.

Moreover, the close link between the pulps and the movie industry, established already in the 1930s, has not been broken but, rather, become even stronger. *The Godfather* (1969), *Love Story* (1970), *The Exorcist* (1971), *Jaws* (1974), *The Da Vinci Code* (2003), and *Twilight* (2008) are perfect examples of this link, since all started out as popular novels written in pulp style that later became blockbuster movies. The venues, plots, and characters may appear different, but they are not. These are essentially updated pulp fiction stories.

Why does pulp fiction have such great emotional appeal? Consider two genres as cases in point—adventure stories and spy stories. Adventure stories are narratives involving heroes or heroines who defeat villains by using superhuman strength and intelligence, or other valiant attributes. Most medieval romances were adventure-plus-romance stories. The hero and his beloved would face a series of challenges. Typically, they would be separated by maleficent circumstances and personages, but the hero would overcome the calamity and be reunited at the end with his loved one in a felicitous reunion. Variations to this basic hero-and-his-lady formula started with writers such as Sir Walter Scott, Victor Hugo, and Robert Louis Stevenson. The adventure genre found a home in the comic book medium early in the twentieth century, beginning with the publication in 1929 of *Tarzan* and *Buck Rogers*—the former adapted from the novels of writer Edgar Rice Burroughs. Both comics became instantly popular. The first comic superhero, Dr. Mystic, was introduced in 1936 by Jerry Siegel and Joe Shuster. In 1938, Action Comics started publishing its Superman comic strip, co-created by the same Siegel and Shuster duo. The 1940s saw the debuts of Batman, The Flash, Green Lantern, Wonder Woman, and Captain America.

Since the 1950s, the adventure story has been regularly recast for new audiences while maintaining the same basic formula, which revolves around the exploits of a hero or heroine who searches for a lost place or treasure, seeks to save someone, or engages in some quest. As Propp had pointed out, it starts with a situation that requires intervention; the protagonist then faces a series of challenging trials, which he or she overcomes, often with the help of a partner or sidekick (which may also be an animal, a machine, a weapon, and so on), triumphantly reaching the objective at the end. Contemporary adventure stories are sometimes modified to include anti-heroes, likable villains (as in *Pirates of the Caribbean*), or dark heroes (as in *The Dark Knight*).

The case of *Watchmen* (released in 1986 as a graphic novel) is particularly relevant. The hero, Rorschach, is a demented vigilante with a morphing inkblot mask (hence his name, which refers to the Rorschach technique in psychology) and the villain is someone called the Comedian. Both Rorschach and the Comedian are strange characters, constituting hero archetypes and antiheroes at once. As Richard Reynolds (1992: 107) states: "While the Comedian is in part a satirical reworking of the state-sponsored, nationalistic breed of superhero most notably exemplified by Captain America or Nick Fury, Rorschach is a version of the night-shrouded hero embodied by characters from Batman through Daredevil." In the 2009 *Watchmen* movie, the Comedian is killed and Rorschach appears with a host of zany characters. The bad guy does a very evil thing but escapes punishment by persuading people that his deed was actually beneficial. The movie reverberates with moral ambiguity rather than certainty (as in the traditional adventure stories).

Spy narratives are adventure stories revolving around the exploits and romantic interests of a spy or secret agent who must battle terrorists or assassins. The classic example of spy fiction is found in the James Bond novels, the fictional English secret agent created by British novelist Ian Fleming. Bond is a debonair, suave, but deadly agent. His code name is 007—the double-0 means that he is licensed to kill at his own discretion. Fleming introduced Bond in *Casino Royale* (1953). The first Bond motion picture was *Dr. No* (1962). The subsequent (and still ongoing) film series has made stars out of actors Sean Connery, Roger Moore, Timothy Dalton, Pierce Brosnan, and most recently Daniel Craig.

The genre traces its origins to James Fenimore Cooper's *The Spy* (1821) and *The Bravo* (1831). Notable early spy novels include Rudyard Kipling's *Kim* (1901), Baroness Emmuska Orczy's *The Scarlet Pimpernel* (1905), Robert Erskine Childers's *The Riddle of the Sands* (1903), Joseph Conrad's *The Secret Agent* (1907), and the over one hundred novels of William Le Queux and E. Phillips Oppenheim published between 1900 and 1914. Also prominent in the genre was John Buchan, whose novel *The Thirty-Nine Steps* (1915) was adapted by Alfred Hitchcock into a popular movie in the 1930s.

The 1970s marked the entrance of Robert Ludlum into the spy genre field, starting with *The Scarlatti Inheritance* (1971). Ludlum's broad success led subsequently to a spate of comparable spy thrillers such as *The Hunt for Red October* (1984) by Tom Clancy, *Harlot's Ghost* (1991) by Norman Mailer, *A Spy by Nature* (2001) by Charles Cumming, and *Dead Line* (2008) by Stella Rimington. The genre is also popular on television, with series such as *La Femme Nikita* (1997–2001), *Alias* (2001–2006), and *24* (2001–2010). It has also crossed over successfully to the video game universe, of which the Metal Gear set of games is the most representative. Spy fiction has spawned several subgenres, including spy-fi, which blends elements of science fiction with the basic spy narrative; spy comedy, which spoofs the traditional spy stories; and spy horror, which combines elements of supernatural thrillers with those of spy fiction.

The critical response to the spy genre has been ambivalent. Some see it as a form of escapism from the real world. As the fictional villain is vanquished, so too are the dangers of the real world (at least in the imagination). Others see it as a vehicle for critiquing governments, especially institutions such as the CIA, in order to provide a better model of how human politics should be run. Whatever the case, spy stories tap into the popular imagination effectively, as can be seen by their longevity and continuity.

NEWSPAPERS

In cities and towns one still finds newspaper dispensing boxes, even though these are diminishing on a daily basis. Newspapers are still delivered to homes and, overall, are still popular reading texts, even though it is unlikely that people will read a newspaper from cover to cover, like they read a novel.

So why do we like our newspapers so much, since they lack the kind of story structure of novels and other popular texts? Newspapers tap into a basic need to know what is going on in our world. They have the same function as village gossip and chatter in oral cultures. And like the power of talk in these cultures, newspapers can influence opinion and, thus, motivate people to initiate social changes. A number of newspapers contain sections that involve a high level of writing. But the kind of journalism that is of particular relevance here is the more popular form that deals with gossip, information about goods and services, and entertainment themes.

Origins and Spread

Handwritten newssheets posted in public places in the ancient world are considered to be the forerunners of newspapers. The earliest was the Roman *Acta Diurna* (Daily Events), dating back to 59 BCE. One of the world's first newspapers, a Chinese circular called *Dibao*, was produced using carved wooden blocks around 700 CE. The first paper-based newspapers with a regular publication and distribution in Europe can be traced to Germany in 1609. The newspaper business expanded considerably in the seventeenth and eighteenth centuries. By the late 1800s, newspapers had become marketplace commodities, as newspapers in large cities tried to outdo one another with sensational reports of crimes, disasters, and scandals.

The year 1690 signals the advent of printed newspapers in the American colonies, with the publication of the *Publick Occurrences, Both Foreign and Domestick*, a three-page paper, printed in Boston. This event showcased the potential power of the written word to bring about social protest. As a consequence, it was suppressed by the government after only one issue. It was in 1704, with the publication of the *Boston News-Letter* that true pop journalism, as it can be called, made its debut. The paper contained financial and foreign news and also recorded births, deaths, and social events. In 1721 James Franklin founded the *New England Courant* in Boston. His younger brother, Benjamin, went to Philadelphia in 1723 to found the *Pennsylvania Gazette* and the *General Magazine*. Although these publications

A NEWSPAPER TIMELINE

1620: *Corantos,* the first news sheets, are published in northern Europe.

1640s: The first daily newspapers are published in England.

1644: English poet John Milton calls for freedom of speech in his pamphlet titled *Aeropagitica.*

1690: Boston printer Benjamin Harris publishes the first American newspaper, *Publick Occurrences, Both Foreign and Domestick.*

1735: Freedom of the press is defended when a jury rules in favor of printer John Peter Zenger, who had criticized the government in print and who had been charged with libel.

1783: The first daily newspaper in the United States, the *Pennsylvania Evening Post and Daily Advertiser,* is published.

1789: Freedom of the press is enshrined in the American Constitution by the enactment of the First Amendment.

1827: The first African American newspaper, *Freedom's Journal,* makes its appearance.

1828: The first Native American newspaper, *The Cherokee,* makes its debut.

1833: The penny press era is ushered in with the publication of the *New York Sun,* costing only one cent.

1848: Six newspapers form the Associated Press, and begin relaying news stories around the country via telegraphy.

1860: The *New York Morning* reaches a circulation of eighty thousand, showing that newspapers had become an integral part of mass communications.

1883: Joseph Pulitzer buys the *New York World,* ushering in the era of yellow (sensationalistic) journalism.

1895: William Randolph Hearst enters newspaper publishing, further promoting yellow journalism.

1896: Adolph Ochs buys the *New York Times* and makes responsible journalism its primary objective.

1914: The first Spanish-language paper in the United States, *El Diario/La Prensa,* is founded in New York.

1917: The Pulitzer Prize is established at Columbia University, to reward achievement in journalism and other areas.

1920s: Newspaper chains spring up, leading to a decline in the number of daily metropolitan newspapers.

1930–1934: Hundreds of syndicated columns start up.

1972: The Watergate scandal stimulates a new era of investigative journalism.

1980: Ohio's *Columbus Dispatch* is the first newspaper to go online.

1982: *USA Today* is launched, the first paper modeled after television.

1998: The *Dallas Morning News* is the first newspaper to break a major story on its website instead of its front page. Increasing use of the Internet leads to the development of blogs, discussion groups, and the like, which take on many of the functions of traditional print newspapers.

2000s: By 2003, most newspapers offer some kind of online news service. More and more people get their news in digital formats, including on mobile devices and tablets. But print newspapers continued to publish with a steady clientele.

2010s–ongoing: Web-based newspapers start appearing and dominating. Some newspapers, like the *Seattle Post-Intelligencer,* move away from print to web publishing. Customized online newspapers appear, offered by MyYahoo, IGoogle, ICurrent.com, and other sites.

failed, Franklin nevertheless gained fame as a writer, editor, and publisher because of them. More importantly, these events heralded the arrival of the contemporary newspaper.

The first New York City newspaper, the *Gazette*, was established in 1725. It was soon followed by the *New York Weekly Journal*, edited by John Peter Zenger, who published acerbic critiques of the British colonial governor of New York and his administration. As a consequence, Zenger was arrested and jailed on charges of libel. He was tried and found not guilty. This trial created the crucial precedent for the tradition of a free press in America.

In 1783, the first daily newspaper in the United States, the *Pennsylvania Evening Post and Daily Advertiser*, was launched in Philadelphia. Until the 1830s newspapers were concerned almost entirely with business and political news, appealing primarily to the privileged classes. All that changed in 1833, when Benjamin Henry Day published the first issue of the *New York Sun*, creating a "penny press" revolution—newspapers for a broad reading public that cost a single cent. The *Sun* included reports of crime and violence and entertainment all in the same issue. With the advent of the first telegraph line in 1844, news could be transmitted quickly across the nation, expanding newspaper culture ever more broadly. In response to this development, an amalgamation of newspapers called the Associated Press (AP) was formed in 1848. The AP emerged as an agency dedicated to the fair reporting of news across the nation, presenting information and commentary in as nonpartisan and objective a manner as possible, a standard that is still pursued today.

As newspapers competed more and more with each other to increase circulation rates, journalism became more and more sensationalistic, which resulted from the competition between two papers, Joseph Pulitzer's *New York World* and William Randolph Hearst's *New York Journal*. To attract larger segments of the reading public, these newspapers used hyperbole in headlines, catchy art design, Sunday supplements containing comic strips and games, and a general editorial sympathy with the "common person" and the "underdog," against authority figures as integral parts of style and content. Hearst published color comic sections that included a strip called *The Yellow Kid*.

The term *yellow journalism* (alluding to the strip) emerged to describe this type of journalism, leading to the *tabloid* genre, which gained wide popularity decades later in the 1920s. The tabloid was smaller, its reports more condensed and sensationalistic, focusing on the occult, the weird, the bizarre (from alien creatures to miraculous cures), and on celebrities and their "private lives."

As yellow journalism showed, newspapers have always depended for survival on quickly and efficiently distributing as many copies as possible. Ironically, as popular as the newspaper continues to be today, high operating expenses, especially the rising cost of labor and newsprint, have driven many out of business. Few cities now have competing dailies. In those that do, the rival publishers typically print their papers on the same presses to reduce costs. Financial problems have hit major metropolitan papers the hardest, in part because they face increasing competition from suburban papers and especially from the Internet. In 1980 *The Columbus (Ohio) Dispatch* launched the first electronic newspaper in the United States. In addition to printing a regular edition, the *Dispatch* began transmitting some of its content to computers in the homes, businesses, and libraries of a small number of subscribers. Today, newspapers offer online versions of their regular editions and even entire issues. The first general news website was the *News and Observer*, originating in Raleigh, North Carolina, in 1994. It began with editors feeding stories from the newspaper's main newsroom onto the website. Today, newspaper websites allow users to add features such as blogs and fan sites onto their home pages, further popularizing the sites.

The Blogosphere

Blogging has become a major form of writing, replacing, in some cases, the traditional print newspaper and magazine article. Blogs originated in the online discussions of chat groups of the early Internet. Blogs have several advantages over print articles. The most important one is that they can be updated continuously, while print articles need to be revised and republished over a period of time. Also, feedback on blogs is rapid and far-reaching, since most blogs allow for readers to respond and leave comments on the site, to which the blogger can reply. This has led to the formation of blogging communities, making up the so-called blogosphere.

Anyone can establish a blog website and promote his or her views freely. One no longer has to submit, in most cases, a piece of writing to an editorial quality-control process, as in the world of traditional print culture. The value of a blog is determined by the inhabitants of the blogosphere. Many print journalists and radio and television commentators now have blogs that allow for the updating of their texts and immediate reader commentary. The rise of the blog to social importance is evidenced by various events in the early 2000s. In one 2002 case, bloggers critiqued comments made by American Senate majority leader Trent Lott at a party in honor of Senator Strom Thurmond. Lott suggested that Thurmond would have made the ideal president. The bloggers portrayed this as implicit approval of racial segregation, since Thurmond had seemingly promoted segregation in his 1948 presidential campaign, as documents recovered by the bloggers showed. The mainstream media never reported on this story until after the bloggers broke it. The end result was that Lott stepped down as majority leader. Blogs were also influential in getting two presidents elected—George W. Bush and Barack Obama. Without going into details here, suffice it to say that the support of the bloggers was shown to greatly influence the outcomes of both elections, superseding and substituting the role of the print newspaper in this domain.

However, this was not the death knell of print journalism. People still seem to want to read newspapers as they ride on public transport vehicles, as they wait for appointments in offices, as they sip coffee in coffee shops and in their homes, and in many other locales. Newspapers still have appeal, even though they have come down considerably from the perch that they enjoyed for centuries before the advent of the Internet.

Reading Newspapers

Why are newspapers so popular? Perhaps because they truly are a pastiche of information, and pastiche, as discussed, is a style that taps into the popular imagination (chapter 1). One of the foremost examples of the power of the press came in 1974 when President Richard Nixon resigned from his office after revelations about the Watergate scandal pointed the finger of blame at him. The scandal had been brought to public attention by the *Washington Post*. Watergate gave rise to investigative reporting as a separate print genre. Today, the same newspapers are coping with the competition of up-to-date news reports on radio. But they remain popular because people buy newspapers not only for their news content and editorial commentaries, but also (if not more so) for their advertising content, for the comics section, for the crossword or Sudoku puzzle, for sports gossip, for classified information, for entertainment news, for reviews of books and movies, for portraits of exceptional individuals, and so on. Newspapers open up a silent (nonvocal) polyphonic dialogue, as Bakhtin might claim (chapter 2).

Needless to say, different types of newspapers attract different kinds of readers. They are thus perceptibly different in how they present their content. Some newspapers, such as the grocery store tabloids, are sensationalistic in form and content; others, like the *New York Times*, are designed to have a much more sophisticated appearance and content. A comparison of the two brings this out clearly.

Table 4.1.   Style Differences between Tabloids and Sophisticated Newspapers

Tabloids	Sophisticated Newspapers
Headlines are large and overstated: *Bodies Found Decapitated!*	Headlines are formal and restrained: *Gruesome Murders Discovered*
Writing style is colloquial and characterized by slang features: *The headless bodies are like part of a horror movie.*	Writing style is more refined and erudite: *The headless bodies were a horrific scene.*
Reporting is sensationalistic and graphic: *There were gory pools of blood splattered all over the place.*	Reporting is subdued and rational: *Blood was found all around.*
Bawdy and occult topics and features are included: horoscopes, ads for sexual services, apocalyptic prophecies, gossip stories about celebrities.	Bawdy and prurient topics are avoided, although some occult features such as horoscopes may be included.
Advertising is blunt: *If you've got a problem having sex, get Viagra.*	Prurient topics and advertising are treated with discretion and prudence: *Sexual satisfaction can be increased with Viagra.*

Reading tabloids is akin to reading circus and carnival posters; reading newspapers like the *New York Times* is akin to reading literary works. Tabloids have the same function as gossip and small-town storytelling. As the American poet E. E. Cummings (1894–1964) aptly put it: "The tabloid newspaper actually means to the typical American what the Bible is popularly supposed to have meant to the typical Pilgrim Father: a very present help in times of trouble, plus a means of keeping out of trouble via harmless, since vicarious, indulgence in the pomps and vanities of this wicked world" (cited by *Vanity Fair,* December 1926). Tabloids entertain audiences by adorning their narrations with hyperbole and sensationalism. They treat topics such as UFOs, alien visitations, and religious apparitions alongside melodramatic exposés of celebrity love affairs, sexual scandals, and the like. Due to its popularity, the tabloid style has spread to other newspapers. The most famous of these is *USA Today*, which began publication in 1982. With its admixture of tabloid-like features and traditional journalism, *USA Today* is a perfect example of how pastiche is becoming an ever-expanding modality.

Advertising

Arguably, advertising would not be the big business it is today without its early partnership with newspapers. The two go hand in hand and, indeed, the rise of modern-day newspapers and persuasive advertising occurred in tandem. On average, newspapers devote half of their space to advertising. Many people read a daily newspaper specifically to check the ads for products, services, and special sales.

The *London Gazette* became the first newspaper to reserve a section exclusively for advertising. Advertising agencies came into existence for the specific purpose of creating newspaper ads for merchants and artisans. In general, they designed the ads in the style of classifieds, without illustrative support. But the ads nonetheless had rhetorical flavor. The following advertisement for toothpaste dates back to a 1660 issue of the *Gazette*. What is captivating about it is the fact that its style is virtually identical to the one used today for the promotion of this very same type of product (cited by Dyer 1982: 16–17):

> Most excellent and proved Dentifrice to scour and cleanse the Teeth, making them white as ivory, preserves [cures] the Tooth-ach [toothache]; so that being constantly used, the Parties [people] using it are never troubled with the Tooth-ach. It fastens the Teeth, sweetens the Breath, and preserves the Gums and Mouth from cankers and Impothumes . . . and the right are only to be had at Thomas Rookes, Stationer.

Hyperbole and exaggeration—"most excellent," "proved," "preserves the Tooth-ach"—constitute hints that bad breath is socially harmful, while the maintenance of a beautiful mouth is portrayed as socially advantageous. Newspaper advertising spread throughout the eighteenth century in both Europe and America, proliferating to the point that the writer and lexicographer Samuel Johnson (1709–1784) felt impelled to make the following statement in *The Idler*: "Advertisements are now so numerous that they are very negligently perused, and it is therefore become necessary to gain attention by magnificence of promise and by eloquence sometimes sublime and sometimes pathetic" (cited by Panati 1984: 168). As advertising became a fixture of print culture, ad creators began paying more attention to the design and layout of the ad text itself. Layouts with words set in blocks and contrasting type fonts became widespread. New language forms (slogans) were coined regularly to serve the persuasiveness of the ad text. As a consequence, newspaper advertising was surreptitiously starting to change the very structure and use of verbal communication, as more and more people became exposed to newspaper advertising. Everything from clothes to beverages was promoted through ingenious new verbal ploys such as strategic repetitions of the product's name in the composition of the ad text, the use of compact phrases set in eye-catching patterns (vertically, horizontally, diagonally), the use of contrasting font styles and formats, and the creation of slogans and neologisms designed to highlight some quality of the product, alongside supporting illustrations. These techniques remain basic to advertising craft to this very day.

MAGAZINES

The pulp fiction magazines discussed above were pivotal in ushering in and spreading popular print culture. Magazines in general are regularly produced publications containing articles, features, photographs, and illustrations on various topics, and sponsored generally by advertising revenues and subscriptions. Unlike newspapers, they are thematic texts—dealing with specific themes, hobbies, special interests, and so forth. Among the most popular kinds of magazines today are those that deal with art and antiques, business, cars, current affairs, entertainment, fashion, health and fitness, history, hobbies, games, humor, music, politics, science, and sports.

Origins and Spread

The earliest magazines published were the German *Erbauliche Monaths-Unterredungen* (1663–1668), the French *Journal des Sçavans* (1665), and the *Philosophical Transactions* (1665) of the Royal Society of London. These were essentially collections of essays on issues and trends related to art, literature, philosophy, and science. In a similar vein, *essay periodicals* followed in the early eighteenth century. Among the most widely read of these were the British publications *The Tatler* (1709–1711) and *The Spectator* (1711–1714)—creations of the renowned essayists Richard Steele (1672–1729) and Joseph Addison (1672–1719)—*The Rambler* (1750–1752) and *The Idler* (1758–1760), founded by Samuel Johnson (1709–1784). In the latter part of the century, some periodicals developed into general purpose magazines. With the publication of *The Gentleman's Magazine* (1731–1907) in England, the modern-day magazine came into being. The event also marked the first use of the word *magazine*. Deriving from the French word *magasin* (through Italian *magazzino* and Arabic *mahazin*), which meant storehouse, the magazine was a veritable literary storehouse of essays, poems, and political writings.

By the mid-nineteenth century, magazine publication increased considerably. *Godey's Lady's Book* (1830–1898), with its colorful fashion

---

A MAGAZINE TIMELINE

1731: The first magazine, *Gentleman's Magazine*, is published in England.
1732: *Poor Richard's Almanack* by Benjamin Franklin is published in the United States.
1741: Colonial magazines appear in Boston and Philadelphia.
1821: The *Saturday Evening Post* is launched.
1836: Sarah Josepha Hales becomes the first editor of *Godey's Lady's Book*, the first women's magazine.
1846: *Harper's Weekly* begins publication.
1879: The Postal Act of 1879 lowers the postal rate for magazines, allowing distribution to thrive.
1880s: The advent of linotype and offset lithography lowers the cost of magazine production.
1922: *Reader's Digest* is launched.
1923: *Time*, founded by Henry Luce, starts publication.
1936: *Life* starts publication.
1953: *TV Guide* is launched.
1954: *Sports Illustrated* begins publication.
1967: Rock and roll gets its own magazine with the launch of *Rolling Stone*.
1969: The *Saturday Evening Post* succumbs to specialized competition.
1974: *People* magazine starts publication.
1980s–1990s: Magazines for all kinds of tastes and hobbies proliferate.
2000s: E-zines start proliferating online. Magazines are also available on mobile devices and tablets. Still, the traditional print version continues to have staying power.
2010s: Magazines become uploaded on mobile devices through special apps (as do newspapers and other print materials). The print versions still exist, but the uploaded option is taking over the market gradually.

---

illustrations, was vastly influential in setting a more open, sexy style in women's clothing, manners, and taste, that seems so common today, yet was controversial at the time. The *Illustrated London News* (1842), the *Fortnightly Review* (1865–1954), *Punch* (1841) in England, *L'Illustration* in France (1843–1944), *Die Woche* (1899–1940) in Germany, and *Leslie's Illustrated Newspaper* (1855–1922) and *Harper's Weekly* (1857–1916) in the United States became staples of an emerging affluent middle class of readers. *Youth's Companion* (1827–1929) and later *St. Nicholas* (1873–1940) were among several children's magazines published in the same era that became highly popular for imparting literacy skills to children. Family magazines such as the *Saturday Evening Post* (1821–) also became vastly popular, indicating that certain days (such as Saturday) could be set aside for entertaining, informative, and wholesome reading.

With the publication of *Cosmopolitan* (1886–), the modern fashion and lifestyle magazine for women came into being. Between 1902 and 1912, this genre became one of the most popular of all magazines. In addition to *Cosmopolitan*, female readers could choose from *Ladies'* (later *Woman's*) *Home Companion* (1873–1957), *McCall's Magazine* (1876–), *Ladies' Home Journal* (1883–), *Good Housekeeping* (1885–), and *Vogue* (1892–). Publications written by women and designed for female audiences would have been unthinkable just a few years previously.

In 1922 the pocket-sized *Reader's Digest* began publication, confirming that people had increasingly little time to read entire books. With the summaries that this magazine regularly published, readers could indulge their need for information and stories and, at the same time, to make up their minds as to whether or not to buy and read an entire book. Since the 1950s, this periodical has had a monthly circulation in the millions. Two other significant developments, dating from the 1920s and 1930s, were the establishment of weekly news magazines such as *Time* (1923) and *Newsweek* (1933), and the emergence of weekly and biweekly magazines, such as *Life* (1936–1972, revived as a monthly in 1978), *Look* (1937–1971), and *Ebony* (1946–), which focuses on issues of African American concern.

Today, magazine publishing is a worldwide phenomenon, and the industry continues to cater to specialized tastes. For example, *National Geographic World* (1888–) contains information from the worlds of science, history, and travel; *Consumer Reports* (1936–) offers comparative evaluations of consumer products; *GQ* (1957–) focuses on issues of concern to urban males; *Rolling Stone* (1967–) is devoted to pop music and pop culture generally; *Ms.* (1970–) deals with women's issues; *People* (1974–) features stories on celebrities; *Discover* (1980–) is a general science magazine; and *Wired* (1993–) looks at issues pertaining to digital culture.

Predictably, in today's digital galaxy the magazine has converged with other media. E-zines are proliferating, and boast various advantages over paper-based magazines. For example, they can be distributed much more quickly and updated regularly. Moreover, given the hypertext capacities of e-zines, they can be linked with other sources of information. The Internet also has created magazine reader sites (on Facebook, Twitter, and other sites). In early 2000, *Vogue* created one of the first such sites, Style.com, where people could get the latest gossip about the fashion industry. Such sites have now become commonplace.

Reading Magazines

While newspapers organize their content in the form of pastiche, magazines present it in the form of collage, a text that revolves around some particular topic split up into articles and features in a cohesive way. Many magazines have a glossy cover with a photograph of a personality or celebrity or, in the case of specialized magazines (for example, car, computer, or travel magazines) of some relevant object or place. The writing level of magazines varies, being consistent with the stylistic characteristics expected by the readership.

Magazines are gauges of what is going on in pop culture. Consider *InStyle* magazine as a case in point. *InStyle* was founded in 1994 (www .InStyle.com). The magazine is very popular and extremely well designed. It offers its readers a collage of items on celebrities, lifestyle, cosmetics, and fashion trends along with numerous ads positioned for upwardly mobile women. Each monthly issue is organized in a set pattern, strategically superimposing continuity between the products advertised, the articles, and the website. Issues often feature a celebrity on the cover, and a relevant article about the celebrity. An issue also provides the reader with advice on where to find fashion items, how to maintain a healthy figure, how to enhance beauty through cosmetics, and the like. The magazine rarely diverges from this format and contents. *InStyle* reveals what can be called *textual syntax*, defined as the technique of linking celebrities, ads, and other content thematically, creating a syntax of sense between products, trends, and people that is compelling and cohesive. For example, a photography magazine attracts photography aficionados who will undoubtedly find its ads helpful in choosing certain photographic equipment and who will, thus, read them as part of the syntax of the text. In effect, the ads complement the articles in a logical fashion.

COMICS

The *comics* have become a target of great interest among pop culture analysts, and stand out as a kind of overarching meta-text characterizing pop culture itself. The predecessors of comics are the caricatures of famous people that became popular in seventeenth-century Italy. Caricature art spread quickly throughout Europe shortly thereafter. In the early nineteenth century, the art was expanded to include speech balloons, giving birth to the comics.

Comics (or *comic strips*) are narratives told by means of a series of drawings arranged in horizontal lines, strips, or rectangles, called *panels*, and read like a verbal text from left to right. Dialogue is presented as written words encircled by a balloon, which issue from the mouth or head of the character speaking. Movement is illustrated largely through the use of lines of different sizes. For example, long thin lines trailing a running horse show speed. Short broken lines indicate jumping.

Origins and Spread

One of the first American texts with the essential characteristics of a comic strip was created by Richard Felton Outcault, appearing in the series titled *Hogan's Alley*. It was published on May 5, 1895, in the *New York Sunday World*. The strip depicted squalid city tenements and backyards filled with dogs and cats, tough-looking characters, urchins, and ragamuffins. One of the urchins was a flap-eared, bald-headed child with a quizzical, yet shrewd, smile. He was dressed in a long, dirty nightshirt, which Outcault often used as a placard to comment on the cartoon itself. Known as the *yellow kid*, it is from this character's name that the term *yellow journalism* derives, as discussed above.

Other early comic strips included the *Little Bears* by James Guilford Swinnerton, which first appeared in the *San Francisco Examiner* in 1892, *The Katzenjammer Kids* by Rudolph Dirks, which first appeared in *The American Humorist* in 1897, and *Mutt and Jeff*, which first appeared as *Mr. A. Mutt* in a November 1907 issue of the *San Francisco Chronicle*. Newspaper syndicates introduced *Mutt and Jeff* to a wider audience, turning it into the first successful daily comic strip in the United States. It became so popular that, to satisfy demand, newspapers published collections of the individual strips, leading to the emergence of an independent comic book publishing industry around 1911. In 1933, a number of comic books, based on well-known newspaper comic strips such as *Joe Palooka* and *Connie*, were even given out as premiums with certain merchandise.

While the Sunday newspaper comic strips were originally designed primarily for children, the daily comic strips were intended to attract all kinds of audiences. Harry Hershfield's *Abie the Agent*, first published in 1914, capitalized on the popularity of the pulp detective and mystery genre of the era. Another early maker of comics was Roy Crane, who created *Wash Tubbs* in 1924. The adventure genre began with the publication in 1929 of *Tarzan* and *Buck Rogers*, as mentioned. Adventure comics became instantly popular and have remained so to this day. Comic and cartoon characters never age and thus can appeal across generations of readers. There have been exceptions to this pattern—starting with *Gasoline Alley* by

Frank O. King where the characters aged day by day—but, by and large, time seems to stand still in the world of the comics.

The adventure genre has always been among the most well-loved comic strip and comic book genres. Great impetus was given to the comic book industry by the phenomenal success in 1938 of *Action Comics*, of which the principal attraction was the *Superman* comic strip, which was later published in separate *Superman* comic books. *Superman* also spawned a series of other comic book hero clones in the early 1940s, from *Batman* to *Captain America*.

The comics have a broad appeal. A number have, in fact, found a devoted following among intellectuals. *Krazy Kat*, for instance, has been regarded by many as one of the most amusing and imaginative works of narrative art ever produced in America. The work of Charles Schultz, as mentioned, also falls into the category of thought-provoking comics. His comic strip *Peanuts* became one of the most popular comic strips ever, appearing in more than two thousand newspapers and translated into more than twenty languages. Its characters—Charlie Brown, his sister Sally, his dog Snoopy, his friends Lucy, Linus, Schroeder, Peppermint Patty, and Marcie, and the bird Woodstock—are part of pop culture nostalgia. The characters are all children, but have much more insight into life than adults do, who are relegated to the margins of the strip. Its tone is one of subtle sadness—a veiled angst that begs the readers to ask questions about life and existence.

Starting in the 1970s, many individuals and small companies began competing with the larger publishers. Indie or alternative artists experimented with new styles, more sophisticated formats, and stories suited to adults. This led to the "graphic novel," which is a book-length comic book that tells a single story. The most celebrated early examples of this genre are *Maus: A Survivor's Tale* (1986) and *Maus II* (1991) by Art Spiegelman. They recount the artist's relationship with his father and the experiences of his father and mother during the Holocaust.

Early on, comics appealed broadly because they became mixed-media (visual and linguistic) narratives for the modern world, both reflecting modern life and helping to mold it. They have inspired plays, musicals, ballets, motion pictures, radio and television series, popular songs, books, and toys. Everyday language is replete with idioms and words created for the comics. For example, the code word for the Allied Forces on D-Day was *Mickey Mouse*, and the password for the Norwegian Underground was *The Phantom*. Painters and sculptors have incorporated comic book characters into their art works; motion picture directors have adapted techniques of the comics into their films; and of course, Bugs Bunny (with his *What's up, Doc?*), Homer Simpson (with his *D'oh*), Rocky and Bullwinkle (with their wry humor), the Flintstones, Fat Albert, Popeye, Scooby-Doo, Arthur, Winnie the Pooh, Mr. Magoo, Felix the Cat, Yogi Bear, Mighty Mouse, Woody Woodpecker, Tom and Jerry, to mention just a few, have become emblems of pop culture generally.

Today, there are many online e-toons. For example, *Gary the Rat* in its original version, was about a ruthless New York lawyer who is transformed into a huge rat, in parodic imitation of Franz Kafka's novella *Metamorphosis*. The rat is hated by his landlord, who wants to evict him, and chased by an exterminator who is out to eliminate him. Yet, Gary is adored by his boss because clients are eager to work with him.

The comic book genre, or at the very least the comic book–style narrative, continues to attract large audiences today, with new titles coming out daily and being showcased through print and electronic channels. TV in particular has taken over from print in some ways, with shows like *Arrow, Falling Skies, Game of Thrones, Grimm, Marvel's Agents of S.H.I.E.L.D., Once Upon a Time, The Walking Dead, Defiance, Supernatural,* and *Sleepy Hollow*—all of which are comic book–style narratives.

Reading Comics

Their very name, *comics*, suggests much about their original nature and how we tend to read them. Comics were about comedy, in all its senses, as in both *the human comedy* and *ribald comedy*. They were once called *the funnies*, and newspapers carried (many still do) a funnies page with strips that are meant to make people laugh or smile. The 1933 *Funnies on Parade*, a magazine-format compilation of newspaper comic features, suggests in its epithet that the comics were about fun.

With the focus on action superheroes in pulp fiction, comics soon fragmented into various genres, becoming visual forms of pulp fiction narratives, many based on the archetypal mythology of the hero, which includes, among other features, the following ones.

- *A life-saving journey in infancy:* Superman had to leave his home planet of Krypton, to avoid being destroyed along with the planet.
- *An obscure childhood:* Little is known about the early lives of most superhero characters. Occasionally, flashbacks are used to enlighten the current situation.

- *Orphanage*: Some superheroes, like Batman, Captain Marvel, Black Panther, and Cyclops, have lost their parents, as had many of the ancient mythic heroes.
- *Superhuman powers*: In one way or other, and to varying degrees, superhuman powers (be they physical or intellectual) are possessed by the fictional superheroes. These are sometimes gained in unusual ways. Spider-Man, created in 1962, has special powers that he developed after being bitten by an irradiated spider gone berserk. This, combined with his unusual blood type, leaves him with superhuman strength, reflexes, a spider sense (which warns him of impending danger), and a spider's adhesive shooter (with which he can climb walls and ceilings).
- *A fatal weakness:* Whether it be exposure to kryptonite, blindness (Daredevil), or psychological problems of various kinds (The Hulk), the fatal weakness is a basic feature of the hero code—Achilles had a weak heel, Samson's strength depended on his long hair, and so on.
- *Selfless dedication to the public good:* Usually at the expense of their own personal lives, the heroes of ancient myths and the superheroes of comic books exist to help common people against evil.
- *A magic weapon:* Many ancient heroes had a magic weapon at their disposal. For example, the Norse god Thor had a powerful hammer. Similarly, Spider-Man has his web shooters, spider-tracers, and a versatile belt; Hellstorm has a trident that can shoot out fire; Iron Man has a sophisticated suit of armor; Batman has a sophisticated car and an array of gadgets; and so on.

The comic book superheroes have also evoked their share of moral panic. In the 1950s concern over violence in comics led to Senate hearings, which led, in turn, to "underground comics" in the 1960s. The artists referred to their strips as *comix* to distinguish them from mainstream comics. But, by the early 1990s, society came to see comics not only as forms of entertainment, but also nostalgically, as the digital age came into existence in full force. The original print comics are now prized items of memorabilia, and new ones still appear and have large, albeit niche audiences.

Comic book heroes are crossing over to all media (as mentioned) and vice versa. *Watchmen*, for example, has been referenced in the TV series *Lost* and *Buffy the Vampire Slayer*. *V for Vendetta*, *From Hell*, and *The League of Extraordinary Gentlemen* have all led to movie versions. In whatever form or medium, the comic has shown itself to be a mirror of changes in the world. Already in 1988 DC Comics published *The New Guardians*, which included an aboriginal girl, an Eskimo man, and an HIV-positive gay man as its superheroes. For years, Japanese manga comic books and anime movies and programs, with characters like Pokémon and Hello Kitty, have become popular (or at least recognized) throughout the world. Comics have a primal quality to them—a fact that was brought out by the movie *Unbreakable* (2002), directed by M. Night Shyamalan. Comics, the movie claims, are modern-day manifestations of something universal, mirroring the kinds of stories imprinted in cave paintings and in writing systems such as the hieroglyphs.

5

RADIO CULTURE

Captured by the radio as soon as she or he awakens, the listener walks all day long through the forest of narrativities.

—Michel de Certeau (1925–1986)

The *War of the Worlds* radio broadcast incident on Halloween night of 1938, mentioned briefly in chapter 2, showed how audiences can blur the line between fiction and reality. Orson Welles (1915–1985) had turned H. G. Wells's novel into a radio docudrama, frightening many listeners into believing that Martians had landed and invaded New Jersey. He created the panic by using a series of "on-the-spot" news reports describing the landing of Martian spaceships—reports that sounded as real as any radio news report. An announcer would remind the radio audience, from time to time, that the show was fictional. Even so, many listeners believed that Martians had actually invaded the Earth. The police and the army were notified by concerned citizens; people ran onto the streets to see what was happening; and some even ran away. The reaction took Welles and his acting company by surprise. They did not expect that people would take the show seriously, after all it was just that, a *show*. They had forgotten (or ignored) Plato's warning, so to speak, that representation and reality are almost impossible for people to take apart psychologically, especially when the former simulates the latter.

The *War of the Worlds* incident is now a famous one in the annals of media and pop culture history, and it underscores the powerful role that its first electronic stage, *radio*, played in the delivery of pop culture. By the 1930s radio had become the primary platform for much of popular fare, from music and comedy to adventure serials. The radio is still around, although it has lost much of its former supremacy. This chapter will look at the radio and its role in pop culture history.

RADIO BROADCASTING

In 1837, the telegraph became the first electronic system of international communications. It was relatively inefficient because it depended on a complex system of receiving stations wired to each other along a fixed route. In 1891, Nikola Tesla (1856–1943) invented a high-frequency transformer, which became a vital component of electronic transmitters, thus setting the stage for Italian engineer Guglielmo Marconi (1874–1937) to send the first radio signal through the air in 1895, when he transmitted an electronic signal successfully to a receiving device that had no wired connection to his transmitter, thus demonstrating that a signal could be sent through space so that devices at random points could receive it. He called his invention a *radiotelegraph* (later shortened to *radio*), because its signal moved outward in all directions, that is, *radially*, from the point of transmission. At first called the *wireless*, radio was introduced into the world. Incidentally, in 1943, the Supreme Court of the United States invalidated many of Marconi's patents, recognizing that Tesla had patented similar inventions prior to his.

In 1901, Marconi developed an alternator appliance that could send signals much farther and with little background noise. This advance led, about two decades later, to the development of commercial technology that established the radio as a mass communications medium, shaping trends throughout society. Radio could reach many more people than print, not only because it could span great distances instantly, but also because its audiences did not have to be print-literate.

Historical Sketch

Evidence of a plan for radio broadcasting to the general public can be found in a 1916 memorandum written by David Sarnoff (1891–1971), an employee of Marconi's U.S. branch, American Marconi, which would eventually become the Radio Corporation of America (RCA). In the memo, Sarnoff recommended that radio be made into a "household utility." The plan was not given any serious consideration by management at first. After World War I ended in 1918, however, several manufacturing companies began to seriously explore Sarnoff's idea for the mass-marketing of home radio receivers.

A RADIO TIMELINE

1890s: Nikola Tesla and Guglielmo Marconi develop radio technology.

1906–1910: Lee De Forest invents the vacuum tube, called the Audion tube, improving radio reception. Reginald Fessenden makes the first radio broadcast from the Metropolitan Opera House in New York City.

1910: Congress passes the Wireless Ship Act, requiring ships to be equipped with wireless radio.

1912: Congress passes the Radio Act, the first piece of government regulation for radio transmission.

1916: David Sarnoff, the commercial manager of American Marconi, writes a famous memo, in which he proposes to his boss to make radio a "household utility."

1916–1920: Frank Conrad founds KDKA in Pittsburgh as the first experimental radio station in 1916. The station's broadcast of the 1920 presidential election results on November 2, 1920, is generally considered to constitute the beginning of professional broadcasting.

1922: The first uses of radio for commercial purposes begin with the airing of the first advertisements by AT&T on station WEAF. This causes an uproar, as people challenge the right of the public airwaves to be used for commercial messages.

1926: The first radio broadcasting network, NBC, is launched by RCA.

1927: A new Radio Act passed by Congress creates the Federal Radio Commission. AM stations are allocated.

1933: FM radio is introduced.

1934: The Federal Communications Commission (FCC) is created by an act of Congress.

1938: Mercury Theatre on the Air broadcasts *War of the Worlds*, demonstrating how a mass medium can cause public panic.

1947: Radio starts to lose audiences to television.

1948: The DJ radio era takes off.

1949: *Red Hot 'n Blue* becomes one of the first radio music shows, broadcasting music that was soon to become the rage (rock and roll).

1955: Top 40 radio becomes a popular type of radio format, indicating that radio was becoming more and more a marketing arm of the recording industry.

1970s: FM radio stations gain popularity, transforming radio into an increasingly specialized medium (with programs for specific musical tastes).

1971: National Public Radio starts broadcasting with *All Things Considered.*

1979: Sony engineer Akio Morita invents the portable Walkman.

1987: WFAN is launched as the first all-sports radio station, making it obvious that the radio has become a narrowcasting medium.

1990s: Talk radio becomes popular. Old and new music genres, from country to gospel and opera, attract niche audiences.

1996: Congress passes the Telecommunications Act, allowing for consolidation in radio ownership across the United States.

2000s: Satellite and web-based radio programs emerge in 2002. File-sharing, online radio programs become highly popular.

2010s–ongoing: Simulcasting becomes a regular aspect of radio broadcasting and online radio stations start cropping up throughout the Internet universe.

In an effort to boost radio sales in peacetime, the Westinghouse Electric Corporation of Pittsburgh established what many culture historians consider to be the first commercially owned radio station, offering a regular schedule of programming to the general public. It came to be known by the call letters KDKA, after it received its license from the Department of Commerce (which held regulatory power over public transmissions at the time) in October of 1920. KDKA gained almost instant popularity with its transmission of recorded music, using a phonograph playing a record placed within the range of a microphone. The station did not charge user fees to listeners, nor did it carry paid advertisements. Westinghouse used KDKA, seemingly, as an enticement for people to purchase home radio receivers.

Other radio manufacturers soon followed suit as KDKA's popularity grew. The General Electric Company, for example, broadcast its own programs on station WGY in Schenectady, New York. Seeing the rise of radio as a mass communications medium, RCA eventually gave Sarnoff permission to develop radio programming for home entertainment. He opened stations in New York City and Washington, D.C., and in 1926 he founded the National Broadcasting Company (NBC), an RCA subsidiary created for the specific purpose of broadcasting programs via a cross-country network of stations. The Columbia Broadcasting System (CBS) radio service was established shortly thereafter in 1928, becoming a dominant force in the American broadcasting industry over the subsequent fifty years. Already in 1922, AT&T (the American Telegraph and Telephone Company) began exploring the possibilities of toll broadcasting, that is, of charging fees to companies in return for airing commercial advertisements on its stations. Fearing legal action, however, it sold its stations to RCA and left the broadcasting business. In return, AT&T was granted the exclusive right to provide the connections that would link local stations to the NBC network.

The sale of radios more than justified the expense to manufacturers of operating broadcasting services. According to estimates by the National Association of Broadcasters, in 1922 there were sixty thousand households in the United States with radios; by 1929 the number had topped ten million. But increases in sales of radio receivers could not continue forever. The systematic sale of advertising time loomed as the only viable solution for the economic survival of radio broadcasting. The merger of advertising with radio programming was the event that, arguably, produced (or reinforced) the business model of pop culture discussed in chapter 3, whereby the marketplace entered the picture to influence the type of content and the schedule of programming in the emerging broadcasting universe. Noncommercial broadcasting would play only a minor role in the United

States from then on—there would not be a coast-to-coast non-commercial radio network until the establishment of National Public Radio (NPR) in 1970. In Great Britain, on the other hand, radio owners paid yearly license fees, collected by the government, which were turned over directly to the publicly run British Broadcasting Corporation (BBC).

Actually, small-scale public broadcasting surfaced in the 1920s and 1930s, with educational radio programming transmitted by a small number of colleges. In 1953, the first noncommercial educational television station (KUHT) was established for nationwide broadcasting at the University of Houston. President John F. Kennedy signed the Educational Television Facilities Act on May 1, 1962. By the mid-1960s, a surge in noncommercial radio stations occurred, with the support of federal funding and funding from the Ford Foundation. The Public Broadcasting Act was passed in 1967, leading in the 1970s to the establishment of the Public Broadcasting Service (PBS) and NPR.

Radio broadcasting reached the pinnacle of its popularity during World War II. In that period, American commentator Edward R. Murrow (1908–1965) changed the nature of news reporting permanently with his sensationalistic descriptions of street scenes during the German bombing raids of London, which he delivered as an eyewitness from the rooftop of the CBS news bureau there. In the same time frame, American president Franklin D. Roosevelt utilized radio as a propaganda device for the first time. The radio allowed him to bypass the press and directly address the American people with his "fireside chats" during the Great Depression. Roosevelt knew that the emotional power of talk would be much more persuasive than would any logical argument he might put into print. Adolf Hitler, too, saw the radio as a propaganda medium, using it to persuade millions to follow him in his quest to conquer the world. Revealingly, a radio appeal from Japanese emperor Hirohito to his nation for unconditional surrender broadcast the end World War II following the atomic bombings of Hiroshima and Nagasaki.

Radio broadcasting dramatically changed social life wherever it was introduced. By bringing information, critical commentary, the arts, and entertainment directly into homes, it democratized cultural reception more than any other previous medium. Historically a privilege of the aristocracy (or the cognoscenti), the arts could now be enjoyed by members of the general public, most of whom would otherwise not have access to venues such as the concert hall and the theater. The parallel growth of network radio and Hollywood cinema in the 1920s created an unprecedented mass culture for people of all social classes and educational backgrounds. While

An early radio (© ThinkStock)

it is true that this was started in the domain of print (as mentioned in the previous chapter), it would not have become as widespread without radio for the simple reason that radio could reach more people for the initial (one-time) cost of a radio receiver.

Radio and the Internet

In the Internet galaxy, radio has shown itself to have remarkable staying power. It is estimated that there are about two billion radio sets in use worldwide. Radio is also technologically adaptive. Digital satellite radio stations, such as XM and Sirius, are now part of that galaxy. The radio may have come down from its top perch, but it continues, nevertheless, to be an integral part of mass communications and a promoter of pop culture fare.

Convergence now characterizes radio broadcasting. *Simulcasting* is the broadcasting of programs across more than one medium at exactly the same time. The term "simulcast" was first used in 1948 at WCAU-TV, Philadelphia. A few years later, in 1952, orchestra conductor Arturo Toscanini's March 15 broadcast of his *NBC Symphony* program is perhaps a first use of radio-TV simulcasting of a concert. In the 1970s, WPXI in Pittsburgh broadcast singer Boz Scaggs's live performance simultaneously on two FM stations in order to produce quadrophonic sound (sound transmitted through four channels). In 1975, the BBC simulcast a recording of singer Van Morrison's London Rainbow concert on television station BBC2 TV and on radio station Radio 2. In 1981, rock musician Frank Zappa's Halloween shows on October 31 at the Palladium of New York City were shown on MTV with the audio-only part simulcast over FM. The July 13, 1985 *Live Aid* telethon concert was broadcast worldwide by TV networks and FM stations. Simulcasting increased throughout the 1980s and 1990s with the advent of video recorders that connected the TV signals to the audio stereo system of the VCRs. With the arrival of the Internet and satellite broadcasting, simulcasting has taken on a slightly different turn—it involves the simultaneous broadcasting on TV or online of a radio program, reversing the previous simulcasting situation. An example of this is *The Howard Stern Show*, which is broadcast on *Sirius Satellite Radio* and *Howard TV*.

Streaming refers to relaying video and audio material over a computer network as a steady continuous "stream," allowing playback while subsequent material is being received. The term refers especially to content delivered in real time over the Internet by means of a source device—a video camera and audio interface or various kinds of software—a digitizing encoder, and a content delivery network to distribute the content. There are also stand-alone Internet radio devices offering the possibility for audiences to listen to radio without computers and to comment on programs directly. YouTube in particular is used commonly to encourage audience interaction through features such as online surveys, live chats, and the like.

Streaming has rendered previous devices such as the CD (compact disc) passé. Many symphony orchestras, for example, now sell live Internet streams of their concerts, instead of CDs, via YouTube and other streaming media. Pop musicians and performers now use this technology to simply get noticed. And, of course, some transmission systems, like Netflix, are based entirely on delivering content through streaming media.

RADIO GENRES

At first, radio was no more than a new platform for delivering previous print and theatrical content. Essentially, it took the various genres of stage drama, pulp fiction, and newspapers and adapted them to the audio medium. For instance, it converted the adventure stories of pulp fiction into action serials; vaudeville acts to comedy-variety programming, newspaper reports into news broadcasts. In the case of the latter, early announcers would simply read selected content from the local newspaper over the air. Because of its capacity to reach large numbers of people, from the 1920s to the early 1950s radio broadcasting evolved into society's primary stage for pop culture. Only after the rise to dominance of television in the 1950s did radio's hegemony begin to erode, as its audiences split into smaller, niche segments. Today, radio is primarily a medium that people listen to in automobiles and at workplaces (while working), or else listen to for special reasons (such as to listen in on talk shows or sports channels). Radio stations present news and traffic information in a regular interspersed fashion throughout their broadcasts, or else present uninterrupted stretches of music during certain periods of the working day. Satellite radio stations offer new interactive ways to receive radio content, such as through the various streaming modalities discussed above.

Overview

Despite obvious differences between radio and television, the development of programming for both media is best understood as a single history comprised of two stages—both in the physical sense of the word (namely as stages on which pop culture is performed), and in the extended sense of periods of time. The sitcom started as a radio genre, crossing over in the 1950s to TV. As an aside, it should be mentioned that sitcoms evoke the traditions of commedia dell'arte, which was especially popular in Italy in the sixteenth and seventeenth centuries. The commedia performances were based on standard comedic plot outlines and stock characters. It was street theater, as opposed to the cultivated theater of the courts and the academies. Common people attended the performances and commedia troupes set up their makeshift stages in piazzas in much the same way as traveling circuses did. The script was open, in the sense that it simply provided an outline (called a *scenario*), with the actors performing a basic plot or routine spontaneously, much like improv comedy today. Each character performed his or her part more or less according to the role, changing details as the routine or skit moved along. The performers wore masks to emphasize their character profile. The same actor always played the same role and wore the same mask, adapting it through improvisation to the unfolding performance and the reactions of the audience. Most of the farcical plots dealt with love affairs, licit or otherwise. Some of the characters, like Harlequin the clown and Pantaloon the old man, became so popular that their masks were worn by people at carnival time.

The sitcom adopted the stock character format and the same kind of plots, dealing comedically with family matters, love, and romance. The difference is that the sitcom unfolds as a series, imitating how the life within a given family or group (such as friends) might evolve in real time and space. The sitcom became very popular on radio, starting with *Amos 'n' Andy*, which premiered on NBC in 1928, and ran for twenty years before moving to television, where it remained popular from 1951 to 1953. Similarly, *The Goldbergs* (1929–1950), *Life with Luigi* (1948–1953), and other ethnic family sitcoms became successful because many (immigrants and non-immigrants) could relate to them. They dealt in a humorous fashion with the problems that everyone faced, especially the relations between parents and children, husband and wife, and so on. Lucille Ball's radio show *My Favorite Husband* (1948–1951) was probably the most popular of all the sitcoms, focusing on the battle between the sexes, arguments among neighbors, and other mundane conflicts.

Variety shows and radio dramas were also popular genres. The former were adapted directly from vaudeville. Radio entertainers such as Jack Benny, Fred Allen, and Edgar Bergen were originally vaudeville comedians. A radio comedy-variety hour consisted of short monologues and skits featuring the host. These were alternated with various acts, including singers, musical performers, and comedians. Radio dramas were presented in one of two formats—*anthology* and *serial*. The former comprised individual plays, such as one would expect to see on stage or in motion pictures. The two most popular radio dramas were *Mercury Theatre on the Air* (1938–1941), created by Orson Welles, and *Theatre Guild of the Air* (1945–1954). Serial dramas, such as police series (for example, *Gangbusters*, 1935–1957), mystery series (*The Shadow*, 1930–1954), and westerns (*The Lone Ranger*, 1933–1955), were all radio adaptations of pulp fiction stories. They became widely loved and followed. Radio drama virtually disappeared by the mid-1950s, as its biggest stars and most popular programs crossed over to television.

A very popular type of serial drama was the soap opera, which was originally developed as a daytime programming format aimed specifically at a female audience. The genre was so named because soap and detergent manufacturers sponsored many of the series. Soap operas dealt with romance, friendship, and familial relations in the lives of common people. Their invention is credited to Irna Phillips in Chicago, with *Painted Dreams*, which premiered in 1930. The genre was essentially a serialized radio version of the romance novel genre. Today, the soap opera no longer claims the popularity it once enjoyed, on radio or on television, indicating that times have changed. But the soap opera was a watershed event in the history of American womanhood, allowing women to engage in fantasy romance in a public way. Instead of portraying women as girlfriends or mothers, subservient to men, the soap operas generally portrayed them as being in charge of their own lives. Many early soap women were lawyers, doctors, and musicians, alongside mothers and housewives. Also, unlike the male-centered hero narrative, the soaps did not bring any conflict to a resounding and climactic conclusion, but left the plots unresolved, thus reflecting real everyday life. Like many other popular texts, the soaps were transgressive, unhinged from traditional narrative themes and representations. All this changed in the 1990s, however, as the soap genre on TV gave way to serials such as *The Sopranos*. By 2009, many of the long-playing soaps were cancelled. Nevertheless, like other radio (and TV) genres today, the soaps are available online (YouTube). But it remains to be seen if in a vastly changed world they will continue to exist, given that their initial subtexts may no longer have meaning today.

In the area of news reporting, radio could offer its audiences live coverage of events—something that newspapers could not do. The immediacy with which radio news reached people redefined the role of news reporting in society. Print journalism became a complementary medium, focusing on in-depth coverage and editorial opinion. Today, radio continues to be a primary source of news reporting. Some stations have news-only formats—National Public Radio's *All Things Considered* and *Morning Edition*, for example.

The Talk Show

Another genre that started on radio is the talk show. The original talk shows were really no more than dialogues between a host and a guest on politics or current affairs. But subsequently, many gossip and "shock talk" programs emerged, becoming very popular, and remaining so to this day. The first such talk show was the one hosted by Father Charles E. Coughlin, which premiered in 1926. A conservative Catholic priest, Coughlin attracted forty-five million listeners to his weekly radio talks. In the 1960s, outspoken hosts Alan Berg and Alex Bennett focused on pressing social issues and events such as the Vietnam War and the civil rights movement. Today, talk shows hosted by radio personages such as Joe Pyne and Rush Limbaugh continue to attract large audiences. There are now also various subgenres, including *hot talk*, which attracts mainly younger male audiences, interspersing contemporary music throughout the show and hosted by "shock jocks" who often use vulgarities to express their radical views of current events, and *sports talk shows*, which also attract mainly male audiences. The talk show has, of course, migrated to the Internet, where it continues to attract huge audiences. Perhaps its popularity can be explained as revealing several inclinations and curiosities, including the interest in gossip, celebrities, sports events, and the like.

THE RADIO STAGE

In taking over print and vaudevillian genres and adapting them to a new medium for broader audience reception, radio was the first important media stage for promoting entertainment culture as a part of the marketplace (chapter 3). Its influence cannot be underestimated. The German Jewish refugee, Anne Frank (1929–1945), wrote the following about radio in her famous diary (from *The Diary of a Young Girl*, 1947, p. 45):

> The radio goes on early in the morning and is listened to at all hours of the day, until nine, ten and often eleven o'clock in the evening. This is certainly a sign that the grown-ups have infinite patience, but it also means that the power of absorption of their brains is pretty limited, with exceptions, of course—I don't want to hurt anyone's feelings. One or two news bulletins would be ample per day! But the old geese, well— I've said my piece!

The radio was (and continues to be in some ways) an effective medium of persuasion. As ex-presidential speechwriter Peggy Noonan aptly phrased it, "TV gives everyone an image, but radio gives birth to a million images in a million brains" (cited in *What I Saw at the Revolution* 1990, p. 34). As in oral cultures, the voice is a powerful conveyor of emotions, in contrast to print culture, which emphasizes literacy and tacit reflection. Listening stimulates a different kind of imagination than viewing or reading. The modalities of the voice move us at a basic sensory-affective level. Radio pop culture can thus be described as a "listened-to" culture and portrayed as having a much more direct impact, in the same ways that oral dialogue has in oral societies and during childhood development.

Radio and Advertising

The newspaper was the first medium to incorporate advertising into its textual format. The two still go hand in hand. The same kind of partnership story can be written for radio. As we saw, a made-for-radio genre—the soap opera—was even named for the type of advertiser that sponsored it. In the United States advertising agencies produced virtually all network radio shows before the advent of network television. Stations often sold agencies full sponsorship, which included placing the brand name in a program's title, as in *Palmolive Beauty Box Theater* (1927–1937) or *The Texaco Star Theater* (1948–1953). The ratings system arose, in fact, from the sponsors' desire to know how many people they were reaching through programs. In 1929 Archibald Crossley launched *Crossley's Cooperative Analysis of Broadcasting*, using telephone surveys to project daily estimates of audience size for the national radio networks. The A. C. Nielsen Company, which started surveying audience size in radio in the mid-1930s, eventually became the leading ratings service. The ratings were used to help determine the price of advertisements and, ultimately, whether the program would stay on the air or be canceled. Only public radio stations have remained exempt from the "ratings game," for the reason that they are financed by government subsidies, individual donations, and corporate grants. Today, the Nielsen system has been updated with streams of data gathered through digital technologies in order to take into account delayed listening patterns. Also, a new type of rating world on the Internet has emerged, with sites such as TV.com, Ratings.net, and Criticker, which advertisers utilize in addition to scientifically based ratings to make up their minds about the popularity of something. The greatest weakness of online ratings is that they represent the views of those inclined to submit ratings in the first place and, thus, they may not be truly representative.

Radio introduced the *commercial*—a mini-narrative or musical jingle about a product or service. The commercial could reach masses of potential customers instantaneously through the power of dialogue or monologue—which could be seductive, friendly, cheery, insistent, or foreboding, as required by the nature of the advertising pitch. Early radio commercials included pseudoscientific narratives ("The product is scientifically tested for effectiveness"), satires of movies and other well-known social personages (much like a mimic would do in comedic situations), and snappy jingles.

The commercial created the first fictitious advertising characters and figures, from Mr. Clean (representing a detergent product of the same name) to Speedy (a personified Alka-Seltzer indigestion tablet). Commercials also became a source of dissemination of recognizable tunes, slogans, and catch phrases throughout society, from "Mr. Clean in a just a minute" (for the Mr. Clean detergent product) to "Plop, plop, fizz, fizz oh what a relief it is" (for the Alka-Seltzer product). From the outset, it was obvious that the commercials themselves were part information and part entertainment. Various jingles, in fact, became hit tunes on their own. Radio commercials were satirized or parodied, thus creating an early form of intertextuality among the domains of pop culture. The entertainment function of ads and commercials persists to this day.

Radio advertising has the advantage that people can listen to commercials while doing other things, such as driving or working. Another is that radio audiences, in general, are more segmentable according to tastes and lifestyle preferences. For example, stations that feature country music attract different kinds of listeners than do those that play rock and, thus, can be identified as consumers of certain types of beverages, automobiles, and the like. By selecting the station in this way, advertisers can strategically target their commercials to the intended market segment.

Orality

Even in a world where television and the Internet dominate, radio remains an important media stage. In its earliest period, it functioned as a storyteller, a source of musical entertainment, a means to get information about the world, and so on. The voices of sitcom actors became their signatures, recognized throughout society. Singers and comedians would become successful not only because of the quality of their songs or acts, but also, and perhaps especially, through the quality of their voices.

In effect, radio revived orality, albeit in a mediated way—true orality involves a face-to-face or audience-to-speaker form of contact, whereas radio mediates the contact. But in so doing it can augment the qualities of the voice through technical modifications. Thus, speech modes such as screaming or whispering can be experienced autonomously, since the speaker cannot be seen, just heard, creating a strong sense of fear or conspiracy, for instance.

In sum, the same kinds of social and communicative functions of the voice that characterize oral cultures are evident in radio. As Benjamin Franklin (1706–1790) so aptly put it in his *Autobiography* (1771–1790, 234), there is no denying the power of the voice to convince and entertain by itself:

> Every accent, every emphasis, every modulation of voice, was so per-
> fectly well turned and well placed, that, without being interested in the
> subject, one could not help being pleased with the discourse; a pleasure
> of much the same kind with that received from an excellent piece of
> music. This is an advantage itinerant preachers have over those who are
> stationary, as the latter can not well improve their delivery of a sermon
> by so many rehearsals.

Radio also was the first medium that converged with recordings in both a technical and business sense. Singers became popular and often famous if their records were played on influential radio stations. A partnership between radio producers and record companies was forged early on. It was a perfect match, since music has always been a part of "listened-to" culture. Therefore, no adaptation was required for radio, as it had been for print culture (see above). The latter required dramatization—that is, the stories had to be dramatized so that they could be listened to. Dramatization made theater more broadly popular. So too, it made pop music more broadly popular. The hit parade concept—a program airing the best-selling records—emerged on radio. If a record made it to the hit parade it became successful; if it did not, it went unnoticed. This gave great power to the record labels, music agents, and radio producers to dictate musical taste and to influence the whole business of pop music. It made musicians celebrities, with many spin-offs. This function of radio continues to some extent, but it has changed somewhat. The hit parade is no longer the means for a singer to gain celebrity status. That function is taken over by talent shows on TV, such as *American Idol*, and even through YouTube uploads. In the latter case the hope is that a song or performance will go viral. Although controlled by a few (the radio producers, labels, and so on), the radio stage for musical performance united people in musical tastes, making possible the rise of specific styles and genres such as jazz, swing, rock, and so on. The fragmented audiences of today make it virtually impossible for any one style to become broadly popular.

Internet Radio

Internet radio (also called web radio, streaming radio, e-radio, online radio, webcasting) is, simply, radio programming transmitted via the Internet. Internet radio has several distinctive features with respect to traditional radio. Some of these can be listed as follows:

- Since a program is streamed or put on a website it can be listened to at any time and at any place. The latter function has made the previous portable radios virtually extinct.
- Internet radio is different from podcasting, which involves downloading instead of streaming as a means of access to a program.
- Some Internet radio services are hyperlinked to traditional radio stations; that is, traditional radio stations offer Internet sites for their listeners to access content subsequent to a transmission or to provide follow-up possibilities (commentary on programs, Q&As about future or past programming, and the like).
- Internet radio programming is accessible from virtually anywhere on the globe, unless censorship or licensing issues are involved in the location where the access is made.
- Surveys show that more people listen to Internet radio than to any other radio platform, including satellite radio, podcasts, or cell phone–based radio combined.

However, apart from these technology-based differences, which have nonetheless led to different ways of listening to radio, Internet radio continues to transmit the same kinds of programming that offline radio does— news, sports, talk, music. The link to the pop culture world, therefore, has not been severed, only altered technologically. The effectiveness of Internet radio to reach today's tech-savvy audiences was already apparent in 1994, when WREK in Atlanta produced the first true Internet multicast transmissions. In the same year, WXYC in Chapel Hill became the first traditional radio station to broadcast on the Internet. Shortly after, companies such as Microsoft released streaming players as free downloads, heralding the era of Internet radio.

THE IMPORTANCE OF RADIO IN POP CULTURE HISTORY

As the first electronic mass entertainment medium, radio played a vital role in the entrenchment of pop culture. Radio became a partner with the movies, the music industry, and other domains of the entertainment world to make pop culture a kind of culture by default. It also blended high and low forms of culture, with programs that ranged from live opera performances to pop music hit parades. From the outset, this showed that the lines between levels of culture were immaterial. What counted was the music, and radio catered (and continues to cater) to all tastes. Grammies are given in all genres of music, from hip-hop to symphonic albums. Radio obliterated, once and for all, the traditional dividing lines between entertainment and engagement. The Saturday afternoon NBC opera radio broadcasts from New York's Metropolitan Opera became popular in the 1920s, showing that opera could be enjoyed by the masses in the same way that they enjoyed pop music. Radio was responsible for making opera artists celebrities, leading to increased sales in the area of classical music records and a kind of parallel recording industry, with specialized labels. Tenors such as Enrico Caruso and Luciano Pavarotti have become household names alongside jazz great Louis Armstrong and contemporary pop singers like Lady Gaga and Justin Bieber.

Radio set the musical agenda, bringing into the living room not only the exciting new music of band leaders like Tommy Dorsey, Duke Ellington, Benny Goodman, Harry James, Guy Lombardo, and Glenn Miller, but also concerts from symphony halls. Radio created the first national (and subsequently international) community of listeners, allowing segments within this community to indulge their preferences. Radio listeners showed allegiance and interest by buying the records of the performers, forming fan clubs, buying magazines that dealt with musical interests, and attending concerts.

In its golden age (from the 1920s to the 1950s), the radio was, in sum, the major source of entertainment. Every night, families gathered in their living rooms to listen to comedies, adventure dramas, music, and other kinds of radio fare. Children hurried home from school to hear afternoon adventure shows and woke up early on Saturday mornings to listen to programming designed specifically for them. In the daytime, home-bound people listened to soap operas. Golden age radio dramas included not only pulp fiction delights such as *Buck Rogers in the 25th Century* and *The Green Hornet*, but also plays by modern-day writers such as Ionesco. Radio soap operas were complemented by documentaries of issues of concern and programs on science. Comedians shared the same spotlight as presidents and scientists who talked about the state of the world or the theory of atomic fusion. This pastiche of content became the defining feature of pop culture.

The radio also became a source for initiating or at least influencing change in society. This was brought out, for instance, by the popularity of *Amos 'n' Andy*, a sitcom that was broadcast throughout the 1930s from 7:00

to 7:15 PM Eastern Standard Time. While the program was being broad-cast many movie theaters stopped their films and turned on radios so that audiences could listen to the program. Some stores and restaurants played radios over public address systems so that customers would not miss an episode. The actors and actresses on the show were whites who portrayed blacks. Many people criticized the program for portraying African Ameri-cans stereotypically. There is little doubt that the controversy stirred up by that program predisposed people to think about racial discrimination in an abstract way, and this, arguably, raised consciousness about this systemic problem. In other words, radio brought it out in the open through comedy, reaching millions of people. Treatises and even newspaper articles could never quite have had the kind of broad impact that the radio stage had.

Radio as a Social Text

An indirect influence that radio has had was that it became an implicit social text. To see what this means, it is useful to step back in time and imagine a village in medieval Europe. Values, ethics, discourses, and daily routines and rituals were informed and guided by a religious text, explicated regularly on Sunday at churches. Residual elements of this text are still around today. Religious dates such as Christmas and Easter, for instance, are planned yearly events around which many people organize social activities, even if they are not necessarily religious. In medieval Europe, the religious text regulated life on a daily basis. People went to church, lived by moral codes derived from the religious text, and listened to the admonitions and dictates of clergymen. The underlying subtext was that each day brought one closer and closer to one's true destiny—salvation and an afterlife with God. Living according to the text no doubt imparted a feeling of security, emotional shelter, and spiritual meaning to people's lives.

After the Renaissance, the Enlightenment, and the Industrial Revolu-tion the religious text lost some of its influence as society became progres-sively secularized. Today, unless someone has joined a religious community or has chosen to live by the dictates of a religious upbringing, the social text by which people in general live is hardly a religious one. We organize our day around work commitments, social appointments, entertainment events, and so on that have nothing to do with salvation; and only at those traditional "points" in the yearly calendar do we synchronize our secular text with the more traditional religious one. This has rendered feasts such as Christmas part of pop culture, with events that do not trace their origin to religion but simply to a new form of entertainment. The secular social text necessitates partitioning the day into "time slots." This is why we depend so heavily upon such devices as clocks, watches, agendas, appointment books, calendars, digital devices that keep track of time, and so on. We would be desperately lost without such things. In this regard, it is relevant to note that in his 1726 novel, *Gulliver's Travels*, Jonathan Swift (1667–1745) satirized the tendency of people to rely on the watch to organize their daily routines—the Lilliputians were baffled to note that Gulliver did virtually nothing without consulting his watch. Like Gulliver, we need to know continually "what time it is" in order to carry on with the normal conduct of our daily life.

Outside of special cases—the textual organization of the day is hardly ever conscious. If we started to reflect upon the value of our daily routines, it is likely that we might soon start to question them and even reject them. This does indeed happen in the case of those individuals who have decided to "drop out" of society, that is, to live their lives outside of the dictates of social textuality.

A social text needs a source of delivery so that the community can receive it. In the 1920s, when it first entered the social scene, radio became that source. As it gained hegemony in the 1940s and early 1950s, it influenced how people listened to information, evaluated it, and ultimately how they lived. It also reflected the structure of sequential events in society. Radio programs were, in fact, pigeonholed into morning, noon, and evening slots, with weekend programming changing the sequence somewhat. Morning programs regularly delivered information content (news, weather, sports). The subtext on weekday mornings was "Wake up people; here's what you need to know." This function is now realized by morning television programming by the major networks. In the afternoon the primary viewing audience was made up of stay-at-home people. The soap opera emerged, as we saw, to cater to this audience. Its romantic narratives, complete with love triangles and various betrayals, evoked ancient narratives in which love trysts, family life, work, and aging all converged. As the soaps changed, so did social mores. One reflected the other.

The third part of the radio sequence came eventually to be called "prime time," the period in the evenings when most people were home. Dramatic serials, music programs, sitcoms, and other genres allowed for evening entertainment. Prime-time programming meshed fictional narrative with moral and social messages for the entire family. Documentary programs in particular showcased real-life events, often bolstered by dramatic portrayals of these events, so that appropriate lessons could be learned.

Needless to say, there are now many more alternatives to this fare, given the huge number of specialty stations that are available and the re-shaping of the radio stage to a niche audience one. The radio stage, in its origins, was communal—everyone listened to virtually the same programs broadcast by the networks at the same time. As television took over in the 1950s, radio lost its social textuality. With technology, however, radio is adapting once again. As discussed briefly above, with new digital and satellite technologies, interest in radio has been rekindled as a new kind of platform in the Internet Age. Internet radio programs can now also be supplemented by images, text, graphics, and other data, rendering it a mul-timodal medium that integrates listening with viewing. But it has lost its community-making function; radio caters to specialized interests, retaining mainly its news and music functions from the past. In effect, as the world of technology changed the locale of the pop culture stage, it also changed how pop culture itself came to be perceived and received.

Information Culture

Radio ushered in the information age, with radio news becoming part information, part social commentary, and part entertainment. The addic-tive need we have for news today is likely traceable to the radio age and its emphasis on the news. Reporters became as well known as entertainers and movie celebrities. Early radio reporters included Edward R. Murrow, Lowell Thomas, and Walter Winchell. As mentioned briefly above, news-casts became especially absorbing during World War II, when millions of people turned to radio every day for the latest news on the war. Murrow won fame during the war for his on-the-scene broadcasts describing Ger-man bombing attacks on London. His listeners back in America, as men-tioned, could hear the bombs exploding in the background, giving them the illusion of being ersatz participants in the war. Shortly thereafter, it is little wonder that governments made widespread use of broadcasts for their own propaganda purposes, knowing the power of orality coupled with dramatization in shaping opinions. The Voice of America, an agency of the U.S. government, began broadcasting overseas in 1942 to inform the world of America's role in the war.

Aware of the growing importance of radio, Franklin Delano Roose-velt (also mentioned) started a new trend in politics—the use of the radio for political campaigning and lobbying purposes. His fireside chats were instrumental in helping him gain support for his policies. Earlier presi-dents, beginning with Woodrow Wilson in 1919, had spoken on radio.

Roosevelt, though, was the first to fully understand the emotional power of this oral medium and the opportunity it provided for taking government policies directly to the people. Other political leaders, including Winston Churchill of the United Kingdom and Charles de Gaulle of France, made similar use of radio to address their nations in times of crisis. In some ways, World War II was fought as much over the radio waves as it was on the battlefield. The fight was for people's minds, and radio proved itself to be highly effective in this regard.

Today, we live in an ever-expanding information culture. Information is itself an integral, not subsidiary, part of entertainment. Newscasts are broadcast at regular times—a trend established during the golden age of radio. In addition, radio stations present on-the-spot news coverage of such events as political conventions, disasters, and similar issues of public importance. Radio stations also broadcast specialized information such as stock market information, reports on celebrities, critiques of new movies, and so on.

Every age is an information age. Only the media for delivering information have changed. The need for information has been present in all eras. But it may have become an obsession today.

6

POP MUSIC

I am fond of music I think because it is so amoral. Everything else is moral and I am after something that isn't. I have always found moralizing intolerable.

—Hermann Hesse (1877–1962)

Pop culture might never have materialized in the first place without music to propel it onto center stage. Pop music and pop culture are virtual synonyms. Trends in pop music have defined each era of pop culture, eventually becoming descriptors of the eras (as in *the jazz era, the swing era, the rock era, the rap era*, and so on). From the Charleston of the Roaring Twenties to the swing music of the 1940s and the techno music of the 2000s, pop music genres have always attracted large audiences.

Although different pop musical styles have been fashionable in different eras, they share a common goal—bringing music to the people. This does not mean that pop music is not art. Many pop music works have risen (and continue to rise) to the level of what is traditionally called "musical art." As discussed throughout this book, pop culture is definable as a pastiche culture with its admixture of levels. In this culture, alongside the daily slush of new songs that hit the marketplace designed to last for a little while as simple commodities, one finds the great jazz works of Louis Armstrong, the rock music of Procol Harum, the early rap music of the Black Eyed Peas, the film scores of Philip Glass, and the songs of Alicia Keys, to mention but a few, that have lasting power. Theirs is music that, once heard, never leaves us. The great British conductor Sir Thomas Beecham (1879–1961) aptly put it as follows (in the *London Sunday Times* September 16, 1962): "Great music is that which penetrates the ear with facility and leaves the memory with difficulty. Magical music never leaves the memory."

145

This chapter will focus on the role of music in the birth and rise of pop culture. Pop music is a central target of analysis, not only because it has always been a source of entertainment, but also because it has been used as a mode of protest and a source for inciting social change.

THE ADVENT OF POP MUSIC

Without technology, pop music would never have had the social impacts that it has had. Its rise to center stage started in the late nineteenth century

A phonograph (© ThinkStock)

A TIMELINE OF POP MUSIC RECORDING

1877: The phonograph is invented by Thomas Edison.

1887–1888: Emile Berliner develops the gramophone, which can play sounds imprinted on mass-produced discs.

1920s: The jazz era is born. The Charleston becomes the first true modern dance craze.

1930s–1940s: The big band era influences trends in lifestyle and influences the spread of nightclub culture.

1947: Magnetic audiotape is developed by 3M. Wynonie Harris records "Good Rockin' Tonight," considered the first rock and roll song.

1948: 33 1/3 rpm records are introduced by Columbia Records and 45 rpm records are introduced by RCA Victor.

1955: Top 40 radio becomes a marketing arm of the recording industry. Rock and roll enters the mainstream, dominating the recording industry.

1956: Stereo recordings are introduced.

1962: Cassette tapes are introduced.

1960s: Rock music is linked with social protest, spearheading the counterculture movement.

1967: The Beatles release *Sgt. Pepper's Lonely Hearts Club Band*, one of the first concept albums.

1979–1980: Rap rises to public attention from clubs in the Bronx.

1981: Music Television (MTV) is born, becoming a new arm of the recording industry. Rock fragments into many genres, from disco to punk, grunge, and techno. Rap and hip-hop start dominating the pop music scene until the early 2000s.

1982: Compact discs are introduced.

1997: DVDs make their debut, offering more storage space than CDs and making music videos popular.

1998: Music download sites proliferate on the Internet.

2000: MP3 technology shakes up the music industry as Internet users share music files on Napster. Napster is eventually ordered to stop unauthorized file-sharing.

2000s: Rap and hip-hop remain popular, but lose their market domination.

2001: Peer-to-peer Internet services make music file-sharing even more popular.

2003: Apple Computer's iTunes music store makes its debut, making it possible to buy music on the Internet.

mid-2000s: Devices such as Apple's iPod enhance access to and availability of music. Because of iTunes and other such sites, the CD starts its demise, with CD stores starting to disappear throughout society.

2010s–ongoing: There is no one dominant style of music, as indie, alternative, pop, rap, and many other styles compete for audiences. YouTube becomes a site for all kinds of musicians to showcase their talents and materials.

with the advent of sound recording technology. It was Thomas Edison who invented the first phonograph (record player) in 1877. A decade later, in 1887, the German-born American inventor Emile Berliner (1851–1929) improved Edison's model, producing the flat-disc phonograph, or gramophone, which was used shortly thereafter for recording and playing back music. About 1920, Berliner's mechanical technology was replaced by electrical recording and reproduction technologies, whereby the vibrations of the phonograph needle were amplified by electromagnetic devices. Pop music had found its technological medium for widespread diffusion.

Historical Sketch

By the early 1920s, the cheapness and availability of mass-produced vinyl records led to a true paradigm shift—the entrenchment of pop music throughout society. New musical styles and idioms, such as jazz, spread quickly because they appealed to mass audiences since recordings of the music could be bought for very little money, as could gramophone machines.

Many music historians trace the origin of pop music to late-eighteenth-century America, when catchy tuneful music was composed by professional musicians for performances in parks in front of large gatherings (generally on Sunday afternoons). By the early nineteenth century, Italian opera had also become popular throughout America, influencing the development of a soft, mellifluous, sentimental type of singing known as *crooning*, which became widespread. Before the advent of sound recordings, the primary medium for disseminating music was printed sheet music. At the threshold of the twentieth century, the growing popularity of crooning and other emerging popular styles created a flourishing music publishing business centralized in New York City, in an area of lower Manhattan called Tin Pan Alley. The first Tin Pan Alley song to sell one million copies was "After the Ball" (1892) by Charles K. Harris. Tin Pan Alley constitutes the first chapter in pop music history.

The songs were simple, memorable, and emotionally appealing. Vaudeville included crooners as part of the show. At about the same time, *ragtime* pieces written by professional composers such as Scott Joplin (1868–1917) also became popular. A small cadre of composers and lyricists based in New York City produced the best-known songs of the 1920s and 1930s. In most cases, the creators worked in pairs (George Gershwin and Ira Gershwin, Richard Rodgers and Oscar Hammerstein, Richard Rodgers and Lorenz Hart, and so forth). Their songs were popularized by Broadway musicals, by well-known singers accompanied by dance orchestras, and by recordings and radio play. Singers such as Bing Crosby and, later, Frank Sinatra became pop icons overnight through recordings, the radio, and public concerts.

The African American influence on mainstream popular music became particularly evident during the Jazz Age, which preceded the Great Depression of the 1930s. In 1935, white jazz musician Benny Goodman boosted the popularity of the style with his band's recordings. From 1935 to 1945, the dominant type of popular music was *swing*, a style modeled on the music of black jazz orchestras. The "big band era" ended after World War II, but the influence of swing music could still be heard in the "jump band" rhythm and blues and dance music of the 1940s.

Important shifts in popular music after World War II were tied to emerging social and technological changes. The massive migration of Southern musicians to urban areas and the use of the electric guitar were particularly influential in shifting the paradigm. These set the stage for the hard-edged Chicago blues of Muddy Waters, the honky-tonk or "hard-country" style of Hank Williams and, in the mid-1950s, the rise of rock and roll music.

Rock grew out of the intermingling of several converging streams of postwar styles, including rhythm and blues, the songs of "shouters" such as Big Joe Turner, gospel-based vocal styles, boogie-woogie piano blues, and honky-tonk music. Promoted by entrepreneurs such as Alan Freed—who introduced the term *rock and roll*—and recorded by small independent labels, rock was an unexpected success story, attracting a newly affluent youth audience in the mid-1950s. The pioneers of rock came from varied backgrounds, musical and nonmusical. Bill Haley and the Comets, whose "Rock Around the Clock" (1955) became the first rock anthem, was a country-and-western bandleader; Fats Domino was a rhythm and blues artist; Chuck Berry was a hairdresser; and Elvis Presley was a truck driver. The golden era of rock and roll—defined by the exuberant recordings of Haley, Berry, Domino, Presley, Little Richard, Jerry Lee Lewis, and Buddy Holly—lasted from 1954 to 1959. The most successful artists of the era wrote and performed songs about love, sexuality, adolescent identity crises, personal freedom in youth, and other issues that were (and continue to be) of central concern today.

In the early 1960s, distinctive regional styles emerged, such as the music of the southern California band called the Beach Boys; the Greenwich Village urban folk movement that included the art of Bob Dylan, the Kingston Trio, and Peter, Paul, and Mary; and the rugged sound of

Northwest groups such as the Sonics. Rock was becoming the musical voice of larger and larger segments of society, and as will be discussed below a voice of protest.

Rock's rise and influence in society became especially noticeable when the so-called "British Invasion" began in 1964, with the arrival of the Beatles in New York City, and as the "rock band" emerged as an artistic phenomenon. British rock bands, raised on the influence of blues, rhythm and blues, and early rock and roll, invigorated mainstream popular music, in part by reinterpreting the early classics of American rock. Each group developed a distinctive style: the early Beatles revisited Chuck Berry's guitar-based rock and roll; the Animals amalgamated blues and rhythm and blues styles to produce a hard-driving musical idiom of their own; and the Rolling Stones incorporated aspects of both early rock and urban blues into their distinctive, thrusting sound.

The mid-to-late 1960s was a period of expansion and diversification in the record industry. The music included not only the influential experiments of the Beatles, but also San Francisco psychedelia, guitar rock by Jimi Hendrix and Eric Clapton, Southern rock, hard rock, jazz rock, folk rock, and other styles. Soul music, the successor to rhythm and blues, emerged with a wide range of highly popular styles, including the gospel-based songs of Aretha Franklin, the funk music of James Brown, and the soulful crooning of Marvin Gaye. Country music—centered in Nashville, Tennessee—also produced a new generation of stars who combined elements of old country-and-western style with rock and roll. Johnny Cash, Waylon Jennings, and Patsy Cline helped contribute to the rising popularity of such music.

In the 1970s, a plethora of distinctive new styles—disco, glam rock, punk rock, new wave, reggae, funk, and so on—surfaced and were pioneered by both the big and the independent labels. As a consequence, pop music became highly fragmented and thus much less profitable for record companies to market to large homogeneous audiences. The industry became cautious, as sales of records dropped dramatically between 1978 and 1982. But a number of factors contributed to its economic revival in the mid-1980s. Among these were the advent of the music video and the debut in 1981 of Music Television (MTV), a twenty-four-hour music video channel, and the introduction of the compact disc in 1982. The video-album *Thriller* (1982) by Michael Jackson became the biggest-selling album in pop music history up to that time, and prompted a pattern by which record companies relied upon a few big hits to generate profits. Popular musicians of the period included Bruce Springsteen, the working-class bar-band hero; the artist known as Prince, whose 1984 single "When Doves Cry" was the first song in decades to top both the mainstream pop charts and the black music charts; and Madonna, the iconoclastic performer from a working-class background who presented herself as a controversial "sex-kitten" in her music videos. MTV, and its subsidiary channels VH1 and MTV2, functioned both as critics of music trends and as purveyors of the same trends, parsing pop music history in programs such as "Behind the Music" and "Beavis and Butt-Head." Today, with Internet music sites, MTV has come down from its high perch as a ruler of the pop music realm. But its influence cannot be denied, taking over at first from radio and now converging with online culture.

Audiences for pop music became even more fragmented in the 1990s, although several main trends rose to the surface. Bands such as Blur, Oasis, Pearl Jam, REM and Radiohead continued the tradition of counterculture rock music. But rap and hip-hop dominated the scene. Today, in the post-rap era, it is becoming increasingly obvious that each new pop music style comes and goes more quickly than ever before. This does not imply that various types of contemporary pop music are not relevant. Pop music has always integrated styles of various degrees of artistic merit. Within this universe, however, there are now many niches that make dominant trends virtually impossible to emerge as in the past.

Interestingly, retromusical trends, as they are called, crystallized in the 1990s. Many newly formed labels devoted themselves to reissuing the classical music repertoire on CD. Their success was fueled in large part by the repeated use of classical music in movie soundtracks. Labels such as Naxos and Chandos, for instance, became highly profitable. A renewed interest in jazz was highlighted by a brilliant ten-part documentary on American PBS by director Ken Burns in early 2001. The main point made by the program was that the jazz phenomenon not only dictated all subsequent pop music trends, but also functioned as a mirror of twentieth-century musical art. One can also discern in jazz a need for liberation at various levels. With its syncopated rhythms and its free-style improvisations, jazz stood in contrast to the stodgy, restrictive outlook of those who brought about the Prohibition movement. Jazz has always been emblematic of a need for freedom from authoritarianism. This is why the Beat writers of the 1950s collaborated with jazz artists at their so-called happenings. It fit in perfectly with their philosophy of separation from the mainstream. Jazz posed a fairly powerful alternative to conventional music and, importantly, promoted the notion of social freedom, and there was an intuitive sense that jazz would bring about change in the rest of society.

In the first two decades of the 2000s eclecticism and pastiche ruled the world of pop music. Radio stations, websites, and other media offered a wide array of genres to increasingly fragmented audiences. Alongside pop music by Beyoncé, Lady Gaga, and Justin Bieber, one finds retro trends throughout the electronic village, not to mention indie music and the rise of indie artists. The move to the online medium has brought about a revolution in how music is produced and sold. Through streaming music services, and YouTube, one can locate any style or genre of music on the web. One can also check the playlists of others and popularity ratings on the sites themselves. Music blogs and social media post new songs for people to evaluate, having thus become reservoirs for new music trends. Often, however, they tend to highlight music by established artists and by those being promoted by record labels. In other words, they have started to take over the traditional role of the radio, MTV, and other media where new music was previously showcased. Mobile device applications also allow users to create and share playlists. But while the technology has made access to music more individualistic and personalized, many of the musical trends continue to be popular for the same reason as previous ones—mixing entertainment and engagement in a pastiche of styles.

Decoding Pop Music

By and large, pop music genres come and go and are enjoyed primarily by the generation of people with whom they were once popular. To this day, there are niche (and sometimes substantial) audiences for jazz, blues, early rock, swing, and so on. Whatever the style, music has great significance to people, because it speaks to them emotionally, stimulating all kinds of feelings. When someone who grew up in the 1950s hears songs by the Platters or Roy Orbison, for instance, he or she tends to be particularly moved by them. Their relevance and meaning becomes more conspicuous with the passage of time, providing indirect evidence of the power of music to sway people. The philosophers of ancient Greece believed that music originated with the gods Apollo and Orpheus, and that it reflected in its melodic and harmonic structure the laws of harmony that rule the universe. They also believed that music influenced human thoughts and actions because it is experienced directly. In some African societies music is considered to be the faculty that sets humans apart from other species. Among some Native American cultures it is thought to have originated as a way for spirits to communicate with human beings.

The question of what constitutes musical art is not an easy one to answer. Why do we still listen and react to Beethoven's *Ninth Symphony* and his last string quartets, even though the music was composed long before we were born? As Adorno and other Frankfurt critics claimed (chapter 2), true musical art can be easily recognized because it moves us beyond the immediacy of the moment in which it was created. On the other hand, most pop music, as Greil Marcus (1976: 18) has put it, will likely fade away because it "is a combination of good ideas dried up by fads, terrible junk, hideous failings in taste and judgment, gullibility and manipulation, moments of unbelievable clarity and invention, pleasure, fun, vulgarity, excess, novelty and utter enervation."

All this might sound elitist to the reader. But it is not. Mozart wrote music that he intended for the enjoyment of common people. The operas of Verdi and Rossini, too, were intended to be popular and populist. But the musical art of a Mozart, a Verdi, or a Rossini could not be so easily managed by entrepreneurs and others as commodities. And no matter what trend emerges in pop music, it likely will never reach the same aesthetic standards as a Beethoven or a Mozart. But then, that is a moot point, since pop culture is a populist culture. Nonetheless, within it, jazz, rock, and rap works have emerged that have aesthetic force and will likely remain beyond their commodity value. When all is said and done, pop music has the same basic function that pulp fiction in the print medium and radio genres in the electronic medium have—to provide entertainment. But, paradoxically, pop music has consistently risen above its entertainment value to become the voice of change, as evidenced by the fact that it spearheaded sweeping social movements in the last century. Without rock, the counterculture movement would literally have been voiceless.

Some music historians and music industry insiders are starting to claim that pop music has reached a critical point, as audiences have fragmented enormously and as musical trends (if any) are in decline or else have become homogeneous. This situation is corroborated by weak music sales, by the loss (or attenuation) of fandom, and waning concert attendance. If this is so, then it has implications for pop culture itself. Pop music has always been the fuel of the pop culture spectacle. If it wanes, then so will the other domains of pop culture. This topic will be taken up in the final chapter.

Genres

Although music genres and performers change constantly, strong continuities can be detected among the genres within the history of popular music. As in other domains of pop culture, music genres have broad appeal because they speak to the themes that engage people emotionally—love, betrayal, sex, and so on. From the Charleston and jazz to swing, rock, rap, and techno, a song will tend to become popular if it has a recognizable melodic structure (that is if it can be sung easily), has a relatively short duration, is associated with a performer who has broad appeal, and speaks to common people. Today, the process of niche-music programming dominates the landscape, as most genres have their own radio stations and websites that cater to particular audiences. These allow for a community of listeners (real and/or virtual) to form around the music and the ancillary interests and activities that ensue from belonging to it. Gone is the global audience that was once united around Top-40 radio.

The spread of multiple music genres today, without a mainstream one uniting fans in a communal way, as did the swing music of the big bands in the 1930s and 1940s, the early rock and roll of the 1950s, and rap of the 1980s and 1990s, is a sign that the hegemony of pop music as a trend-setting force across the realms of pop culture may have come to an end. Whereas once a single style or genre dominated, today, everything from rock and jazz to classical and gospel have their own audiences, each with its recording artists, radio stations, websites, accompanying fan blogs and magazines, and so on and so forth.

In addition to an American-based typology of genres, the music styles of other countries have gained widespread appeal through satellite technologies and the Internet, making their way into pop culture. The expression that "anything goes" certainly applies to the pop music scene today. In a way, this has always been the case. The Argentine tango, for instance, gained worldwide popularity already during the 1910s, initiating a craze for Latin ballroom dancing in Paris, London, and New York City. Its carnal sensuousness was revived by Shakira in her "Assassination Tango" video in which she cleverly emphasizes the role of the woman in the dance form. The Cuban rumba also became popular around the world in the 1930s

---

MAJOR POP MUSIC GENRES

Adult contemporary/Easy Listening: a mix of oldies, light opera, and softer rock hits (Celine Dion, il Divo, Andrea Boccelli, Mariah Carey, Amy Winehouse, Whitney Houston, Barbara Streisand, Nat King Cole, Barry Manilow, Alanis Morissette, the Carpenters, Olivia Newton-John, Shakira, Nellie Furtado, Michael Bublé)

(*continued*)

MAJOR POP MUSIC GENRES (*continued*)

Eclectic Pop: all kinds of styles "mashed" together, including pop, rap, rock, techno, and other styles (Jay-Z, Usher, Adele, Beyoncé, Katy Perry, Lady Gaga, Rihanna, Bruno Mars, LMFAO, Nicki Minaj, Drake, Justin Bieber, Lil Wayne, Madonna, Michael Jackson)

Country: all subgenres, including traditional, urban, rock country, and others (Hank Williams, Dolly Parton, Dixie Chicks, Lee Ann Womack, Shania Twain, Garth Brooks, Johnny Cash, Leeann Rimes, Taylor Swift, Blake Shelton and Miranda Lambert, Carrie Underwood, the Eagles)

Rock: all forms of rock, past and present, including old rock and roll, classic rock and roll, jazz rock, folk rock, hard rock, metal rock, industrial rock, grunge, punk, and so on (Elvis Presley, Rolling Stones, Chuck Berry, the Beatles, Steppenwolf, Led Zeppelin, Foo Fighters, Sex Pistols, Green Day, Pink Floyd, Elvis Costello, Coldplay, Radiohead, Nirvana, Nine Inch Nails, the Supremes, AC/DC, Kiss, Chicago, Credence Clearwater Revival, Bob Dylan)

Disco: classic disco from the 1970s and 1980s and current techno (the Bee Gees, KC and the Sunshine Band, Kool and the Gang, Village People, Rasputin, ABBA, Diana Ross, Donna Summer, David Guetta, deadmau5, Afrojack)

Rap and hip-hop: works by rap and hip-hop stars, classic and current (Ludacris, Jay-Z, 50 Cent, Eminem, Kanye West, Queen Latifah, Snoop Dogg, N.W.A, Salt-N-Pepa, Tupac Shakur, Beastie Boys, Chris Brown, Lil Wayne, Nas, Sista Souljah, Public Enemy, LL Cool J, Black Eyed Peas, Drake, Wiz Khalifa)

Rhythm and Blues: rhythm and blues music and all its subgenres such as Motown by classic and contemporary performers (Tina Turner, Luther Vandross, Aretha Franklin, James Brown, Otis Redding, Ray Charles, Sam Cooke, Marvin Gaye, Wilson Pickett, the Supremes, Percy Sledge, Ike and Tina Turner, Smokey Robinson, Gladys Knight, Stevie Wonder, The Temptations, Waylon, T-Wayne)

Experimental: music styles promoted mainly by college and university radio stations

Latin: music composed and performed by Hispanic artists, and "salsa" music generally (Pepe Aguilar, Ricky Martin, Christina Aguilera, Jennifer Lopez, Julio and Enrique Iglesias, Pit Bull, Nelly Furtado, Sérgio Mendes, Gloria Estefan, Shakira, Laura Pausini, Selena, Thalia, Santana)

Classical music: music of the great composers (Bach, Mozart, Beethoven, Chopin, Tchaikovsky, Rachmaninoff, and so on)

Jazz and Blues: jazz, blues, and swing music from all eras and in all genres (Herbie Hancock, Louis Armstrong, B. B King, Miles Davis, Stan Kenton, Chuck Mangione, Dave Brubeck, John Lee Hooker, Taj Mahal, John Coltrane, Billie Holiday, Count Basie, Thelonius Monk, Dizzy Gillespie, Ella Fitzgerald, Charlie Parker, Charles Mingus, Mary Lou Williams, Nat King Cole, Frank Sinatra, Tony Bennett, Wynton Marsalis)

Gospel: gospel music intended to appeal to lovers of both current and traditional gospel performers

Opera: mainly from the Romantic era (operas by Rossini, Verdi, Puccini, Bizet, and so on)

primarily through recordings and radio. In the Internet era, such styles have made a comeback, becoming popular with new audiences across the world, highlighted on television programs such as *Dancing with the Stars*. Indian film music, produced in studios in New Delhi and Mumbai, is gaining the attention of multiethnic audiences across the world, as is African music, which includes a number of distinctive regional styles, such as the juju music of Nigerian bandleader King Sunny Adé, central African soukous, a blend of indigenous songs and dance rhythms with Afro-Cuban music, and South African isicathamiya, the Zulu choral singing style performed by Ladysmith Black Mombazo.

Never before have so many music styles been so available to whoever wants to listen to them. Pop culture has literally brought music to the people. Music has also functioned as a "support art form" used in movies and TV programs, frequently defining them. The *William Tell* overture gallop movement by Rossini, for instance, has become so closely linked with the *Lone Ranger* radio and TV series of the 1940s and 1950s that the two are hardly ever perceived as separate by those who grew up in that era. Similarly, another Rossini overture, the one he composed for the opera *The Barber of Seville*, has become so broadly associated with a famous *Bugs Bunny* cartoon episode that the two are now inseparable in many people's minds.

SOCIAL CHANGE

The swing music that became the rage in the mid–1930s and early 1940s reflected a new open lifestyle, breaking away from the Puritan past of America. Swing had also become a powerful form of escapism, as people saw it especially as a way to cope with the stark economic realities of the post-Depression era and the moral ravages of world war. But already in that era, swing culture showed a tendency to develop in a particular new direction. In 1942, Frank Sinatra wowed "bobby-soxers" at the Paramount in New York, giving America a foretaste of the teenage-based rock and roll culture that was just around the corner and the kinds of changes it was to bring about. By the mid-1950s, rock culture had emerged to replace swing culture as the dominant one, gaining popularity at first with adolescents.

Historical Sketch

The Jazz Age of the 1920s heralded a change in the way America experienced music and in how it viewed social life. It was music created and played at first by African American musicians; but white young people took to it from the outset, despite biased reactions to it by many in society at the time. The music was too much fun to ignore, and it caught on broadly as it gained popularity through recordings and radio play. Jazz was a gauge of change to come. This dynamic has defined the role of pop music since the 1920s.

In the mid-1950s rock and roll tapped into this dynamic. The first rock songs actually reflected a blend of styles, including swing, blues, the gospel-based vocal-group style known as doo-wop, boogie-woogie, and the country music style known as honky-tonk (made popular by Hank Williams). They were recorded and released by small, independent record companies and promoted by controversial radio disc jockeys such as Alan Freed (as mentioned). The term *rock and roll* was used by the Boswell Sisters in 1934 in their song titled "Rock and Roll," although it referred to the back-and-forth movement of a rocking chair, not to the meanings it developed in the 1950s. By the time Elvis Presley recorded "Good Rockin' Tonight" in 1954, which was a remake of Wynonie Harris's 1948 rendition of the song, rock and roll had established itself as the voice of young people, reflecting a new social emphasis on youth. Harris's song was a rhythm and blues number, triggering the use of the word *rock* shortly after Bill Haley and the Comets recorded "Rock around the Clock" in 1955 as a moniker of something truly new and exciting. The song was the theme music for *The Blackboard Jungle*, a 1955 motion picture about teenagers coming of age in the 1950s.

The link between rock and roll and young people was visible from the outset. Changes in the rock and roll music scene became sources of change in youth culture and lifestyle. It reinforced the "generation gap," as adults reacted negatively to rock and roll at first, with some calling it the "devil's music." But the adult world could not stem the tide; rock was seemingly "here to stay," as a 1958 song by a rock band of the era, Danny and the Juniors, so aptly put it. The fervent popularity of rock and roll caught the attention of media moguls and the entertainment and celebrity-making industries generally. Hollywood jumped on the bandwagon early on, producing movies, such as *The Blackboard Jungle*, which were all about the growing social and political power of young people in the world, featuring rock and roll as the voice of the new generation. Some movies were nothing more than proto-rock-videos. The 1956 movie *Rock, Rock, Rock*, for instance, included acts by rock stars and groups of the era. It also featured an appearance by disc jockey Alan Freed. Similarly, *Rock, Baby, Rock It* (1957) and *Go, Johnny, Go!* (1958) were nothing more than screen concerts. Rock and

A SCHEMATIC OUTLINE OF ROCK HISTORY

1950s: Elvis Presley ("Heartbreak Hotel," "Hound Dog," "Love Me Tender," "Jailhouse Rock"); Jerry Lee Lewis ("Great Balls of Fire"); Chuck Berry ("Johnny B. Goode"); the Platters ("Only You"); Buddy Holly ("That'll Be the Day," "Peggy Sue"); American Bandstand is launched in 1957, spreading new trends in rock and roll music; Ed Sullivan hosts rock and roll stars on his Sunday evening TV variety show; jukeboxes proliferate in diners throughout society promoting rock and roll broadly; radio DJ Alan Freed helps spread rock and roll with his show *Moondog Rock 'n' Roll Party*

1960s: the Beatles (albums: *Revolver, Sgt. Pepper's Lonely Hearts Club Band, The White Album, Abbey Road*); the Rolling Stones; Bob Dylan; James Brown; the Who; Janis Joplin; Jimi Hendrix; the Doors; the counterculture movement adopts rock and roll music as its voice of change; Woodstock (the open air concert); Elvis Presley makes a comeback with his 1968 special on NBC; rock is featured in a number of stage works, including *Hair* (1967)

1970s: rock fragments into several genres including metal (Led Zeppelin, Steppenwolf) and (early on) neo-counterculture bands (Procol Harum, the Moody Blues), jazz rock (Chicago); disco emerges (the Bee Gees, K. C. and the Sunshine Band, Donna Summers); the movie *Saturday Night Fever* (1977) glorifies the disco scene; punk rock emerges (Sex Pistols, Clash, Talking Heads) in stark opposition to disco culture; new wave (a blend of punk and disco) appears (Blondie); *The Rocky Horror Picture Show* introduces cross-gender trends and a carnivalesque form of rock and roll, adopted by bands such as Kiss; *Saturday Night Live* introduces rock musical acts, spreading rock music even more into the mainstream; other influential rock artists and bands include Bruce Springsteen, King Crimson, and Emerson, Lake and Palmer; with Elvis's death in 1977, early rock and roll is about to fade from center stage

1980s: Madonna (video album: *Like a Virgin*); Michael Jackson (video album: *Thriller*); Guns n' Roses (album: *Appetite for Destruction*); U2 (album: *The Joshua Tree*); the Police; Cyndi Lauper; Boy George; heavy metal (AC/DC), satanic rock (Black Sabbath), and other hard trends compete with softer forms of rock (Wham) and residues of counterculture rock; MTV makes its debut in 1981 with "Video Killed the Radio Star," by the Buggles, taking over from radio as the primary promoter of new music trends; rap starts to make its way to center stage

1990s: rock and roll becomes a music of nostalgia as the Rock and Roll Hall of Fame and Museum opens up in Cleveland, Ohio, in 1995; rap and hip-hop rise to dominance among youth; only grunge rock rivals rap, with Kurt Cobain and Nirvana (album: *Nevermind*)

2000s: rock becomes simply one of a myriad of alternatives vying for popularity; old rock and roll revivals abound; the World Wide Web becomes the new stage for new rock works generally; "neo-genres," such as neo-punk (Green Day) and alternative rock, emerge

2010s–ongoing: rock has virtually disappeared from the scene, constituting a retro form of music; it is still liked, but it no longer attracts large audiences even at nostalgic revival concerts.

roll was the first true "generational music," written by and for teenagers. Teens loved it; parents hated it.

In the 1960s, rock fragmented into diverse styles—Motown, California surfer rock, folk rock, and so on. The British Invasion began in 1964 with the arrival of the Beatles in New York City—a key moment in the history of society, since it gave momentum to the counterculture movement that was burgeoning in America. The movement surfaced in San Francisco around 1966, and was associated from the outset with the use of hallucinogenic drugs, psychedelic art, light shows, public displays of sexuality, antiwar protests, sit-ins demanding change in universities and society at large, and above all else, a new form of music. Counterculture musicians such as Jerry Garcia and the Grateful Dead experimented with long, improvised stretches of music called *jams*. The new music spearheaded and sustained a political movement whose objectives were the rejection of traditional bourgeois consumerist society. It came into favor with intellectuals, such as Herbert Marcuse of the Frankfurt School (chapter 2), and psychologists such as Timothy Leary. The movement denounced the business, military, and political complex as the cause of all social ills. The rock concert became an ideological "happening," spurring on youths to social activism. At concerts such as Monterey Pop (1967) and Woodstock (1969), drugs were consumed to induce or heighten the aesthetic experience of the music, and sexual activities were performed openly, in obvious defiance of moralism.

But the movement faded by the early 1970s. Various analyses have been put forth to explain its demise—the end of the Vietnam War (a major reason for protest in the 1960s and early 1970s), effective social changes brought about by the movement itself, the aging of counterculture youths, and so on. Suffice it to say here that, like all trends and movements in pop culture, change is inevitable, whatever its reason. The music of the counterculture era, like the music of all previous eras, entered the realm of nostalgia, where it could be tamed and relegated to pop culture history.

By the mid-1970s, a plethora of new trends appeared, showing that audiences were fragmenting more and more into distinctive musical communities and subcultures. Initially associated with the gay lifestyle of New York City, disco drew upon African American dance styles of the past, attracting a large following. After the release of the motion picture *Saturday Night Fever* (1977) and its hugely successful soundtrack featuring the Bee Gees, disco rose to dominance, but only for a very short period. Around 1976, punk rock originated in London and New York as a reaction against both the superficiality of disco and the artistic pretentiousness of 1960s counterculture rock. Punk rock was raw and rude. In its original intent, it was a throwback to the golden era of rock and roll—to the abrasive sounds of Little Richard and Chuck Berry. But, unlike the early rockers, punk bands such as the Sex Pistols and the Clash eliminated melody and harmony from their musical text, transforming it into an angry, shrill, brutal style. Eventually, such punk bands as the Ramones, Blondie, and Talking Heads adopted a softer, more melodic style, called new wave. Punk continues to have appeal, and is still around. Also in the mid-1970s, reggae music—developed by musicians in Jamaica—began to attract attention among a sizable number of young people, especially after the release of the 1973 film *The Harder They Come*, which starred reggae singer Jimmy Cliff in the role of an underclass gangster. The superstar of the style was, however, Bob Marley, who by the time of his death in 1981 had become one of the most popular musicians in the world.

By the end of the 1970s, record sales plummeted and, for a little while, it appeared that the final chapter on rock and roll had been written. However, a new generation of video rock stars, such as Michael Jackson and Madonna, gave it new life. The success of video rock highlights the role that the media have played in the propagation of rock throughout its history. Rock and roll became popular across the teen world after Elvis Presley appeared on *The Ed Sullivan Show* in 1956. The same program catapulted the Beatles to fame in 1964. An estimated seventy-three million people watched the Beatles' first appearance on the show. Arguably, without television rock would have remained confined to the teen world. Its crossover to the musical mainstream was fostered and nurtured by television. In a book titled *If It Ain't Got That Swing* (2000), Mark Gauvreau Judge argues that "adult pop music" was marginalized with the advent of rock in the 1950s. Judge may have forgotten that the adult music to which he refers (jazz, for example) started as part of youth culture.

Decoding Rock

From deafening amplification and onstage performances that come across as pure corporeal spectacle, to dance trends, fashions, and lifestyles they initiated, rock musicians have influenced pop music trends. Early rock had two genres—one was the fast, hard type, which was louder and more intensely rhythmic than any of its predecessors, and the other was the ballad type, which continued, in many ways, the tradition of crooning music. It was the hard type, needless to say, that created panic. When compared to crooning music, the differences were blatant.

Table 6.1. Characteristics of Crooning Music and of Early Rock Music

Crooning Music	Early Rock Music
Soft and tender	Loud and rough
Restrained rhythms	Hard-driving rhythms
Flowing melodies	Hard-edged melodies
Romantic lyrics	Lyrics tinged with allusions to sexuality
Accompanied by traditional (non-electric) instruments	Accompanied by electric instruments with the capacity to amplify the music significantly

The instrument that truly set rock apart from all previous pop music styles was the electric guitar. It allowed the music to be louder and more strident. Beginning in the late 1960s a new generation of rock guitarists, including Jimi Hendrix, Eric Clapton, and Carlos Santana, experimented

The electric guitar remains a powerful symbol within pop music (© ThinkStock)

with more amplification, extending the potential of the instrument considerably. Other instruments commonly used in early rock music included the stand-up bass or the electric bass guitar, the piano, and the drums. But the guitar is the heart and soul of rock, giving the music masculine power. Only in the 1980s when women started using the instrument in bands such as Chrissie Hynde and the Pretenders did the guitar start losing its masculine symbolism, becoming a veritable weapon of revolution.

It is interesting that the punk rockers would often end their stage performance by smashing their guitars, perhaps to symbolize the end of masculinist rock. Like the carnival jesters of the medieval era, punk rockers were "lords of misrule" celebrating vulgarity, destruction, and obscenity through parodic performances and the costumes (clothing) they wore. Although these elements were subtly implicit in the music and stage acts of early rock stars like Little Richard and Jerry Lee Lewis, they became explicit in punk rock. Rage, horror, and irony were united in the musical text and performance. Bands such as the Sex Pistols sang about the absurdity of the effete sexual practices of society. One of their slogans was "F . . . Forever!" alluding to sex as a simple animal act. They also vomited on stage, wore garbage bags held together with safety pins, and performed gross forms of spectacle, such as urination. After the death of bassist Sid Vicious in 1979, the band sported T-shirts with the words *Sid Lives* on them. The Sex Pistols made fun of the monarchy, the government, the human body, multinational corporations, and rock itself. Nothing was sacred, including their own instruments. However, while punk rock created moral panic, it never really had a disruptive impact on the social mainstream. But it did raise awareness to several things, such as the superficiality and banality of bourgeois life.

DISSENT

By standing against stodgy moralism and bourgeois pseudo-morality in its musical texuality, rock, like jazz before it, was an indirect voice of dissent. Since the mid-1980s, the word *rock* started being used less and less to refer to new styles of music. One particular style, called rap, seemed to come out of nowhere to attract the allegiance of a new generation of teens. At first, rap was a semi-monological genre, whereby vocalists performed rhythmic speech, accompanied by music snippets, called samples, from prerecorded material or from material created on purpose for the rap song. The first rap records were made in the late 1970s by small, independent record companies, mirroring the birth of rock as a trend. Although rapper groups such as

A RAP AND HIP-HOP TIMELINE

1970s/1980s: The first rap-only radio station, KDAY-AM in Los Angeles, goes on the air. Russell Simmons and Rick Rubin start Def Jam Records. The label and its artists push rap closer into the musical mainstream.

1979: DJ Flash recruits local emcees and records the first true rap hit, "The Message." In the same year, a trio created by the owner of Sugar Hill Records, called the Sugarhill Gang, produces the first rap hit song, "Rapper's Delight," but then fades fast. Also in that year the charismatic performer MC takes rap to national television.

1980: Blow's single "The Breaks" becomes rap's first gold record.

1981: Blondie records "Rapture," considered to be the first rap song that did not rely on samples from previously recorded music. It became the first number one rap single.

1983: Run-D.M.C. emphasize hard rhymes and beats to the rap musical style. Right after, Too Short makes so-called "pimping" (displaying sexual behavior that is imitative of pimps) a central theme in rap. Rap gets its first video on MTV—Run-D.M.C.'s "Rock Box." Grandmaster Flash and Melle Mel release the anti-cocaine anthem "White Lines (Don't Do It)." Hip-hop fuses with jazz on "Rock It" by Herbie Hancock and Grandmaster DST.

1985: 2 Live Crew get into legal trouble because of their sexually explicit lyrics.

1986: Run-D.M.C. join Aerosmith to record "Walk This Way."

1987: Public Enemy uses explicitly subversive political messages in their lyrics. The group N.W.A put gangsta rap on the map.

1988: Geto Boys spread gangsta rap. De La Soul adds an element of parody and goofiness to rap culture by toting daisies. Queen Latifah challenges male rap hegemony with her overpowering presence and romantic musical style. Public Enemy releases *It Takes a Nation of Millions to Hold Us Back*, which is widely regarded as rap's greatest album. N.W.A, featuring Ice Cube and Dr. Dre, record *Straight Outta Compton*, the first gangsta album to become widely known.

1990: Ice Cube translates black youth's rage into incisive, controversial lyrics. The erotic lyrics of 2 Live Crew's album *As Nasty as They Wanna Be* are declared obscene by a Florida judge, whose decision is overturned on appeal.

1992: The first controversy associated with rap comes to the forefront when rapper Ice-T records "Cop Killer." Dr. Dre becomes infamous due to his sexist lyrics, and starts Death Row Records with partner Suge Knight, an ex-con. The label releases *The Chronic*, which makes a star out of another ex-con, Snoop Dogg.

1994: Bone Thugs-N-Harmony spread a new melodic trend in rap, at the same time that the Fugees inject a soulful style.

1995: Eminem comes onto the scene as "the white rapper." His music decries the social conditions of poor people and the dispossessed.

1996: Lil' Kim projects a powerfully sexual persona, spawning a horde of female rapper copycats. Lil John uses images that appear to have been filmed in strip clubs or spliced in from pornographic movies.

(*continued*)

A RAP AND HIP-HOP TIMELINE (*continued*)

1997: Puff Daddy (P. Diddy), Wyclef Jean, and Missy Elliott become icons by making rap more and more palatable, musically and lyrically, to the mainstream.

1998: Big Pun, Lauryn Hill, and Ja Rule turn rap into a multi-layered spectacle. 50 Cent adds a new gangsta swagger to rap.

1999: Lauryn Hill is the first woman to be nominated for ten Grammy awards in a single year. She wins five of them.

2001: Four hip-hop albums make VH1's list "The 100 Greatest Albums of All Time."

2003: Kanye West symbolizes rap's evolution into big business, becoming one of the most successful producers in rap history. Eminem's "Lose Yourself," from his film *8 Mile*, wins the Oscar for Best Original Song.

2004: Tupac Shakur surpasses 37 million in total album sales, making him one of the top forty best-selling pop artists of all time. Eminem, Jay-Z and the Beastie Boys surpass the milestone of 21 million albums sold.

2005–ongoing: Sales and downloads of rap music start to diminish considerably, as fragmentation and diversification spread throughout rap culture. Like all previous forms of pop music, rap starts to become a part of pop culture lore. It still has niche audiences given its ability to change and adapt musically to emerging trends.

Sugarhill Gang had national hits during the late 1970s and early 1980s, rap did not enter the mainstream until 1986, when rappers Run-D.M.C. and the hard rock band Aerosmith collaborated on the song "Walk This Way," creating a new audience for rap among white, middle-class teen audiences. By the end of the 1980s, MTV had launched a program dedicated solely to rap, and the records of rap artists such as MC Hammer and the Beastie Boys achieved multi-platinum status.

Impact and Evolution

Rap and hip-hop are terms that are frequently used interchangeably. But the former, which was spread broadly from a recording by Sugarhill Gang called "Rapper's Delight" (1979), refers more specifically to the musical style itself, whereas the latter refers to the attendant lifestyle that those who follow rap tend to adopt—including a new colorful name (like the rap artists themselves) and a panache in demeanor and attitude. The word *hop*, actually, has been around since the 1920s, when so-called *Lindy hop* dancing, also known as *jitterbug*, was popular in Harlem. The word was also used to describe 1950s fast rock dancing, as captured by Danny and the Juniors in their 1958 hit "At the Hop." It is useful, if not necessary, to understand the history of the rap and hip-hop movements, at least in bare outline form, as one basic story line.

The rise of hip-hop in many ways parallels the birth of rock and roll in the 1950s. Both originated in African American culture and both were initially aimed at black audiences. In both cases, the new genre gradually attracted white musicians, who made it popular among white audiences. For rock and roll that musician was Elvis Presley; for rap it was, as mentioned above, the band Aerosmith. Also influential was a white group from New York City, called the Beastie Boys, who released the rap song "Fight for Your Right to Party" (1986), which quickly reached the Billboard top-ten list of popular hits.

Early rap emphasized lyrics and wordplay over melody and harmony, achieving interest through rhythm and variations in the timing of the lyrics. Rap's themes can be broadly categorized under three headings: those that are blatantly sexual; those that chronicle and often embrace the so-called gangsta lifestyle of youths who live in inner cities; and those that address contemporary political issues or aspects of black history. All three themes have one subtext—dissent—from racism and hypocrisy. It was originally a voice of dispossessed black youth. However, by the mid-1990s rap artists started borrowing from folk music, jazz, and other music styles, developing an eclectic pastiche of sound that started to attract larger audiences. The dissent had faded, and the rap artists themselves became more and more just pop music stars, rather than angry voices of dissent.

Abrasive Spectacle

As in rock and roll, the dissent inherent in rap emanated from the musical style, the performance, and the lyrics. These three constituted "abrasive spectacle." In 1988, the rap group N.W.A released the first major album of gangsta rap, *Straight Outta Compton*. Songs from the album generated an extraordinary amount of controversy because of their suggestions of violence. As a result they brought about moral panic, drawing protests from a number of organizations, including the FBI. So too did the early music of Ice-T, Dr. Dre (an original member of N.W.A), and Snoop Dogg. However, attempts to censor gangsta and sexually explicit rap only served to publicize the music more widely, and, thus, to make it even more attractive to youths. The "in your face" attitude noticeable in rap videos to this day, some of which appear to be little more than erotic videos, continues to be polemical.

The hip-hop lifestyle became attractive to many youths in the mid-1990s. The salient features of the lifestyle included the practice of assuming a new name, known as a *tag*, and a dress code that emphasized a gangster image. Hip-hop was an abrasive spectacle culture, allowing youths to literally show their rage over social inequalities and racism. But like all previous forms of spectacle, the rage soon subsided. Often criticized for its harsh lyrics and negative images, by 2000 rap music had started to garner a second reading from the mainstream, which started to see it as a legitimate artistic vehicle rejecting the racist inclinations of the past so that something could be done to change the situation once and for all. Given the overall lack of opportunity afforded to young African Americans in contemporary society, rap music came to be seen as a vehicle through which they could secure a voice and a place in the public sphere and, above all else, their own sense of history and tradition. This is why hip-hop artists spell their performance names differently—*Dogg* instead of *Dog, Sista* instead of *Sister*, and so on. It is a practice of dissent.

A *New York Times* 2002 survey found that most of the top rap artists at the time were already "historical figures" in the rap movement—Dr. Dre, Warren G, Puff Daddy, Shaggy, Nelly, Ludacris, Coolio, Salt-N-Pepa, and Snoop Dogg. With its own magazines, movies, radio and television programs, footwear, clothing, beverages, and jewelry, hip-hop had become big business. But hip-hop had left a mark. In the song "Changes," Tupac Shakur, an artist who was murdered at the age of twenty-five by unknown assailants, emphasized the need for change to occur not only in the larger society, but also in black communities themselves. With lines such as "Tired of being poor and even worse I'm black, my stomach hurts so I'm looking for a purse to snatch" Tupac encapsulated the tragic irony of the situation facing many blacks. Tupac suggested that there was a conspiracy from the higher echelons of mainstream society to make sure that black communities had access to guns and drugs so that they could destroy themselves: "First ship them dope and let them deal the brothas, give them guns step back and watch them kill each other." When basic survival needs such as food become unattainable, antisocial behaviors surface.

Today, rap continues to have a following. New songs and new trends within the movement continue to appear, suggesting its continuing vitality, but it is less and less abrasive. This has always been the pattern in pop culture, as discussed throughout this book. A look at the lyrics and forms of current musical styles reveals that certain things are the same as they always have been. Sexuality and its sentimental counterpart, romance, still dominate. Protest and a general dissenting critique of society still can be found in a variety of musical genres. Late 1990s groups such as Rage Against the Machine attempted to continue the tradition of Bob Dylan and Crosby, Stills, Nash, and Young, expressing rage against "the system." But although such musical voices remain important vehicles for stimulating social awareness and protest, they seem either to pass much too quickly from the public eye, or else tend to have very little effect other than to get people to buy the music.

A definite break from the pattern can be seen in the fact that abrasive spectacles no longer have the same panic-inducing effect of the past. Even the sexual antics of a Nickie Minaj or a Miley Cyrus have little effect. Another pattern is that pop music has become more and more retrospective. The music stars of yesteryear are as much in the limelight as are current ones. The halftime Superbowl show has been headlined by names of the past like Janet Jackson, Paul McCartney, the Rolling Stones, Prince, the Black Eyed Peas, and Madonna. Bored with the onslaught of new musical fads, fleeting pop icons, and simply bad music, many people today seem to be opting to engage in nostalgic fads, such as ballroom dancing, rather than adopt new trends blindly. Perhaps the thrill of new music, with its antisocial subtext, has weakened in the context of the global village.

POP MUSIC IN THE INTERNET AGE

Western pop music has spread throughout the world because of the Internet. But there are changes. Some non-Western countries have developed their own thriving pop music industries. In addition, the marketplace for pop music has changed drastically. Recordings, radio, and television no longer constitute a partnership to promote pop music trends. Today, virtually anyone with access to the Internet can showcase himself or herself musically. Amateur YouTube musicians are often as popular as professional ones. Even the latter could probably not become popular without YouTube and other online media. But while the new cadre of online musicians may be garnering international attention, the attention is short-lived. Only sporadically, does the online musician cross over to the traditional media stages and become truly popular. Television is still dominant in showcasing new talent, as it was in the past, but not new music, as it did with shows such as *American Bandstand* in the 1950s and channels such as MTV in the 1980s. In the Internet Age, three trends have brought about the demise of the traditional music scene and industry—indie music, iTunes (and its derivatives), and YouTube. The first two will be discussed briefly here;

the last one (YouTube) will be taken up more extensively in a subsequent chapter.

Indie music is music produced independently from major record labels, thus involving a DIY ("do-it-yourself") approach to the creation, production, and sale of music. The term also describes a particular genre that is not necessarily produced independently but aims to set itself apart stylistically from major trends. The term is also applied to record companies such as Sun Records and Stax. These are minor labels when compared to major corporate ones; they often sprout up to record emerging new artists and trends that the major ones ignore at first. This was the case with early rock, early rap, and other styles. Typically, however, if the artists become popular, these companies are either bought out by major labels or else merge with them.

The Internet has truly changed everything. One can easily upload "homemade" songs and albums on YouTube, which can be inserted alongside those of major-label artists, thus creating a true pastiche that blurs the traditional line between recognized artists and everyone else. Those who become celebrities through YouTube, such as Psy with his Gangnam Style video that went viral in 2012, gain fame. The video got the artist to appear in other media and it spread across the globe in various ways, from being imitated to creating dance competitions. The advent of such nano-celebrities who now compete with true celebrities has clouded the pop music world with ambiguities and with a new type of expectation on the part of audiences. But nano-celebrities have always been a part of pop culture. In the past, the "one-hit wonder" performer was an ipso facto nano-celebrity; today, a viral phenomenon such as the Gangnam one has taken its place, but in so doing has reduced the period of nano-celebrity so drastically that it has impacted deleteriously on both the notions of celebrity and popularity. Thus, today it is difficult to identify what will become popular, and whatever does is unlikely to last for very long.

The Internet has also made it possible, through iTunes, to be one's own music agent, producer, and manager. Virtually anyone can sell their music through iTunes and similar sites. Of course, it is the established artists who benefit more from iTunes. But the musical works of so many independent musicians available on iTunes has made it virtually impossible to identify new trends. iTunes has also made all previous technologies of music storage and reproduction obsolete. The record, the audiotape, and the CD are all remnants of previous technologies and either exist only as a subsidiary alternative to the Internet source of music or have completely vanished, remaining only as items of memorabilia.

In sum, pop music culture is becoming more and more what can be called a "Mashpedia culture," where music videos are selected by Internet users in a mixed fashion and offered on YouTube sites. This may mean that the traditional world of pop music in relation to pop culture as its voice has morphed dramatically, as will be discussed subsequently.

7

CINEMA AND VIDEO

The cinema, that dream factory, takes over and employs countless mythical motifs.

—Mircea Eliade (1907–1986)

The great French director Jean-Luc Godard once wrote, "All you need for a movie is a gun and a girl" (Godard 1992: 8). Godard's witticism not only seems to capture the essence of popular cinema, but also two key components of pop culture generally—sex and violence. Perhaps no other media stage has been as influential as cinema in spreading and making sex and violence part of the overall spectacle. But that is not all that cinema is about. Some of the first celebrities were born on the silver screen; fashion trends spread from that screen to society at large; and so on. No other media stage has stimulated as much artistic creativity as has the movie screen. And no other art form has had the capacity to hold up a mirror to the contemporary world as has cinema. As the late Swedish director Ingmar Bergman stated in a 1991 interview in London: "No art passes our conscience in the way film does, and goes directly to our feelings, deep down into the dark rooms of our souls."

This chapter will discuss the role of cinema in the rise and spread of pop culture. Cinema is especially important for understanding pop culture, since the film industry has produced outstanding examples of both "trash" and "high art." It is also the media stage that gave rise to the style of representation known as *postmodernism*. Cinema remains the art form to which most people today respond most strongly and to which they look for recreation, inspiration, and insight.

171

MOTION PICTURES

Photographic technology is the predecessor of cinema. Photography dates back to the Renaissance, when the first crude camera, called a *camera obscura* (dark chamber), consisting of a box with a tiny opening in one side that allowed light to come in, was used mainly by painters as a sketching aid. In 1826 the French physicist Joseph Nicéphore Niépce (1765–1833) pro-

Muybridge's horse photos (© ThinkStock)

duced the first modern camera. Photographic technology was developed shortly thereafter by French painter Louis J. M. Daguerre (1787–1851), who worked as Niépce's partner for several years, and the British inventor William Henry Fox Talbot (1800–1877). The first successful "moving photographs" were made in 1877 by Eadweard Muybridge (1830–1904), a British photographer working in California. Muybridge took a series of photographs of a running horse, setting up a row of cameras with strings attached to their shutters. When the horse ran by, it broke each string in succession, tripping the shutters.

Muybridge's creation influenced inventors in several countries to work toward developing devices for recording moving images. Among them was Thomas Edison, who invented the first functional motion picture camera in 1888 when he filmed fifteen seconds of one of his assistants sneezing. Shortly thereafter, Auguste Marie Louis Nicolas Lumière (1862–1954) and his brother Louis Jean Lumière (1864–1948) gave the first public showing of a "moving picture" in a Paris café in 1895.

The public film screenings came to be known as *movies* in America. Traveling projectionists would bring the movies to smaller cities and towns. The movies were without sound, so the projectionists often employed live actors to provide dialogue. A little later, titles were inserted within the films, replacing the actors.

Historical Sketch

Historians trace the origin of cinema to the year after the Lumière demonstration (1896), when the French magician Georges Méliès made a series of films that explored the potential of the new medium. In 1899, in a studio on the outskirts of Paris, Méliès reconstructed a ten-part version of the trial of French army officer Alfred Dreyfus and filmed *Cinderella* (1900) in twenty scenes. Méliès is chiefly remembered, however, for his clever fantasies, such as *A Trip to the Moon* (1902), in which he exploited the movie camera's capacities to capture the emotional subtleties of human expression through close-up and angle techniques. His short films were an instant hit with the public and were shown internationally. Although considered little more than curiosities today, they are significant precursors of an art form that was in its infancy at the time.

American inventor Edwin S. Porter produced the first major American silent film, *The Great Train Robbery*, in 1903. Only eight minutes long, it greatly influenced the development of motion pictures because of its intercutting of scenes shot at different times and in different places to form

FILM AND VIDEO TIMELINE

1877: Eadweard Muybridge captures moving images on film.

1888: Thomas Edison develops the first motion picture camera.

1889: Hannibal Goodwin develops technology that allows movies to be created.

1894: Thomas Edison opens up the first kinetoscope parlors with coin-operated projectors.

1895: The Lumière brothers show the first short films in Paris.

1896: Thomas Edison invents the Vitascope, which is capable of large-screen projection.

1903: Edwin S. Porter's *The Great Train Robbery*, an early western, gains popularity, indicating that the era of cinema is just around the corner.

1907: Storefront movie parlors, called *nickelodeons* because the price of admission was a nickel, begin to flourish.

1910s: Silent films become popular. The first movie celebrities emerge in the late 1910s and early 1920s.

1914: Movie theaters start opening up in New York City.

1915: D. W. Griffith's *Birth of a Nation*, a racist film, gains unexpected success.

1920s: The Big Five studios (Paramount, MGM, Warner Brothers, Twentieth Century Fox, RKO) and the Little Three studios (Columbia, Universal, United Artists) are founded in the late 1920s.

1922: The American movie industry establishes voluntary censorship.

1927: Soundtrack technology is invented. The first *talkie* is *The Jazz Singer* (1927), starring Al Jolson.

1930s: The golden age of cinema arrives.

1946: Cinema becomes extremely popular, as over ninety million people attend movies weekly.

1947: The House Un-American Activities Committee starts holding hearings on communism in Hollywood.

1957: In the *Roth vs. United States* case the Supreme Court sets community standards as the criteria for defining obscenity.

1968: MPAA movie ratings are introduced.

1976: VCRs are launched, creating a new movie rental and purchase industry. *Star Wars* initiates a new era of big-budget blockbusters.

1990s: Independent films become popular and successful.

1995: The first megaplex movie theater is built in 1995 in Dallas leading to a wave of megaplexes and a new cinema-going culture. *Toy Story* is the first completely computer-generated movie, starting a new trend in movie production.

1997: DVDs come onto the scene in 1997, displacing videotapes.

2000s: Movies converge with the Internet, where trailers are shown and where even full features can be seen.

2010–ongoing: Movies start being cast in new kinds of digital formats: on cell phones, iPods, and other mobile devices.

a unified narrative, culminating in a suspenseful chase scene. So-called nickelodeon theaters opened up in major American cities around 1905, located mainly in small stores. With the successful production of D. W. Griffith's *The Birth of a Nation* (1915), small theaters sprang up throughout the United States. Cinema was evolving rapidly into a mass entertainment art form. Most films of the era were short comedies, adventure stories, or vaudevillian performances.

Between 1915 and 1920, the construction of movie theaters (also called palaces) proliferated throughout the United States. The film industry established itself primarily in Hollywood. Hundreds of films a year poured from the Hollywood studios to satisfy the cravings of a fanatic movie-going public. The vast majority of them were westerns, slapstick comedies, and romantic melodramas such as Cecil B. De Mille's *Male and Female* (1919). After World War I, motion-picture production became a major business, generating millions of dollars for successful studios.

The transition from silent to sound films was so rapid that many films released in 1928 and 1929 had begun production as silent films but were hastily turned into sound films, or *talkies*, as they were called. Gangster films and musicals dominated the new "talking screen" of the early 1930s. The vogue of filming popular novels, especially of the pulp fiction variety, reached a peak in the late 1930s with expensively mounted productions, including one of the most popular films in motion-picture history, *Gone with the Wind* (1939). In the same era, many studios also started tapping into pulp fiction's successful foray into the realms of fantasy and horror with films such as *Dracula* (1931), *Frankenstein* (1931), and *The Mummy* (1932), plus sequels and spin-offs. One of the most enduring films of the era was the musical fantasy *The Wizard of Oz* (1939), based on a book by L. Frank Baum—a children's movie with a frightful theme that reflected the emerging cynicism of society at large, namely, that all human aspirations are ultimately make-believe, that the Wizard at the end of the road of life is really a charlatan. The fun of living is getting to Oz, not finding out the truth about Oz. The era also saw the appearance of the thriller as a popular genre. British director Alfred Hitchcock led the way with *The Thirty-Nine Steps* (1935) and *The Lady Vanishes* (1938).

The era was also known for its movie serials, consisting of a set of episodes (known as *chapters*), designed to keep audiences waiting anxiously to see the next episode, because each episode (except the last one) would end often when the hero or heroine would become entangled in some cliffhanger situation (being trapped in a car that was about to fall over a hill) from which escape seemed unlikely. Readers waited restlessly for the succeeding episode of the serial to see how the situation was resolved. By the 1930s and 1940s the movie serial attracted huge audiences. A typical serial had from twelve to fifteen chapters. Accompanying the hero was the sidekick or partner of the hero or heroine, who typically provided comic relief, and the romantic partner.

The first movie serial dates, actually, back to the 1910 production of *Arsene Lupin Contra Sherlock Holmes* (in five chapters). The same decade saw the rise of popularity of the genre with *What Happened to Mary?* (1912), *The Adventures of Kathlyn* (1913), the *Perils of Pauline* (1914), *The Ventures of Marguerite* (1915), and *The Hazards of Helen* (1914–1917). Interestingly, the protagonists in the silent serial movies were primarily women, showing implicitly that pop culture was indifferent to gender roles in society, highlighting the sexual appeal of womanhood on the screen. The studios producing the serials were the Weiss Brothers, Mascot, Universal, Columbia, Victory, and Republic Pictures. It was the latter studio that took over mass production in 1937. Serials were especially popular with children. A typical Saturday afternoon at the movies from the 1920s to the 1950s included a chapter of a serial, along with feature films and animated cartoons. The serial style was adopted by Walt Disney with his early television series featuring heroes such as Davy Crockett and Zorro. The original movie serials disappeared in the 1950s—the last one was the 1956 serial produced by Columbia called *Blazing the Overland Trail*. In the 2000s, Cliffhanger Productions produced several serial formats for YouTube. Although the serial may have disappeared from the screen, its descendants are movie series such as the Indiana Jones, Jason Bourne, Mission Impossible, and James Bond films in which there is considerable crossover material from movie to movie.

Among the most popular genres of the early serials were the westerns—stories about the American West with its rugged landscape and dangers. The western movies made the cowboy the American hero par excellence. Some of America's first celebrities were movie cowboys, including John Wayne, Roy Rogers, The Lone Ranger (Clayton Moore), Hopalong Cassidy (William Boyd), Kit Carson (Bill Williams), among others. From the 1920s through the 1950s, hundreds of cowboy movies were produced by Hollywood, many in serial form. In these, the enemy was often the Native American, producing a representational bias that became endemic in society. The intent for bias was probably not there; adventure was emphasized along with conquest of the land. But the exploitation subtext was inevitable. A more serious treatment of westerns and of Native Americans started to appear in the 1950s with movies such as *High Noon* (1952) and *Shane* (1953) and much later with *Unforgiven* (1992) and *Dances with Wolves*

(1990). The western has lost much of its popularity today. Its demise is undoubtedly due to the fact that the "wild wild west" is an empty metaphor to contemporary audiences.

The movies and other media started converging already in the 1920s, but it was in the late 1930s and early 1940s that the convergence became common. One American filmmaker who crossed over to Hollywood from radio was the writer-director-actor Orson Welles. Welles experimented with new camera angles and sound effects that greatly extended the emotional power of film. His *Citizen Kane* (1941) and *The Magnificent Ambersons* (1942) influenced the subsequent work of virtually every major filmmaker in the world. In Italy, for example, cinema achieved an intimacy and depth of emotion that has since become associated with the cinematic medium generally, starting with Roberto Rossellini's *Open City* (1945) and Vittorio De Sica's *The Bicycle Thief* (1949).

One of the most distinctive and original directors to emerge in post–World War II cinema was Sweden's Ingmar Bergman, who brought an intense philosophical and intellectual depth to moviemaking that has rarely been equaled, treating the themes of personal isolation, sexual conflict, and religious obsession in compelling ways. In his film *The Seventh Seal* (1956) he probed the mystery of life and spirituality through the trials and tribulations of a medieval knight playing a game of chess with Death. In *Wild Strawberries* (1957) he used the technique of flashbacks to penetrate the depressing life of an elderly professor. He then dissected the human condition starkly in a series of films—*Persona* (1966), *Cries and Whispers* (1972), *Scenes from a Marriage* (1973), and *Autumn Sonata* (1978)—which examined the futile penchant in the human species to search for meaning in existence.

In 1948, the U.S. Supreme Court required studios to rid themselves of their theaters. This eliminated studio control and liberated the movie marketplace from Hollywood's strict distribution rules. A number of theaters started specializing in films by foreign directors. Italian director Federico Fellini's *La strada* (1954) and *Nights of Cabiria* (1957) became unexpected hits throughout the United States. The so-called French New Wave had a particular impact on moviemaking with films such as *Le beau Serge* (1958), directed by Claude Chabrol, *The Lovers* (1958), directed by Louis Malle, *The 400 Blows* (1959), directed by Francois Truffaut, and *Breathless* (1960), directed by Jean-Luc Godard.

Starting in the late 1950s, color movies gradually started replacing black-and-white ones. But some filmmakers occasionally made use of the latter, striving for "naked" realism. *Psycho* (1960) by Alfred Hitchcock, *The Last Picture Show* (1971) by Peter Bogdanovich, *Raging Bull* (1980) by

Martin Scorsese, *Zelig* (1983) and *Shadows and Fog* (1992) by Woody Allen, and *Schindler's List* (1994) by Steven Spielberg are notable examples.

Of the many Hollywood directors, perhaps no one has been as successful at exploiting the film medium as a versatile art-and-entertainment form as has Steven Spielberg. Capitalizing on our fear of the unknown and the grotesque, Spielberg has been able to sanitize this instinctual emotion into a "family-friendly" form. His *Jurassic Park* (1993), for instance, taps into the same sense of fear that the traditional grotesque horror genre does while at the same time rendering it palatable through characterization and tinges of humor.

In the early 1970s, a new system of movie distribution—releasing a film in many cities at the same time, supported by television advertising—was used successfully to promote *The Godfather* (1972), directed by Francis Ford Coppola. The results exceeded all expectations—the movie became the most commercially successful film produced up to that time. A new generation of filmmakers came to the forefront, including Spielberg and George Lucas (*Star Wars*, 1977), who introduced spectacular visual effects into filmmaking. The serial movie was revived with *Raiders of the Lost Ark* (1981), *Indiana Jones and the Temple of Doom* (1984), *Indiana Jones and the Last Crusade* (1989), and *Indiana Jones and the Kingdom of the Crystal Skull* (2008), which recalled the cliff-hangers of the 1930s and 1940s. Spielberg also made one of the most successful films in Hollywood history, *E.T.: The Extra-Terrestrial* (1982).

By the 1980s and the 1990s, the influx of movies from Europe, Asia, Africa, the Middle East, Australia, and elsewhere attracted increasingly larger American audiences. Independent movie production also started to gain widespread popularity. Independent directors included Quentin Tarantino (*Pulp Fiction*, 1994), the Coen brothers (*Fargo*, 1996), and John Sayles (*Lone Star*, 1996). New channels of distribution (cable television, video, mobile devices) resulted in an increased variety of films from across the globe. Although Hollywood maintained its dominance, filmmaking had evolved into a truly global art in the global village. Movies such as *Crouching Tiger, Hidden Dragon* (2000), a United States–Taiwan coproduction directed by Ang Lee, and Chinese director Zhang Yimou's *Hero* (2002) and *House of Flying Daggers* (2004) are cases in point.

Digital technologies started making an impact on moviemaking in the same era, and continue to do so. Movies started featuring characters from video games and using techniques simulating reality television (e.g., a roving camera). The first movie to do so was *The Blair Witch Project* (1999). Three film students set out into the Black Hills Forest to make a documentary on the legendary Blair Witch with a 16 mm camera, a video camera, and a DAT recorder. With these they capture every word and sound. After wandering around the forest, the three become lost and hunted. They were never to be seen again. A year later, a bag full of film cans, DAT tapes, and video tapes was found. The video footage and the film make the movie seem truly real.

Today, some movies are made specifically for the online world. YouTube allows anyone to upload his or her movie and gain an instant audience for it. However, as in the case of indie music (see chapter 6) this does not guarantee popularity. The online medium is becoming basically an audition locus for aspiring artists, directors, actors, scriptwriters, and the like to gain access to viewers. With 3D releases, DSLR cameras, and free Internet distribution, the age of digital filmmaking is slowly changing the way in which movies are made and received.

Types of Film

There are, traditionally, three main categories of film—*feature films, documentaries,* and *animated films,* also called *cartoons.* The feature film is a work of fiction, almost always narrative in structure, which is produced in three stages. The preproduction stage is the period of time when the script is procured. The script may be an adaptation from a novel or short story, a comic book, a play, or a video game; it may also be something written specifically for the screen. The production stage is the period of time when the filming of the script occurs. Finally, the postproduction (editing) stage is the phase when all the parts of the film, which have been shot out of sequence, are put together to make one cohesive story.

The documentary is a nonfiction film depicting real-life situations with individuals often describing their feelings and experiences in an unrehearsed manner to a camera or an interviewer. Documentaries are rarely shown in theaters that exhibit feature films. They are seen regularly on television, however. The traditional creation of an animated motion picture nearly always begins with the preparation of a *storyboard*, a series of sketches that portray the important parts of the story. Additional sketches are then prepared to illustrate backgrounds, décor, and the appearance and temperaments of the characters. Today, animated films are produced digitally on computers.

Movies have brought about various new conceptualizations. Whereas in print works, the author(s) can be easily identified as the creator(s) of the text, in films the question of authorship is much more complex, since a screenwriter and a director are involved in a partnership (although many times the two are one and the same person). The function of screenwriters varies greatly with the type of film being produced. The screenwriter may be called upon to develop an idea or to adapt a novel, stage play, or musical to the special requirements of the screen. But the writer is not the only "author" of the film—the director is as well because he or she is the individual who interprets the script and guides the production crew and actors in carrying out his or her vision of the story. The director has artistic control over everything, although in reality various circumstances compromise this ideal of the director's absolute artistic authority. Nonetheless, it is the director's sense of the theme or intent, along with his or her creative visualization of the script, that transforms it into a motion picture.

The role of writer, director, and actors was explored brilliantly by Federico Fellini in *8½* (1963), which is essentially an analysis of what film is all about, with actors filling in parts as the action moves along within a given frame by the director and, in this case, the director's cut being literally what he felt was relevant to the story. The movie is a meta-text—a film text about film texts in general—bringing out the relationship between the various individuals involved in realizing a movie and how the movie achieves verisimilitude.

For some films, alongside the screenwriter and director is the composer, who is assigned the task of creating a musical score to accompany scenes in the story. Music can identify a person as being suspicious when there is nothing visible on the screen to suggest such a thing. It can also function as a bridge from one scene to another in order to prepare the audience for an impending change of mood. One or two characters may also be associated with their own musical themes, either related to or separate from the main theme. Film music has become a genre of its own and, in some cases, the score has eclipsed the film itself. An example of this is the theme music written for *Love Story* (1970).

The Movie Theater

Even though the Internet and mobile devices have made it easier and more convenient to view movies anywhere and at any time, going to the movies still remains a popular activity. This bears testimony to the fact that a movie, like any other spectacle in pop culture, is best experienced communally, inside a movie theater, with food fare and other social rituals included in the event. Today's megaplexes feature not only movies and the usual fast-food fare, but video game sections, restaurants, and various recreational outlets and devices. The movie theater has become a self-contained entertainment locale, much like an amusement park.

The movie *Cinema Paradiso* (1988) dealt with this aspect of cinema, emphasizing how important the movie theater was for common people in times of poverty, war, and desperation. It brought people together to experience escapism and to fantasize as a community. When cinema became a mass cultural form of entertainment in the 1930s, on every corner of urban America one was bound to find a movie theater, which was often the center of attraction of that part of town. All that seemed to change in the late 1980s with the advent of VCR technology, which, combined with the spread of cable television featuring relatively current films on special channels, seemed to seriously threaten the survival of movie theaters. As a result, film companies increasingly favored the production of blockbusters with fantastic special effects in order to lure the public back to the big screen. Today, with specialty movie channels, large home screens, and movies-on-demand technologies, the traditional movie theater may have finally lost its hegemony, as independent movie theaters are disappearing all over the world. Megaplexes, as mentioned, have taken their place. And even though the megaplexes are entertainment centers, the fact that people still go to see movies in a theater bespeaks the power of movies as an art form that is experienced communally.

The threat to the movie theater is now coming from the same source that is threatening traditional forms of pop culture—the Internet. It remains to be seen, however, if the social function of movie theaters will be transferred to other locales (if indeed it can or will be replaced). As it has turned out, so far the advent of movie channels and the Internet has not led to the demise of the movie theater. The new technologies have given options to the viewers, who can now access movies in different media and formats and in a time-independent fashion. But it has not brought about the end of the movie theater, as such.

Genres

The study of movie genres is a central one within pop culture studies. Early filmmakers drew upon novels, pulp fiction, vaudeville, the circus, and other popular sources of entertainment for their film scripts, projecting cinema directly onto the evolutionary momentum that pop culture was gaining in other domains at the turn of the twentieth century. Current films, television series, made-for-TV movies, miniseries, and even new forms of video and online multimedia productions often follow the genre

Table 7.1. Movie Genres (A Selection)

Genres	Examples
Crime, Detective, and Gangster Drama	*Little Caesar* (1930), *The Maltese Falcon* (1941), *The Godfather* (1972), *The Zodiac* (2007), *Public Enemies* (2009), *Kaufman's Game* (2014)
Science Fiction	*A Trip to the Moon* (1902), *Star Wars* (1977), *Blade Runner* (1982), *The Matrix* (1999), *Children of Men* (2006), *Star Trek* (2009), *Dawn of the Planet of the Apes* (2014), *Lucy* (2014)
Animation	*Snow White and the Seven Dwarfs* (1937), *Toy Story* (1995), *Shrek* (2001), *Ice Age* (2002), *Wall-E* (2007), *Frankenweenie* (2010), *Penguins of Madagascar* (2014)
Comedy (including romantic comedy)	*It Happened One Night* (1934), *Gentlemen Prefer Blondes* (1953), *Pillow Talk* (1959), *You've Got Mail* (1998), *White Chicks* (2004), *Bridesmaids* (2011), *Sex Tape* (2014), *Ride Along* (2014)
Character Drama	*Citizen Kane* (1941), *Cool Hand Luke* (1967), *Raging Bull* (1980), *Brokeback Mountain* (2005), *Slumdog Millionaire* (2008), *Midnight in Paris* (2011)
Historical Drama and Documentaries	*Intolerance* (1916), *Nanook of the North* (1921), *Quest for Fire* (1981), *JFK* (1991), *Schindler's List* (1993), *Fahrenheit 9/11* (2004), *10,000 BC* (2008), *Video Games: The Movie* (2014)
Youth Rebellion and Coming-of-Age	*The Wild One* (1954), *Rebel without a Cause* (1955), *A Clockwork Orange* (1971), *The Breakfast Club* (1985), *Youth in Rebellion* (2009)
Adventure, Spy, and Action	*Thief of Baghdad* (1921), *James Bond* movies (*Dr. No, Goldfinger*, and so on), *Indiana Jones* movies (*Raiders of the Lost Ark, Indiana Jones and the Temple of Doom*, and so on), *Mission Impossible* movies (*Mission Impossible, Mission Impossible II*, and so on)
Thriller, Mystery, and Suspense	*M* (1931), *Rear Window* (1954), *Psycho* (1960), *The Usual Suspects* (1995), *Seven* (1995) (*Memento* (2001), *The Da Vinci Code* (2006), *Inception* (2010), *The Equalizer* (2014)
Monster and Fear	*King Kong* (1933), *Godzilla* (1954), *Jaws* (1975), *Jurassic Park* (1993), *Monsters* (2010), *Ragnarok* (2014)
Horror (and vampire movies)	*Nosferatu* (1922), *The Phantom of the Opera* (1925), *Dracula* (1931), *Rosemary's Baby* (1968), *The Shining* (1980), *Interview with the Vampire* (1994), *Twilight* (2008), *Zombieland* (2009), *Dark Shadows* (2012), *Dracula Untold* (2014)
Gore and Slasher	*Friday the Thirteenth* (1980), *I Know What You Did Last Summer* (1997), the *Saw* movies (starting in 2004), the *Hostel* movies (starting in 2005)

Genres	Examples
Musical (including rock and roll and rap movies)	*Flying Down to Rio* (1933), *The Wizard of Oz* (1939), *Jailhouse Rock* (1957), *A Hard Day's Night* (1964), *The Sound of Music* (1965), *Spice World* (1998), *8 Mile Road* (2002), *Barbershop* (2004), *Les Miserables* (2012), *Jersey Boys* (2014)
War	*Birth of a Nation* (1915), *Wings* (1931), *Casablanca* (1942), *Apocalypse Now* (1979), *Full Metal Jacket* (1987), *Braveheart* (1995), *Saving Private Ryan* (1998), *Inglourious Basterds* (2009), *Fury* (2014)
Film Noir (and neo-noir)	*Double Indemnity* (1944), *Sunset Boulevard* (1950), *The French Connection* (1971), *Blue Velvet* (1986), *American Psycho* (2000), *The Dark Knight* (2008), *Gone Girl* (2014)
Western	*The Great Train Robbery* (1903), *Rio Bravo* (1959), *The Good, the Bad, and the Ugly* (1966), *Unforgiven* (1992), *3:10 to Yuma* (2007), *The Dark Valley* (2014)
Romance, Melodrama, and "Chick Flicks"	*The Perils of Pauline* (1914), *The Sheik* (1921), *Bridget Jones' Diary* (2001), *The Notebook* (2004), *Sex and the City* (2008), *About Last Night* (2014), *The Fault in Our Stars* (2014)
Superhero	*The Mark of Zorro* (1974), *Superman* (1978), *Batman* movies (starting in 1995), *Spider-Man* movies (starting in 2002), *The Fantastic Four* (2005), *X-Men: Days of Future Past* (2014), *Captain America* (2014)
Martial Arts	*Enter the Dragon* (1973), *The Karate Kid* (1984), *Rush Hour* (1998), *Crouching Tiger, Hidden Dragon* (2000), *Ninja Assassin* (2009), *Skintrade* (2014)
Sword and Sorcery	*Excalibur* (1981), *Conan the Barbarian* (1982), *Lord of the Rings* movies (starting in 2001), the *Harry Potter* movies (starting in 2000), *Beowulf* (2007), *47 Ronin* (2013)
Disaster and Apocalyptic	*The Towering Inferno* (1974), *Titanic* (1997), *The Perfect Storm* (2000), *Lost Souls* (2000), *Left Behind* (2001), *The Day after Tomorrow* (2004), *2012* (2009), *The Maze Runner* (2014)
UFO and Alien	*Invasion of the Body Snatchers* (1978), *Alien* movies (starting in 1979), *Independence Day* (1996), *X-Files* (1998), *Cowboys and Aliens* (2011), *Alien Uprising* (2013)
Slapstick, Dumbness, and Hilarity	*The Circus* (1928), *The Three Stooges* movies, *Dumb and Dumber* (1994), *Jackass* movies (starting in 2002), *Hangover* movies (starting in 2009), *Dumb and Dumber To* (2014)
African American Themes	*Superfly* (1972), *The Color Purple* (1985), *Do the Right Thing* (1989), *Boyz n the Hood* (1991), *Jungle Fever* (1991), *No Good Deed* (2014)

formulas of pulp fiction—crime stories, mystery, romance, adventure, horror, thriller, spy, and so on—thus catering to the populist imagination. But cinema has also created new genres and has evolved into a veritable art form for the modern world.

The list in the table can easily be expanded to include various other genres and subgenres such as automobile movies *(Fast & Furious* movies) and, of course, many of the categories in it have a lot of overlap with each other.

One could argue, of course, that the new genres are really reconstructions of previous ones. The chick flick, for example, is really an offshoot of the romance genre, although, unlike traditional romance stories, it puts the spotlight on the difficulties facing women in the age of women's liberation. The genre constitutes a new "site" in the struggle for women to come to grips socially with their new sense of freedom. The chick flick challenges the traditional views of womanhood, tracing its roots to writers such as Virginia Woolf and Daphne Du Maurier, and to movies such as *Gone with the Wind* and the TV miniseries *The Thorn Birds*, which were far ahead of their eras.

Movies have become our contemporary storytellers. In his first full-length animated feature of 1937, *Snow White and the Seven Dwarfs*, Walt Disney showed the power of cinema as a raconteur of mythic stories in modern guise. Based on, but significantly differing from, the original 1810 story by the Brothers Grimm, the movie evokes the mythic power of womanhood beneath its textual surface. The only truly powerful characters in the story are, in fact, two women—Snow White and the evil queen. The men are either dwarves, serving their newfound mistress faithfully, or else merely perform a perfunctory role, like offering a romantic kiss at the end. Snow White is a ruler of Nature. All respond to her command, from the animals to the dwarves and even the Prince, who is beckoned to her side by an implicit natural instinct. Disney further explored the power of womanhood in *Cinderella* (1950) and *Sleeping Beauty* (1959).

Not all critics would agree with this assessment. Pinsky (2004: 77), for instance, claims that movies such as *Snow White* are "archetypal female rescue fantasies with essentially passive heroines." However, I read a different story in the movies. Snow White, Cinderella, and Sleeping Beauty are hardly passive. Indeed, they motivate those around them. More importantly to the present discussion, the Disney movies show the power of cinema to rework and reconstruct the mythic stories of human understanding. One cannot underestimate the influence of Disney and the Disney Studios on the evolution of contemporary America. Cinema was, and continues to be, a powerful force in shaping belief systems and in changing the world.

The Thriller

A genre that has stimulated great interest among pop culture analysts is the thriller, which traces its origins to the cliffhanger serials of the 1920s and 1930s. Thrillers often overlap with crime, mystery, spy, and adventure stories. There are also subgenres now, including the action thriller, featuring a hero in a race against time to save someone or to stop a villain from destroying something; the conspiracy thriller, which revolves around a hero facing some conspiracy and struggling to expose it or unravel it; the crime thriller, which involves a hero crime fighter; the disaster thriller, which revolves around some disaster, human-made or natural; the erotic thriller, in which a dangerous erotic situation brings about a thrilling outcome; the horror thriller, which is intended to a evoke suspense or a feeling of unease; the legal thriller, featuring lawyers as protagonists solving crimes; the spy thriller, in which a hero must fight terrorists or assassins; the psychological thriller, which features a conflict in the mind of the hero or antihero; the supernatural thriller, which incorporates elements of the occult and the supernatural into the thriller format; and the techno thriller, which features technology as intrinsic to the plot.

The early director most closely associated with the thriller is Alfred Hitchcock (1899–1980), noted for his technically innovative and psychologically complex treatments of the genre. Hitchcock entered the moviemaking business in 1920 as a designer of silent-film title cards and worked as an art director, scriptwriter, and assistant director before directing his first picture, *The Pleasure Garden*, in 1925. It was Hitchcock's third picture, *The Lodger* (1926), about a man suspected of being Jack the Ripper that thrust the thriller genre into cinematic center stage. In 1929, Hitchcock made his first talking film, *Blackmail*, which was acclaimed for its imaginative use of sound in evoking suspense and a feeling of "creepiness." The term *spine-chiller* became widespread shortly thereafter to describe movies that induced the same kinds of reactions. In *Blackmail*, Hitchcock used a continually clanging shop bell to convey the heroine's feelings of guilt, making her situation a psychologically chilling one. During the 1930s and 1940s he gained international fame with a series of immensely popular suspense thrillers, including *The Man Who Knew Too Much* (1934), *The 39 Steps* (1935), *The Lady Vanishes* (1938), *Suspicion* (1941)—about a woman who imagines that her husband is a murderer—*Shadow of a Doubt* (1943), and *Notorious* (1946).

Hitchcock embarked upon the most creative period of his career in the 1950s. In rapid succession, he produced and directed a series of inventive films, beginning with *Strangers on a Train* (1951) and continuing with

Rear Window (1954), a remake of *The Man Who Knew Too Much* (1956), *Vertigo* (1958), *North by Northwest* (1959), *Psycho* (1960), and *The Birds* (1963). The plots of these pictures are surreal nightmares that take place in daylight—a small town appears calm on the surface but reveals dark tensions underneath; an innocent man finds himself suddenly the object of suspicion; a wholesome-looking motel clerk is actually a psychotic killer who impersonates his dead mother; and so on. Influenced by the montage experiments of Russian director Sergei Eisenstein, such as the use of a series of quick shots to evoke strong emotions in the viewer, Hitchcock's movies are mirrors of the fragmented nature of the psyche and its fears. They are existential essays on terror and horror.

So effective was Hitchcock's cinematic art that all subsequent thriller movies are now in his shadow. The adjective "Hitchcockian" has entered the movie lexicon permanently. The American Film Institute's 2001 listing of the one hundred most popular thrillers of all time, voted on by eighteen hundred cinemagoers, showed that Hitchcock's *Psycho* was number one. Two other Hitchcock films made the top ten: *North by Northwest* at number four and *The Birds* at number seven.

A film that falls into the category of the Hitchcockian thriller, meriting comment here because it has become a common point of reference in pop culture studies, is the 2001 film *Memento*, written and directed by Christopher Nolan and based on a short story written by his brother Jonathan Nolan (*Memento Mori*). The plot is both chilling and spine-tingling in true Hitchockian style. The main character, Leonard, is forced to live entirely in the present, unable to create new memories after suffering a head injury, as he seeks revenge for the rape and murder of his wife. Leonard writes notes on his body, takes Polaroid photos, and keeps pieces of paper so that he can remember what he has discovered—hence the title *Memento* to indicate that his memory is a series of mementos, which he is unable to connect in any coherent way to understand the passage of time. The narrative's time sequence is presented in bidirectional manner (going forward in color and backward in black and white). In this way, the audience is denied the key clues of which the protagonist is also deprived, due to his amnesia. Much like the protagonist in *North by Northwest*, the viewer is projected directly into the character's sense of horror of having lost his memory. This leads to doubt about the reality of consciousness.

We know that at the very start Leonard's wife was killed. Leonard was apparently hit on the head during an intruder's commission of the brutal act, and he is consequently left without short-term memory. He carries with him a picture of a man he suspects of the murder. The death of this man, and the inference that Leonard killed him, ends the tale. Leonard goes on to write a letter, in the style of previous mementos, perhaps to himself, knowing that he will otherwise forget what happened.

As in many of Hitchcock's thrillers, surreal symbolism is used by Nolan to evoke a sense of fear of the unknown in viewers. The movie is replete with symbols of time—alarm clocks ringing, a wristwatch, notepads, and so on. However, the movie destroys the sure sense of time normally evoked by such artifacts by showing the plot in both forward and reverse time, distinguishing the two sequences as mentioned above—color sequences show what actually happened; black-and-white ones show what Leonard believes happened. The first color scene, in which Leonard shoots and kills Teddy (the suspected murderer of Leonard's wife) is chronologically the last scene of the narrative. In that clip we see a Polaroid undeveloping, a bullet flying back into the barrel of a gun and Teddy coming back to life. This is followed immediately by a black-and-white scene of Leonard in a motel room talking to an anonymous person on the phone, explaining his circumstances.

To make the movie even more spine-chilling, Nolan intersplices the parallel story of a man named Sam Jenkins into the narrative. As an insurance investigator, Leonard came across a medical claim from Sam Jenkins, who eerily had the same memory problem that he has now. Leonard investigated the case, and denied Sam the money he sought because he believed that Sam was faking his condition. Sam's wife also was not sure if her husband was faking. So, she came up with a memory test. She had diabetes and it was Sam's job to administer shots of insulin to her. If, in a short time frame, she repeatedly asked for the shots and he repeatedly gave them, she would be able to prove that his condition was real. Sam administered the shots each time she requested them, forgetting that he had just given her one. Eventually, she slipped into a coma from the overdoses and died, leaving Sam a patient in a mental institution. The Sam Jenkins subplot clearly creates a surreal sense that Leonard may, himself, be a patient in the same mental institution, and that he also killed his wife.

Why do we get so much pleasure from thrillers, from childhood stories of unknown spirits haunting us to modern-day tales such as *Psycho* and *Memento*? The Greek philosopher Aristotle claimed that stories are often motivated by our sense of fear. This sense becomes sublimated through the cathartic effect stories produce in us. In the Hitchcockian thrillers and in *Memento* catharsis is suspended and not allowed to be released, owing to the lack of any real resolution at the end of the movie. Perhaps that is why we find them powerful, as we search for catharsis outside of the movie context.

Horror and Monster Movies

The horror and monster genres are also highly popular ones. In a way, horror movies have the same function as the freak sideshows of the carnivals, stimulating our fear of the grotesque in the form of fictional monsters like Frankenstein and King Kong and of the unknown in ghost and paranormal movies.

The horror genre entered the realm of the popular scene through the pulp fiction medium, although it traces its origins to the Gothic novel of the nineteenth century. It is still a staple of current movie fare. From the zombie films of the 1950s and 1960s to current-day bloody movies like the *Hostel* and *Saw* series of films, the horror movie is essentially a treatise in fear and freakishness. Not all critics would agree with this assessment, however. Some have looked at a monster movie such as *King Kong* (1933) in terms of how the ape's predicament parallels that of exploited groups, such as African Americans. Do such movies thus legitimize exploitation by allowing it to become sublimated in fictionalized form and thus purge people of the guilt that they bear? It is one of many interpretations, given that critics see in texts what they are predisposed to see. Another reading of the horror genre is that it caters to an unconscious scopophiliac instinct (the pleasure of viewing women as erotic objects). In this interpretive frame, therefore, the heroine who falls for King Kong is seen as a victim, succumbing to masculine pleasures. In my view, neither interpretation (although legitimate in some ways) seems to grasp the psychic origin of the genre in folklore traditions based on existential fear. The use of grotesque images throughout the ages, especially with marionettes and puppetry in ancient and medieval plays, suggests a deeper motivation for the appeal of horror stories—horror projects us into the "other side" of fantasy, the dark horrific side. To put it differently: movies such as the Disney ones are to sweet dreams what horror flicks are to nightmares.

No director has shown a greater understanding of the psychic roots of horror than the Canadian David Cronenberg. In his classic, *Videodrome* (1983), Cronenberg shows that the real horror is the video genre itself. In the film, a video virus emits infectious rays that induce hallucinations (a television screen, for example, becomes a huge pair of lips, a video cassette is forced into a woman's genitals). At the end, the protagonist mutates into a videocassette, prepared to bring about hallucinations in others.

The first known example of the Gothic novel is *The Castle of Otranto* (1764), written by Horace Walpole. The stories were called Gothic because they took place in gloomy Gothic castles with secret passageways, dungeons, and towers where strange happenings occurred unexpectedly. The first true horror-monster story, *Frankenstein* (1818), was penned by Mary Shelley (1797–1851). She took the name of a Swiss physician called Frankenstein who created a monster from parts of corpses. Through ghosts, vampires, zombies, the undead, monsters, serial killers, slashers, and the like, we are really putting into visual filmic form our fear of and fascination with the dark instincts of the body and the dark side of the mind. In *The Texas Chainsaw Massacre* (1974), a hitchhiker slits his hand open just for the thrill of it. Onlookers recoil in horror, except for the invalid Franklin, who realizes that what lies between the body and the outside world is really only a small membrane of skin, protected merely by a social taboo against its violation. The gap between inner and outer worlds is blurred in horror stories through what French psychoanalyst Jacques Lacan (1901–1981) called *glissage*, whereby the inner body "spills out" into the world, becoming nothing but matter. The horror of the contemporary slasher movie lies, arguably, in its visual depictions of the body's inner organs (brains, intestines, eyeballs and so on) spilling out into the world. But slasher movies were not the first to make explicit this glissage of the body. It has been a central feature of horror stories from the start. Tod Browning's 1932 movie *Freaks*, for example, included a brief shot of an armless, legless man crawling with a knife in between his teeth, and emerging from under a circus wagon like a gigantic worm. At the end of the movie, the high-wire artist is somehow transformed into a chicken with the head of a woman.

Monsters are the visual forms of fear, while ghosts and supernatural creatures are manifestations of the Shadow archetype. By facing death in art, it is easier to grasp mortality psychologically. Many horror movies have extended the concept of Shadow horror to include human relations, which may turn dark. In *The Exorcist* (1972) it is parent-child relationships that provide the context for the horror (Regan's parents are divorced, her father neglects her, and Father Karras's mother dies in poverty). If the family can survive the crisis together in spite of everything, the evil entity will die; if the family collapses, the evil will have successfully destroyed the collapsing moral system at the heart of society. The subtext is a transparent one: the ultimate threat to humanity comes from within the human heart itself.

POSTMODERNISM

The term *postmodernism* was coined originally by architects in the early 1970s to designate a style that was meant to break away from an earlier modernist style (including box-like skyscrapers and apartment buildings) that had degenerated into sterile and monotonous architectural formulas. Postmodern architects called for greater individuality, complexity, and eccentricity in design, along with structural allusions to historically meaningful symbols and themes. Shortly after its adoption in architecture, the term started to catch on more broadly, coming to be used to name emerging trends in philosophy and the arts. In postmodernism, nothing is for certain, and even science and mathematics are seen as constructs of the human mind, as subject to its vagaries as are the arts. The essence of postmodern narrative was, and continues to be, irony and parody. As the sociologist Zygmunt Bauman (1992: vii–viii) perceptively remarked, postmodernism constitutes "a state of mind marked above all by its all-deriding, all-eroding, all-dissolving destructiveness."

Nowhere has postmodernism become as powerful an art form as in the movies. It is on the movie screen that postmodern techniques were first displayed. In this regard, several movies merit discussion in this section.

Future Worlds

The fear of the future has been a major theme within postmodern cinema. Stanley Kubrick's cinematic masterpiece of 1971, *A Clockwork Orange*, is a perfect example of this kind of film (as already discussed). The setting for the movie is Britain in the future. A teenager, Alex De Large (played by Malcolm McDowell), lives a life of wanton and reckless crime and sex. His physical appearance, and especially his face, are scary and menacing of the status quo. He is Chaos in person.

Arrested and imprisoned for murder, he volunteers to receive shock treatment therapy designed to brainwash him to become nauseated by his lifestyle. However, Mr. Alexander, one of his victims, traps him with the aim of avenging himself. He hopes to drive Alex to commit suicide to Beethoven's Ninth Symphony. But Alex is supported by the media and soon afterward is released and restored to health through therapy.

The movie ends with no resolution. But the film's showcasing of reckless violence perpetrated by a teenager and glorified by media attention is a stark postmodern portrait of contemporary life. Alex is a goalless and ruthless adolescent trapped in a weary, meaningless environment. His psychic escape is through sex, intimidation, and crime. He is always ready to explode. Alex feels an acute and urgent need to change and to "save" the world by turning it upside down. But he does not know how to save it or what to save it from. The modern world is what it is. The film's fragmented images of a decaying society on the streets reinforce the view that life is absurd, without a purpose, and that human actions are a montage of senseless movements.

Some of the movie's scenic techniques were emulated by Ridley Scott in his 1982 masterpiece, *Blade Runner*, based on a science fiction story titled *Do Androids Dream of Electric Sheep?* by Philip K. Dick (1928–1982). The movie still attracts considerable interest from movie buffs, being scripted in a style of postmodern science fiction writing known as *cyberpunk*. The target of cyberpunk writers was dehumanized societies dominated by technology and science, emphasizing the failure of progress to bring about meaningful change in the human condition.

Rick Deckard is one of a select few futuristic law enforcement officers, nicknamed *blade runners*, who have been trained to detect and track down *replicants*, powerful humanoid robots who have been engineered to do the work of people in space. The replicants need to be tracked down because they have gone amok. They have somehow become conscious and developed the desire for immortality, made all the more urgent by the limited lifespan programmed into them. A desperate band of these killer replicants has made its way back to Earth seeking to have their programs changed. They hunt down the corporate tycoon responsible for their creation so that he can reprogram them for immortality. Deckard's assignment is to find these runaway replicants and terminate them.

His search takes place in an urban wasteland where human mutants control the streets while pathetic inhabitants in endless blocks of gloomy high-rises remain glued to their television sets. Deckard relies on a VCR, complete with stop action and precision image-enhancers, to search for the replicants through dark alleys abandoned to the forces of anarchy.

The method used by Deckard to identify a suspect as being either human or replicant is an implicit rejection of a classic test used by artificial intelligence theorists. The British mathematician Alan Turing (1912–1954) suggested, shortly before his untimely death, that one could program a computer in such a way that it would be virtually impossible for anyone to discriminate between its answers and those of a human being. His notion has become immortalized as the *Turing test*. Deckard's detection technique rejects the validity of the Turing test because he focuses on the reactions of his interviewee's eyes, not on the simple content of the interviewee's answers. The eyes are a mirror of the soul, as the expression goes, and their expressive reactions to emotional situations can never be replicated artificially. The replicants in the movie are icons of the human form. But there is one feature that differentiates human anatomy from artificially made anatomies—the eye. Replicants use their "eyes" exclusively to see; humans also use them to show feeling. Aware of the mysterious power of the human eye, the replicants kill their maker by poking out his eyes. Interestingly, we are never sure throughout the movie if Deckard is a human or a replicant himself, since the camera never provides a close-up of his eyes.

In this postmodern world the replicants, paradoxically, are more "human" than the human characters. Deckard even falls in love with one of them, Rachel, whose name has obvious intertextual connections with the biblical character of the same name. She helps him track down his prey, falling in love with him (or so it seems). The film makes many other references to the Bible. For example, near the end, a naked replicant, Roy, wearing only a white cloth around his waist, in obvious allusion to the scene of Christ's crucifixion, saves Deckard's life at the cost of his own. The white dove that appears when Roy "expires" is reminiscent of the dove that was sent to Noah's ark in the midst of torrential rain to help the ark find a safe place away from the deluge—a symbolic quest for a safer future. Soon after Roy's demise, Deckard and Rachel succeed in reaching safety, escaping the gruesome city scene by rambling off into the countryside. The dark, gloomy atmosphere suddenly clears up, the sun comes out, and a new day dawns. The scene calls to mind the biblical Garden of Eden. This ending of the movie was not the original one, but rather one that the producers insisted upon. Nevertheless, given the subtext of the movie, it is as valid as the version in the director's cut.

Blade Runner asks the fundamental questions of philosophy in a new way: What is a human being? What is real? Is there any purpose to existence? By making the replicants icons of human beings, and by transforming their struggle to survive and to know who they are into a reflection of our own struggle, the movie shows that sophistication is possible in postmodern moviemaking, which integrates pulp fiction (the movie is, in fact, basically a film noir detective thriller) with philosophical inquiry.

This postmodern movie can also be inserted into a larger philosophical discourse called *post-humanism*, or the view that humans should no longer dominate the world but instead must merge with their machines to create a new world with humans sharing an equal partnership with machines and other animals. This requires a new view of reality and a revisitation of all of previous philosophy. The theorist most associated with this view is Donna Haraway (1989, 1991). Haraway's perspective, known as *cyborg theory*, claims that the machines we make are extensions of ourselves. Since the cyborg can have masculine and feminine traits, and mixed racial traits, it will rise, claims Haraway, to efface the isms of traditional human-centered worlds. She also claims that the cyborg will efface all traditional notions of a Self contained inside the human body as well as the traditional notions of the uniqueness of human consciousness.

Blade Runner raised the same questions. The difference is that the movie is fiction and allows us to entertain the prospect of future worlds on our own terms; cyborg theory is philosophical speculation that might be ignoring even more profound questions, such as the spiritual nature of humanity—a topic that the movie does not avoid.

Images over Words

Perhaps the most often discussed example of postmodern cinematic technique in pop culture studies is Godfrey Reggio's 1983 film *Koyaanisqa-tsi*—a film without words that unfolds through a series of discontinuous, narrativeless images. On the one hand, the movie shows us how disjunctive and purposeless the modernist world based on technology has become; on the other hand, it is an example of what postmodern art is all about. The film has no characters, plot, dialogue, or commentary—that is, it has nothing recognizable as a narrative. The camera juxtaposes contrasting images of cars on freeways, atomic blasts, litter on urban streets, people shopping mindlessly in malls, decaying housing complexes, buildings being demolished, and other scenes of the modern world into a visual pastiche. We see the world as the camera sees it, as a series of incongruous disconcerting images with no language to describe them and give them an interpretation. It is a turgid, gloomy world with no identifiable purpose or meaning. People move around like mindless robots. To emphasize the insanity of a world with endless chains of cars on intricate road networks and crowds bustling aimlessly about, Reggio incorporates the mesmerizing music of Philip Glass (b. 1937) to act as a guide for understanding the images. We can thus hear the senselessness of human actions in the contrasting melodies and rhythms of Glass's music. His slow rhythms tire us with their lugubriousness, and his fast tempi—which accompany a chorus of singers chanting dementedly in the background—assault our sense of balance. When the filmic-musical frenzy finally ends, we feel an enormous sense of relief.

In a certain sense, the whole film can be conceived of as a musical sonata with an opening part or exposition, a middle developmental section, and a final recapitulation with a coda. The exposition is a glimpse into a vastly different world—the world of the Hopi peoples of the southwestern United States, a world based on a holistic view of existence that does not separate humans from nature through technology. Glass's choral music is sacred and profound, imitating Gregorian chant. It inspires reverence for the bond that links humans and nature. This initial segment stands in dark contrast to the development of the filmic sonata—a cornucopia of dissonant images of a rotting, absurd, modern world. Then we are taken back, at the end, to the Hopi world. As in any recapitulation, the opening strains of the choir return, hauntingly, awesomely, and with a warning this time (the coda), which is projected onto the screen: "*Koyaanisqatsi* (from the Hopi language)—crazy life, life in turmoil, life out of balance, life disintegrating, a state of life that calls for another way of living."

Jean-François Lyotard (1984: xxiv) observed that in postmodernism "narrative function is losing its functors, its great heroes, its great dangers, its great voyages, its great goal." However, in making us more conscious of our narrative presuppositions, postmodernism has actually engendered a serious reevaluation of belief systems. Today postmodernism may have run its course, although residues of its approach can be seen even in comedic films, such as *Burn after Reading* (2008) by the Coen brothers, which emphasizes the absurdity of decision making in daily life, which can literally turn on a dime. Life is a series of random events that lead us nowhere and everywhere. There is no teleological plan behind human actions—just the random actions themselves. In *Fight Club* (1999), directed by David Fincher, the character Tyler puts it rather insightfully at the end of the movie: "We're the middle children of history, man. No purpose or place. We have no Great War, no Great Depression. Our Great War is a spiritual war. Our Great Depression is our lives."

THE BLOCKBUSTER

Blockbuster is a term that comes up often in the study of cinema. The word derives from theater slang referring to a highly successful play; in film parlance it refers to a movie that earns an excessive amount of revenue or one that involves famous stars and captures public attention, even if the movie does not meet financial expectations. The directors who are particularly associated with the blockbuster are Cecil B. De Mille (1881–1959), Steven Spielberg (b. 1947), and George Lucas (b. 1944).

Birth of the Blockbuster

Although it has come to the forefront as a major type of film since the mid-1970s, the originator of the blockbuster was Cecil B. De Mille, an early American motion picture director and producer whose spectacular historical epics and biblical film extravaganzas brought the filmic blockbuster into existence. In the 1910s, De Mille made a number of distinctive silent films dealing with romance, including *The Warrens of Virginia* (1915), *Joan the Woman* (1916), and *Male and Female* (1919). In a short time, he carved out, through his own personal lifestyle, the image of the dashing Hollywood director that continues to hold sway over the public's imagination.

In 1923, he produced the first true blockbuster with *The Ten Commandments*, an overblown spectacle that contained the blueprint for the blockbuster formula. The movie was enormously successful at the box office. He followed this success in the subsequent decade with other blockbusters, including *The Sign of the Cross* (1932), *Cleopatra* (1934), and *The Crusades* (1935). Subsequently, De Mille's big-budget films became legendary with a string of pictures that included *The Plainsman* (1936), *The Buccaneer* (1938), *Union Pacific* (1939), *Northwest Mounted Police* (1940), *Reap the Wild Wind* (1942), *Samson and Delilah* (1949), and a sensationalistic remake of *The Ten Commandments* (1958)—his final movie as a director.

The blockbuster is to moviemaking what P. T. Barnum's circus was to spectacle in general. It introduced sensationalism into movies. In fact, one of De Mille's most insightful blockbusters was the 1952 epic about the circus called *The Greatest Show on Earth*.

Entrenchment of the Blockbuster

There is very little doubt that De Mille's successors are Steven Spielberg and George Lucas. Spielberg's earliest efforts were television movies, among which *Duel* (1971), a suspense film about "road rage," brought him wider recognition. *Sugarland Express* (1974), his first theatrical feature film, was an expertly crafted variant of *Duel*. He followed it up with *Jaws* (1975), a thriller based on American author Peter Benchley's novel of the same name. *Jaws* proved to be such a tremendous success that Spielberg's name became a household word.

Jaws marked a turning point in the fortunes of the American film industry. Blockbuster-type films had been part of the Hollywood production mix, as mentioned above, but *Jaws* rewrote the formula and, above all else, proved that in conjunction with effective marketing strategies a movie could produce unprecedented revenues. *Jaws* lacked big-name stars; it focused, instead, on the frightening special effects of a mechanical monster shark. The movie impressed upon Hollywood that an important segment of the moviegoing audience was young people and children, as George Lucas's *Star Wars* (1977), certainly understood.

The *Star Wars* phenomenon showed that blockbuster movies were spectacles for the whole family, bringing children and parents together to the movie theater, and that they took over the role of storytelling within families. The *Star Wars* set of six movies, which wrapped up in 2005, is a pastiche version of several pulp fiction genres, including the superhero tale and the sci-fi story. It also recycles ancient Greek mythology. In a Greek tragedy the story begins typically with a prologue or monologue that explains the tale's topic (as discussed previously). Each episode of *Star Wars* begins in the same manner through the use of rising text against the background of space: "A long time ago in a galaxy far, far away." The *Star Wars* saga is also divided into individual episodes, released in a sequence that starts in medias res, with the fourth episode being the first one to be recounted. The unifying theme of all the *Star Wars* episodes is the universal mythic struggle between evil (the Dark Side) and good (the Force). The villains appear in futuristic white armor, but their leader, Darth Vader, stands out from the foot soldiers by dressing in black and speaking with a low foreboding tone of voice. He is the leader, after all, of the Dark Side. As the story unfolds, Luke Skywalker, the last Jedi Knight left to fight against the Dark Side, discovers that his father was a Jedi Knight. Luke yearns to know who his father was. In line with the Greek tradition of tragic irony, as in the Oedipus myth, Luke learns that his father is the very person he has destroyed—Darth Vader.

Following the standard set by the *Star Wars* saga, the term blockbuster today usually involves a series of sequels (the *James Bond, Harry Potter, The Lord of the Ring* movies, and so on). James Bond (as mentioned) strode onto the pop culture stage in the novel *Casino Royale* in 1953, by writer Ian Fleming (1908–1964) (South and Held 2006). The character became a pop icon, however, only after his filmic debut in *Dr. No* (1962). As a modern-day superhero spy, he is adaptive to change yet retains his essential character. The Bond blockbuster series achieves its appeal by virtue of the fact that it is perceived to be an ongoing narrative. Similarly, the *Harry Potter* movies (based on the novels by J. K. Rowling) are cast in chronological order, with the characters aging in tandem with their audiences. In this case, audience members and movie (book) characters experience the coming of age dynamically together.

VIDEO CULTURE

The late 1980s saw a revolution in the history of the movies, with major releases being made available for home video viewing very soon after they left the movie theater. The first home videotape recorder to be sold was the Beta machine, invented by the Sony Corporation in the late 1970s. The popularity of that device was quickly eclipsed by the VHS videotape format, introduced into the market through clever advertising by the Radio Corporation of America.

The videocassette recorder (VCR), with its capacity to play pre-recorded videotapes, rented or purchased at video shops, and to record programs shown on television for later playback, made a noticeable dent in moviegoing at first. So too did the cable television systems that emerged at about the same time, which vastly expanded the number of channels available to the home viewer and provided access to recent movies via a pay-TV format. As these new technologies came into widespread use, movie studios were understandably worried. But they needn't have. The studios had forgotten a major lesson of cinematic history—being in a movie theater with a real audience is part of the communal effect that cinema is intended to create.

However, there was another video-based competitor that came onto the scene at about the same time—the video game. The video game concept has actually complemented cinema in more ways than one.

Video Games

Video games played on a video console started out as arcade games, which originated perhaps as far back as the Roaring Twenties, according to some historians. A home video game is really an arcade game with expanded capabilities. In the early 1970s the electronic tennis game named Pong introduced the video game industry to the United States. After this industry nearly collapsed in the mid-1980s, Japanese companies, especially the Nintendo Corporation, assumed leadership, improving game technology and introducing popular adventure games such as Donkey Kong and the Super Mario Brothers, thus spawning a video game culture that has blossomed into a major form of entertainment rivaling cinema.

The term *video game* is now used to refer to any electronic game, whether it is played on a computer with appropriate software, on a game console, on a mobile digital device, or online. There are now genres of video games and various formats in which they can be played. Particularly relevant to the present discussion is the role-playing game, which gained popularity at first with Dungeons & Dragons. Participants pretend to be in a situation or environment, such as a battle or newly discovered place; each situation has its own rules and each participant plays a specific role or character in the scenario. Rather than filmmakers or others creating the storyline, the games let users do so themselves. The increase in the popularity of online gaming of this type has resulted in the formation of subgenres. One example is that of multiplayer online games, which, as T. L. Taylor (2006) has remarked, are designed for sociability and interaction, more than for the thrill of the game.

Participants create a character, known as an *avatar*, by inputting descriptions of appearance and behavior into the game. Other participants have no way of knowing if the avatar corresponds to the real physical appearance or personality of the player, or not. In this way realism and fantasy mesh completely.

Why are video games so popular? The probable answer is that they make the escapism provided by cinema even more powerful by taking the make-believe element from the screenwriter and director and putting it directly into the hands of the viewer. In video game scripts, the player(s) is the scriptwriter, actor, and director at once. The *spectator* is no longer a passive viewer of the *spectacle*, but a participant in it. Video games give participants the feeling of being immersed in a simulated world that resembles the real world. The line between the imaginary and the real is thus totally

Video games incorporate many popular film genres, including mythic and fantasy war, adventure, and science fiction (© ThinkStock)

blurred. Video gaming has spawned its own subculture, with attendant websites, blogs, magazines, and the like.

As Steven Johnson (2005) has cleverly argued, video games may actually be enhancing intelligence, since they provide a locus for the same kind of rigorous mental workout that mathematical theorems and puzzles do. The complex plots and intricacies of video games are thus making more people sharper today. Johnson calls this the "Sleeper Curve" effect. The term comes from Woody Allen's 1973 movie *Sleeper*, in which a granola-eating New Yorker falls asleep but reawakens in the future, where junk and rich foods actually prolong life, rather than shorten it. According to Johnson, the subtext of the movie is clear: the most apparently debasing forms of mass diversion turn out to be nutritional after all.

We are a "problem-solving species," Johnson claims, hence the addictive power of video games. Johnson's argument may or may not be true. One thing is for certain; video games, like any other prop in pop culture, provide great enjoyment. If fun enhances cognition, so much the better. The lesson to be learned from studying pop culture is not that it is intertwined with intellectual or cognitive growth, but rather that it taps into our basic needs.

CINEMA IN THE INTERNET AGE

The movie theater has shown remarkable durability in the Internet Age. With all kinds of media platforms for viewing movies today, from You-Tube to Netflix, it is truly amazing that people still go to the movies and that new movies are showcased first on the traditional movie screen. This says a lot about the emotional power of communal viewing, as *Cinema Paradiso* certainly understood. The technology for making and delivering movie fare may have changed, but the social locus for enjoying the movie experience has really not changed all that much.

Of course, the indie movement and the general DIY attitude that now undergirds the conduct of pop culture fare is also characteristic of the world of cinema making. The number of movies that are being added to or produced for online venues such as Apple iTunes, Amazon Instant Video, and Google Play is increasing exponentially. The growing stock of digital tools and realtime analytics that are offered by self-serve platforms like Vimeo, VHX, and Gumroad is changing the whole marketplace for cinema. And so is the way popularity for movies is gained, since it is occurring more and more by word-of-mouth social media like Twitter and Facebook. Overall, there are three ways in which the Internet has reshaped or complemented cinema:

1. The Internet is now a new distribution channel for new films. It is also a pirating source, since it can present films that can be downloaded free.
2. It promotes films with online trailers.
3. It allows for the production of films made especially for the Internet, called web films.

We will return to the features of the Internet in this regard subsequently; for now, it is sufficient to point out that movies, like music and other popular forms of entertainment, are migrating more and more to cyberspace. New releases can now be seen on YouTube alongside indie and DIY productions. The distinction between what can be called "quality-controlled" and "market-researched" culture versus DIY culture is impinging on the very foundation of populism in all the arts.

8

TELEVISION

In Beverly Hills they don't throw their garbage away. They make it into television shows.

—Woody Allen (b. 1935)

Through cinema, pulp fiction magazines, recordings of music, newspapers, and radio, pop culture had become, by the 1950s, an intrinsic part of American society. This state of affairs was further cemented by the advent of television, the media stage that has remained a dominant one for showcasing pop culture and its trends ever since. Like the other stages, television has had its critics from the outset who claim (or at least worry) that the medium has negative effects on people, especially children. As American literacy lobbyist Frederic Glezer phrased it in a *Newsweek* article in 1986, television is a "four-to five-hour experience with nothingness." Before the advent of video games and the Internet, television was the main scapegoat in the "culture wars" that occur occasionally in the United States. Ultimately, however, there is no evidence for any of the alarming claims or any basis to the fears. The Australian critic Clive James (1983: vi) has aptly put it as follows: "Anyone afraid of what he thinks television does to the world is probably just afraid of the world."

The purpose of this chapter is to take a look at the television–pop culture partnership that has been in place since the late 1940s. Why do we continue to love television, even to the point of spending considerable amounts of money on new television systems and technologies? The writer Barbara Ehrenreich (1990: 12) answers this question cleverly and insightfully as follows:

So why do people keep on watching? The answer, by now, should be perfectly obvious: we love TV because TV brings us a world in which TV does not exist. In fact, deep in their hearts, this is what the spuds crave most: a rich, new, participatory life.

Ehrenreich may have put her finger directly on the reason why we spend, according to some estimates, over fifteen years of our waking lives watching television.

TELEVISION BROADCASTING

The scientific principles underlying the technology leading to the invention of television were established by John Logie Baird, a British electrical engineer, at the end of the nineteenth century. The prototype for television was devised as early as 1884 by the German inventor Paul Gottlieb Nipkow, who invented a scanning device that sent pictures over short distances. The research led to a workable television camera that was developed in 1923 by the Russian-born American engineer Vladimir K. Zworykin (and perfected in 1927 by the American inventors Philo T. Farnsworth and Allen B. DuMont). The first television receiver was exhibited in Schenectady, New York, in 1928, by the American inventor Ernst F. W. Alexanderson. In 1936, the Radio Corporation of America (RCA) installed television receivers in one hundred and fifty homes in the New York City area. NBC (which was owned by RCA) began trial telecasts to these homes, starting with a cartoon episode of *Felix the Cat*. By 1939, NBC produced regular broadcasts, which were suspended when the United States entered World War II. After the war, six television stations were built, each broadcasting for only a few hours a day. As early as 1941 the FCC (Federal Communications Commission) turned its attention to setting standards for television broadcasting. By 1948, thirty-four all-day stations were in operation in twenty-one major cities, and about one million television sets had been sold. By the end of the 1950s national television networks had been established in most industrialized countries. As the twentieth century came to a close, television entered the Internet Galaxy with the advent of digital television and online television formats.

Television is everywhere—in hotel rooms, airports, schools, elevators, office waiting rooms, cafeterias, washrooms, and even outer space. The successful landing on the moon in July 1969 was documented with live broadcasts made from the surface of the moon. Television technology is also applied to other systems, such as medical devices, security systems, and computer-aided manufacturing.

Television has, like all other mass entertainment media, been a two-edged sword. On the positive side, it has been instrumental in bringing about significant and important changes in society. The television images of the Vietnam War broadcast daily in the late 1960s and early 1970s brought about protest. It was thus a factor in ultimately bringing an end to the war. The constant exposure and treatment of sexual themes on sitcoms has, through the years, helped shatter the hypocritical silence that previously existed with regard to sexual matters in society at large. On the other hand, whereas reading books requires various degrees of critical reflection, processing television images does not. This may have surreptitiously induced a shift away from reading to viewing. However, there is no evidence that people living before television were more avid readers and intellectually more energetic than are those who were born after the advent of television.

Many of the early television programs were taken directly from radio, including westerns such as *Gunsmoke*, soap operas such as *The Guiding Light*, and sitcoms such as *The Jack Benny Show*. Television at first was little more than "visual radio."

The Radio Corporation of America (RCA) showed the American public how effective and appealing television was with its live coverage of the 1939 New York World's Fair. Immediately thereafter, the National Broadcasting Company (NBC), the Columbia Broadcasting System (CBS), the American Broadcasting Company (ABC), and the DuMont Television Network (which went out of business in 1955) became the first television networks in the United States. By the mid-1950s NBC, CBS, and ABC—collectively known as the Big Three—had successfully secured American television audiences as their exclusive domain. In the mid-1980s, the Fox television network went on the air, capturing a segment of that domain. So, before cable television ended channel scarcity in the late 1980s, viewing choices were largely limited to the programming that the major networks provided.

With the widespread growth of cable television and then of Direct-Broadcast-Satellite (DBS) services, many new channels and types of programming became available to people across the globe. As a consequence, debates about television's impact on children, world culture, global politics, and community life became common. On the one side, critics said that television fed a constant stream of simplified ideas and mindless images to unwitting viewers, that it negatively influenced politics and voting patterns, that it destroyed local cultures in favor of a bland generic entertainment

TELEVISION TIMELINE

1880s: The cathode ray tube is invented, making television technology possible.

1884: Paul Nipkow patents the electrical telescope in Germany, which becomes the basis for television technology.

1927: Philo T. Farnsworth transmits the first television picture.

1935: Farnsworth conducts the first public demonstration of television in Philadelphia.

1936: First television service debuts, in Britain.

1939: NBC starts regular television broadcasts from New York City.

1941: The FCC sets standards for television broadcasting.

1948: Milton Berle and Ed Sullivan go on air with the first television variety shows, ushering in the golden age of television. The first community antenna television (CAT) is established.

1950: The A. C. Nielsen Market Research Company starts tracking television audience behaviors. The first swear words are heard on *The Arthur Godfrey Show*.

1950s: Television becomes a dominant medium, with previous radio genres and personalities crossing over to television. Programs such as *I Love Lucy* (starting in 1951), *The Today Show* and *The Tonight Show* (1952), and later *The Beverly Hillbillies* (1964) establish the standards for television broadcasting.

1954: Color television technology is introduced, but does not become marketable until the 1970s. The U.S. Senate begins hearings on the purported effects of television violence on juveniles.

1958–1959: Quiz show scandals tarnish television's image.

1960: The first satellite system, called Telstar, is established. The Kennedy-Nixon presidential debate shows the power of television to influence public opinion.

1961: A second round of Senate hearings on television violence takes place.

1966: Prime-time programs are broadcast in color.

1967: Congress creates the Corporation for Public Broadcasting, leading to the establishment of public television channels.

1968: *60 Minutes* starts broadcasting. The National Commission on the Causes of Violence concludes that television violence encourages violent behavior. The first interracial kiss is seen on a *Star Trek* episode.

1971: *All in the Family* changes the character of sitcoms, introducing controversial social issues into the content of prime-time programming.

1972: The FCC makes cable available to cities. The U.S. Surgeon General releases a report on the relation between television and social behavior.

1975: HBO (Home Box Office) begins broadcasting via satellite. VCRs are introduced. Under FCC pressure, broadcasters adopt a "family hour" format to provide wholesome early-evening family programming.

1976: Cable comes onto the scene. Ted Turner's WTBS in Atlanta, which uplinks to satellite technology, becomes the first "superstation."

(continued)

TELEVISION TIMELINE (*continued*)

1977: The eight-part miniseries *Roots* sets new standards for television broadcasting with its probe of the African American experience. The miniseries also shows the first bare female breasts on television.

1980s–1990s: The popularity of sitcoms like *M*A*S*H* (1972–1983), *The Cosby Show* (1984–1992), *The Simpsons* (1989–), *Seinfeld* (1989–1998), and *Friends* (1994–2004) leads some media critics to define this decade as the "era of the sitcom."

1980: CNN premieres as a twenty-four-hour cable news network, owned originally by Ted Turner, revolutionizing newscasting and making news a part of genre television.

1981: MTV is launched.

1986: Rupert Murdoch's Fox Television makes its debut.

1985–1990: New channels and networks start up. Specialty cable channels also emerge.

1990: The Children's Television Act mandates children's programming.

1991: The first homosexual kiss on American television is seen on an episode of *L. A. Law.*

1994: The direct broadcast satellite (DBS) industry debuts.

1996: The Telecommunications Act abolishes most television ownership restrictions.

1997: Parental advisories are mandated for television programs.

1998: The V-chip is introduced. HDTV broadcasting starts.

2000s: Specialty channels start proliferating: TBS, Spike, ESPN, Weather Channel, TLC, USA Network, and so on. Television and the Internet merge to create a co-broadcasting system, whereby television channels and Internet websites deliver the same or complementary content.

2002: The FCC rules to end antenna-based broadcasting by 2007, transforming the television medium gradually into a digital format.

2003: VOD (video on demand) is introduced.

2005–ongoing: Television starts to compete with sites such as YouTube. Television is received on mobile devices. Internet TV emerges and competes with traditional TV. TV programs have Internet sites for further viewing, follow-up, and commentary.

---

culture, and that it encouraged passivity. On the other side, defenders said that television provided a great deal of high-quality educational and cultural programming and that it was the major source of local, national, and international news for many people who would otherwise remain uninformed. Whatever the truth, one thing is certain—television turned out to be, before the Internet, the technological invention that consolidated McLuhan's (1962, 1964) global village.

As in the case of radio, advertising is the fuel that propels television broadcasting. In the United States and Europe advertising agencies underwrite commercial network programming. Only in the area of public broadcasting, and on specialty channels such as HBO, is this not the case. Public television services are generally supported by government funding, contributions from viewers, corporate gifts, and foundation grants. Direct Broadcast Satellite (DBS) now provides viewers with a system capable of capturing satellite signals. However, most channels available from satellites require subscription fees and licenses.

Interactive Television

Online television services offer interactive formats that give viewers more of a choice to watch what they want to watch and when they want to watch it. But the concept of interactive television is not new. In the winter of 1953, in the infancy of television broadcasting, a kids' show called *Winky Dink* featured an interactive component. Viewers bought a kit that included a piece of plastic to cover the television screen and a magic crayon. Kids could then help the hapless Winky character out of jams. Prompted by the show's announcer, they could draw a bridge for him, for example, so that he could cross over a ravine and then erase the bridge, as instructed by the announcer, so that the bad guys would plunge into the ravine. The show ran for four years and was revived briefly in 1970.

The next chapter in interactive television dates back to December 1, 1977, in Columbus, Ohio, where cable companies made a "relay box" available to customers so that they could order movies whenever they wished. The system also showed city council meetings during which viewers could express their opinions through the box. There was also a "Your Call Football" service whereby viewers could anticipate the plays in semi-professional football games. By the early 1990s, some specialty channels provided by cable companies devised systems that would allow viewers to watch shows whenever they chose to do so. In the mid-1990s, interactivity became a regular feature, as channels and programs started websites, which viewers could visit during, before, or after regular broadcasts of shows. With cable technologies, moreover, viewers could pause live television and record shows onto low-cost hard drives with the click of a button. Today, online television sites allow users to pull up detailed information while they are watching a news or documentary broadcast.

Webcasts are now common. They have allowed events, such as local sports events, to gain a broad international audience (Rowe 2011). In the past, amateur sports or sports from other countries would hardly ever be showcased on the broadcast media. Webcasting has allowed these events to garner a relatively large audience. With all kinds of video devices people throughout the globe can become producers of their own programs. Their actors can be taken from real life and webcast with or without their knowledge. The boundaries between the private and the public, between fact and fiction, have thus become blurred.

Genres

As mentioned, many early TV programs were taken directly from radio. *I Love Lucy* (1951–1957), which starred Lucille Ball, was adapted from her radio show *My Favorite Husband* (1948–1951). It established the dramatic elements that have been adopted by subsequent sitcoms, such as family entanglements and gender conflicts. Some television sitcoms, such as *Father Knows Best* (1954–1960) and *The Cosby Show* (1984–1992), leaned instead toward the moralistic narrative, often focusing on child rearing. Some sitcoms have also occasionally used fantasy characters—for example, *Bewitched* (1964–1972) and *I Dream of Jeannie* 1965–1969). Others had a social criticism function. Prime examples were *All in the Family* 1971–1979) and *M*A*S*H* (1972–1983). An interesting early example was a short-lived sitcom called *It's a Man's World*, which premiered on NBC in 1962. It followed the daily lives of four young men: a refugee from a rich Chicago family, a folk singer, and two orphaned brothers. The episodes of the sitcom were truly forward-looking. They dealt with premarital sex, feminism, and the generation gap. Mass audiences were not ready for this type of sitcom, however, and after only nineteen episodes, NBC canceled it.

The television *comedy-variety* genre is a hybrid of vaudeville and nightclub entertainment. In the early years of television, many of the medium's first stars were, as a matter of fact, comedy-variety performers. The *Ed Sullivan Show* (1948–1971), for example, hosted by newspaper columnist Ed Sullivan on CBS, featured entertainers as diverse as Elvis Presley and the Bolshoi Ballet.

The early years of television also offered many highly regarded anthology dramas. Hour-long works by Paddy Chayefsky (1923–1981), Rod Serling (1924–1975), and other playwrights were presented on programs such as *Goodyear-Philco Playhouse* (1951–1960) and *Studio One* (1948–1958). As with radio, however, serial dramas proved to be much more popular and, therefore, the anthologies gradually faded from the screen. The serials included police dramas, such as *Dragnet* (1952–1959, 1967–1970), *The Mod*

Squad (1968–1973), and *Hawaii Five-O* (1968–1980); private-eye series, such as *77 Sunset Strip* (1958–1964), *The Rockford Files* (1974–1980), and *Magnum, P.I.* (1980–1988), in which the character of the detective was as important as the criminal investigation; and westerns, such as *Gunsmoke* (1955–1975), *Wagon Train* (1957–1965), and *Bonanza* (1959–1973), which focused on the settling of the west and the human dramas that this entailed. Other distinct types of television series included war programs, such as *Rat Patrol* (1966–1967); spy series, such as *The Man from U.N.C.L.E.* (1964–1968); and science-fiction series, such as *Star Trek* (1966–1969). Many dramatic series were based on the exploits of lawyers, doctors, or rich business entrepreneurs. These included *Perry Mason* (1957–1966), *L.A. Law* (1986–1994), *Ben Casey* (1961–1966), and *Marcus Welby, M.D.* (1969–1976).

Television soap operas, like their radio counterparts, explored romance, sex, friendship, and familial relations. Among the most popular of the early television era were *The Guiding Light* (1952–2009) and *The Edge of Night* (1956–1984). The history of the television soap opera is also the history of gender relations in society (as already discussed).

The earliest years of television offered little in the way of news coverage that was different from radio. But this changed in 1956, when NBC introduced *The Huntley-Brinkley Report*, a half-hour national telecast presented in the early evening and featuring filmed reports of the day's events. The other networks followed suit shortly thereafter. With the invention of videotape, the cost of such coverage dropped significantly, allowing individual stations to initiate and expand local news coverage. Network and local news have now become an integral part of television programming. In addition to daily news coverage, the networks have capitalized on the popularity of news reporting by developing weekly prime-time newsmagazine series, such as *60 Minutes* (starting in 1968) and *20/20* (starting in 1978). Such programs consist of a mixture of investigative reporting and human-interest stories. They have proliferated, with some focusing on crime or criminal investigations of common people, such as *48 Hours* and *Dateline NBC*. All-news cable channels have become popular since the mid-1980s. The first of these, CNN (Cable News Network), was founded in 1980 by American businessman Ted Turner. CNN was the first twenty-four-hour television network devoted entirely to news broadcasts. In 1991, the network received wide publicity when its reporter Peter Arnett remained in Iraq during the Persian Gulf War to broadcast his reports. Arnett gave a "play-by-play" account of the conflict, not unlike what a television sportscaster does in describing a football or baseball match. A similar approach occurred during the initial phases of the Iraq war, when "embedded" news reporters actually jumped on army vehicles and took us, the viewers, directly into the action, at least the type of action where the gore of war did not come through. Coverage of 9/11 and the wars in Afghanistan, Iraq, and Syria have followed this model. News reporting is as much entertainment and "reality drama" as it is information programming. War is real; television broadcasts, however, transform the events of the war into a daily adventure serial imbued with all the elements of a fictional narrative.

With cable television, the range of genres has expanded considerably. Reality television, contestant shows, CSI programs, specialized sports channels and programming, and many more are now options that viewers can select as they please. Many programs become popular because of social trends. For example, makeover and cookery genres have now emerged as very popular ones. Dating shows have always been popular—so, programs revolving around TV courtship, such as those of the eligible bachelor or bachelorette kind, are now also highly popular. In a phrase, television translates into program form what society is interested in.

A brief perusal of the kinds of TV shows that were popular in the early 2010s indicates how much TV has changed over the years and yet, paradoxically, continues to offer programming that reflects the same kinds of social emphases. In 2012 the first broadcasts of *Duck Dynasty*, *Dog with a Blog*, and *Push Girls* (featuring disabled women) and an increase in sports and children's programs showed that a pastiche of emerging concepts and perceptions in society have made their way to the TV screen. The concept of blockbuster has also migrated to the TV screen with the premieres in 2011 of *Game of Thrones* and in 2013 of *House of Cards* (debuting on Netflix)

THE COMEDIC AND THE REAL

Comedy is one of the meta-genres of popular culture—a genre that dominates within that culture. As Berger (2005, 38–39) aptly puts it, the reason for this is that "People crave humor and laughter, which explains why there are so many situation comedies on television and why film comedies have such widespread appeal." Narrating the "real" is also a meta-genre, as people try to understand their own lives through a portrayal of the lives of others. This is the likely reason why reality shows and reality channels such as A&E and TLC have become part and parcel of television textuality.

Sitcoms

As mentioned in chapter 4, the concept of the sitcom traces its ancestry ultimately to the improvised theatrical genre known as the commedia dell'arte. The same actor always played the same role. Most of the lively, farcical plots dealt with love affairs, family relations, and sexual conflicts, as do modern-day sitcoms. It is not known how the commedia originated, but by 1575 the companies that performed it had become extremely popular in Italy. Commedia troupes started appearing throughout Europe shortly thereafter.

Traditionally, sitcoms have featured largely self-contained individual episodes, as in commedia performances. Events of previous episodes would rarely be mentioned. This changed somewhat with *The Beverly Hillbillies*, in the 1960s and early 1970s, where allusions to past episodes were sometimes

---

SEX HIGHLIGHTS FROM SITCOM HISTORY

1952: *I Love Lucy* is forbidden to script the word *pregnant* when Lucille Ball (the main female character) is actually pregnant. Lucy and Ricky Ricardo sleep in separate beds.

1961: On *The Dick Van Dyke Show* Mary Tyler Moore wants to wear capri pants, with CBS allowing the tight pants to be worn only sporadically.

1964: On *Bewitched* married couple Darrin and Samantha Stevens are seen sharing a double bed.

1965: On *I Dream of Jeannie*, Jeannie must hide her belly button, according to the censors.

1971: On *All in the Family*, the Bunkers address taboo subjects such as menopause, homosexuality, and premarital sex.

1972: On *Maude* middle-aged Maude decides to have an abortion.

1974: Circumcision is discussed on *All in the Family*.

1977: On *Three's Company* John Ritter's character pretends to be gay to share an apartment with two women roommates.

1987: On *Married . . . with Children* jokes about vibrators and nymphomania abound.

1989: *Thirtysomething* shows male lovers in bed, even though they do not touch or kiss.

1991: On *Murphy Brown* Candice Bergen's unmarried character decides to have a baby.

1992: On *Seinfeld* refraining from masturbation is described as being "master of your domain."

2000s–ongoing: Sitcoms generally take an explicit approach to discussing all topics of sexual concern. Traditional sitcoms are being supplemented more and more by reality shows that are, essentially, sitcoms in their overall format, including E!'s *Keeping Up with the Kardashians* and MTV's *Jersey Shore*, which both show explicit sexual activities and drinking.

made. Sitcoms started introducing ongoing story lines systematically in the late 1990s. *Friends*, for instance, provided an overall story architecture similar to that of soap operas, often with two or three ongoing episodes taking place simultaneously. *Friends* also used end-of-season cliffhanger episodes.

Stock characters are what make sitcoms appealing and connect them to the commedia. The sage character, who might be someone with a superior intellect, an elderly person, or else an outsider wryly commenting on a situation in which the other characters have put themselves, can be seen in the persona of Wilson on *Home Improvement* and Sheldon on *Big Bang Theory*. Some characters provide constant comic relief, like the Pagliaccio of the commedia. Cosmo Kramer on *Seinfeld* was such a character; Ed Norton on the *Honeymooners* was another. The antagonist is yet another stock character found in sitcoms. This character functions as a rival of the sitcom's principal character or protagonist. Michael Stivic on *All in the Family* was one such character, opposing the bigotry of the main character, his father-in-law Archie Bunker. On *The Simpsons*, Homer often makes an antagonist of his neighbor, Ned Flanders.

Other stock figures in sitcoms include the following:

- The promiscuous character who is constantly involved in sexual exploits: the Fonz (*Happy Days*), Blanche Devereaux (*The Golden Girls*), Roz Doyle (*Frasier*), Larry Dallas (*Three's Company*), Joey Tribiani (*Friends*), Glenn Quagmire (*Family Guy*), Penny (*The Big Bang Theory*), and Haley Dunphy (*Modern Family*).
- The meddler who is always curious about others and a spreader of gossip: Ralph Furley (*Three's Company*), Mitchell Pritchett (*Modern Family*), Mike Sorrentino and Ronnie Ortiz-Magro (*Jersey Shore*).
- The complainer or grouch, who is continuously criticizing others and grumbling about life: Archie Bunker (*All in the Family*), Lou Grant (*Mary Tyler Moore Show*), Ralph (*The Honeymooners*), Frank Barone (*Everybody Loves Raymond*), Jay Pritchett (*Modern Family*), Sammi Giancola, Angelina Pivarnick, and Nicole Polizzi (*Jersey Shore*), Sheldon Cooper (*Big Bang Theory*).
- The lovable loser who cannot do anything right, yet is amiable and liked by everyone: Cliff Clavin (*Cheers*), Noel Shempsky (*Frasier*), Gunther (*Friends*), Phil Dunphy (*Modern Family*), Vinny Guadagnino and Deena Nicole Cortese (*Jersey Shore*).
- The sarcastic servant who, like Leporello in *Don Giovanni*, provides satiric commentary on events in the sitcom: Florence Johnston (*The Jeffersons*), Geoffrey (*The Fresh Prince of Bel-Air*), Niles (*The Nanny*),

Rosario Salazar (*Will & Grace*), Cameron Tucker (*Modern Family*), and Paul Delvecchio (*Jersey Shore*).

- The overprotective parent who attempts to save his or her children from socially induced woes: Cliff Huxtable (*The Cosby Show*), Paul Hennessy (*8 Simple Rules for Dating My Teenage Daughter*), Danny Tanner (*Full House*), Claire Dunphy and Gloria Delgado Pritchett (*Modern Family*), and Jennifer Farley (*Jersey Shore*).
- The entertainer who wants to make everybody happy, no matter what the situation requires emotionally: Jess (*New Girl*), Raymond Barone (*Everybody Loves Raymond*), Leslie Knope (*Parks and Recreation*).
- The thinker/intellectual or "know-it-all" who assumes an air of superiority and is often condescending to other characters: Lisa Simpson (*The Simpsons*), Alex Dunphy (*Modern Family*), Sheldon Cooper (*Big Bang Theory*)

Stock characters have appeal because they represent people in real life. Indeed, the comedic mode of representation has always been a mode for understanding everyday life, exposing the more ridiculous aspects of human behavior. Since comedies have a playful mood and end happily, they contrast markedly with tragedy, which takes the same aspects of everyday life and gives them a more serious treatment. In a way, comedy is, as British writer Angela Carter (1991: 56) aptly puts it, "tragedy that happens to other people." Through the egregious mistakes, weaknesses, infidelities, betrayals, acts of deception, mischievous actions, and the like of comedic characters we can see the true tragedy of life, as Carter suggests, through the lens of laughter. And through the comedic we come to see, and even accept, the absurdity of many of our own systems of belief. As writer Gore Vidal puts it: "Laughing at someone else is an excellent way of learning how to laugh at oneself; and questioning what seem to be the absurd beliefs of another group is a good way of recognizing the potential absurdities of one's own cherished beliefs" (Vidal 1974: 78).

Perhaps the sitcom that can be used to sum up its social functions is *South Park*. The show is a modern-day version of the ribald satiric comedy, in the tradition of, for example, the comedic plays of Aristophanes (450–385 BCE). The prime targets of its satire are religion, politics, and pop culture itself. With its double entendres, the sitcom carries with it a political, moral, or social subtext from episode to episode. It is carnival at its very best, poking fun at America's overly sensitive political correctness and obsession over everything from gay marriage to Lindsay Lohan's drinking habits, Bono's hypocritical self-adulation, and Scientology. In episode 912, "Trapped in the Closet," Stan is believed to be the reincarnation of Scientology founder and prophet L. Ron Hubbard. A group of Scientologists, including John Travolta and Tom Cruise, assemble to celebrate Hubbard's second coming. When told that his acting pales in comparison to others, Cruise locks himself inside Stan's closet and refuses to come out of it. Eventually John Travolta and R. Kelly join Cruise and also refuse to come out of the closet. In the end Stan reveals he is actually not Hubbard's reincarnation, proclaiming that "Scientology is just a big fat global scam."

Episode 704 is an attack on Reality TV. After discovering that they are in a reality show Stan explains why the whole thing is "messed up." "Why? Because you're playing with people's lives. You're turning people's problems into entertainment." To this Cartman adds, "Yeah! We'd never do that on Earth!"

Nothing is sacred on *South Park*. In "Mr. Garrison's Fancy New Vagina" (episode 901), the children's' teacher, Mr. Garrison, feels that he is a woman on the inside; so, he decides to undergo a sex change operation to make himself female. After becoming a woman, Garrison becomes distraught at one point when he discovers that he has missed his menstrual period, believing that he is pregnant, and thus cheerfully deciding to terminate the pregnancy. The episode is a social critique of moralistic attitudes, bringing the debate over gender issues to the national stage in a comedic manner. In "D-Yikes!" (episode 1106), the now "Mrs. Garrison" decides she is a lesbian and spends the entire episode defending the town's local lesbian bar, Les Bos, from the people who wish to buy it and convert it into a heterosexual dance club. A group of lesbians spearheaded by Garrison win the battle and get to keep their bar.

Unlike other sitcoms, which are pleasantly subdued in their portrayals of American life, *South Park* is a powerful moral comedy, challenging hypocrisy, political correctness, fads and trends, celebrities, and so on, because it is ideologically opaque—never revealing its political orientation perhaps because politics itself is hypocritical. One of the most disturbing episodes (1010), "Miss Teacher Bangs a Boy," brings this out emphatically. The episode focuses on Kyle's little brother, Ike, who is in kindergarten and is having a sexual relationship with his teacher, Ms. Stephenson. The episode touches on several aspects of aberrant sexuality: a teacher who is sleeping with her student, child molestation, and statutory rape. However, when Kyle reports the crime to the police, they just respond with "Nice!" because the boy is having a sexual affair with an attractive female. Even the citizens of South Park do not mind that the teacher is sexually abusing a kindergartener, because she is a female. The absurd irony of gender hypocrisy in America is ludicrously transparent in this distressing episode.

Reality Television

Reality TV programs clutter the prime time airwaves, as did unscripted programs such as *Survivor* and *Temptation Island* in the early 2000s, which pitted real-life people into situations involving all the dramatic elements of the soaps—intrigue, danger, betrayal, romance, and sex. The appeal of such programs, which blur the line between reality and fiction, lies in their "text-in-the making" nature. As in the 1921 play by Luigi Pirandello (1867–1936), *Six Characters in Search of an Author*, the audience is presented with real-life characters in search of a script and a narrative. The fun is in figuring out how this will come about.

Consider an early reality show, *Temptation Island* (2001). A group of common people in bathing suits was put on an idyllic island so that their emotional and romantic lives could be wrecked on purpose through "temptation" schemes. Who would overcome temptation? Who would yield to it? The reason the couples in the show agreed to be in it was, purportedly, so that they could test their devotion to each other. Because the characters were common people, the show provided a voyeuristic template against which viewers could evaluate themselves (Would I react in the same way? Would I become unfaithful under similar circumstances?). Reality television caught on and, today, it is more than a meta-genre, it is a symptom of the inability to distinguish between fiction and reality. On television, people can become famous (*American Idol*), choose a romantic partner (*Bachelor* and *Bachelorette* programs), showcase their problems (*Intervention, Hoarders*), and so on and so forth.

Unscripted television is not new. It has been a staple of cable networks and public broadcasting outlets for years. The fine series *1900 House* on Britain's Channel 4 was much more intriguing than any *Survivor, Temptation Island*, or *Bachelor* format, since it followed the misadventures of a family that agreed to live as the Victorians did for three months. The series combined elements of narrative with those of documentary and drama producing a television sociology of family life that was truly powerful. Similarly, the 1971 American documentary of the Loud family—involving seven months of uninterrupted shooting and three hundred hours of nonstop broadcasting—created a text-in-the-making program that reflected the banality of bourgeois family life. The Loud family fell apart, begging the question: Did the television cameras cause the rift? Would all families fall apart in the same situation?

Historically, reality television dates back to 1948, when Allen Funt's *Candid Camera* first aired. The program was itself based on the radio show. *Candid Camera* showed everyday people reacting to contrived situations unknowingly. Coinciding with the radio-to-television trend, there was a popular radio series called *Nightwatch* in the early 1950s that followed Californian police officers in Culver City, prefiguring TV shows such as *Cops* and *48 Hours*. In 1992, the kind of reality television we are familiar with today began with MTV's *The Real World*, whose episodes took place in a house, where seven strangers from different backgrounds and circumstances were filmed as they carried out their lives for several months. A host of similar shows followed, such as *The Osbournes*, *The Simple Life*, and *The Biggest Loser*. The name *reality TV* surfaced in 2002, when CBS's *Survivor* aired, which was an accumulation of filming and production techniques originating from *The Real World*.

Why has reality television become so popular? Does it result from television blurring the lines between the imaginary and the real? These questions made up the theme of a truly remarkable 1998 movie called *The Truman Show*. Directed by Peter Weir, and written by Andrew Niccol, the film features Jim Carrey as Truman Burbank, the unsuspecting star of his very own reality television show. Burbank is the first baby to be legally adopted by a corporation, which films every moment of Truman's life for television audiences to witness. Burbank goes about his life in the largest studio ever constructed, a world within a world, without knowing that he is in it. His life is captured by over five thousand cameras, all controlled from a room at the top of the domed studio. Truman's friends, family, and wife are carefully selected actors. *The Truman Show* becomes one of the most popular television shows ever, with an income equivalent to the gross national product of a small country. All revenues are generated by product placement. Eventually Truman learns the truth about his life, despite attempts to conceal it from him. He steps through the door of the set back into real life, leaving viewers in a quandary as to what to do and looking for something else to view on TV.

The world manufactured for Truman is a hybrid of both the old and the new, blending the society of the 1950s with the technology of the late 1990s. The idea of recreating the feel of the 1950s was to evoke the optimism and hope associated with the era. The citizens of Truman's world are polite and friendly, biking cheerfully to work and taking strolls down tree-lined boulevards. The setting is nostalgic. However, its integration with new technologies is a jarring one, conveying the feeling that something is amiss. Truman drives a recent car model, uses an ATM card, and works on a computer. Viewers watch him bathe, sleep, and go through the motions of everyday life. The show becomes addictive for viewers. The subtext of the movie is an obvious one—television has eliminated the difference between itself and reality. Significantly, advertising is at the core of the success of *The Truman Show*, since revenues are generated by product placement. Companies fight each other to have Truman use their particular brand of coffee, eat their particular brand of chicken, and so on. Viewers can flip through *The Truman Show* catalogue and place an order, since everything on the show, from the wardrobes to the furniture, is for sale. When Truman and his wife discuss a new kitchen product, their conversation comes off sounding like a commercial. By the end, we yearn for Truman to escape from his studio prison cell, at the same time that we remain completely obsessed with his life. Ironically, we need Truman both to stay where he is and to escape his artificial reality.

Current reality television taps into the appeal of *The Truman Show*'s principle that contemporary people can no longer distinguish, or want to distinguish, between reality and fantasy. It is a perfect exemplification of the concept of the *simulacrum*, put forward by French philosopher Jean Baudrillard (1983), whereby the borderline between representation and reality has vanished, turning real life into simulation and vice versa simulated life into real life. With programs like *Toddlers and Tiaras*, *Hoarders*, *Say Yes to the Dress*, and others, which, although scripted, simulate reality (*The Office*, *The Kardashian Show*), reality television is eclipsing fictional television.

TELEVISION AS A SOCIAL TEXT

Television entered the world hesitatingly in the 1950s. It has morphed, since then, into a powerful social text that most people alive today read on a daily basis to evaluate reality and to extract principles of life from it. It also explores social issues constantly. ABC's *Pan Am*, for example, takes us back to 1963 to allow us to appreciate the plight of stewardesses and their role in promoting an incipient feminism. *Mad Men* evokes an era when sexual relations were seemingly more straightforward, albeit not simple.

Contemporary programs have also taken on a different, darker complexion. *Breaking Bad*, which debuted in 2008, is a case in point. It is about a chemistry genius named Walt who due to a bad business deal now teaches at a high school and works part time at a car wash. When he is diagnosed with terminal lung cancer, he teams up with a former student, Jesse, a small-time dealer, to cook meth in order to make enough money to keep his family out of poverty after he dies. His cancer goes into remission, but although he is conflicted, he continues to make meth. The episodes deal insightfully with this inner conflict. The show's black humor and moral dilemmas are evidence that the dynamics of television textuality are changing as social dynamics change. A program such as *Breaking Bad* would have been meaningless in the simpler 1950s era of law and order versus evil. Likewise, the social dynamics of sitcoms have changed. When *Father Knows Best* was on the air, women stayed at home to raise the children and men went out to work (with exceptions, of course). In 2010 the U.S. Census Bureau revealed that 154,000 stay-at-home fathers took care of 287,000 children under the age of fifteen, up from 49,000 stay-at-home dads in 1996. The contemporary slate of sitcoms and other programs are showcasing men and women wrestling with their roles in a world far different from that of the 1950s and 1960s.

Decoding TV

As implied in the *Truman Show*, TV has become a mind world. It has also become a kind of village square. Rather than go out and chitchat or gossip in the village square, as medieval people tended to do, we do virtually the same thing by peering daily into the complicated lives of reality television personages. Talk shows allow modern-day people to reveal and confess their "sins" or heart-wrenching stories in public. A large viewing audience can thus participate cathartically in other people's acts of self-revelation, repentance, or emotional healing. Television is a locus for discussing moral issues, acted out upon a media stage that has replaced the pulpit as the platform from which they are discussed publicly. Television hosts, like medieval priests, comment morally upon each case, deriving general moral principles from it.

Television programming meshes fictional narrative with moral and social messages. Documentary programs in particular showcase real-life events, often bolstered by dramatic portrayals of these events, so that appropriate social lessons can be learned. And genre channels allow individuals to navigate the social universe through the screen. The channels include: cultural/educational channels (Discovery Channel, Arts & Entertainment Channel, the Learning Channel), movie channels (Home Box Office, Showtime, the Movie Network), news channels (CNN, the Weather Channel, Fox News), music channels (MTV, VH-1), religious channels

(Vision television, the Christian Network), government channels (C-Span, S-Span), sports channels (ESPN, TSN), shopping channels (Home Shopping Network, QVC), animation channels (the Cartoon network), and the list could go on and on. Television also provides access to many other kinds of specialized programs, from erotic movies to wrestling and boxing tournaments, video game channels, musical channels for highly specialized tastes, and services specializing in news headlines, program listings, weather updates, and the like.

But this plethora of choices has actually started to erode the unifying power of TV to influence society as a group. People once watched programs such as *All in the Family* and debated the issues presented on that program in their social milieus. Now, it is unlikely that people will watch the same programs at the same time as a communal audience. This fragments interpretation and reaction to programs and, consequently, diminishes the control that television has over social trends. As a consequence, television is starting to lose its hegemony as a social text. Nonetheless, the impact television has had on society cannot be overstated, as discussed in this and previous chapters.

The postmodernist culture has also diminished TV's power. When cleverly designed programs such as *24* attempt to bring out the absurdity of war, they do so in a stylistic thriller fashion, which leaves audiences thrilled but not necessarily socially motivated. The protagonist in the series, Bauer, appears tired of war, which has cost him not only physically but psychologically as well. He keeps fighting, but for people, rather than for political ideologies. In typical postmodern fashion, the series has a few good guys, a few bad guys, and in between a lot of question marks. The audience is suspended in the simulacrum. There are no James Bond–type victories over evil; just nagging questions.

But, in its own way, TV continues to be a locus for debating social issues even in the Internet Age. Take, for example, the changing views of masculinity in American Society. Early sitcoms like *Father Knows Best* and *The Adventures of Ozzie and Harriet* sculpted the father figure to fit the template of the traditional patriarchal family. The father was in charge, with his wife working behind the scenes to maintain harmony among the family members. Males were portrayed as strong, silent, but family-bound people. There were two notable exceptions to this portrayal pattern: *The Honeymooners* and *I Love Lucy*, both of which revolved around strong-willed wives who were, in effect, precursors of later feminist characters on television.

In the 1960s and early 1970s the mythology of masculinity changed drastically. The television father was portrayed more as a ludicrous character than as a sage. The sitcom that reflected this new subtext perfectly was *All in the Family*. In the early 1970s, the North American continent was divided, ideologically and emotionally, into two camps—those who supported the views and attitudes of the sitcom's father figure, Archie Bunker, a staunch defender of the Vietnam War, and those who despised the war and thus the persona of Archie Bunker. What was happening inside the fictional Bunker family was apparently happening in families across the continent. North American society had entered into a period of turmoil and bitter debate over such controversial issues as war, racism, the role of women in society, and the workability of the patriarchal family. The 1950s mythology of men as sages was also challenged in the same decade by sitcoms such as *The Mary Tyler Moore Show*, *Rhoda*, *Maude*, *The Days and Nights of Molly Dodd*, *Cagney and Lacey*, and others that portrayed strong, independent women.

The total deconstruction of the mythology took place in sitcoms from the mid-1980s to the late 1990s. A typical example was *Married . . . with Children*, a morbid parody of fatherhood, macho men, and the nuclear family. The father on that program, Al Bundy, was little more than a physical brute, who was hardly deserving of the title of *father*. Indeed, as the name of the sitcom suggested, he was merely married and just happened to have children (who incidentally were just as shallow as he was—Bud, his boorish, sex-crazed son, and Kelly, his empty-headed and over-sexed daughter.

It is interesting to note that in the midst of the reconfiguration, *The Cosby Show*—a throwback to the 1950s—achieved success throughout the 1980s. In hindsight, there were a number of likely reasons for its success. First and foremost, was the fact the Bill Cosby himself was a great comedian who could easily endear himself to a large audience. (This was, of course, long before allegations surfaced in 2014 that he had abused numerous women over the past decades.) But, more importantly, *The Cosby Show* was an appropriate counterpart to *Married . . . with Children*, reflecting an escalating cultural war in America over representations of the family, masculinity, and womanhood on television. Some audiences were searching for television father figures who were more traditional, albeit gentle and understanding, rather than stern. Bill Cosby, at least according to the public perception of him at the time, fit this image perfectly. But there was a difference. Unlike the wife in *Father Knows Best*, Cosby's wife had a more assertive role to play in the family. The "new-look" patriarchal family provided a symbolism of reassurance in traditional values to those who perceived that the world was in moral flux.

In the 2000s, the representation of masculinity in sitcoms became highly diversified, with gay fathers, single fathers, and other "father types" becoming the subject matter of the sitcoms, showing that television was indeed a social mirror, reflecting what is going on in society and adapting to it textually. Television is fiction, but its representations come off as real because of its ability to tap into trends and changing ideologies. The meshing of the imaginary and the real have always been part of its power. Many of today's sitcoms are designed specifically for audiences with diverse views of traditional symbols and mores.

While there are now more inclusive masculinities, no longer ensconced in homophobia, marginalization, or subordination, it is difficult to pinpoint where masculinity is going. Once again, TV is stepping into the debate with programs such as *Big Bang Theory*, which premiered in 2007. It is centered on five characters living in Pasadena, California, as roommates: Leonard and Sheldon are physicists; Penny is a waitress and aspiring actress who lives across the hall; and engineer Howard and astrophysicist Raj are geeky coworkers of Leonard and Sheldon. Other characters have been scripted into the sitcom in subsequent years. Scientific theories are discussed and debated on virtually every episode, highlighting how much masculinity has changed in sitcom humor—nerds and geeks are as attractive and charming as are macho men. Science is also the basis upon which romantic partnerships are formed on the program—the "sexiness" of having an interest in science is, in fact, a subtext of the sitcom. The main male characters revel in reading and collecting comics, reflecting a geeky attitude to the modern world itself. Dating and romance revolve around the interests of the partners, not just sentimental feelings. There is no macho courtship tradition here, just connecting through intellectual interests. In portraying masculinity in ways that contrast with past portrayals, this sitcom is a treatise on changing gender roles, relations, patterns of understanding.

EFFECTS

Marshall McLuhan was among the first to decry that television had an impact far greater than the content it communicated. Indeed, television has constituted a platform-medium for blending the comedic and the real into a simulacrum. As Orson Welles so aptly put it, we hate to love it, in the same way that we hate to love fattening foods: "I hate television. I hate it as much as peanuts. But I can't stop eating peanuts" (Welles 1956: 12).

Mythologization

One effect of television can be called the *celebrity-making* or the *mythologizing effect*, joining the movies and other media in this function. Like

any type of stage (or more accurately screen in this case), television transforms its personages into mythic characters by simply showcasing them on
the screen, where they are seen as suspended in real time and space, in a
mythic world of their own. This is why meeting television personalities
causes great enthusiasm and excitement in many people. They are otherworldly figures who have "stepped out" of the screen to take on human
proportions. Television personages are the contemporary equivalents of the
graven images of the Bible. The same effect is produced by other media, as
we have seen. But since television reaches more people, the mythologizing
effect is more widespread.

In the 1950s Clayton Moore, the actor who portrayed the Lone
Ranger, and Fess Parker, who played Davy Crockett, became nationwide
heroes to children and their parents alike. Spin-offs ensued, with Lone
Ranger and Davy Crockett toys, costumes, comics, pop songs, and so on.
They became icons that children idolized and that could easily influence
children in various subtle ways. In 1977, after the Fonz (the main character
on *Happy Days*) got a library card in one of the sitcom's episodes, nearly
five hundred thousand young viewers apparently did so as well. However,
in the Internet Age everything is increasingly short-lived, including TV
celebrities. While in the 1950s a personage such as Ed Sullivan would be
known across society, today an announcer or a talk show host has a more
limited celebrity status.

Fabrication

The term *history fabrication effect* can be used to refer to the fact that
television has often been the maker of history, not just its documenter.
As agenda-setting theory has pointed out (chapter 2), the events that are
showcased on television are felt as being more significant and historically
meaningful to society than those that are not. A political or military conflict
that gets airtime becomes a historical event; one that does not is ignored.
Television imbues a cause with significance. Political and social protesters
frequently inform the news media of their intentions, and then dramatically stage their demonstrations for the cameras. Sports events such as the
World Series, the Super Bowl, the Stanley Cup Playoffs or the World Cup
of soccer are transformed by television coverage into battles of Herculean
proportion. Events such as the John Kennedy and Lee Harvey Oswald assassinations, the Vietnam War, the Watergate hearings, the Rodney King
beating, the O. J. Simpson trial, the death of Lady Diana, the Bill Clinton
sex scandal, the 9/11 attack, the Iraq war, the election of a black presi-

dent, the Ebola crisis, and so on are perceived as portentous and prophetic historical events through the filter of television coverage. People make up their minds about the guilt or innocence of others by watching news and interview programs; they see certain behaviors as laudable or damnable by tuning into talk shows or docudramas; and the list could go on and on.

People experience history through television, not just by reading about it in a book or studying it at school. Edward R. Murrow of *CBS News* became a society-wide hero when, on his *See It Now* documentary in 1954, he fought back against fanatical senator Joseph McCarthy, who at the time was leading a campaign against a purported Communist subversion of the media. Murrow used footage of McCarthy's own press conferences to expose the excesses of his campaign. Murrow's rebuke led to the Senate's reprimand of McCarthy, which paralyzed him from taking further political action. The horrific images of the Vietnam War that were transmitted into people's homes daily in the late 1960s and early 1970s mobilized social protest, bringing about an end to the war. Significantly, an MTV flag was hoisted by East German youths over the Berlin Wall as they tore it down in 1989. More people watched the wedding of England's Prince Charles and Princess Diana, and later Diana's funeral, than had ever before in human history observed such events communally. The Bill Clinton–Monica Lewinsky sex scandal allowed common people to become privy to the sexual flaws of a powerful political figure. The images of the two planes smashing into the World Trade Center buildings on September 11, 2001, brought about an international reaction, whose consequences are still being felt.

The history-making power of television has led many to actually stage events for the cameras. The social critic W. T. Anderson (1992: 125–130) calls these appropriately "pseudoevents," because they are never completely spontaneous, but somewhat planned for the purpose of playing to television's huge audiences. The American invasion of Grenada on October 25, 1983, the Gulf War in 1991, the attack on Afghanistan in 2001, and the war in Iraq starting in 2003 were concomitantly real events and pseudo-events. The actual military operations and conflicts were real events. But the reporting of those wars was part news reporting, part drama. As propaganda theory predicted (chapter 2), reporters were censored and kept away from the more brutal action so that the news coverage could be stylized and managed more effectively. The idea was to fabricate a military and moral victory for the viewing public. Pseudoevents constitute unscripted reality television at its best, because they mesh reality (the real killing and terrorizing of people) with news commentary and docudrama representations. As Anderson (1992: 126–27) aptly puts it, the "media take the raw material of experience and fashion it into stories; they retell the stories to us, and we call them reality."

Of course, other media fabricate (or have fabricated) history as well. Books written about wars, historical eras, and so on have shaped how we perceive certain events of the past. However, with the rise of television in the 1950s, there is little doubt that most people started perceiving history through the television screen rather than through print. The history-making power of television has changed the way we perceive history itself—not as a story with a long arc, but rather as a kaleidoscopic pastiche of narrative, bits of information, and images. Channels such as CNN are formatted in precisely this way, with sidebars and captions giving information on sports, the weather, and subsidiary news items as announcers recite the news or discuss social issues. Such a format affords viewers little time to reflect on the topics, implications, and meanings contained in televised information. The camera moves in to selected aspects of a situation, to show a face that cares, that is suffering, that is happy, that is angry, and then shifts to the cool face of an anchorman or anchorwoman to tell us what it's all about. The news items, the film footage, and the commentaries are all fast paced and brief. "Within such a stylistic environment," remarks Stuart Ewen (1988: 265), "the news is beyond comprehension." Thus it is that as "nations and people are daily sorted out into boxes marked 'good guys,' 'villains,' 'victims,' and 'lucky ones,' style becomes the essence, reality becomes the appearance" (Ewen 1988: 265–66).

The above discussion is not meant to imply that television has not been used as a powerful medium of social protest or as an agent for social change, as mentioned several times in this chapter. When asked about the stunning defeat of Communism in Eastern Europe in the late 1980s, the Polish leader Lech Walesa was reported to have said that it "all came from the television set," implying that television had undermined the stability of the communist world's relatively poor and largely sheltered lifestyle with images of consumer delights seen on Western programs and commercials. The paradox of TV is the paradox of pop culture generally; it involves both fiction and reality, blending them in such ways that are imperceptible and thus subconsciously powerful.

TV IN THE INTERNET AGE

Like previous media, television has converged with the Internet, as programs on TV now have websites that provide either more coverage, possibilities to see programs at any time, follow-up commentary, and so on. The digital distribution of TV content through the Internet by streaming technology by the major broadcasters is now called Internet TV. The term *Web TV*, on the other hand, is more specifically used to refer to programs or videos created specifically for the Web. An example is Netflix's *House of Cards*, which was nominated for an Emmy. In practice, though, the two terms are used synonymously.

The Internet has actually bolstered the power of conventional television to entertain and influence audiences in time-independent ways. However, in so doing it has lost its communal audience power—that is, it has lost its ability to bring audiences together at the same time to view the same content and then to debate it broadly. On sitcoms such as *All in the Family* and *Seinfeld*, large audiences watched the shows at the same time and then developed opinions about social issues that they discussed at workplaces, at coffee shops, and the like. The new distribution media have fractured the "communal audience effect," as it can be called, rendering television less influential as an agent of change.

Web TV programs such as *Husbands, My Gay Roommate,* and *Dr. Horrible's Sing-Along Blog* are becoming popular, often eclipsing in content value those on regular TV. Distributed by YouTube, Netflix, Newsgrounds, Crackle, and Blip.tv, these programs have made it possible for a new type of television industry to emerge, with its own producers, executives, script-writers, and actors. In 2013 Netflix made TV history when several of its programs—*House of Cards, Arrested Development, Hemlock Grove*—were nominated for Emmys. Given the rise of Web TV, the International Academy of Web Television was founded in 2009 to adjudicate programs and give out their Streamy Awards. So successful is Web TV becoming that major entertainment industries are now planning to produce Web-based programs on a regular basis.

As in the case of pop music, it is now possible to get involved in DIY television because of easy-to-use uploading and streaming software. Anyone can now produce a TV show him- or herself, edit it, and upload it for international viewing virtually for free. Incredibly, such programs are becoming popular, with their own celebrities, and thus have the potential to transform television marketing. Some Web shows have become so popular that producers are building studio facilities and now entering into partnerships with sponsors and conventional TV producers. Web TV shows have fervent niche audiences and new technology platforms, such as Blip .tv and Vimeo, which are proliferating and making professional production an easy thing to access. Advertisers have taken notice and are putting their ads more and more on Web TV programs, in pop-up, pre-roll, post-roll, and mid-roll formats.

Unlike conventional TV, it is obviously impossible to categorize the Web TV text into genre categories, to decide what constitutes a webisode, and what differentiates it from a conventional TV episode. It is thus changing not only the way we view TV but also the critical apparatus used to understand it, making most previous critical approaches virtually irrelevant. What makes Web TV attractive to people is that it provides opportunities to watch content that matches one's individual tastes, whereas network and cable TV producers focus on audiences and thus on general content that can be appreciated communally. As Bob Dylan aptly put it in one of his songs, "The times, they are a-changin'."

9

ADVERTISING AND BRANDING

It is useless to invent something that can't be sold.

—Thomas Edison (1847–1931)

As discussed in chapter 3, the constitution, development, and spread of pop culture are tied to mediation and the marketplace. In the decade following World War I, the American economy embarked on a period of spectacular growth. Spurred on by the good times and a desire to assume a modern and forward-looking worldview, large numbers of Americans adopted new freer lifestyles, making entertainment an objective. The booming economy and fast-paced life of the decade gave it the nickname of the Roaring Twenties. It was at that point in time that a veritable pop culture emerged in stage spectacles, music, cinema, print, and radio. In the same decade shopping for the fun of it became widespread as department stores started spreading all over the United States. Advertising became a part of the overall social system, developing a partnership with pop culture that has remained indelible to this day. As the Frankfurt School philosopher Herbert Marcuse (1964: 18) suggested, everything started to be "sold" and "packaged" in the same way as commercial products.

> If mass communications blend together harmoniously, and often unnoticeably, art, politics, religion, and philosophy with commercials, they bring these realms of culture to their common denominator—the commodity form. The music of the soul is also the music of salesmanship. Exchange value, not truth value, counts.

The purpose of this chapter is look at this partnership. Advertising has become so intrinsically intertwined with pop culture that it is difficult, if not impossible, to keep the two distinct in our minds. Indeed, advertising itself has become a veritable genre in pop culture fare, being both a sponsoring source and a creative impulse.

ADVERTISING

The contemporary advertising industry was founded at the threshold of the twentieth century on the premise that sales of a product would increase if the product could be linked to lifestyle and socially significant trends. Indirect proof that product advertising has achieved its goal of blurring the line between the product and reality can be seen in the fact that it is now used as a persuasion technique by anyone in society who wants to influence people to do something—to endorse a political candidate, to support a cause, and so on and so forth. Business firms, political parties, candidates, social organizations, special-interest groups, and governments alike use advertising routinely to create favorable images of themselves or of their causes.

Using both verbal and nonverbal techniques to make its messages as persuasive as need be, advertising has become an integral category of pop culture studies. Many ads and commercials are often more entertaining than are the programs they sponsor.

Historical Sketch

The term *advertising* derives from the medieval Latin verb *advertere* "to direct one's attention to." Advertising designates any type or form of public announcement intended to promote the sale of specific commodities or services, or to spread some kind of social or political message. The first advertising materials of human civilization were the many outdoor signs displayed above the shop doors of ancient cities of the Middle East, as early as 3000 BCE. The ancient Greeks and Romans also hung signs outside their shops. Since few people could read, the merchants of the era used recognizable visual symbols carved in stone, clay, or wood for their signs. Throughout history, picture signs in marketplaces and temples have constituted popular media for disseminating information and for promoting the barter and sale of goods and services. With the invention of the printing press in the fifteenth century, signs and posters could be printed quickly and cheaply, and posted in public places or inserted in books, pamphlets, newspapers, and the like. The printing press also spawned a new form of advertising, known as the *handbill*—literally a leaflet distributed by hand.

AN ADVERTISING TIMELINE

1625: The first ad appears in an English newspaper.

1704: The first classified ads in Colonial America run in the *Boston News-Letter*, featuring land deals and ship cargoes.

1735: Benjamin Franklin sells ad space in the *Pennsylvania Gazette*.

1830s: The penny press becomes the first advertising-supported media outlet.

1841: A proto ad agency is established in Boston by Volney Palmer.

1860s: Advertising is incorporated into magazines.

1869: The first true ad agency is established by N. W. Ayer in Philadelphia.

1871: P. T. Barnum establishes his Greatest Show on Earth, creating a wave of publicity stunts, posters, and the like, which brings about the modern advertising age.

1887: *Ladies Home Journal* is designed for consumer advertising.

1914: The Federal Trade Commission is established in 1914 to help monitor advertising practices.

1922: Newspaper columnist Walter Lippmann publishes a controversial book, *Public Opinion*, in which he illustrates how slogans and other persuasive strategies shape public perception. The first radio commercial is aired.

1950s–1960s: Thirty-second and sixty-second television commercials interrupting programs become routine.

1957: Vance Packard's *The Hidden Persuaders* is published, warning people of the dangers of advertising.

1984: Apple's Macintosh commercial at the halftime of the Super Bowl shows that advertising had become an art form in itself.

mid-1980s: Brand placement and a general partnership between advertising and pop culture solidifies.

1994: Internet banner advertising gets started.

1995: The Internet advertising agency DoubleClick is founded.

2000s: The Internet and the World Wide Web become increasingly attractive as sites for advertising. New forms of advertising, such as pop-ups, appear. The Internet is also used to assay consumer likes and dislikes of products and of ads themselves. Brand logos are scattered everywhere, from hockey rink boards to all kinds of common objects. Google and Facebook become increasingly important sites for advertisers.

2010s–ongoing: Advertising becomes common on smart phones and tablets and app-based computing; in effect, mobile advertising becomes huge, as advertising migrates to all kinds of locales and sites.

This was more effective than posters or signs because it could be reproduced and distributed to many people living near and far apart.

By the latter part of the seventeenth century, print advertisements started appearing regularly in newspapers. The *London Gazette* became the first newspaper to reserve a section exclusively for advertising purposes for

a fee. Several businesses were established in England for the specific purpose of creating newspaper ads for merchants and artisans. They designed
the ad texts in the style of modern classifieds, without illustrative support.
However, the ads showed some of the same rhetorical zest of contemporary
ads, tailoring the language style to suit the wealthy clients who bought and
read newspapers.

The increasing use and influence of advertising in the nineteenth century led to the establishment of advertising agencies. Among the first was
the one by Philadelphia entrepreneur Volney B. Palmer in 1842. By 1849,
Palmer had offices in New York, Boston, and Baltimore in addition to his
Philadelphia office. In 1865, George P. Rowell began contracting with local newspapers as a go-between with clients. A few years later, in 1869, N.
W. Ayer and Son, another Philadelphia advertising agency, became a rival
of Rowell and Palmer. In time, the firm hired writers and artists to create
print ads and to carry out complete advertising campaigns for clients. It
thus became the first ad agency in the modern sense of the word. By 1900,
agencies in the United States were writing ads for all kinds of clients and
were starting to assume responsibility for full advertising campaigns. By the
1920s, such agencies had become themselves large business enterprises. The
agencies were constantly developing new design techniques and strategic
methods designed to influence shopping patterns. At this point in time
advertising came to be perceived primarily as an instrument of persuasion
by corporate executives. Business and psychology had joined forces, which
helped the former build a conceptual bridge between the commodity and
the consumer's desires and aspirations. Advertisers started to pay close attention to trends in the ever-expanding pop culture world, and often used,
in the form of jingles and slogans, the same kinds of popular musical and
linguistic styles found in pop culture.

In the 1920s, the increased use of electricity led to the possibility of
further entrenching advertising into the social landscape through the use of
new technologies. For example, electricity made possible the illuminated
outdoor poster. At around the same time, photoengraving and other new
printing technologies helped both the editorial and advertising departments
of magazines create truly effective illustrative material. The radio commercial—a mini-narrative or musical jingle—became a highly popular form of
advertising, since it could reach masses of potential customers, print literate
or not, instantaneously. The commercial became even more influential
with the advent of television in the early 1950s. Recently, the Internet has
come forward to complement and supplement both the print and commercial (radio and television) forms of advertising. Internet advertisers use

graphics, audio, and various visual techniques to enhance the effectiveness of their messages. Advertising mirrors and shapes cultural trends in a synergistic fashion. And most of us simply enjoy them. There are now even websites that feature ads for their own sake, so that people can view them for their aesthetic qualities alone, and thus enjoy them as they would any other type of modern performance or spectacle. Needless to say, advertising can now be found on mobile devices and virtually any other digital locus that involves large numbers of consumers.

There are several general techniques of advertising, no matter on which media it appears, including *positioning, image-creation, mythologization, aestheticization, reality advertising*, and *simulation. Positioning* is the placing or targeting of a product for a specific group, known as a market segment. For example, ads for Budweiser beer are normally positioned for a middle-class young male audience, whereas ads for Chanel perfume are positioned for a middle- to upper-class female audience. Ads for these products are found in media that cater to the interests of those two demographic markets. The advertising of the Mercedes Benz automobile is aimed at socially upscale car buyers; the advertising of Dodge vans is aimed, instead, at middle-class suburban dwellers. Similarly, the respective ads and commercials will be positioned in media that cater to the interests of each market demographic.

Creating an *image* for a product inheres in fashioning a "personality" for it so that it can be positioned for specific market populations. The image is an amalgam of the product's name, packaging, logo, price, and overall presentation that makes it recognizable as a symbol standing for a personality type. Take beer as an example. What kinds of people drink Budweiser? And what kinds drink Stella Artois instead? Answers to these questions would typically include remarks about the educational level, class, social attitudes, and so on of the consumer. In other words, for the advertiser the personality of the one who drinks Budweiser is deemed to be different from the one who drinks Stella Artois. In many ads we see the former as a down-to-earth character who simply wants to "hang out with friends"; the latter can be seen instead as a smooth sophisticated type who hangs out in upper-scale venues. The idea behind creating an image for the product is to speak directly to particular types of individuals, not to everyone, so that the targeted individuals can see their own personalities represented in the lifestyle images created by the relevant advertisements.

Mythologization refers to the use of unconscious themes to create an image for some products. For instance, the quest for beauty, the conquest of death, among other such themes, are constantly being worked into the specific images that advertisers create for some beauty and cosmetic products. The people who appear in the relevant ads and commercials are attractive people, with an unreal, mythic quality about the way they look. The modern advertiser stresses not the product, but the unconscious or mythic meanings that may be associated with the product.

The term *aestheticization* refers to the use of the same kinds of techniques employed by visual artists. Perfume ads that show women surrounded by a dark void or appearing mysteriously out of nothing, as in a dream, are created according to the principles of surrealist art, based on the workings of the subconscious through fantastic imagery and the incongruous juxtaposition of subject matter. Many ads for perfumes are essentially surrealist artworks.

Real-life advertising refers to the use of real people and celebrities in ads and commercials, rather than professional actors. Real people and celebrities are often more interesting to consumers than are actors. The subtext is a transparent one—anyone can become beautiful, sexy, and young-looking with a little help from a brand of perfume, a clothing item, and so on. The strategy connects with consumers in the same way that reality television does.

Simulative advertising can be defined as the use of styles, trends, and language present in various domains of popular culture to create advertising texts. A classic example goes back to 2002, when Mazda commercials simulated the surrealistic feeling of looking at a computer screen. The suggestion was that cars are toys that can be manipulated on a screen, permitting an escape from reality into a fantasy world of total control. In the commercial, a young boy was shown looking at the cars, turning to his audience with the childish exclamation, "Zoom, zoom."

Advertisers have always been among the most creative users of new technologies. Google is, actually, threatening the survival of the traditional ad agency because it collects money from advertisers not on the basis of promise, but on the basis of performance. In addition, it sells directly to advertisers and provides free services, such as templates for creating ads, for which agencies have traditionally charged. The same kinds of advantages are offered by mobile device advertising. Currently, advertisers are adapting their ads to mobile devices, creating ads designed specifically for this channel of communication.

Advertising has always been an issue of debate and a target of legislation across the world. In some countries, there are laws prohibiting or restricting the use of women in advertisements unless the product is relevant for women as consumers. In other countries, advertising for sanitary products and toilet paper is forbidden for reasons of modesty. Clearly, in the global village some societies are scrambling to protect themselves against the images that emanate from the advertising image factory.

But already in 1922, the American journalist Walter Lippmann argued that the growth of advertising had a powerful effect on people, changing human behavior for the worse, and affecting people's politics, familial relations, and general worldview. In 1957 Vance Packard's book *The Hidden Persuaders* led to a public outcry against the use of brainwashing techniques by advertisers. But advertising carries on, simply because it is good for business. It has succeeded more than any economic process or sociopolitical movement in promoting consumerism as a way of life. It has done so primarily by proposing marketplace solutions to emotional and social problems. Ads and commercials offer the same kinds of promises and hopes to which religions and social philosophies once held exclusive rights. To counteract advertising's hegemony, a movement consisting of anti-advertising activists called *culture jammers* (Lasn 2000) was formed in the early 2000s. Through their website and magazine *(Adbusters)*, culture jammers provide satirical critiques of advertising, with clever parodies of ads (called *subvertisements*), along with articles and discussions on how to recognize the advertiser's manipulation. But people like advertising and may resent others telling them that such enjoyment is victimization. Moreover, advertising is not in itself disruptive of the value systems of the cultural mainstream; rather, it reflects shifts already present in the mainstream.

Integrating with Pop Culture

We hardly reflect upon the degree to which pop culture celebrities, spectacles, and events have become integrated with sponsors. Whereas once the boards of hockey rinks were white, today they display all kinds of brand names, logos, and other advertising material. This branding of hockey can be seen even more dramatically in European hockey leagues where even players' jerseys are filled with brand logos. A similar portrait could be drawn for other sports and, indeed, for almost any popular spectacle or event.

The line between advertising and pop culture is now virtually nonexistent. The same styles and trends characterize both. For instance, naming practices in the advertising world are adapted to changing times. Brands named with alphabet and number symbols, or with acronyms, are now common. These cleverly suggest techno-savvy and a text-messaging style of writing brand names (Frankel 2004, Cook 2004):

- iPod
- Xbox
- PS3
- 2BFree (clothes)
- Spex Appeal
- Xylocaine
- Glam Gurlz
- Minds@Work

Actually, this strategy was used long before the advent of text messaging on mobile devices. Brands such as Cheez Whiz, Spic and Span, Wheetabix, Kool cigarettes, and others were named in a similar way. Brand names such as Pret-O-Lite, U All Kno After Dinner Mints, Phiteezi Shoes, and U-Rub-IN actually go back to the 1920s (Cook 2004: 44).

The integration with pop culture can also be seen in such trends as Dove's Self-Esteem or Real Women campaign, where real women, with "real curves," were enlisted to be the models in ads and commercials. In contrast to professional models who are attractive, sexy, ultra-thin, and have a flawless complexion, the Dove models hit closer to home with female consumers.

As mentioned, campaigns against advertising have sprung up from time to time. Aware of the popularity of such campaigns, advertisers have created their own anti-advertising forms, producing ads that spoof other ads. The rise of digital media makes it possible for advertisers to reach people at all times of the day and anywhere on Earth. But as people become more and more skeptical of the traditional "sales pitch," and now have the capacity to critique ads through social media, the advertiser has joined the mix by adopting the satirical tone that anti-advertisers have used in the past. An example is Newcastle Brown Ale, which used the Internet to mock the big advertising campaigns on conventional media, implying that it could communicate its message on a shoestring budget. The satirical approach of the brand went viral on social media, catapulting it onto mainstream media and making its campaign hugely successful. The Internet is averse to traditional advertising; it has its own attitudes. In effect, ads and commercials that make fun of advertising acknowledge the fact that most people today know that it is psychologically manipulative. The anti-advertising mode of advertising thus connects empathically with potential consumers. It is a contemporary example of co-option—that is, of tapping into emerging groupthink and then using it cleverly for advertising purposes.

AD CULTURE

As the foregoing discussion implies, advertising has become an intrinsic part of modern society. It even has its own prize categories at film festivals. Advertising is adaptive, constantly seeking out new forms of representation and media channels reflecting fluctuations in social trends and values. Although we may be inclined to condemn its objectives, as an aesthetic experience we invariably enjoy advertising, in the same way we enjoy any spectacle or performance. Advertisements sway, please, and seduce.

Aware of this, restrictive legislative measures to constrain advertisers are now common. Such restrictions mirror the prohibitionists' efforts to ban alcohol and its attendant lifestyle during the Roaring Twenties. Campaigns of this kind often backfire. In early 1998, the U.S. Congress was mulling over banning all lifestyle symbols from cigarette advertising. In response, the ad creators came up with ingenious alternatives. For instance, an ad for Salem cigarettes featured a pair of peppers curled together to look like a pair of lips, with a cigarette dangling from them. Benson and Hedges ads in the same year portrayed cigarettes acting like people—floating in swimming pools, lounging in armchairs, and so on. Ironically, such government-permissible advertising was a huge success, as cigarette-smoking rates among young people rose dramatically.

The Ad Campaign

The integration of advertising into the cultural system of a society is perpetrated and reinforced by *advertising campaigns*, which can be defined simply as the use of a series of slightly different ads and commercials based on the same theme, characters, jingles, and techniques over a specified time period. An ad campaign is comparable to a musical piece, consisting of theme and variations. One of the primary functions of ad campaigns is to guarantee that the product's image is in step with the times. The Budweiser ad campaigns of the 1980s and early 1990s emphasized rural ruggedness and female sexuality. The actors in the commercials were untamed, rugged, handsome men and the women their prey. In the early 2000s, the same brand changed its image to keep in step with the changing times. Its new ad campaign showed young urban males who hung around together, loved sports, and did whatever such males tend to do together. So appealing was the *Whassup!* campaign that its signature catch phrase was joked about on talk shows, parodied on websites, mimicked in other media, and used by people commonly in conversations. In the 2010s Budweiser has again changed its approach, showcasing young people, male and female, at parties and simply hanging around to have fun. The makers of Budweiser have clearly adapted their advertising style to be sensitive to social changes and trends.

Campaign slogans normally announce a new chapter or phase in a brand's history. For example, McDonald's had, for many years, used the slogan *We do it all for you*, indicating that the eatery was there to serve those families in which both partners worked. The restaurant catered to children with built-in playgrounds, free toys, a clown named Ronald McDonald, and so on. The campaign lasted too long. In the early 2000s, the world had changed drastically, and McDonald's was on the verge of bankruptcy. Cleverly, the company changed its slogan and, thus, its campaign strategy to *I'm lovin' it*, recognizing a new form of individualism in society. It also altered its menu to accommodate those who espoused a healthier view of fast food. As a consequence, the company rebounded substantively.

Co-option

As the Budweiser and McDonald's cases illustrate, the most effective advertising strategy is not only to keep up with the times, but also to co-opt trends. In the 1960s, for example, advertisers co-opted the lifestyle images and imitated the language of the hippies to promote their products. The strategy worked brilliantly, given that the images and language were counterculture ones. Advertising models wore counterculture clothing fashions to promote all kinds of products; counterculture music style was used as background in commercials, and so on. In this way, people could feel that they were ersatz participants in the ongoing youth revolution.

Campaigns such as the Pepsi Generation and the Coke universal brotherhood (*"I'd like to teach the world to sing in perfect harmony"*) ones directly incorporated the rhetoric and symbolism of counterculture youths, thus creating the illusion that the goals of the hippies and of the soft drink manufacturers were one and the same. Rebellion through purchasing became the subliminal thread woven into the ad campaigns. The campaigns for the Dodge Rebellion and Oldsmobile Youngmobile followed the soft drink ones, etching into the nomenclature of the cars themselves the powerful connotations of rebellion and defiance. Even a sewing company came forward to urge people on to join its own type of surrogate revolution, hence its slogan, *You don't let the establishment make your world; don't let it make your clothes.* By claiming symbolically and rhetorically to "join the revolution," advertising created its own real revolution. Since the late 1960s, the worlds of advertising, marketing, youth trends, and entertainment have become synergistically intertwined.

Today, the integration of ad campaigns into groupthink has become so ubiquitous that we hardly realize how powerful it is. The anti-advertising strategy mentioned above is a case in point. As Canadian social activist Naomi Klein (2000) has emphasized, modern-day consumerist economic systems depend almost entirely on the partnership that has been forged among the previously autonomous worlds of business, media, and entertainment. It is no exaggeration to say that the history of pop culture is intrinsically interwoven with the history of advertising. In looking back over the last century, it is obvious that the language of advertisers, the style of ad campaigns, and their peculiar textualities are taken from creative domains, from cinematography to pop music. As McLuhan (1964: 24) aptly put it, advertising is the "art of the modern world."

BRANDING

The technique of integrating products into pop culture is called *branding*. The intent of the technique is to tap into cultural tendencies that govern emerging lifestyles, values, beliefs, and the like, turning the product into a symbolic means for becoming part of those tendencies. As Alex Frankel (2004: 81) aptly puts it: "The most common marketing definition of a brand is that it is a *promise*—an unspoken pact between a company and a consumer to deliver a particular experience."

In the medieval and Renaissance eras, sponsorship of the arts fell to the Church or the nobility. In the modern world the sponsors are brand companies. They are the ones who pay for the show. Thus, trends in pop culture cross over to advertising and advertising styles mirror what is emerging in pop culture. This is why pop culture celebrities, from movie actors to sports figures, are often advertising celebrities as well. As P. T. Barnum had cleverly anticipated, consumerism can be fun, especially if advertised to be so.

Consider the case of McDonald's. The hamburger sandwich was introduced to America at the St. Louis World's Fair in 1904. The first hamburger stand was opened up in 1940, in a drive-in near Pasadena, California, by movie theater co-owners Richard and Maurice McDonald. The McDonalds then opened up the first burger joint in 1948. The modern-day restaurant chain was founded in 1955 by Raymond A. Kroc, a distributor of machines for making milk shakes. Kroc learned of a hamburger stand that had eight of the machines. Kroc visited the stand, which was run by the McDonald brothers, and was impressed with how quickly customers were served. Kroc persuaded the owners to let him start a chain of fast-service restaurants under the same name. Kroc opened the first McDonald's restaurant in Des Plaines, Illinois, in 1955. It is significant to note that this event coincided with the rise of youth culture in the 1950s. The number of McDonald's eateries began to proliferate, as young people flocked to it. By 1961 Kroc had established more than 200 restaurants, building McDonald's into a powerful business.

The astute Kroc realized that in order to survive in the long run, he needed to attract adults as well. Aware that fewer and fewer families had the time to prepare meals within the household, he wisely decided to change the image of McDonald's into a place where the family could eat together. His plan worked beyond expectations. En masse families started to eat at McDonald's more and more often. The golden arches logo reflected the chain's new image perfectly. Arches reverberate with mythic symbolism—they beckon good people to march through them where they can expect a world of cleanliness, friendliness, hospitality, and intrinsic values. Kroc made sure that McDonald's was run like a religion. From the menu to the uniforms, he exacted and imposed standardization, in the same way that religions do.

Kroc's advertising campaigns reinforced this new image effectively, entrenching it throughout society. McDonald's was a place that would *do it all for you*, keeping family members united at meal times. Many outlets even installed miniature amusement parks in them for children. Kids' meals were introduced throughout the restaurant chain. As a family-oriented company, McDonald's started sponsoring Ronald McDonald House Charities, which operates hundreds of Ronald McDonald Houses worldwide in which the families of critically ill children may stay when the young patients undergo medical treatment away from their homes.

The world soon changed and McDonald's was also bound to change, in order to fit in with new patterns and trends in society. Its *I'm lovin' it* campaign came to the rescue, as did a change in its menu to accommodate healthier foods. The eatery also advertises new movies and other events in popular culture. The same pattern of merging with changes in the world can be witnessed throughout the marketplace, as businesses attempt to keep up with changes in the world and incorporate them into their brand image.

Placement

Brand-name computers displayed visibly in movies, designer clothes shown prominently in sitcoms, and so on and so forth are now so common that hardly anyone realizes that it is a branding strategy, known more specifically as *placement*. In the 1940s and 1950s placement was a simple matter. In radio programs such as Texaco Theater, General Electric Theater, Kraft Theater, the program itself was associated exclusively with one sponsor. The same pattern extended to early television programming. The movies entered the placement world in 1982 when the extraterrestrial creature in Steven Spielberg's *E.T.* was seen snacking on Reese's Pieces—increasing sales for the product enormously.

In 1983 movie actor Tom Cruise donned a pair of Wayfarers in *Risky Business*, and sales for the product shot up, as did generally the wearing of sunglasses.

Computer and digital devices now appear everywhere, from movies such as *Legally Blonde* (2001), in which the main protagonist, Elle, can be seen using a tangerine clamshell iBook, to *Confessions of a Shopaholic* (2009), where the character Rebecca owns a MacBook. Actually, a list of movies from 2014 shows how extensive brand placement has become, as in each movie numerous brands appear:

- *Non-Stop:* Samsung, Casio, *Eating Well* magazine, *Town & Country* magazine, *New York Times*, SIG Sauer, LG, and others
- *The Lego Movie:* DC comics, Apple, Titleist, and others
- *Ride Along:* Apple, Adidas, BMW, Cheez-It, Samsung, Coca-Cola, Dodge, Xbox, Toyota, Sprite, Ford, Glock, Nike, Powerade, Skillz, and many more
- *Lone Survivor:* Budweiser, Coors, Domino's Pizza, Pepsi, Gatorade, Nestlé, Panasonic, *Time* magazine and others.

It is interesting to note that before the age of modern placement, a number of Hollywood movies from the late 1940s to the early 1960s commented on the psychological dangers posed by advertising's insertion into the social paradigm, becoming indistinguishable from it. Below is a list of relevant movies:

- *The Hucksters* (1947). Clarke Gable plays a New York adman. His duties take him to Hollywood, where he creates a successful radio commercial for "Beautee Soap," which mimics the jingle style of the era. A transparent subtext of the movie is to show how ad agencies control what people see.
- *Mr. Blandings Builds His Dream House* (1948). Cary Grant (also a New York adman) wants to create a blockbuster campaign for the ham product called "Wham." The movie spoofs the ever-broadening advertising culture that was shaping social values more and more.
- *A Letter to Three Wives* (1949). Ann Sothern is a writer of radio soap operas. Her husband is a critic of the media and advertising worlds, which he critiques as vulgarizing American culture. In one scene, the husband states: "The purpose of radio writing, as far as I can see, is to prove to the masses that a deodorant can bring happiness, a mouthwash guarantee success and a laxative attract romance."
- *Callaway Went Thataway* (1951). Fred MacMurray and Dorothy McGuire are partners in an agency that creates a successful TV program based on old western movies, a program sponsored by a cereal called "Corkies." The movie satirizes early television and its dependence on cinematic clichés.
- *A Face in the Crowd* (1957). Andy Griffith plays a hobo who is hired to act in commercials because of his ability to charm consumers by poking fun at the sponsors of programs. The movie constitutes a black parody of advertising culture.
- *Lover Come Back* (1961). Rock Hudson and Doris Day portray executives of rival ad agencies. Hudson lands clients by providing them with sex and alcohol.

Placement is a form of subliminal advertising, that is, the use of some stimulus below the threshold of awareness, perceived by or affecting someone's mind without being aware of it. The publication of Vance Packard's 1957 work on the effects of advertising, *The Hidden Persuaders*, which inspired an outpouring of subsequent studies examining the effects of advertising on individuals and on society at large, is the starting point for analyzing advertising as a subliminal form of persuasion—a field of inquiry that is still prolific and typically contradictory in its findings, theories, and social responses.

The actual theory of subliminal advertising was first enunciated by a market researcher named James Vicary in a 1957 study that he admitted to be fraudulent a few years later. Vicary had apparently flashed the phrases "Eat Popcorn" or "Coca-Cola" on a New Jersey movie theater screen every five seconds as the movies played. The phrases lasted barely three-thousandths of a second so that the audience would not consciously be aware that it had seen them. Sales of popcorn and Coca-Cola, Vicary claimed, soared in the theater at intermission. Vicary's claims were discussed by Vance Packard in his book, which led to a public outcry against the use of brainwashing techniques by advertisers. However, when broadcasters and researchers attempted to repeat Vicary's experiment, they met with little or no success. Vicary admitted in 1962 that he had fabricated the findings in order to generate business for his market-research business.

The question that most of the studies have entertained, but without answering in any definitive fashion, is whether advertising has become a force molding cultural mores and individual behaviors or whether it constitutes no more than a "mirror" of deeper sociocultural evolutionary tendencies within affluent societies. Without going into the debate here, suffice it to say that there is one thing with which virtually everyone agrees—advertising has become one of the most dominant and appealing forms of social textuality ever devised. The images and slogans that advertisers promulgate on a daily basis delineate and, some would say, define the contemporary world.

But to what extent are the warnings contained in research papers and monographs on the effects that advertising purportedly has on society accurate or justified? Is advertising to be blamed for causing virtually everything, from obesity to self-indulgent promiscuity? Are media moguls the shapers of behavior that so many would claim they are today? Has advertising spawned contemporary worldviews? Are the victims of advertising and the media generally, as Key (1972: 13) suggests, people who "scream and shout hysterically at rock concerts and later in life at religious revival meetings?" There is no doubt that advertising has played a role in shaping behaviors in people generally. But, in my view, even though people mindlessly absorb the messages disseminated constantly by advertisements, and although these may have subliminal effects on behavior, common people accept images, by and large, only if they suit their already-established preferences. It is more accurate to say that advertising produces images that reinforce already-forged lifestyle models in individuals, mirroring them and often co-opting them. Advertisers are not intent on spreading commercially risky innovations. They do not aim to be disruptive of the value systems of the cultural mainstream; rather, they want to reflect "shifts" already present in that mainstream and even anticipate them. If they are indeed psychologically effective, then, it is primarily because advertising, like other social texts (including religious ones) tap into deeply engrained expressive and archetypal structures that constitute the human being's quest for symbolic meaning to life.

It is true, however, that advertising is an integral part of emerging social patterns, forming a synergy with them. Arguably, the most successful campaigns have been those that have co-opted themes, trends, and fads present in popular culture generally, or else made use of well-known personalities or celebrities, creating a dynamic interplay between advertising and popular culture, whereby one influences the other through a constant dynamic back-and-forth flow. The concept of emergent code is sometimes used to explain why the co-option strategy is effective and is an idea inspired by the work of the late culture critic Raymond Williams (1982). According to Williams, cultural behaviors and codes can be subdivided into dominant, residual, and emergent. The dominant code is the set of ideas, values, and lifestyles that define current or middle-of-the-road norms in cultural behavior; residual codes are those that were dominant in the past but are still in circulation in minor ways; and emergent codes are those that dictate future norms, revealing their elements in bits and pieces at the present time. Some of the more effective ad campaigns are those that tap into the emergent codes of a culture (in lifestyle, music trends, and so on).

In the end, as McLuhan pointed out in various writings, advertising is effective because it is both persuasive and entertaining. Among the various persuasion-entertainment strategies used are the following:

- the "bandwagon" strategy, which consists of exaggerated claims that "everyone" is using a particular product/service, inviting the viewer to jump on the bandwagon
- the "disparaging copy" technique, whereby one brand is overtly critical of another company's products or campaigns
- the "educational" strategy, which is designed to educate or inform consumers about a product/service, especially if it has only recently been introduced into the market
- the "nostalgia" technique, which consists in using images from previous times when, purportedly, life was more serene and less dangerous

- the "plain-folks" pitch, whereby a product/service is associated with common people who use it for practical purposes
- the "something-for-nothing" lure, also known as "incentive marketing," which consists in giving away free gifts in order to give a favorable image to the product/service or company ("Buy one and get a second one free!" "Send for free sample!" "Trial offer at half price!" "No money down!")
- the "help your child" tactic, whereby parents are induced into believing that giving their children certain products will secure them a better life and future
- the "ask mommy or daddy" technique, whereby children are exhorted to ask their parents to purchase some product for them
- the "scare copy" or "hidden fear" tactic, which is designed to promote such goods and services as insurance, fire alarms, cosmetics, and vitamin capsules by evoking the fear of poverty, sickness, loss of social standing, impending disaster, and so forth
- the use of "jingles" and "slogans" in order to enhance recognition of a product/service through music and rhetorical language
- "satisfied customer testimonials," which are statements made by satisfied customers who endorse a product/service
- the "formula" tactic, which consists in the use of formulaic or trivial statements that sound truthful or authoritative ("A Volkswagen is a Volkswagen!" "Coke is it!")
- the "history" technique, whereby a significant historical event is incorporated into the ad, either by allusion or by direct reference
- the use of humor to make a product appealing and friendly, as is the case in many beer ads, which associate drinking beer with a recreational and youthful lifestyle
- the "imperative verb" technique, consisting in the use of the imperative form of verbs in order to create the effect that an unseen authoritative source is giving advice ("Join the Pepsi Generation!" "Have a great day, at McDonald's!")
- the "benefits" ploy, which emphasizes the advantages that may accrue from purchasing a product/service, such as the nutritional value of some food, or the performance of some car
- the "mystery ingredient" technique, whereby a mystery ingredient in a drink, detergent, and so on is identified as being the source behind the product's appeal

- the "alliteration" technique, whereby the initial consonant sound of a brand name is repeated ("The Superfree Sensation," "Marlboro Man")
- the "positive appeal" strategy, intended to demonstrate why a product is attractive or important to possess
- the "prestige" advertising tactic, whereby a product/service is placed and advertised in high-quality magazines or media programs so as to enhance the company's reputation
- the "rational appeal" technique, consisting of logical arguments that demonstrate how the product/service might fulfill some need
- the "reminder" technique, whereby an ad or commercial is designed to recall an advertisement that viewers are familiar with
- the "secretive statement" strategy, consisting in the use of statements designed to create the effect that something secretive is being communicated, thus capturing people's attention by stimulating curiosity ("Don't tell your friends about . . ." "Do you know what she's wearing?")
- the "snob-appeal" approach, which aims to convince consumers that using a product/service will enable them to maintain or elevate their social status
- the "soft sell" method, which uses subtle, rather than blatant, forms of persuasion (for example, the type of TV commercial that tells you what a product can do, in comparison to some other product in the same line)
- the "teaser" technique, whereby little information about a product is given, thus making people curious to know more about it
- the "viral advertising" technique, which consists of statements that attempt to capture people's attention by encouraging them to "pass it on" (like a virus) to others
- the "absence-of-language" tactic, consisting in the intentional omission of language, suggesting, by implication, that the product "speaks for itself"; many perfume ads are constructed in this way
- the "self-criticizing" or "post-advertising" approach, which involves a brand's critique of its own advertising, pretending to be on the consumer's side but actually promoting itself in a clever way
- the "retro-advertising" strategy, whereby a previous ad campaign, or the style of a previous ad campaign, is recalled to promote the same product/service or something similar to it
- the "shock effect" technique, which consists in constructing ads that are designed to shock, thus garnering attention

ADVERTISING IN THE INTERNET AGE

The Internet has made it possible for advertisers to employ new ways to get a message across, complementing and expanding traditional ad campaign strategies. For example, in 2001 BMW hired several famous movie directors to make short online films featuring its cars, which clearly blurred the line between art and advertising. Each film was only six minutes long, but it featured a prominent actor driving the car in an adventure-style way.

Online advertising today includes not only e-mail marketing, but also search engine marketing, social media marketing, display advertising, and mobile advertising. Like other advertising media, the online versions tap into the same kinds of themes, strategies, and overall delivery. The difference is that in the online world, every ad is really part of a placement strategy. And like all other areas of pop culture, advertising has undergone convergence, whereby the same ad is delivered on radio, in print, on TV, and on websites and various social media. The point to be made is that advertising is the fuel for the delivery of pop culture and is itself an art form within it—this situation has not changed in the Internet Age. Without the marketplace aspect of pop culture, as explicated in the chapter 3 model, there would be no pop culture as we have known it since at least the 1920s. However, the Internet is changing virtually everything about how pop culture is delivered, as will be discussed in the last two chapters.

One area that has truly exploded in this area is social media advertising. The main advantage of advertising on sites such as Facebook, Friendster, Orkut, Bebo, and others is that ads can be targeted demographically more accurately. Ads are distributed to users on the basis of information gathered from group profiles. Moreover, social media users may like an ad so much that they pass it on to others in the social network. This makes advertising truly part of a new form of social dissemination and distribution. In 2012, Facebook implemented so-called *Promoted Posts*, whereby businesses could pay to feature their ads in news feeds. This was followed in 2013 with the launch of video ads that play in news feeds. Similarly, Twitter launched *Promoted Tweets* and *Accounts* already in 2009. In 2013, Twitter allowed ad makers to use data from browser histories to insert ads that relate to the purported interests of Twitter users. This story can be told for all other social media sites. In 2013, Instagram allowed advertisers to sponsor photos and videos.

Social media are fast becoming part of the advertising-pop culture pastiche, as people become immune to ads, processing them unconsciously. Moreover, the ads on social media are highly entertaining and appealing.

They are fun to watch and thus are likely to be passed on to others in a network. Advertising, like all other domains of pop culture, is now a truly "socialized" form of textuality. It will be interesting to see in the next few years how advertising will evolve in all kinds of virtual spaces and what critical reactions to it will emerge.

10

POP LANGUAGE

Slang is a language that rolls up its sleeves, spits on its hands and goes to work.

—Carl Sandburg (1878–1967)

In the 1950s a term was used by young people that became a shibboleth for the lifestyle that the golden era of rock entailed. That term was *cool*. Simply put, it meant (and continues to mean) knowing how to look, walk, and talk in socially attractive ways.

How can a simple word stand for so much? Words are powerful symbols that document social trends and movements. Language has always played, and continues to play, a key role in the constitution and evolution of pop culture. Pop language, as it may be called, is as much a part of the whole spectacle as is dance and music, manifesting itself in trendy words that are spread by the media. The purpose of this chapter is to look at the forms and functions of pop language. Although this is a topic that rarely finds its way into pop culture studies, it is as crucial a theme as any other. Pop culture is not only performed; it is also spoken.

WHAT IS POP LANGUAGE?

The word *cool* is a perfect example of what pop language is all about and what kinds of meanings this type of word encodes. The word has been used by young people to describe attractive lifestyle images since at least the 1920s. Flappers were cool; rock stars are cool; rappers are cool; celebrities are cool; and so on. Synonyms for *cool* have cropped up throughout pop culture history. These include *hip* and *groovy*, of which only the former is still around today, while the latter is now relegated mainly to the hippie era. It is not a coincidence that the counterculture youths of the 1960s were called *hippies*. They were *hip*, rejecting the customs, traditions, and lifestyles of mainstream society. The same kind of meaning is imprinted in the *hip-hop* term that emerged in the 1980s to describe the lifestyle associated with rap music.

Words like these have crystallized constantly throughout pop culture's history, as have certain phrases and discourse styles that became popular through hit songs, movies, jingles, and the like. Pop language allows people to "talk the talk." One of the shrewdest showmen of all time, P. T. Barnum (1810–1891), understood the power of pop language. To promote his attractions, Barnum relied on hyperbole and exaggeration to create interest in them. Barnum introduced expressions such as the following:

Don't miss this once-in-a-lifetime opportunity!
Limited edition at an unbelievably low price!
All items must go!
Not to be missed!

Barnum realized that language could be used to create a mood of fanfare in people. The same type of fanfare discourse is found today throughout the pop culture landscape, from advertising, sportscasting, and movie trailers to news headlines.

Most people would categorize words such as *cool* and *hip* as slang. But this is incorrect. They are items that bespeak a lifestyle connected to the popular. They have become a part of our everyday vocabulary, not as slang items, but as part of a popular style of discourse that blends in with trends in the larger popular culture. Like never before, common discourse is being shaped by the ever-changing categories of pop language, not because the latter is better than other forms of language, but because it is everywhere.

Defining Pop Language

The conversational style and vocabulary used in pulp fiction magazines and dime novels penetrated the speech of society, showing up surreptitiously in newspaper and magazine articles and in the speech of radio announcers. The term *pop language* was introduced by journalist Leslie Savan in her book, *Slam Dunks and No-Brainers: Language in Your Life, the*

Media, Business, Politics, and, Like, Whatever (2005), to describe the kind of language that rises from popular spectacles and texts, spreading throughout society through mediation and reinforced by the marketplace (chapter 3). Throughout society, Savan notes, people are using a style of speech that carries with it a built-in applause sign or laugh track. Phrases such as "That is so last year," "Don't go there," "Get a life," "I hate it when that happens," "It doesn't get any better than this," and the sneering "I don't think so" come from television sitcoms and popular movies and have spread broadly to other media and become part of everyday speech habits. Pop language is unconsciously attractive, claims Savan, because it emanates from popular media and is thus felt to be "hip" and in synch with the times. Like sitcom dialogue, it is light; self-conscious; ironic; and replete with put-downs, catchy phrases, and exaggerated inflections (*Whatever!*). Savan compares the 1953 Disney cartoon *Peter Pan* with the 2002 sequel *Return to Never Land*, pointing out how remarkably free the former one was of packaged phrases and trendy catchphrases. The sequel, on the other hand, is replete with them, including such phrases as "In your dreams, Hook," "Put a cork in it," "Tell me about it," "You've got that right," and "Don't even think about it."

Pop language is the voice of pop culture. It is really a modern-day version of the type of profane speech used at carnival time, satirizing the boredom of serious talk. As Jonathan Lear (2011) has recently argued, it allows for the profane and comedic side of the human mind to express itself without reprobation. In this sense, it is actually a kind of therapeutic talk, rather than senseless verbiage. In the 1920s, jazz culture introduced a whole series of buzzwords and catchphrases into everyday discourse, including words such as *hip, stylin', cool,* and *groovy.* The words *pot* and *marijuana,* which were part of a secret criminal jargon in the 1940s, became everyday words in the 1960s when the hippies adopted them and spread them through lifestyle images, recordings, and other media. In the 1990s hip-hop culture introduced expressions such as *bad, chill,* and *nasty* into conversational style. Pop language is, and always has been, an oppositional counterpart to standard forms of speech, as can be seen in how it turns vocabulary on its head to give it a different range of social meanings. Take *bad* as an example. The trend of using this word in a nonliteral antonymic way (meaning attractive) was initiated by Michael Jackson with his album titled *Bad* in 1987. Then, in the same year, hip-hop artist LL Cool J introduced the phrase *not bad* "meaning bad, but bad meaning good," as he defined it in his song *I'm Bad.* Similar pop language etymologies can be drafted for words such as *sick* (meaning good).

Pop language has so many sides to it that it would require a treatment that is well beyond the scope of the present chapter. Savan decries its abuse in common conversation. She equates it, thus, with slang. Her point seems to be that in the past, the primary conduits of slang vocabulary were writers. Shakespeare, for instance, brought into acceptable usage such slang terms as *hubbub*, *to bump*, and *to dwindle*. But not before the twentieth century did it become routine for the conduits to be pop culture and the media. The number of slang words that have entered the communal lexicon since the 1960s is truly mind boggling, constituting strong evidence that pop culture in all domains of modern-day life has become a major social force.

The way actors speak in popular movies influences how people speak on the streets. *Animal House* (1978) introduced terms still used today, such as *wimp*, which is a commonly used term for someone who is scared or has no courage, and *brew* which means a beer. *Clueless* (1995) introduced such forms as *as if*, an exclamation of disbelief, and *whatever* to convey disinterest in what another person is saying. In 2004, the film *Mean Girls* helped spread a new form of pop speech used by young females across North America, with words such as *plastic*, meaning fake girls who look like Barbie dolls, and *fetch* which is an abbreviation of *fetching* to describe something cool and trendy.

Pop language is to be distinguished from the artificial or constructed languages that writers and filmmakers sometimes create for effect. J. R. R. Tolkien, for example, created several languages for his books; Richard Adams constructed Lapine, spoken by the rabbit characters in *Watership Down*; Anthony Burgess invented Nadsat for his book *A Clockwork Orange*; Klingon was the artificial language used on the *Star Trek* TV series; Valyrian was created for the TV series *Game of Thrones*; and the list could go on. These languages do not spread outside of, maybe, a group of fans for the novels, movies, or programs, becoming a kind of in-group code for them. Pop language is, like music, a product of trends and changes in pop culture representations and spectacles. This is why it changes as the broader culture changes. It may leave traces, however, and if these accumulate they lead to changes in the grammar and lexicon of the standard language.

Because the screen has become a powerful disseminator of linguistic trends, British playwright Peter Shaffer (1926–) calls it "Screenspeak." In a post-script to the published version of his play *Amadeus*—which became an Oscar-winning 1984 movie—he comments insightfully as follows (1993: 109):

> The cinema is a worrying medium for the stage playwright to work in.
> Its unverbal essence offers difficulties to anyone living largely by the

spoken word. Increasingly, as American films grow ever more popular around the world, it is apparent that the most successful are being spoken in Screenspeak, a kind of cinematic esperanto equally comprehensible in Bogotà and Bulaway. For example, dialogue in heavy-action pictures, horrific or intergalactic, now consists almost entirely of the alternation of two single words—a cry and a whisper—needing translation nowhere on the planet: *Lessgidowaheer* and *Omygaad*.

The way celebrities speak on the silver screen becomes, immediately thereafter, an unconscious Streetspeak. As celebrities change and as scripts change for the screen, so too will pop language change, leaving only residues. As mentioned, if these accumulate then it has an effect on language generally. And if one reads novels from the nineteenth century and compares the language in them to fictional narratives today, that cumulative effect becomes highly transparent. It is not just a matter of linguistic change; it is also a matter of stylistic practices in writing that are at play.

SLANG

Pop language is not equivalent to slang. However, it easily and willingly absorbs slang features into its grammar. Indeed many of its words come from a kind of media slang that is curt and to the point, and, as mentioned, often ironic. Slang and pop language also share the characteristic of compression; that is, both are characterized by trendy abbreviation patterns. Technically called *clipping*, examples are *demo* (demonstration), *psycho* (psychopath), and *wacko* (wacky person), *DJ* (disc jockey), and *kidvid* (kids' video). Yet another slang feature of pop language is its incorporation of profanities. In other words, pop language shares with slang the function of going against the learned style of formal language that extols long sentences and elaborate words.

Words that gain popularity, such as *duh* and *dude*, are at first promulgated by media outlets, being perceived initially as slang items, but becoming colloquialisms over time and, eventually, becoming part of pop language. *Duh* surfaced in the late 1990s, and was, at first, much criticized by language purists, spreading throughout the media, from movies to television programs, making its way, for a while, into common everyday speech. Although it has lost some of its appeal, it is an example of how a media slang item can catch on with the general public. As Laroche (2007: 48) comments:

> The media not only help spread new language from all quarters, they also produce it when they coin terms to describe themselves and their

activities. Media-related words are especially interesting because they often have social resonance. They're not just appropriate or imaginative describers of a certain medium, but also say something important about our larger world. The hybrid "infotainment," for example, merges information and entertainment, just as some media increasingly do. The hybrid word not only reflects the fact, but it also tells us something about our society and our society's values, pressures, trends.

The spread of the word *dude*, a descriptive term referring to inarticulate personages (Kiesling 2004), is another case in point. It is used in greetings ("What's up, dude?"), as an exclamation ("Whoa, dude!"), to convey commiseration ("Dude, I'm so sorry!"), to one-up someone ("That's so lame, dude!"), and to convey agreement, surprise, or disgust ("Dude!"). In all these uses it is suffused with the same style of situational irony of other slang items of pop language. *Dude* began its foray into the pop language lexicon with the 1981 movie *Fast Times at Ridgemont High*, making significant appearances in *The Big Lebowski* (1998) and *Dude, Where's My Car?* (2000).

Another characteristic feature of various forms of slang is profanity. Glorified by movies and music videos, profane language affords many people the opportunity to talk tough, just for the sake of it. In such use, however, the profanity becomes neutralized or at least diminished in its impact. The four-letter "F-word" is a case in point. It is used with regularity in movies, in a matter-of-fact manner that hardly captures people's attention any longer. It has also developed a noun form on the pop culture stage: "What are you doing, you f★★★?" Originally, however, the word had a more subversive function in pop culture performances. For instance, the late controversial comedian Lenny Bruce used it as a transgressive technique in his act. Unlike many other comedians, Bruce did not tell simple jokes. Instead, he attacked hypocritical attitudes toward sex, politics, and religion, by speaking in a conversational manner, injecting frequent Yiddish words and profanities into his material, especially the F-word. Many were offended by his use of that word, and he was frequently arrested on obscenity charges. His speech clearly had a subversive impact; its use today in movies and television programs, on the other hand, has no such impact. Robert Wachal (2002) found that four-letter words are so common in all types of media that they go largely unnoticed. In a single two-hour episode of the HBO series *The Sopranos* alone, Wachal recorded one hundred uses of the F-word.

The neutralization of profanity content, as it can be called, can be seen in the use of many words today, such as *slut*. Along with *ho* and *pimp* to describe a fiancée and fiancé respectively, *slut* is used in complimentary, rather than derogatory ways, designating an attractive female. The word *slut*, which actually originated in the Middle Ages, has now been appropriated by pop culture to make fun of its previous meaning. In a duet with Eminem, Nate Dogg describes his search for a "big old slut" in the single *Shake That*; in the Broadway musical *Avenue Q*, an ample-bosomed puppet is named Lucy the Slut; shops and websites now promote a brand of cosmetics called *Slut*; and so on. It seems that in pop culture, subversion quickly becomes conversion.

Social Media Language

For a particular form of linguistic trend to spread it needs mediation and actual usage by large groups of people. Today, social media such as Facebook and Twitter provide that mediation. Actually, these media have generated their own forms of pop language. The word "friend" on Facebook has a different designation than it does in real life, although sometimes the line is a blurry one indeed. Facebook now has its own slang, with words and abbreviations such as the following having become part of its grammar:

Table 10.1.

dead	funny, hilarious
DGYF	Dang girl, you're fine
facestalking	browsing through someone else's Facebook pictures
fbc	Facebook chat
fbf	Facebook friend
GPOY	gratuitous picture of yourself
PC4PC	picture comment for picture comment
SD	sweet dreams
seltering	sticking out one's rear in a fitness pose
shelfie	picture of objects arranged on a shelf

Twitter has also generated its own lexicon, forming a veritable dialect vis-à-vis other social media dialects. Here are some examples:

Table 10.2.

follower	someone who subscribes to receive updates
followFriday	calling attention to a user's favorite followers
FOMO	fear of missing out
friendapalooza	situation whereby a twitterer adds many friends in a short period of time
friendscrapping	adding all of a friend's friends as one's own
twabe	young woman, sweetheart, dear
twabstinence	refers to the decision to cut back on Twitter time
twabulous	fabulous tweet
twalking	tweeting while walking
tweeple	Twitter user
twitterati	A-list Twitter users
ztwitt	to tweet extremely fast

The interesting thing is that such language or more accurately, style, is spreading to all forms of language, becoming dialects of pop language. As Marwick (2013) and Boyd (2014) have cogently argued, the rise of social media have led to a "context collapse," whereby events in distinct social worlds collide online, causing outpourings of drama, including linguistic drama. But it is probably more accurate to say that the new media have generated new rituals of linguistic interaction, imprinted in the new words and styles. These create and affirm social bonds, regardless of the content. The social media have generated the kinds of rituals that they need for communication to be fluid and resilient on their platforms.

SPELLING STYLE

Pop language is, as mentioned, a compressing language, using abbreviations not just for the reason of enhancing the rapidity of communication, but also for communicating subtle nuances of meaning. This can be seen, for instance, in how some artists spell their names. The phonetic style adopted by rap artists, for example, bespeaks of an attitude that says "I'll do it my way, not the way of white American speakers of English." Here is a small sampling of rap artists' names with their peculiar spelling patterns:

- Snoop Dogg
- Ja Rule
- Eazy-E
- Lil Jon
- LL Cool J
- Timbaland
- Busta Rhymes
- Coolio
- Jay-Z
- Mystikal
- The Notorious B.I.G.
- Bubba Sparxxx

These are not simple quirky spelling forms. Spelling is not just a system of rules for writing words correctly; it is part of implicit social or political commentary. By flying in the face of orthographic and grammatical traditions, which bespeak whiteness, rap artists are declaring a kind of sui generis linguistic autonomy from the hegemony of white culture. Correct spelling, like correct speaking and correct grammar, are more than signs of education. The different spelling styles symbolize how young blacks feel about traditions that have historically excluded them from the mainstream. Here are some examples of such language (taken mainly from rap lyrics):

- i dont know why
- you da right person
- how ya doin
- wanna know why
- i got enuf
- it wuz lotsa fun
- i fine
- me is 31
- Supadupa fly
- Tupac is da gangsta of da sky

The attitude of noncompliance with standard linguistic rules built into such constructions is instantly apparent. As such artists know, to speak the language of a culture according to its rules of grammar and spelling is to validate that culture. Ironic language exudes linguistic empowerment, giving African Americans control over an alien tongue—English—that was forced upon their ancestors during their days of slavery. The driving force that attracted hundreds of inner-city ghetto African American and Hispanic youths to rap music was its anti-hegemonic attitude and its ability to give expression to socially powerless voices. As mentioned previously, today, mainstream rap culture is more a part of general pop music culture than a form of protest culture. This does not mean that rap's original anti-hegemonic subtext has been completely obliterated. Like other trends in pop culture, present and past, it can and often does resurface as a voice of alterity (otherness).

The spelling style used by rap artists is now symptomatic of pop language generally. Even before rap, spelling trends were part of the pop music scene. For example, a number of rock groups used different spellings for their names: Guns N' Roses, Led Zeppelin, the Monkees, and so on. Current spelling oddities in pop music naming are really no more than modern-day manifestations of a tendency that seems to have always existed within pop culture (Cook 2004: 22–23). It is relevant to note that the use of spaces between words was introduced as a writing practice in European languages in the eighth century, as people discovered how useful they could be for facilitating the reading of texts. The space, like the zero in mathematics, allows us to detect boundaries, thus facilitating the reading process. The elimination of word spaces in pop language is more for special effects than anything else. The poet E. E. Cummings (1894–1962), who wrote in lower case, and used distortions of syntax, unusual punctuation, new words, and elements of slang, also eliminated spaces in many of his works.

The spelling trends in pop language, therefore, are not new. The history of English shows a constant attempt to reform spelling practices for various reasons. All one has to do is look at the writings of authors such as Chaucer and even Shakespeare to realize the extent to which spelling has changed over the years. Many of the actual features of pop language spelling today are the same ones proposed by many in the past. In 1828 Noah Webster proposed the elimination of *u* in words such as *colour, harbour, favour,* and *odour.* His proposal was accepted, and the resulting spelling difference is a feature that distinguishes American from British English—and that, by extension, divides America from its British past. Changes of this kind have always come about to symbolize a break with tradition. American English itself was once considered to be subversive by the British (since it was not the king's English). So, although rap spelling style implies a break with white culture, it is, paradoxically, also a contemporary symptom of a larger tendency in America to constantly break from the past. As Vivian Cook (2004: viii) has perceptively remarked:

> Our discussions of spelling often suggest that there is an ideal of perfect spelling that people should strive for. Correct spelling and punctuation are seen as injunctions carved on tablets of stone; to break them is to transgress the tacit commandments for civilized behavior. Spelling and punctuation can become an emotional rather than rational area of dispute.

The writer George Bernard Shaw often made fun of English spelling, pointing out, for example, that the word *fish* could be legitimately spelled *ghoti* given that *gh* was used in place of *f* in a word such as *enough, o* for *i* in a word such as *women*, and *ti* for *sh* in a word such as *nation*.

Sexuality

As discussed throughout this book, sex and romance have always been part of popular representations and expressions, from poetry to music. It comes as no surprise, therefore, to find, that sex and sexuality are common themes in pop language. Some pop language forms, like profane words, are symptomatic of the kind of sexually charged language used at carnival time. 2 Live Crew, for example, is a rap group that has developed a reputation of being "too nasty," because of the blatantly sexual nature of their lyrics. In their song "S & M," one finds lines such as "So I pulled a little girlie, this is what I did, Jumped in the ride, took her to the crib." This type of language has always characterized pop music, although it was much more euphemistic in the past. When Bill Haley and the Comets sang about *rocking around the clock*, or Jerry Lee Lewis about *great balls of fire*, in the 1950s, the metaphorical allusion to sex was unmistakable. In rap lyrics, the sexual phraseology is simply much more explicit. Words like *hump* (or *trunk*) for the female buttocks and *lumps* for the breasts are also found throughout rap lyrics. Black men, on the other hand, are depicted as endowed with unique sexual prowess—an image satirized, by the way, by Beyoncé in "Me, Myself, and I," a song about how disappointing sex turns out to be. Throughout the history of pop music, female voices have always been prominent in bringing out the power of their own sexuality, along with their ownership of it. From the Shangrilas to Madonna, the Spice Girls, and Nikki Minaj, pop music has consistently provided a vehicle for female voices to articulate their slant on sex, romance, and relationships.

TEXTSPEAK

Many of the spelling and vocabulary patterns discussed above that appear in social media can be classified under the general rubric of *textspeak*, the kind of language used to send written messages through various digital channels, especially mobile devices. Essentially, textspeak is a form of shorthand (based on abbreviations, acronyms, alphanumeric symbols, and so on) that makes it possible to carry out real-time written communication quickly and effectively. But as we have seen it entails much more from a semantic and cultural angle. Textspeak is found across languages. In Mandarin Chinese, for example, numbers that sound like words are used in place of the words. Today there are even websites such as *transl8it* (translate it) that standardize textspeak so that it can be used more systematically and broadly for communication, like the Morse code before it. There are now standard dictionaries and glossaries of textspeak available online.

Clipping

The basic characteristic of textspeak (TS) is the shortening of a word or phrase in some logical way. For example, *I love you* is shortened to *i luv u* or even *ilu*. Deciphering the TS form depends on user familiarity. Words and expressions that are used frequently in communication get shortened systematically. TS is now used by professionals such as doctors and lawyers to interact with colleagues. In the absence of face-to-face communication, TM has made it much easier for professionals to communicate quickly and efficiently with colleagues.

Some critics are decrying TS as a product of modern-day versions of inertia and ennui. Helprin (2009), for instance, cautions that this form of language has an addictive effect on people and how they process information, rendering them much less reflective and less inclined to appreciate literary diversity. Others (Crystal 2008) respond that TS is no more than an efficient way to create written messages for informal communication and that people are aware of the different forms of writing according to context. It is relevant to note that no less an authority on language trends than the Oxford English Dictionary has incorporated many items from TS, acknowledging that it is part of linguistic evolution, not devolution. Ironically, people and the media are now attacking textspeak through the media. Facebook groups, ironically and paradoxically, are sprouting up to decry textspeak as endangering the survival of genuine language—despite the fact that Facebook is itself a major source of linguistic compression. On an episode of NBC's *Parks and Recreation*, we see the main character, played by Rob Lowe, explaining the clipped form *OMG* to a taxi driver while sitting in the back seat of the cab. In anger, the driver drowns him out by turning up the radio.

Actually, compression in language is nothing new. Scholars and scientists have always used various kinds of abbreviations to facilitate technical communications among themselves. Abbreviations such as *etc., et al., op. cit., N.B.* are still part and parcel of "scholarspeak." But what sets the reductive tendencies in TS apart from all abbreviation tendencies of the past is the speed and extent to which its forms are spreading and becoming part of communicative behavior throughout the online world and, seemingly, spreading to offline language.

Clearly, technology and language are intertwined, and always have been. As a part of pop language, textspeak is no better or no worse than previous forms of communication based on popular trends.

Table 10.3.

TS Form	Translation
afk	away from keyboard
brb	I'll be right back.
btw	by the way
g2g	Got to go.
hhok	Ha ha; I'm only kidding.
imho	in my humble opinion
lol	laugh out loud
tttt	to tell the truth

There are five clipping patterns that are at work in writing systems such as TS: abbreviation, acronymy, phonetic replacement, compounding, and letter symbols. Abbreviations are shortened words: *ppl* for *people, b/c* for *because.* Acronyms are forms composed of the first letter of every word within a phrase: *OMG* for *oh my God, LOL* for *laugh out loud.* Phonetic replacements occur when certain letters and numbers replace entire words because they represent the pronunciation more compactly: for example, *cu* for *see you* and *18r* for *later.* Compounding consists of the combination of separate words, or parts of words, to make a new one that is shorter than the forms it combines taken separately: *mousepad, webonomics, netlag, netizen, hackitude, geekitude.* A letter symbol is a letter, such as *e-,* used in place of words: *e-zine, e-commerce,* and so on.

Are such trends radical? Do they spell out (literally) the end of language as we have known it for millennia? Actually, such trends are nothing new, since they can be explained under the rubric of the Principle of Least Effort (PLE), identified in the 1930s by the Harvard linguist George Kingsley Zipf (1902–1950). Zipf claimed that many clipping phenomena in language could be explained as the result of an inborn tendency for humans to make the most of communicative resources with the least expenditure of effort (physical, cognitive, and social). The PLE is, Zipf suggested, the reason why speakers shorten the length of words and utterances if these gain currency and the meaning of the clipped form is clear. For example, the word *advertisement* is commonly shortened to *ad* because it is used frequently and the meaning of the clipped word is evident. Zipf demonstrated that there exists an intrinsic interdependence between the length of a specific word (in number of phonemes) and its rank order in the language (its position in order of its frequency of occurrence in texts). The higher the rank order of a word (the more frequent it is in actual usage), the shorter it tends to be (made up with fewer phonemes). The PLE manifests itself, therefore, in the tendency for phrases that come into popular use to become abbreviated (*FYI, UNESCO, Hi, Bye, ad, photo, Mr., Mrs., Dr., aka, VCR, DNA, laser, GNP, IQ, VIP*).

Nowhere is the operation of Zipf's Law as apparent today as it is in the forms that are created in textspeak. This increases the speed at which messages can be inputted and received, lowering the effort required to write out entire words.

Writing takes time and effort. Today, both come at a premium. Not answering the barrage of e-mails or text messages that people receive on a daily basis is perceived negatively. Logically, the clipping of forms helps counteract the situation by making it possible to get back to one's sender of messages quickly and rapidly. Textspeak is now the underlying spelling and grammatical system for much of pop language; the two go hand in hand. Textspeak is integrated into pop and mainstream codes more and more as children start using mobile text messaging devices at earlier ages. Some school systems are responding to this by allowing textspeak on essays and exam papers. It has also introduced pictographic features into written language broadly, such as emoticons, symbol substitutions ("@" for "at"), and the like. Studies now show that textspeak is penetrating all kinds of writing styles, from journalistic to academic. In a way, this is rendering classical canons of writing anachronistic. What was once considered to be informal writing is now just writing. In her 2011 master's thesis at the University of Calgary, *What Does Txting Do 2 Language?*, Joan H. Lee argues that expo-

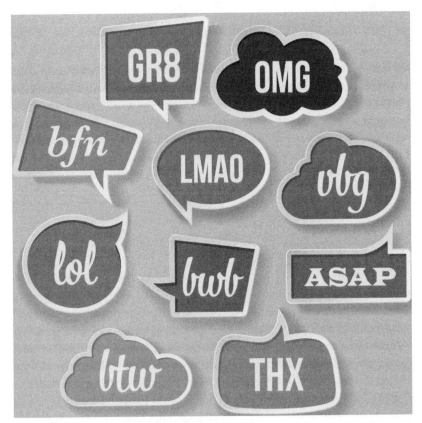

Abbreviations and other shorthand forms of words are staples of text messaging (© ThinkStock)

sure to and use of textspeak leads to a diminution in people's knowledge of vocabulary, thus reducing it considerably. Lee discovered that students with more exposure to traditional print media (books and articles) were more open to expanding their vocabulary. This goes contrary to many studies that suggest that textspeak is not harming language: "Our assumption about texting is that it encourages unconstrained language," Lee argues, "but the study found this to be a myth." Lee suggests that reading traditional print materials exposes people to linguistic variety and creativity that is not found in textspeak.

Of course, Lee is referring to different forms of creativity—the creativity of a Dostoyevsky cannot be compared to the creativity of a Twitter user. What needs to be seen is what literary genres Twitterspeak and textspeak will produce and if they stand up to traditional literary texts. Novels in textspeak have already been written, of course. But so far they have not become popular or relevant as traditional novels have. One of the first, titled *The Last Messages*, written by Hannu Luntiala, came out in Helsinki in 2007. It consisted entirely of mobile phone text messages by the Nokia Corporation, telling the story of an IT Finnish executive who quits his job and decides to travel through Europe and India, keeping in touch with friends and family through roughly one thousand text messages, listed in sequential order. The novel speaks to Generation Textspeak, but it also shows that it can communicate nuances of meaning and even expand upon them. And indeed, it is a new pop language that has emerged to literally capture the "sense" of the age. In 2012, the short story *Two Bad Thumbs*, by novelist and journalist Will Cohu, made it to a list of twenty titles competing for the *Sunday Times* literary award. The relevant aspect of the story was that it used text messages throughout to unravel a lurid tale of a sexual affair. Text messages are exchanged by lovers constantly and profusely, and the short story captured the ethos of contemporary love affairs in the manner of delivery in which the text messages unfold. Needless to say, this could be a temporary trend, since textspeak is bound to change or morph into other forms of language and even disappear. But such novels and stories capture the ethos of pop culture in the contemporary age through the template of current forms of pop language, especially textspeak.

Pop language has always been an intrinsic part of pop culture. The slang of the Roaring Twenties, the slang of hippies in the 1960s, the spelling style exemplified by rap artists and text messages are all an embedded part of that culture. Research on slang throughout the world shows that popular coinages and linguistic patterns have a very short lifespan. However, the same domain of research also shows that there are many terms that gain general currency, cutting across age, class, and gender boundaries. The language used on screen stages (television, cinema, Internet) entertains us as well as makes us debate important things—such as the nature, role, and evolution of language. That is the paradox of pop culture, as we have seen throughout this book.

11

ONLINE POP CULTURE

The new electronic independence re-creates the world in the image of a global village

—Marshall McLuhan (1911–1980)

The model adopted in this book (see chapter 3) to explicate how pop culture emerged and spread, in contrast to local folk cultures and various "high" forms of culture, includes as a main component the media, thus emphasizing the role of technology in the model. Without mass communications technologies, only localized forms of pop culture would have emerged, and they would have quickly receded from the scene. Mass printing technologies made it possible for the emergence of pop literary forms, such as the dime novels and pulp fiction magazines; recording technologies projected pop music styles onto the national and international stages; radio became a major stage in the 1920s, spreading pop culture fare ever more broadly and permanently; and in the 1950s television became a veritable social text based on the expansion of pop culture genres. All of these technologies constituted paradigm shifts in pop culture and in society. In other words, social change was reflected in pop culture content and, vice versa, this content influenced social change. Perhaps no one was more aware of this synergy than was Marshall McLuhan (chapter 2). As he aptly put it (1951: 46): "As the unity of the modern world becomes increasingly a technological rather than a social affair, the techniques of the arts provide the most valuable means of insight into the real direction of our own collective purpose." Substituting "arts" with "pop culture" brings out the importance of the latter in changing the world.

In order to grasp the meaning of the relation between technology and pop culture especially in the age of the Internet, and because of the paradigm shift toward the online stage for the delivery of such culture, it is essential to revisit McLuhan's ideas at least schematically first in this chapter, before discussing online pop culture. As he also pointed out several times in his writings (McLuhan 1951, 1964), which are relevant to repeat here, we hardly ever realize how much the electronic world has changed us, from politics to entertainment. Here is a sampling:

- "Anyone who tries to make a distinction between education and entertainment doesn't know the first thing about either."
- "Politics will eventually be replaced by imagery. The politician will be only too happy to abdicate in favor of his image, because the image will be much more powerful than he could ever be."
- "The new electronic independence re-creates the world in the image of a global village."
- "As technology advances, it reverses the characteristics of every situation again and again. The age of automation is going to be the age of 'do it yourself.'"

These are truisms, of course, but without their articulation we would hardly be aware of their truth value. It is in such anecdotal and aphoristic ways that McLuhan provided us with a truly insightful commentary on the relations among media, pop culture, and technology. His own style, which has often been criticized as being too compressed and prone to being used simply as a collection of sound bites, is actually a perfect critical language for describing pop culture. It provides snapshots that allow us to think more profoundly about the content they espouse.

BACK TO McLUHAN

McLuhan's 1951 book, *The Mechanical Bride: Folklore of Industrial Man*, constitutes, arguably, the first true study of pop culture in the modern sense of this term. Using what he termed a "mosaic approach"—a series of short essays and aphorisms—he started off each chapter with a quote from a newspaper article, a magazine article, or an ad. Using the material of one's subject matter to critique it has become a standard critical technique ever since. Perhaps the two most relevant ideas in that book and subsequent ones for the present purposes can be paraphrased as follows: in modern secular societies, as technology changes so does pop culture and as pop culture changes so does society.

Technology

The academic study of the media traces its roots to America in the 1930s. It was not until the late 1950s, however, that the formal study of pop culture emerged, right after the publication of McLuhan's pivotal book mentioned above. In his lectures, McLuhan warned his students at the University of Toronto that the media to which they were exposed on a daily basis, and the popular culture that they contained, constituted a blessing and a curse at the same time. While the electronic media do in fact make information and culture instantly available and accessible to larger and larger groups of people, they also tend to engender a general feeling of alienation in us because the medium in this case separates us from others and physically becomes their replacement—hence his expression the "medium is the message." Our modern mediated world is indeed a two-edged sword. The alienation that McLuhan warned about decades ago has, seemingly, become widespread in the Internet Age, at the same time that more and more people gain access to information that was once the privilege of a few. Despite this we are drawn to changes in media, which become sources of new pop culture forms, tapping into our populist imagination. The psychological reason why this is so is, McLuhan insisted, because media are extensions of ourselves.

What did he mean by this? Before the advent of alphabets, people communicated and passed on their knowledge primarily through the spoken word. They also established their cultures through orality. So, rituals and stories were spoken and transmitted orally from one generation to the next. But even in early oral cultures, tools had been invented for recording and preserving ideas in durable physical forms. The forms were invariably pictographic. Pictography has not disappeared from human life, even though most of our written communication is based on the alphabet. Pictography is a *medium* in McLuhan's sense (from Latin *medius* "middle or between")—a means of recording ideas on some surface (a cave wall, a piece of wood, papyrus) with appropriate technology (a carving tool, pigment, a stylus).

McLuhan was among the first to realize that changes in media lead to changes in social structure and in knowledge systems. Pictography did not alter the basic oral nature of daily communication, nor did it alter the oral mode of transmitting knowledge of early civilizations. That occurred after the invention of alphabetic writing around 1000 BCE—an event that brought about the first true paradigm shift in the world's social structure. The move away from pictographic to alphabetic writing constituted the initial step toward the establishment of a worldwide civilization. Simply put, alphabetic writing made *print* the first viable global medium for storing and exchanging ideas and knowledge.

The second step in the establishment of a worldwide civilization was taken in the fifteenth century after the development of movable type technology—an event that made it possible to print and duplicate books cheaply. McLuhan designated the type of social order that ensued from that technological event the "Gutenberg Galaxy," after Johannes Gutenberg (1400–1468) the German printer who invented movable type in Europe. The Gutenberg Galaxy did indeed, as McLuhan pointed out, establish print culture as the primary medium for recording and preserving information and knowledge. But it did more than that. It also established the book as the first true "mass distraction" device of history. And, indeed, to this day we read books not only for educational or reference purposes, but also to while away our leisure hours.

The third step toward the founding of a worldwide civilization was taken at the start of the twentieth century, after advancements in electronic technology established sound recordings, cinema, radio, and (a little later) television as new media for communicating information and, above all else, for providing distraction to larger and larger masses of people. Since electronic signals can cross borders virtually unimpeded, McLuhan characterized the world that was being united by electronic media as the "global village." Near the end of the twentieth century, the fourth step toward establishing a worldwide civilization was taken right after computers became widely available and the Internet emerged as a global medium.

A tool, McLuhan explained, is anything that extends some sensory, physical, or intellectual capacity. An ax extends the power of the human hand to break wood; the wheel of the human foot to cover great distances; the telescope of the eye to see farther; and so on and so forth. McLuhan claimed that the actual tools developed to record and transmit messages determine how people process and remember them. This is so because they are themselves based on the senses. Human beings decipher information with all the senses. Our *sense ratios*, as he called them, are equally calibrated at birth to receive information. However, in social settings, it is unlikely that all the senses will operate at the same ratio. One sense ratio or the other increases according to the modality employed to record and transmit a message. In an oral culture, the *auditory sense ratio* is the one that largely shapes information processing and message interpretation; in a print culture, on the other hand, the *visual sense ratio* is the crucial one. This raising or lowering of sense ratios is not, however, preclusive. Indeed, in our own culture, we can have various sense ratios activated in tandem. For example, if one were to hear the word *cat* uttered by someone, the auditory sense ratio would be the operational one in processing the meaning of the word. If, however, one were to see the word written on a sheet of paper, then the visual sense ratio would be activated instead. A visual depiction of the *cat* accompanied by an utterance of the word would activate the auditory and visual sense ratios in tandem.

Pop Culture

Any major change in how information is encoded or, better, "in-mediated" brings about a concomitant paradigm shift in social systems. Ancient cuneiform writing allowed the Sumerians to develop a great civilization; papyrus and hieroglyphics transformed Egyptian society into an advanced civilization as well; the alphabet spurred the ancient Greeks on to make extraordinary advances in science, technology, and the arts; the alphabet also made it possible for the Romans to develop an effective system of government; the printing press facilitated the dissemination of knowledge broadly and widely, paving the way for the European Renaissance, the Protestant Reformation, and the Enlightenment; radio, movies, and television brought about the rise of a global pop culture in the twentieth century; and the Internet and the World Wide Web ushered in an interconnected world as the twentieth century came to a close.

Because of the fact that media are tools extending bodily and cognitive processes they have brought about several paradigm shifts over the course of human history. The first one was a consequence of the invention of writing and the spread of literacy. Literacy engenders the sense that knowledge and information are disconnected from their human sources and thus that they have "objectivity"; orality does not. This perception is bolstered by the fact that printed information can be easily categorized and preserved in some durable material form such as books.

But orality has not, of course, disappeared from human life. The spoken word comes naturally; literacy does not. Through simple exposure to everyday oral dialogue, children develop the ability to speak with little or no effort and without any training or prompting whatsoever. Literacy, on the other hand, does not emerge through simple exposure to printed texts. It is learned through instruction, practice, and constant rehearsal. Schools were established, in fact, to impart literacy and print-based knowledge.

The second event that changed the course of history occurred in the twentieth century—millennia after the advent of alphabetic writing—with the emergence and diffusion of the electronic mass media. These not only facilitated distance communications, but they also brought about a global form of culture. In effect, to paraphrase McLuhan, participating in pop culture content is an activity of engagement in our senses and emotions.

THE ONLINE STAGE

With the rise and spread of online pop culture, it is no longer possible to approach its study with the traditional critical apparatus and theoretical stances put forward since the 1930s (chapter 2). Such culture now resists the traditional parameters of critical analysis, since it unfolds on a DIY stage; literally it can mean something different to every person. Certainly, the dichotomy between entertainment and engagement is still there, since we can glean both from online spectacles and texts. Celebrities, genres, lifestyles, fads, and other aspects of the popular are also still around, but in different ways. Most importantly, it is now a global phenomenon, since a website can reach everyone instantaneously.

Convergence Again

A main theme in this book has been that each previous stage for the delivery of pop culture does not disappear as a new one emerges from technological innovation. Rather it converges with it. The online stage is now where all previous stages converge, making it the most powerful of all.

McLuhan pointed out, again perceptively, that the content of one medium is always another medium. In the Web 2.0 world, we now experience the media stage as a two-way process, not the one-way process that characterized virtually all previous stages. The online world, as Guertin (2013) has argued, captures and transforms previous media, allowing them to interact with each other—a process called *remediation* by Bolter and Grusin (1999). In effect, the online stage is a stage where constant flux and change create constant instability in cultural content (Briggs and Burke 2005). Mark Deuze (2010) observes that the technologies associated with the online stage, especially the mobile ones, make content personalized and transportable and thus more and more embedded in all aspects of everyday life and just as ephemeral.

Jenkins (2001, 2006) breaks down the contemporary meaning of convergence into various categories:

- *Technological convergence*, or the digitization of all content and the manufacturing of devices that contain recording and camera functions, so that anyone can record, videotape, and upload content.
- *Economic convergence*, whereby supermedia companies buy up media content more and more.
- *Social convergence*, which involves channel switching, multimodal navigation, and multitasking.
- *Cultural convergence*, or participatory culture unfolding in such media as social networking sites.
- *Global convergence*, which is the admixture of hybrid cultural products arising from global exchanges.

Mashpedia Culture

Given the effects of the various forms of convergence, the online stage is no longer concerned only with celebrities, pop music, movies, TV programs, video games, fads, and the like. It now includes, as McLuhan predicted, religion and politics and everything else that is of relevance to everyday life—everything is easily transformed into entertainment. The primary use of the Internet is for entertainment, even though it now meshes in all other areas of human endeavor, from science, philosophy, and education to business and religion. Vaudevillian stages, the radio, movies, television, and other previous media, located a pop culture spectacle or event in time and space. So entertainment was more compartmentalized and thus separate from other kinds of affairs in everyday life. As more and more of the population fills its daily life with entertainment, it is bound to have an effect on how we view non-leisure activities. Even intellectual presentations are now compressed radically to fit the online compression mode, as the Ted (Technology, Entertainment, Design) Talks indicate. These started in 1984, but in the contemporary Internet Age they have evolved into online presentations of both profound ideas and entertainment that last typically under fifteen minutes—recalling Andy Warhol's prophetic characterization of the electronic age as one in which everyone will have fifteen minutes of fame.

The term *Mashpedia culture* can be used to indicate the ever-expanding pastiche culture evolving online whereby anything can be put together within the mixture, from physics to momentary fads in music and humor.

This state of affairs has truly transformed the world, blurring the lines between serious culture and entertainment culture. People seem to be increasingly more focused on video games, celebrities, sports events, and the like, without distinguishing them from philosophical, artistic, and other forms of culture. If it is not fun, then it probably will not garner much attention, unless we are looking for some specific kind of information (such as medical). And if it is, then the fifteen-minute Ted Talk is sufficient to bring its importance out.

Mashpedia culture, however, is really not a threat to serious culture— medicine and other sciences are too important to us and to the industries set up around them to become totally enmeshed in a popularization purée. This type of culture will always exist and can be called, simply, serious culture. The other forms of culture are short-lived more and more as the online world requires constant innovation, lending validity to Barthes' (1957) notion of *neomania*, giving it a new meaning. Barthes coined the term to refer to the constant craving for new things, new spectacles, new fads, new celebrities, and so on, a state of mind fueled by advertising. Obsolescence is, in a consumerist culture, something to be avoided, whether it is the type of television set one has or the mobile digital device one has recently purchased. In the Internet Age, neomania seems to have become an unconscious mind-set as we are bombarded more and more by neo-fads, neo-styles, and neo-celebrities. The Internet has been a powerful democratizing force, giving everyone a voice and a locus for bringing to light new ideas, new artistic forms, and the like. But it has also given a powerful strident voice to faddishness and trendiness. As in all previous eras of human life, there needs to be a balance between the serious and the faddish, the serious and the comedic. Indeed, the survival of pop culture depends on the restoration of this balance.

Cyberspace

Cyberspace is the term coined by American novelist William Gibson in his 1984 novel *Neuromancer*, a novel that was the inspiration for the emergence of cyberpunk science fiction writing (as discussed previously). Cyberpunk narratives take place typically in a bleak, dehumanized future world dominated by technology and robotic humans. Gibson's description of cyberspace is worth repeating here:

> Cyberspace. A consensual hallucination experienced daily by millions of legitimate operators. A graphic representation of data abstracted from

the banks of every computer in the human system. Unthinkable complexity. Lines of Light ranged in the nonspace of the mind, clusters of constellations of data. Like city lights, receding. (Gibson 1984: 67)

Cyberspace now has its own communities (Facebook communities, Second Life, Multiple User Domains, and so on) and its own set of conventions for communicating and interacting (as discussed in the previous chapter). Movement and interaction in cyberspace are, of course, virtual. This makes it hyperreal. As Mikael Benedikt (1991: 1) notes, in cyberspace "the tablet becomes a page becomes a screen becomes a world, a virtual world. Everywhere and nowhere, a place where nothing is forgotten yet everything changes." The modern human lives in two universes, that of physical reality and that of hyperreality. What is online about ourselves will define us well beyond our mortal lives. In the past, only artists, writers, musicians, and other important individuals would have been able to leave behind their memories for posterity through their work; now virtually anyone can do something similar. Our Facebook pages and our tweets define us, remaining in cyberspace well beyond our physical lives. In cyberspace we can leave a record of ourselves for future generations to read. This is affecting not only how we remember and live, but also how we view mortality. Cyberspace is strangely uniting us (which can be called the communal mind) at the same time that it is making personal choice and activity important (which can be called the individualist mind). This might explain why pop culture now has a virtual but highly fractured audience (communal mind) and a highly personalized DIY form at the same time (the individualist mind).

SOCIAL MEDIA MEMES

In previous eras of pop culture, a few people decided what would be put on a stage in view of gaining popularity. That has changed in the Internet Age. Now the decision of what becomes popular is influenced by virality (viral videos on YouTube) and memes—the spreading of information through cyberspace. Facebook and Twitter, among other social media sites, are where popularity is now made and ensconced. Memes have replaced agents, radio announcers, TV producers, and the other previous makers of pop culture. Memes are the new marketers. However, they carry only the content that is truly popular, as decided by social media users. This implies that pop culture is now becoming a mimicry (memetic) culture. Posting a photo of people involved in humorous situations is replacing TV's *Funniest Home Videos* and people dancing some new style is replacing previous dance shows—at least in part.

As an example, take the Internet resident Grumpy Cat Tard, a cute kitten that became a meme as did the LOLcats, which were featured at *I Can Has Cheezburger*. These sites became memes through social media and the comments of people on their Facebook sites that highlighted their humor. So, LOLcats are turned into image macros consisting of funny pictures of cats with superimposed textual commentary in the form of textspeak English called *lolspeak*. This became a social media meme reinforced by the ritual of *Caturday* on *4chan*.

Facebook

Facebook is one of the most frequented social networking sites, having become an intrinsic part of everyday virtual life in cyberspace. A person's Facebook page includes a personal profile consisting of biographical information, audio-visual supports (photos, videos, music, and so on), and a listing of personal preferences (hobbies, music, movies, and so on). It can be characterized as a constantly "open line" of communication among the "friends" who belong to the same Facebook community.

The earliest social networking sites can be traced back to the mid-1990s, becoming somewhat popular with the establishment of Friendster in 2002. Facebook was created in 2004 at Harvard University by student Mark Zuckerberg for use by the students there. By 2005, Facebook had eclipsed Friendster, migrating to other Ivy League schools and by 2006 to universities and colleges across the globe. In that same year, Facebook opened its membership to anyone thirteen years of age or older. Microsoft Corporation bought a share in Facebook a year later, making it available to virtually anyone on Earth. It is now a digital business, collecting revenue mainly from banner advertising (since membership is free).

Television networks, artists, and musicians also have Facebook sites for communicating with fans, followers, and audiences generally. Facebook has become a major agency for the spread of trends in pop culture. Screen-to-screen communication is thus now as much a part of life as face-to-face communication, leading to writing as a complement of orality, not an alternative to it. Some social critics are pointing out that Facebook is leading to a superficial form of interaction. Others claim instead that Facebook is actually allowing people to feel more comfortable about themselves, giving people the opportunity to construct their own identities and to prepare them emotionally to negotiate face-to-face contact more successfully. It all depends on which expert one reads or believes.

The question of why people expose themselves online, through profiles, photos, and other private artifacts, is a major one in the social sciences, especially given the fact that the "fad effect" of Facebook has subsided. Is Facebook replacing the confessional or psychoanalyst's couch, allowing people to confess in public? When Facebook came into wide use, it was heralded as bringing about a liberation from conformity and a channel for expressing one's opinions freely. But this view is an anachronism. Counting the number of friends on Facebook is seemingly more crucial than venting one's philosophical or aesthetic viewpoints. Facebook is being used more and more to construct a popular persona for oneself. For this reason it has become addictive for many, as we seek out other people's reactions to our daily updated diaries (Lanier 2010, Kirkpatrick 2010). The triumph of Facebook lies in its promise to allow human needs to be expressed individualistically, even though most users soon start to realize that its true force lies in the compulsive attachment it instills in them.

Facebook has offered a broad range of utopian options for gaining control over meaning and experience, emancipating people from the bonds of traditional patterns of socialness. Yet under the spell of the new medium, these options have become strangely similar to those of the past at best, or degenerated into fetishized practices of self-enhancement. On the other hand, as the Frankfurt scholars predicted, maybe a medium such as Facebook is the revolutionary tool that will finally jolt humans out of their intellectual and artistic lethargy and awaken in them the sense of individual power that is crucial for true creativity to occur in the first place.

Certainly, Facebook (and other social media sites) has become a locus where popular trends are gathered and disseminated throughout cyberspace; if these become memes, then their popularity is virtually guaranteed, albeit likely short lived. The power of Internet memes and their distribution through social media sites became dramatically obvious, when in December of 2014, the Gangnam Style video (see chapters 3 and 6) became the first YouTube clip to be viewed more than 2.1 billion times. After its great success in 2012 thousands responded by creating and posting their own variations of the video on YouTube and on Facebook, including "Mitt Romney Style," "NASA Johnson Style," and "Egyptian Style." Gangnam Style, and its parodies, imitations, and derivations, is now the most well-known example of an Internet meme. Other well-known Internet memes include "Leave Britney Alone," the pepper-spraying cop, LOLcats (as discussed above), Scumbag Steve, and Occupy Wall Street's "We Are the 99

Percent." As Shifman (2013) argues, there are now popular meme genres, which reveal some of the most fundamental aspects of the Internet and of participatory Web 2.0 culture.

Internet memes not only compete for attention, generally resulting in a shorter life for a trend or fad, but also, through user creativity, to collaborate with each other and achieve greater survival, as the cats example mentioned above shows. Also, paradoxically, an individual meme that experiences a high degree of popularity does not survive unless it is unique, whereas a meme with no such popularity level but that keeps being used together with other memes has greater survivability.

For the purposes of the discussion on online pop culture, it is sufficient to point out that Facebook is a major propagator of memes. Take a well-known example. In September 2009, nearly 500,000 Facebook users posted this statement as their status update: "No one should die because they cannot afford health care, and no one should go broke because they get sick. If you agree, post this as your status for the rest of the day." At a certain point in the propagation, a user posted a variant starting with "Jim thinks that no one . . ." which was itself copied over 60,000 times. Other variants surfaced leading to over one million status updates. In the past, any agent, such as a record marketer or a TV producer, would have killed to have access to such a powerful marketing system. Indeed, the traditional agents are now constantly on Facebook (their own and others' pages) to help get the memes propagating to create celebrity status for someone, get a song to become popular, and so on. Interestingly, fans of a TV program, such as *The Big Bang Theory*, now post quotes from the show on Facebook and these spread throughout the Internet to become part of a growing new language that can be called "meme language." Facebook can even start its own fads, not adopt them and pass them on from other sources such as YouTube. On the official *Facebook Lying Down Game* page it is claimed that the idea to encourage the game of lying down in random public places started on Facebook to become a temporary fad in 2012 before the Olympics.

Twitter

Twitter has become highly popular throughout the world since it was co-founded in 2006 by Jack Dorsey. The messages on Twitter are known as *tweets*—a terminology that is intended to suggest the sounds made by birds and thus, by association, the role of aviary communication both in terms of its perceived gentleness and its previous role in human communication (carrier pigeons). Tweets are inserted on a user's profile page and delivered to subscribers known as followers, suggesting a kind of bird-pet relation between people. Twitter is essentially an SMS (short message service) on the Internet, since it allows for text messaging to take place without text-messaging devices. As the site claims, Twitter sees itself more as an "information network" than a social networking site, although it incorporates both functions.

Twitter became broadly popular after the 2007 South by Southwest Festival, during which over 60,000 tweets were exchanged by the participants daily on plasma screens in the hallways of the conference. In this way, the conference-goers were able to keep in touch constantly throughout the event. The enthusiasm of the conference-goers soon spread across cyberspace, leading to the emergence of Twitter as a major social network site and tweeting as a common communicative activity. Like all other such sites, Twitter is now delivered on mobile devices and is now largely financed by advertising.

Most tweets are purely conversational—exchanges between friends, associates, colleagues, and acquaintances. Despite what the company says, information is not the main attraction of Twitter—indeed, only around 10 percent of its contents can be considered to be purely informational. Some have designated Twitter as providing a venue for social grooming, that is, for presenting oneself in a favorable way to others in order to gain attention and to gather followers. Institutions of various kinds, from NASA to universities, now use tweeting as a source of contact with clients and colleagues.

Some critics claim that the limited length of each tweet, the desire for followers, and the constant flow of tweets are all leading to a withdrawal from meaningful communication and to an engagement in superficial exchanges. While this may be true, the critics may be missing the historical point that informal daily interaction has probably always been this way. Twitter has simply made it possible for people to enlarge the range of informal communication, not introduce it into social life.

More importantly for the present purposes is the fact that Twitter has become another site for the dissemination and entrenchment of fads, trends, celebrities, and the like, as well as reinforcing the popularity of existing spectacles, programs, and celebrities. In the Twitterverse a meme is announced by a hashtag, thus already giving it prominence. In a way, that has been the story of all previous forms of pop culture. What is different is how pop culture trends are spread and the fragmentation of audiences into Internet communities.

Sometimes, however, an Internet meme can cross over into the art world. The best example of this is the Grumpy Cat phenomenon—which has migrated from the Internet to other areas of society, including to art museums and other referential points in pop culture—that is, it has made its way into other media and other channels of dissemination.

One can claim that this is the ultimate in banality, but there is much more to it than literally meets the eye. The cat fits in with contemporary perceptions of animals as pets and ersatz humans, which has always been a part of pop cultural representations—from the Disney animated movies to the *Looney Tunes* cartoons. Grumpy Cat is a meme that has become a celebrity, no more, no less. The cat symbolizes how truly populist pop culture is. Frankfurt School theorist Walter Benjamin (chapter 2) addressed this issue already in the 1930s when mechanical reproduction technology made art reproductions common. He suggested that this was part of an ever-growing democratization of art, leading to a demise in the notion of originality and the ways in which art was viewed and appreciated as something truly unique. A successful meme is, in fact, something that is highly reproducible, recognizable, and easily shared.

The fact that a paradigm shift has truly occurred was evidenced by the fact that the PBS Idea Channel discussed in 2013 the idea of memes as new forms of art. In the end, if people enjoy something, such as the photo of a grumpy cat, and it becomes part of pop culture, then all one can say is that it is just that—popular.

YOUTUBE

YouTube is a video-sharing website, founded in 2005 by Chad Hurley, Steve Chen, and Jawed Karim. It features videos posted by individuals as well as by musicians, artists, TV networks, and other professionals and institutions. It allows users to comment on and rate videos. YouTube members can also start a discussion about a video, transforming YouTube into a social networking site. They can also e-mail YouTube video links to others. Today, YouTube offers advertising, video diaries known as vlogs, made-for-YouTube movies, and material created by professors for use in courses. YouTube was purchased by Google in 2006, with a consequent burgeoning of viewership, a fact that forced television networks to use YouTube to promote their programs. In 2007, YouTube joined CNN for a series of presidential campaign debates in which users could post videos asking candidates questions.

As Strangelove (2010) has argued, the YouTube phenomenon cannot be easily categorized in terms of traditional theories of media and popular culture. One can see an anonymous musician playing classical music in a clip that has been viewed over sixty million times. An inebriated David Hasselhoff attempting to eat a hamburger also gets millions of views. A cat playing the piano goes viral. It is difficult to say what this tells us about viewers and users of YouTube, other than it has opened up the performance stage to virtually everyone and that anything captured on video and uploaded to YouTube will attract the interest of someone else somewhere in the world. In effect, the online stage is virtually synonymous with YouTube.

Viral Videos

The concept of memes can be traced, arguably, to the emergence of the viral video, a video (usually on YouTube) that becomes popular through social media and other forms of Internet sharing. Anything can potentially go viral, such as the Grumpy Cat meme mentioned above, but it is typically either televised sketches, "candid-camera" type videos, musical performances by established celebrities, embarrassing videos, and anything that is hilarious. A perusal of the content of famous viral videos shows that they have some traits in common, including the following:

- the length of the title—the shorter the better
- the running-time—again, the shorter the better
- the degree of humor or irony in the video—the more ludicrous or satirical the better
- the element of surprise
- talent—the more someone displays talent in some area, the better.

But sometimes virality cannot be so easily predicted. In 2008, a YouTube video showed a New York band playing one of its songs, "Take Me Out," using only iPhones. Over two million people viewed the video on YouTube. The large audience for a clip such as this one illustrates the larger phenomenon in the world of YouTube of the apparent unpredictability of success. The videos that go viral have included clips of animals and people dancing, playing instruments, singing, falling, and so on.

The viral video is thus a key to understanding how pop culture, or at least how the notion of "popularity" has changed in the Internet Age.

Merging with All Other Media

Everything can be seen on YouTube, from old rock and roll records and performances, to current jazz compositions, replays of sitcoms, and on and on. YouTube is also home to millions of DIY videos. If the latter go viral, there is a strong chance that the musicians, actors, or performers in them will cross over to other media. In effect, YouTube is now the locus where media converge with DIY productions. YouTube is the leading source of Internet traffic, attracting over more than a billion unique visitors per month, who watch more than six billion hours of video.

In November 2008, YouTube forged an agreement with MGM, Lions Gate Entertainment, and CBS, allowing the companies to post full-length films and television programs on the site, accompanied by advertisements. This merging with traditional media occurs on other sites, of course—for example, websites such as Hulu feature content from NBC, Fox, and Disney. But YouTube now offers many more options than do other sites. It also introduced an online film rentals service, of over six thousand films. In 2011, YouTube joined forces with the Google+ social networking site, allowing YouTube videos to be viewed on the site.

YouTube has redefined the "popular" in pop culture. Both private individuals and traditional production companies have used YouTube to attract audiences. Independent content creators have, actually, built grassroots fans at very little cost or effort. Older media celebrities have progressively moved their acts over to YouTube, attracting international audiences that are much larger than those attainable by television or cinema. YouTube has become a populist voice, and for this it was was awarded a 2008 Peabody Award that described it as a modern-day "Speaker's Corner" that embodies and promotes democracy. Its most subscribed channels feature minorities, contrasting with mainstream media in which the stars are still largely white.

YouTube has also spawned a new form of populist visual journalism, whereby citizen eyewitnesses anywhere and established news institutions share content. YouTube has also allowed government to more easily communicate with citizens. It is relevant to note that the White House's official YouTube channel is one of the top news producers on the site. Since government videos can be accompanied by columns of other videos, some of them critical, it is easy to see why YouTube has indeed become part of a new form of democratization. It is also a place where the horrors of war are showcased, where crimes are caught in action and in situ, and on and on. The implications of the online stage are enormous for the future of pop culture, as will be discussed in the next chapter.

12

FOREVER POP

Man consists of two parts, his mind and his body, only the body has more fun.

—Woody Allen (b. 1935)

Pop culture is everywhere today, thanks to the global village in which we live—on TV, on the radio, in ads, on YouTube, on Facebook, and on and on. And where it is not, more than likely the reason is that a particular society has taken steps to keep it away, fearing that it might radically alter its existing (more traditional) culture. Pop culture is both appealing and controversial (and has always been so). This is why in America the debate on what constitutes legitimate or acceptable culture seems to be always ongoing. One of the themes of this book has been that despite the fact that pop culture has been controversial it has nevertheless survived and spread because it is appealing to common people. It provides an outlet for an engagement in the profane (through music, dance, spectacle, and so on)—an engagement that is clearly as crucial for maintaining a psychic balance as is engagement in the sacred or serious forms of culture.

The purpose of this brief final chapter is to go over some of the more relevant themes that have been interwoven throughout this book, tying some loose ends together, and to take a closer look at the shift of platforms in the delivery of pop culture from traditional media stages to the Internet. In the world of memes and Mashpedia culture, which show no discrimination between a work of high culture, such as a symphony, and the photo of a grumpy cat, the power of pastiche has become saliently obvious.

THE SHOW MUST GO ON

The 2002 movie *Chicago* has been cited throughout this book. The reason is that it deals with why and how pop culture evolved to become so dominant. The movie is about fame-hungry Roxie Hart, who hopes to flee from her boring husband, Amos, and who dreams of a successful life on the vaudeville stage, in the bright lights of Chicago's nightclub scene. Roxie is in awe of club singer Velma Kelly (who has been arrested for the murder of her husband and sister, on discovering their affair). Roxie meets Fred Cassely, a man who convinces her that he can make her showbiz career take off. However, after catering to his sexual desires, Roxie discovers that he has no more connections in show business than she herself does. She thus shoots and kills Fred. Upon discovering her infidelity, Roxie's husband refuses to take the blame for the murder and Roxie is sent to jail to hang. In jail she finally meets Velma Kelly, her idol, who is receiving media attention for the double murder she committed. She also meets other women awaiting trial for the murders of their own partners.

The subtext of the movie (based on a 1976 musical play) is clear—the vaudevillian stage has empowered females to metaphorically kill their controlling men. When Roxie hires slick Chicago lawyer Billy Flynn, he convinces her to get the media to think of her as an innocent victim. The tabloids react positively to the new girl on the cell block, and Roxie finally becomes a star. All this hardly would ever have transpired, or even been contemplated, in an era before pop culture.

As the makers of *Chicago* clearly understood, pop culture is an emotional culture, expressing its inherent sexuality through unconscious subversive power of jazz music and pop music generally. The expression *The show must go on* can be applied to pop culture. As *Chicago* suggests, the power of sexuality works even better when society attempts to prohibit it. *Chicago* takes place in the era of Prohibition, when illegal nightclubs (known as speakeasies), with booze and romance available "after midnight," became the rage for young men and women alike. Known as flappers, the women dressed, smoked, drove cars, danced, and lived a new form of sexual freedom. This shocked the society of the era. Moral panic set in. Linda Scott (2005: 167) puts it eloquently as follows:

> The flapper's dress was particularly well-suited to her nightlife. Going without a corset left the girl free to move—and all the fringe, beads, and spangles shimmied with her. Just as has happened with every other musical sensation coming from the African American community in the

twentieth century—ragtime, swing, rock, blues, rap—the conservatives charged that jazz would corrupt the morals of white youth.

Portrayals of "loose women" have always caused great consternation and reprobation throughout time. With the rise of pop culture, women were still seen as morally corrupt if they expressed their sexuality, but because they were part of the show their roles as women started changing, leading, arguably, to the women's lib movement starting in the 1950s. The stage empowered women rather than victimized them. Maria Elena Buszek (2006) has shown how the so-called subverting images of women in erotic movies, pin-ups, and the like actually made sexual womanhood an open and public affair, not a repressed aspect of the female gender. Starting with burlesque and later *Playboy*, Buszek argues that the story of erotic pop culture is a story of true feminism. In a similar vein, Linda Scott (2005) has argued that the type of feminism that denounced women's roles in erotic spectacles in the 1980s and 1990s was, in effect, an attempt by puritan-minded women intellectuals to control all women, not free them. As Scott (2005: 9) writes, the women on stage were "social activists, who argued passionately for the rights of women to have beauty and pleasure, especially in sexual expression." Similarly, Lynn Peril (2006) points out that the freedom that pop culture has ascribed to women has been met, generally speaking, with hypocrisy or suspicion. But the fact remains that pop culture has been good for women.

However, the line between sexism and sexuality has always been a thin one in pop culture. And perhaps no one has known this more than Eve Ensler, creator of *The Vagina Monologues*, which have been translated and performed throughout the world. Ensler's objective originally was to stop violence against women. The *Monologues* are the result of interviews with more than two hundred women. The subtext is that violence can be stopped if women's sexuality is understood, openly and frankly, and not shrouded in myth and misunderstanding. Clarissa Smith (2007) has also argued this very point in a truly insightful study showing that women should hardly consider themselves to be enslaved by the sexuality of the images coming out of popular media, debunking the myth that women are objects of the male gaze.

Carnival

Of all the theoretical frameworks proposed for explaining pop culture from a psychological viewpoint (chapter 2), the one that seems most

capable of providing a truly meaningful understanding of the phenomenon is carnival theory. Carnivals and spectacles have functioned historically as vehicles for expressing the need for the profane within human
beings to balance their spiritual side. Simply put, pop culture, like traditional carnivals, circuses, and fairs constitutes a release valve for the need
to enjoy oneself even in bizarre ways, giving it a communal expressive
form, and thus rendering it harmless. Pop culture is cathartic, as philosopher Walter Benjamin also argued (chapter 2). For this, Benjamin became
a sidelined member of the School. Jürgen Habermas, a late member of
the School, also broke somewhat with its rigid Marxist philosophy, seeing
in pop culture the power of individual human agency. If there is to be
progress, he claimed, then it must come from the people, not from intellectuals. As John Lough (2002: 219) has aptly phrased it, the Frankfurt
model "presupposes an audience as powerless dupes, with all constituents
making the same reading."

Pop culture is really nothing more than a contemporary descendant of
carnivals. This explains why sexuality, occultism, comedy, satire, and the
like are so intrinsic to pop culture, and why their attempted eradication by
puritanical elements has never succeeded. The Dracula legend, for instance,
is not only the stuff of occult narrative traditions; it is now as intrinsic to
pop culture as are sitcoms. It was introduced to the modern world through
the pen of Bram Stoker (1847–1912), whose novel *Dracula* was first published in 1897 and has remained in print ever since. His treatment became
the yardstick by which all future vampires in pop literature and film would
be measured. The figure of Dracula challenges all authority and simultaneously resuscitates the mythical search for eternal youth and immortality in
the imagination of common people. Stoker's Dracula was the embodiment
of this search, but the Dracula that finds its way into modern-day pop
culture is a much more ambivalent creature. His offspring include ersatz
vampires today who base their lifestyle on drinking blood and dressing up as
Dracula look-alikes (McLelland 2006). Life and the stage are truly simulacra
of each other.

Pop culture is a safeguard against the spread of dangerous forms of
sexism and occultism, since it is always prepared to satirize deeply rooted
notions. Alongside a scary Dracula movie, a television series like the *Ad-
dams Family* satirizes the horror genre, turning it into a channel for laughter.
From ancient times, spectacles and performances evoking tears and laughter
have balanced the psychic tension between the sacred and the profane present within us. The laughter is the laughter of all people, not just intellectuals and cognoscenti. Because it mocks and derides both the sacred and the

profane, it is emotionally powerful. It brings the sacred (politics, religion, business) under the microscope of comedy, where it can be examined cathectically. As Beatrice Otto (2007) has carefully documented, this is why fools and jesters are found across time and across cultures, from the courts of ancient China and India to the courts of medieval Europe, Africa, the Middle East, and the Americas. Not surprisingly, they have had the same function everywhere—to mock and entertain. As Jung claimed, in every person there exists a predilection for puerile mischief. So, at the personal level, the Trickster archetype (as he termed it) may manifest itself as a desire for frivolity, in playing devil's advocate in a discussion, in a sly craving to mock someone's success, in an urge to steal something for the sheer thrill of it, and so on. The Trickster surfaces in Dickens's Artful Dodger, in the fabled character known as Rumpelstiltskin, in Shakespeare's Puck in *A Midsummer Night's Dream*, in the roles assumed by many modern-day comedians, and so on and so forth.

Perhaps no other stage act has come to characterize the essence of pop culture than *The Rocky Horror Picture Show*, mentioned briefly in chapter 1. It was a spectacle blending vampirism, rock culture, transvestitism, pornography, and all the other aspects that make up the carnival. The film debuted in 1975 and, remarkably, is still being shown in some cities. Its appeal is due, in large part, to its blatantly carnevalesque vulgarity. It constitutes a theatrical engagement in rudeness, tastelessness, profanity, crudeness, and impropriety—all those attitudes and behaviors that are constantly suppressed in proper society. It has become a tradition in some cities for it to be shown at midnight on Halloween, when audiences can show up dressed in drag and lingerie without any critical reactions on the part of the people on the streets. The film, the accompanying theatrical performance, and the audience are part of the show. The master of ceremonies, Dr. Frank-N-Furter, instructs his audience at the outset with the following Dionysian advice: "Give yourself over to absolute pleasure. Swim the warm waters of sins of the flesh—erotic nightmares beyond any measure, and sensual daydreams to treasure forever. Can't you just see it? Don't dream it, be it." With that signal, the audience is supposed to start indulging in drinking, smoking, and in various forms of debauchery without interruption by the theater staff.

The men in the show wear corsets and fishnet stockings, while the women wear erotic costumes and act in an overtly sexual fashion. The film itself is replete with sexual themes and fetishes, from Dr. Frank-N-Furter's animated corpse sex-toy, to the liberalization of the uptight, morally hypocritical couple Brad and Janet. As in traditional carnivals, the audience dances and sings along, shouting lewd comments at the screen, and throwing objects at certain points in the film. Such spectacles have emancipatory power, allowing people to engage in fantasy forms of anarchy through a ritualistic ridiculing of the artificial norms that society imposes.

The sacred was mythologized in Greek culture as the realm of Apollo—the god of beauty and of the fine arts—and the profane as the realm of Dionysus—the god of wine, representing the irrational, undisciplined, and orgiastic side of human nature. Pop culture is Dionysian. It impels us to come to grips with our carnality and mortality, before tackling our divinity and spirituality.

Intertexuality

Pop culture is characterized by intertextuality—one text suggesting another (chapter 2). This imparts to it a sense of continuity and structural coherence. Sometimes even an object or prop becomes a means for creating the intertextuality. Take cigarettes in movies as a case in point. In *Casablanca* (1942), cigarettes are used as part of the nightclub scene in Rick's café. Swaggering imperiously in his realm, Rick (Humphrey Bogart) is rarely seen without a cigarette in his mouth or in his hand. So captivating was this image of nightclub cool to cinemagoers, that it became a paradigm imitated by hordes of young males in the 1940s and 1950s. That very paradigm was satirized by Jean Luc Godard in his 1960 film, *Breathless*. In one scene, Jean-Paul Belmondo stares at a poster of Bogart in a cinema window. He takes out a cigarette and starts smoking it, imitating Bogart in *Casablanca*. With the cigarette dangling from the side of his mouth, Belmondo approaches his female mate with a blunt "Sleep with me tonight?" In Nicholas Ray's 1955 movie *Rebel without a Cause*, the sexual cool associated with smoking comes out forcefully in the "car chicken" scene, in which James Dean can be seen dangling a cigarette from a side of his mouth, just before he gets ready to duel his opponent to death with his car. In the 1980 movie, *Caddyshack*, there is a scene parodying smoking as a come-on, when actor Chevy Chase smiles at a woman as smoke comes out of his mouth in a ludicrous, farcical way. There are various other movies that employ the cigarette in similar intertextual ways, ultimately alluding to the *Casablanca* text, including the 2006 movie *Thank You for Smoking*, directed by Jason Reitman, which was designed to show the absurdity of the prohibitionist mentality against smoking.

POP CULTURE SPREAD

Business (the marketplace) has played a critical role in the institution and spread of pop culture. Early in the twentieth century, records by American pop musicians were bought in other countries because the music held great popular appeal. With the advent of television in the 1950s, the spread gained momentum, reaching international proportions with satellite television in the 1990s. Today, with YouTube, the spread has become truly international. Censorship or censorious actions against vulgar elements in pop culture have become virtually moot. Censorship is ineffectual in any case and can even backfire. As Peter Blecha (2004) has documented, some of the most famous songs of Billie Holiday, Elvis Presley, Woody Guthrie, the Beatles, the Rolling Stones, Jimi Hendrix, Frank Zappa, the Sex Pistols, Patti Smith, Public Enemy, Ice-T, 2 Live Crew, Nirvana, Bruce Springsteen, Eminem, the Dixie Chicks, and many more, were either censored or stifled in some way at the start. But all this did was to make them even more popular than they probably would otherwise have been. Prohibition seems to do more to pique interest in the prohibited item than does any intrinsic merit it might have. Moreover, the imposition of censorious strictures in a democratic society raises the question of *what* content is appropriate and *who* has the right to decide so.

Most people can easily distinguish between what is good and what is bad. The answer to the presence of any harmful influences in pop culture is not to be found in censorship; it is to become aware of the meanings embedded in popular representations and media images. When the human mind is aware of these, it will be better able to fend off any undesirable effects that they may cause.

This is in fact what some groups have suggested (chapter 9). In *Culture Jam* (2000), the Canadian activist Kalle Lasn makes a case for "jamming" the messages found in advertising. Lasn founded *Adbusters* magazine to do exactly that. He believes that corporate America is no longer a country, but one overarching marketplace shaped by the cult of celebrity and the spectacles that generate it. Culture and marketing are, according to Lasn, one and the same. What is of interest here is not Lasn's political take on capitalist culture, but how he has approached the problem of how to counteract the images that emanate from it. As a simple example of what jamming implies, take a slogan such as McDonald's *I'm lovin' it!* As it stands, this catchy phrase means nothing and yet everything, since it can allude to almost anything (the food fare, the lifestyle associated with it, and so on). It has rhetorical force. Its ambiguous message can be "jammed" by adding a simple phrase to it, such as *I'm lovin' it, as my arteries clog up with cholesterol!* This phrase deconstructs the rhetorical structure of the message effectively.

POP CULTURE IN THE GLOBAL VILLAGE

Because of trends starting in the Roaring Twenties, there are today many more tolerant attitudes around. As Scott (2005: 166) has aptly observed: "This era brought a wave of sensualism, in which legions of young women—particularly though not exclusively those of modest means—asserted themselves by their dress, their dancing, and their romances." The interplay between levels of culture, as discussed several times, is a distinctive feature of pop culture, whereby alongside numerous spectacles and texts that are nothing but ephemeral entertainments, one finds works with lasting value. But all this might be changing on the Internet stage, which has made DIY culture a reality. The definition of pop culture as a culture by the people for the people has thus taken on a much more literal designation.

As in previous eras of pop culture history, the DIY trend is not unexpected, highlighting the role of common people in the constitution of pop culture. But, unlike the trends of the past, the new stage allows for self-expression to be showcased like never before. This, again, is not without precedence. Letters to the editor and graffiti on city walls are all examples of previous forms of self-expression. But the current Mashpedia form of pop culture may be damaging the integrity of the pop culture experiment itself—an experiment designed ironically to empower common people to express themselves. As Manuel Castells (2001) has cogently argued, cyberspace has made it possible for people to put themselves on display and to establish their identities in public, and this is altering traditional notions of the Self and human experiences of all kinds (from the sensory to the cognitive and social). In the global village, pop culture, as we have known it for over a century, has taken on a new ephemeral form. As mentioned several times in this book, the term *global village* was coined by McLuhan to characterize how people have become interconnected by electronic technologies, which have virtually eliminated the limitations of time and space, contracting the globe into a village. The Internet is an extension of the central nervous system and has thus heightened our awareness of others. This is exactly what once happened in real tribal villages. In the electronic village a form of global tribal consciousness has emerged, as human minds from traditionally foreign cultures interact and produce language and art forms that transcend the traditional national borders, leading to a unified mind that makes it possible to translate any language or code into any other.

The use of electronic media, McLuhan claimed, constitutes a break with the linear forms of mentality produced by print technologies. Along with a change in mentality, the electronic revolution is reconfiguring societies and cultures. On the negative side, McLuhan suggested, a world united by electronic media creates a hyper-stimulated environment that threatens to overwhelm the nervous system itself. The Internet leaves us unaware of its effects by rendering them invisible. In an influential study, the anthropologist Arjun Appadurai (2001) calls these effects *disjuncture* and *difference*, implying that the flow of capital, images, ideas, and artistic textualities do not unfold in a planned and coordinated fashion, as they did in previous worlds, but crisscross constantly along an unpredictable variety of paths.

Global audiences are changing the very nature of how pop culture is created and received. Multilingual audiences are now unified by the Internet. Paradoxically, this seems to have made American pop culture even more widespread, as other countries adopt it and adapt it to their own cultural codes. On the other hand, the popularity of the spectacles of other countries has never been higher in the history of the American pop culture experiment. In the global village, the origin of a cultural product becomes less crucial than how it is circulated and appropriated. In this village, with the proliferation of social media, the global expansion of the major media corporations, and the rise of indie artists and their niche audiences, who have never before had such opportunities to create their own media texts, the world of pop culture has changed drastically.

The implications of the global village for the constitution and evolution of pop culture are, clearly, rather profound. Above all else, cultural products are now available literally at people's fingertips, by either clicking or touching screens. Aware of the power of this new form of access, traditional media outlets now have social media sites for communicating with audiences. It is relevant to note that some psychologists suggest that using mobile devices and social media sites may tap into the same brain areas that make compulsive behaviors addictive, generating the feel-good neurotransmitter dopamine. If this is so, then it corroborates McLuhan's idea that our technological objects are extensions of ourselves, rebounding back into us and affecting psychological and emotional changes.

As Lori Andrews has recently argued, sites such as Facebook have become a veritable Big Brother, being able to track our navigation patterns and use them for various purposes. As such, she writes (2011: 56) that Facebook is redefining the social contract: "There may be a contract between Facebook and its users, but it's surely not the social contract of democratic theorists." Essentially, people seem to be willing to surrender their privacy in exchange for communicative immediacy and self-expression.

The advent and utilization of the Internet stage raises many obvious questions. One of these involves copyright and authorship. The noble idea of opening up the performance stage to everyone via Google is highly idealistic. In October 2005, Google faced a class action suit by authors and publishers, which was resolved in 2009. The settlement created a registry that represents the copyright holders. In return, Google can sell access to copyrighted books. Overall, the Internet allows people to do what they used to do offline, but in a more efficient and expanded way. And it has given common people the power of agency. A new pop musician can be discovered and become a celebrity overnight after appearing on YouTube. But, as it all too often turns out, the popularity generated online quickly fades from public favor, the YouTube video remaining a sad memento of the musician's fifteen minutes of fame. Statistics and popularity rule the digital universe. Using the algorithm called PageRank, Google can easily determine the relevancy of sites and thus, by implication, assign value to information through measurement. Rather than just ranking sites according to the number of times a particular searchword is used, Google ranks them on the basis of the number of links the sites have. If a popular site is linked to a page, then that link is given even greater relevancy. Relevancy is thus tied to statistically determined popularity. As Carr (2008) argues, Google has thus conditioned us to process information statistically, not in terms of understanding. So, Google may in fact be leading to selective and superficial browsing, and that may signal the end of the pop culture experiment.

WILL POP CULTURE SURVIVE?

Pop culture is a form of culture expressed in stories, spectacles, music, and the like that is appealing because it springs from the people and appeals to them directly, not through the interpretive templates of cognoscenti. It has made personal choice a reality. Fragmentation and dispersion now rule the digital stage. And, importantly, pop culture now has its own true theorists—namely, the makers of pop culture texts themselves. In effect, pop culture is itself becoming a meta-theory of who we are. The best theory of the cinema is the movie *Cinema Paradiso* (1988) and the best theory of rock music is Bob Seger's signature tune "Old Time Rock and Roll." Marshall

Fishwick (2002: 24) has commented appropriately on this aspect of modern life as follows:

> Popular culture has many facets, like a diamond, and can be subversive and explosive. Scorn may be mixed with the fun, venom with laughter; it can be wildly comical and deadly serious. Popular culture is at the heart of revolutions that slip in on little cat feet. Those most affected by them—the elite and the mighty—seldom see them coming. Popular culture sees and hears, being close to the people. If the medium is the message, then the reaction might be revolution.

The pop culture experiment might continue, despite fragmentation, dispersion, convergence, and other such trends. In fact, it is probably more accurate to say that it is no more an experiment but an unconscious pattern of mind. This is so, in large part, because of its democratic nature—culture by the people for the people. However, the forces fueling its evolution are changing. It remains to be seen if pop culture, as we have known it for so long, will actually survive or will morph into something new and different. After all, newness and innovation are values that have always undergirded the experiment.

EXERCISES AND DISCUSSION

CHAPTER 1

1. Can you give examples of high, mid, and low forms of pop culture that are currently found in different media?
2. Give examples of conceptual, material, performative, and aesthetic forms of culture.
3. Do you think that trends in youth culture are still the ones today that make their way into the mainstream of pop culture? If so, give examples.
4. Are there any objects, like the jukebox of the past, that symbolize pop culture today? If so, which ones? If not, why do you think they are no longer there?
5. Give your own list of movies, TV programs, and websites where automobiles are featured stars.
6. List anything from the pop culture of previous years that has become part of nostalgia today.
7. How would you approach the study of pop culture today?

CHAPTER 2

1. Use the SMCR model to describe any TV program or webcast today.
2. Explain the difference among the terms broadcasting, narrowcasting, and multicasting.
3. Explain Agenda Setting Theory in your own words. Does it apply today to the Internet?

4. Defend or critique culture industry theory. Does it apply to the world of the Internet today?
5. Explain the following theories or movements in your own words: propaganda theory, feminism, post-feminism, and postmodernism.
6. Listen to the 1938 broadcast of the *War of the Worlds* online. What features made it realistic? What kind of program could be created today to produce a similar effect?
7. Of all the theories explained in this chapter, which ones do you think apply to pop culture today?

CHAPTER 3

1. How would you explain the concept of mega-company in your own terms? Are there any current examples?
2. Add other fads that you think should be among the selection in the chapter.
3. Give a list of any toys you played with in childhood and why you did so.
4. Are T-shirts in fashion today? If so, what do they mean? If not, why not?
5. Give examples of famous chefs on TV and why you think they are popular.
6. Add celebrities and icons that you think should be among the selection in the chapter.
7. Why do you think cars have played a role in pop culture history?

CHAPTER 4

1. Do you read print books for entertainment or do you use some device (such as a tablet)? Which medium do you prefer and why?
2. List your favorite ten fiction books and explain why you like them.
3. Use Propp's Model to analyze any current superhero in pop culture.
4. Do you read a newspaper? If so, in what medium (print or electronic)? Why do you read the newspaper?
5. What type of magazine do you think is popular today? Why?
6. Are comics still popular? Why or why not?

7. Do you think that print popular culture will disappear? If so, why? If not, why not?

CHAPTER 5

1. Do you listen to the radio regularly? On what platform or medium do you listen? Why?
2. What radio programming do you like?
3. List the kinds of specialized radio media that exist today.
4. Use the stock character notion to describe the characters in any adventure hero flick you have seen.
5. Which radio commercials do you remember the most? Why?
6. Explain the difference between entertainment and engagement in your own words.
7. Do you think the radio might still play a role as a social text?

CHAPTER 6

1. What kinds of music do you listen to? Which are popular in general?
2. Add to the list of music genres in the chapter any other genres that you think should be there. Explain your choices.
3. Why do you think changes in pop music dovetail with changes in society?
4. Add to the list of rap and hip-hop events in the chapter any other ones that you think should be there. Explain your choices.
5. What is indie music? Does it constitute its own genre? How so?
6. On what platform do you access your favorite music? Why?
7. Do you think that pop music is as influential in changing society today as it once was?

CHAPTER 7

1. Do you go to the movies or do you prefer to watch movies on some platform? Why?
2. Add to the list of movie genres in the chapter any other genres that you think should be there. Explain your choices.

3. Do you like thrillers? Why do you think they appeal so broadly?

4. Do you like horror flicks? Again, why do you think they appeal so broadly?

5. Which blockbuster movies have you seen? Which are your favorites? Explain why.

6. Do you think that moviemaking today might be too dependent on the blockbuster formula?

7. Do you think YouTube might eventually displace all other means of seeing movies?

CHAPTER 8

1. Do you watch TV regularly? Why and when?

2. What are your favorite programs on TV? Explain why you like them.

3. Discuss the role of the TV sitcom in bringing about social changes.

4. Why do you think Reality TV is so popular?

5. Watch the *Truman Show* online and then discuss it in class.

6. Describe any TV mythology today.

7. Do you think traditional TV will survive in the Internet Age? Explain your answer.

CHAPTER 9

1. List the ads that you think are the most interesting and popular today. Explain why this is so.

2. Give your own examples of product placement in the movies.

3. Give your own examples of product placement on TV programs.

4. Give other types of persuasion strategies that ads seem to employ in addition to the ones mentioned in the chapter.

5. What kind of advertising do you think is the most effective?

6. Why do you think advertising has become popular?

7. Design an ad campaign for your favorite pop celebrity. Discuss it in class.

CHAPTER 10

1. Give examples of pop language today. Where do you think they came from?
2. Take any recent children's movie and analyze its language in terms of trendiness.
3. Define urban slang in your own words. Give examples of current urban slang.
4. Why do you think profanity is intrinsic to many types of slang?
5. Give examples of social media slang in addition to the items in the chapter.
6. Do you use Twitter? If so, list the kinds of linguistic patterns that apply to Twitter.
7. Do you think that textspeak is leading to an impoverishment of language? Defend your position.

CHAPTER 11

1. Explain in your words McLuhan's idea that technology extends human faculties. Give some examples of your own.
2. Why do you think pop culture is so tied to changes in technology?
3. Explain convergence theory in your own words.
4. Do you agree that online culture is a "Mashpedia culture"? Defend your response.
5. Give a list of your favorite Internet memes.
6. What roles do you think Facebook and Twitter play in the world of pop culture other than the ones mentioned in the chapter?
7. Why do you think Grumpy Cat went viral and became a major meme?

CHAPTER 12

1. Watch the movie *Chicago* and pick out the parts and aspects that fit in with the kinds of ideas about pop culture expounded in this book.
2. Do you agree that humans need to engage in the profane every once in a while? Defend your response.
3. Give examples of intertextuality of your own.

4. What trends from non-American cultures have gone viral and have become part of a new global pop culture?
5. Explain why you think that something like Gangnam Style would become a meme.
6. Why do you think junk food became ordinary food?
7. Do you think pop culture will survive? If so, how do you think it will be different?

GLOSSARY

The following glossary contains many of the terms used in this book that might require a formal definition. Those that are used in a descriptive manner (such as *carnivalesque*) are not included here. Also excluded are terms for technological devices such as *iPods* and *cell phones* and terms that are well known generally (for example, *broadcasting*).

acronym a word formed from the initial letters of a series of words. WAC = Women's Army Corps; radar = *r*adio *d*etecting *a*nd *r*anging; laser = *l*ight *a*mplification by *s*timulated *e*mission of *r*adiation; UNESCO = *U*nited *N*ations *E*ducational, *S*cientific, and *C*ultural *O*rganization. Acronymy is a major feature of the language used in text messages and other types of digital forms of communication: *cm* = *call me, ruok? = Are you OK?*

addressee the receiver of a message; the individual(s) to whom a message is directed.

addresser the sender of a message; the creator of a message.

advertising any type or form of public announcement designed to promote the sale of specific commodities or services (primarily through persuasion).

aesthesia the experience of sensation; in art appreciation it refers to the fact that our senses and feelings are stimulated holistically by art works.

alliteration the repetition of the initial consonant sounds of words: *super sounds; pitter patter.*

anagram word or phrase made from another word or phrase by rearranging its letters: *won = now; dread = adder; drop = prod; stop = pots.*

archetype an original model or type after which other similar things are patterned.

audience the specified group of individuals toward whom media products are directed or who attend or engage in specific kinds of pop culture spectacles.

binary opposition term referring to the fact that many aspects of meaning are perceived in terms of opposites, such as *good vs. evil, night vs. day,* and so on. An opposition often leads to a connected set of derived oppositions. So, for example, in a narrative the *good* characters are opposed to the *evil* ones in terms of derived oppositions such as *us vs. them, right vs. wrong, truth vs. falsity* and so on. These categories are manifested in actions, statements, plot twists, and the like. In cultural theory, some binary oppositions—such as *self vs. other, us vs. them, man vs. woman, young vs. old*—are seen as potentially dangerous because of the tendency of people to identify with one of the two elements in the opposition, seeing the other negatively or as a derivative.

blockbuster   a film or book that gains widespread popularity and achieves enormous sales.

brand image   the recognizable traits or "personality" of a product created through its name, packaging, price, and style of advertisement.

brand name   the name given to a product.

branding   the integration of products with media and pop culture events, programs, celebrities, and so forth.

bricolage   the technique of putting together different elements to create something new. The notion has been used in particular to describe subcultures' appropriation of elements from the mainstream culture in order to transform or subvert their meanings (as in punk fashion).

bull's-eye model   a model that depicts communication as a process consisting of a sender aiming a message at a receiver as if in a bull's-eye target range.

burlesque   a comic performance characterized by ridiculous exaggeration. Burlesque first appeared in the plays of the Greek dramatists Aristophanes (448? –388? BCE) and Euripides (480?–406 BCE), and the Roman playwright Plautus (254?–184 BCE). The seventeenth-century French playwright Molière (1622– 1673) made dramatic burlesque a high art form. In the United States, the word *burlesque* was applied to a form of theatrical production, especially popular in the 1920s and 1930s, characterized by ribald comedy and scantily clad women, and often including stripteases.

cabaret   live entertainment in a locale such as a club or restaurant consisting of singing, dancing, and comedy.

carnival   traditional form of outdoor amusement that consists of exhibits, games, rides, shows, feasting, and merrymaking. The carnival event has been used to explain the appeal of pop culture spectacles.

cartoon   drawing, often with a caption, caricaturing or symbolizing some event, situation, or person of topical interest; a strip of drawings that tell a story; an animated humorous film intended primarily for children (also called *toon*).

catharsis hypothesis   claim that the representation of sex, violence, and aggression in media and pop culture spectacles has a preventive purging effect, since an involvement in fantasy aggression may provide a release from hostile impulses that otherwise might be acted out in real life.

celebrity   person in the public eye primarily because of media exposure. A celebrity is usually an actor, a television personality, a pop musician, or the like.

censorship   control of what people may say, hear, write or read by some institution (usually governmental).

channel   the physical means by which a signal or message is transmitted.

character   a person portrayed in an artistic piece, such as a drama or novel.

Charleston   a dance style characterized by kicking out the feet sideways while the knees are kept together. The dance popularized the image of stylish young women of the 1920s called *flappers*.

chick flick   a film that is intended or perceived to appeal primarily to women, given its romantic, sentimental, or human relations plot, or else its focus on the changing role of women in society.

closed text   a text that elicits a singular interpretation or a very limited range of interpretations.

codex   a proto-book used in the Middle Ages, generally dealing with classic works or the scriptures.

collage   an artistic arrangement of materials and objects pasted on a surface or computer screen, often with unifying lines and color.

comic book   a magazine using cartoon characters. Most comic books tell stories, though they have also been used for education, artistic expression, and other purposes.

commedia dell'arte   a type of comedy developed in Italy in the sixteenth century, characterized by improvisation from standard plot outlines and stock characters, who often wear traditional masks and costumes.

commercial   an advertisement on the radio, television, or Internet, normally involving a story or skit and/or a jingle. Commercials were first developed for radio in the 1920s.

communication   social interaction through the exchange of messages; the production and exchange of messages and meanings; the use of specific modes and media to transmit messages.

consumerist   overly concerned with material goods.

contact   the psychological and social connections that inhere between interlocutors in a communication situation.

context   the situation (physical, psychological, and/or social) in which a text or spectacle is performed or occurs, or to which it refers.

convergence   the erosion of traditional distinctions among media due to concentration of ownership, globalization, and audience fragmentation; the process by which formerly separate technologies such as television and the telephone are brought together by a common technological base (digitization) or a common industrial strategy.

culture jammers   a group of social activists with a popular website and magazine that are critical of the advertising process.

culture wars   any clash of tastes and ideologies with regard to cultural products.

cyberspace   the realm of communication over the Internet. The term was coined by American writer William Gibson in his 1984 science fiction novel *Neuromancer*, in which he described cyberspace as a place of "unthinkable complexity."

decoding   the process of deciphering a text on the basis of its code or codes (systems of meaning) and the medium or media used.

Digital Galaxy   the new social order ushered in by the Internet.

digital media   computer-based systems of transmission.

e-book   digital book (published on the Internet).

effects models   models of media and pop culture texts attempting to explain any effects (psychological, social, and so on) they may have on people, societies, and cultures.

Electronic Galaxy   the social order ushered in by electronic media.

electronic media   devices such as radios and computers that allow for the sending and reception of electromagnetic signals.

emotive   containing emotional intent (for example in communicating something).

encoding   the use of a code or codes (systems of meaning) to select or create a text using a specific medium or media.

e-toon   a digital comic or cartoon (published on the Internet).

e-zine   a digital magazine (published on the Internet).

feedback   reaction to transmitted messages that informs the sender as to the nature of its reception.

feminism   a movement advocating the same rights and opportunities for women as are enjoyed by men. Feminist beliefs have existed throughout history, but feminism as a social movement did not become widespread until the mid-1800s, when women were barred by law from voting in elections or serving on juries and when most institutions of higher education and most professional careers were also closed to women. Many historians regard the feminist movement as a turning point in the history of modern societies.

feminist theory   a theory devoted to showing how media-pop culture texts and social power structures coalesce to define gender categories; a framework for studying the images and portrayals of women in the media.

fetish   an object that is believed to have magical or spiritual powers, or to cause sexual arousal.

fiction   a text whose content is produced by the imagination and is not necessarily based on fact.

flappers   stylish and fun-loving young women of the 1920s who showed disdain for the traditional social conventions associated with women.

Frankfurt School   a school of critical inquiry founded at the University of Frankfurt in 1922. It was the world's first Marxist institute of social research. Its aim was to understand the way in which human groups create meaning collectively under the impact of modern technology, capitalist social systems, and culture industries. The school was highly pessimistic about the possibility of genuine individuality under modern capitalism and condemned most forms of popular or mass culture as a type of incessant propaganda that indoctrinated the masses and disguised genuine social inequalities. The school's main con-tention was that typical pop culture fare was vulgar, functioning primarily to pacify ordinary people.

gangsta rap   a style of rap music in which the lyrics deal with themes involving gangs, gangsters, and/or criminal lifestyles.

genre   a group of classification for works of literature, art, music, and so on. A genre is recognizable as distinct because of the subject matter it deals with, the themes it embodies, the style it adopts, and so forth.

global village   a world that has become dependent upon electronic media for information and is thus united, electronically, as if in a village. The term was coined by Marshall McLuhan.

globalization   the process by which formerly separate, discrete, or local cultural phenomena are brought into contact with one another and with new groups of people in an interactive fashion.

goth   a form of punk music and lifestyle characterized by the wearing of dark clothes, the use of dark cosmetics, and other macabre forms of symbolism.

Gutenberg Galaxy   the radical new social order ushered in by the invention of the printing press. The term was coined by Marshall McLuhan.

hegemony   the far-reaching power of the dominant class in a capitalist society. The term is most closely associated with the Italian Marxist Antonio Gramsci.

hermeneutics   the art and method of interpreting texts.

hippies   the members of a youth movement of the 1960s and 1970s that started in the United States and spread to many other countries.

hypertextuality   a system for linking different texts and images within a computer document or over a network.

icon   a celebrity who gains culture-wide status.

image   a representation of a personality, product, or service used to enhance the aesthetic, social, or economic value of the product or service represented.

Internet   the matrix of networks that connects computers around the world.

interpretation   the process of figuring out what something (word, text) means.

intertextuality   allusions within a text to another text or texts.

irony   use of words to express something different from and often opposite to their literal meaning, usually for satirical effect.

jingle   a catchy tune used in commercials.

logo   a distinctive signature, trademark, colophon, motto, or nameplate of a company or brand.

magazine   a paper-based publication consisting of a collection of articles or stories, or both, published at regular intervals.

marketing   the business of positioning goods and services to the right audience.

Marxism   a socioeconomic and philosophical theory developed by Karl Marx and Friedrich Engels. It constitutes the blueprint ideology behind Communism, holding that all people are entitled to enjoy the fruits of their labor, but are prevented from doing so in capitalist systems, which divide society into two classes—non-owning workers and nonworking owners.

mass media   media such as radio, television, newspapers, periodicals, and the Internet that have the capacity to reach a large audience.

media convergence   the transferal of all media into digital formats and, thus, their integration into a single transmission system.

medium   the physical means or process used to encode a certain type of message and deliver it through some channel.

meme   an idea, a photo, a song, and so on that becomes popular through the Internet.

message   information transmitted by words, signals, or other means from one person, station, or group to another with a specific function or meaning.

multimedia   combined use of several media, such as images, music, print, and so on in the construction of a text or in the performance of some spectacle.

mythology   a set of latent mythic themes or symbols in some media product or pop culture spectacle.

narrative   something told or written, such as an account, story, tale, and so on.

narrator   the teller of the narrative.

narrowcasting   broadcasting designed to reach specific types of audiences.

newspaper   a paper-based publication, usually issued on a daily or weekly basis, the main function of which is to report the news.

noise   any interfering element (physical or psychological) in the channel that distorts or partially effaces a message.

novel   a fictional prose narrative of considerable length, typically having a plot that is unfolded by the actions, speech, and thoughts of the characters.

open text   a text that entails a complex interpretation of its meaning.

opposition   the psychological process by which ideas and forms are differentiated in binary pairs (for example, *good vs. evil* and *night vs. day*).

parody   a work imitating the characteristic style of someone or another work in a satirical or humorous way.

pastiche   a media product or pop culture text or spectacle that is created in imitation of another similar one; or is constructed with a blend of borrowed styles.

plot   a plan or sequence of events in a narrative.

pop art   an artistic movement depicting objects or scenes from everyday life and employing techniques of commercial art and design.

pop culture   culture produced by the people for the people.

pop language   language that is spread through media spectacles.

pop music   music intended to be appreciated by ordinary people, usually for entertainment and pleasure.

pop star   an individual in media who has become an icon in his or her field.

positioning   the placing or marketing of a product for the right audience.

post-feminism   an approach to pop culture and media that still holds on to basic feminist criticism, but which expands it considerably, especially with respect to the previous restrictive feminist view of women's sexuality.

postmodernism   the belief that all knowledge is relative and human-made.

print media media based on paper (or similar) technology.

propaganda a systematic dissemination of doctrines, views, and so on reflecting specific interests and ideologies (political, social, and so on).

pulp fiction magazines and novels produced on cheap paper, dealing with very popular and titillating themes, such as crime, horror, and sex.

radio a system for sending audio signals through the air without wires via electromagnetic waves.

receiver a person or group at whom a message is aimed.

reception theory a theory that attempts to explain how audiences interpret texts and spectacles.

redundancy the repetition of parts of a message to counteract noise in a channel.

representation the process of giving a form to some idea, ritual, and so on.

semiotics the discipline that studies signs and their uses in representation.

sender the transmitter of a message.

setting the place, space, or context in which a narrative unfolds.

slogan a catchword or phrase used to advertise a product.

subtext the concealed or implicit system of meanings within a text.

synesthesia stimulation of different sensory reactions by juxtaposition: *loud colors*.

tabloid a small-format newspaper that is roughly half the size of a standard newspaper, usually containing sensationalistic coverage of crime, scandal, gossip, violence, and news about celebrities.

television the system for sending audio and visual signals through the air via electromagnetic waves.

text a message meant to be interpreted.

transmission the sending and reception of messages.

vaudeville the principal form of popular entertainment in North America before the advent of cinema in the late nineteenth and early twentieth century.

World Wide Web an information server on the Internet composed of interconnected sites and files, accessible with a browser program.

youth culture the various forms of music, clothing, and other features that are adopted by young people.

REFERENCES AND
FURTHER READING

The following bibliography contains both the works referenced in this text and those that have been consulted but not cited. Overall, this extensive bibliography can be used for further reading and advanced research purposes.

Abercrombie, N. (1996). *Television and Society*. Cambridge: Polity Press.

Abrams, N., I. Bell, and J. Udris. (2001). *Studying Film*. London: Arnold.

Ahern, S., ed. (2006). *Making Radio*. Sydney: Allen and Unwin.

Alesso, P., and C. F. Smith. (2009). *Thinking on the Web: Berners-Lee, Gödel and Turing*. Hoboken, NJ: John Wiley.

Anderson, W. T. (1992). *Reality Isn't What It Used to Be*. San Francisco: Harper Collins.

Andrews, L. (2011). *I Know Who You Are and I Saw What You Did: Social Networks and the Death of Privacy*. New York: Free Press.

Ang, I. (1995). *Living Room Wars: Rethinking Media Audiences for a Postmodern World*. London and New York: Routledge.

Appadurai, A. (2001). *Globalization*. Durham, N.C.: Duke University Press.

Artz, L., and B. Murphy. (2000). *Cultural Hegemony in the United States*. Beverly Hills: Sage.

Atwan, G. (2008). *The Facebook Book*. New York: Abrams.

Auletta, K. (2009). *Googled: The End of the World as We Know It*. New York: Penguin.

Austin, T. (2002). *Hollywood, Hype and Audiences: Selling and Watching Popular Film in the 1990s*. Manchester, UK: Manchester University Press.

Bakhtin, M. (1981). *The Dialogic Imagination: Four Essays*. Austin: University of Texas Press.

Bakhtin, M. (1986). *Speech Genres and Other Late Essays*. Austin: University of Texas Press.

Bakhtin, M. (1993). *Rabelais and His World*. Bloomington: Indiana University Press.

Baran, S. J. (2004). *Introduction to Mass Communication, Media Literacy, and Culture*. New York: McGraw-Hill.

Barbour, A. G. (1970). *Days of Thrills and Adventure*. New York: Macmillan.

Barker, D. C. (2002). *Rushed to Judgment: Talk Radio, Persuasion, and American Political Behavior*. New York: Columbia University Press.

Baron, N. S. (2000). *Alphabet to Email: How Written English Evolved and Where It's Heading*. London: Routledge.

Baron, N. S. (2008). *Always On*. Oxford: Oxford University Press.

Barthes, R. (1957). *Mythologies*. Paris: Seuil.

Barthes, R. (1967). *Système de la mode*. Paris: Seuil.

Barthes, R. (1975). *The Pleasure of the Text*. New York: Hill and Wang.

Barthes, R. (1981). "Theory of the Text." In *Untying the Text*, edited by Robert Young, 31–47. London: Routledge.

Bataille, G. (1962). *Erotism, Death and Sensuality*. New York: City Light Books.

Baudrillard, J. (1983). *Simulations*. New York: Semiotexte.

Bauerlein, M. (2008). *The Dumbest Generation: How the Digital Age Stupefies Young Americans and Jeopardizes Our Future or, Don't Trust Anyone under 30*. New York: Penguin.

Bauman, Z. (1992). *Intimations of Postmodernity*. London: Routledge.

Belasco, W. (1989). *Appetite for Change: How the Counterculture Took on the Food Industry 1966–1988*. New York: Pantheon Books.

Bell, D. (2007). *Cyberculture Theorists: Manuel Castells and Donna Haraway*. London: Routledge.

Benedikt, M. (1991). *Cyberspace: First Steps*. Cambridge, MA: MIT Press.

Bennett, T., et al., eds. (1981). *Culture and Social Process: A Reader*. London: Open University Press.

Berger, A. A. (1992). *Popular Culture Genres: Theories and Texts*. Newbury Park, CA: Sage.

Berger, A. A. (1996). *Manufacturing Desire: Media, Popular Culture, and Everyday Life*. New Brunswick, NJ: Transaction Publishers.

Berger, A. A. (2000). *Ads, Fads, and Consumer Culture: Advertising's Impact on American Character and Society*. Lanham, MD: Rowman & Littlefield.

Berger, A. A. (2005). *Making Sense of Media: Key Texts in Media and Cultural Studies*. Oxford: Blackwell.

Berger, A. A. (2007). *Media and Society: A Critical Perspective*. Lanham, MD: Rowman & Littlefield.

Bernard, S. (2000). *Studying Radio*. London: Arnold.

Biagi, S. (2001). *Media/Impact: An Introduction to Mass Media*. Belmont, CA: Wadsworth/Thomson Learning.

Bignell, J. (2005). *Big Brother: Reality TV in the Twenty-First Century*. New York: Palgrave Macmillan.

Bissell, T. (2010). *Extra Lives: Why Video Games Matter*. New York: Pantheon.

Blecha, P. (2004). *Taboo Tunes: A History of Banned and Censored Songs*. San Francisco: Backbeat.

Bolter, J. D., and R. Grusin. (1999). *Remediation: Understanding New Media*. New York and London: MIT.

Boon, M. (2002). *The Road of Excess: A History of Writers on Drugs*. Cambridge, MA: Harvard University Press.

Borland, J. (2008). Crossover Camera. *Technology Review* (22 April 2008). http://www.technologyreview.com/computing/20657/?a=f.

Bottomore, T. (1984). *The Frankfurt School*. London: Routledge.

Boyd, D. (2014). *It's Complicated: The Social Lives of Networked Teens*. New Haven, CT: Yale University Press.

Braudy, L. (1997). *The Frenzy of Renown: Fame and Its History*. New York: Vintage.

Briggs, A., and P. Burke. (2005). *A Social History of the Media: From Gutenberg to the Internet*. 2nd ed. Cambridge: Polity Press.

Briggs, A., and P. Cobley, eds. (1998). *The Media: An Introduction*. Essex, UK: Addison Wesley Longman.

Britton, W. (2005). *Beyond Bond: Spies in Fiction and Film*. Westport, CT: Praeger.

Britton, W. (2006). *Onscreen and Undercover: The Ultimate Book of Movie Espionage*. Westport, CT: Praeger.

Brooker, W. (2001). *Batman Unmasked: Analyzing a Cultural Icon*. New York: Continuum.

Bruhn Jensen, K. (2010). *Media Convergence*. London: Routledge.

Buszek, M. E. (2006). *Pin-Up Grrrls: Feminism, Sexuality, Popular Culture*. Durham, NC: Duke University Press.

Campbell, R., C. R. Martin, and B. Fabos. (2005). *Media and Culture: An Introduction to Mass Communication*. Boston: Bedford/St. Martin's.

Carr, N. (2008). *The Shallows: What the Internet Is Doing to our Brains*. New York: Norton.

Carter, A. (1991). *Wise Children*. New York: Chatto and Windus.

Cashmore, E. (2006). *Celebrity Culture*. London: Routledge.

Castells, M. (2001). *The Internet Galaxy*. Oxford: Oxford University Press.

Cawelti, J. (1971). *The Six-Gun Mystique*. Bowling Green, OH: Bowling Green University Popular Press.

Cleland, S., and I. Brodsky. (2011). *Search and Destroy: Why You Can't Trust Google Inc*. New York: Telescope.

Cobley, P. (2000). *The American Thriller*. New York: Palgrave.

Cohen, S. (1972). *Folk Devils and Moral Panics: The Creation of Mods and Rockers*. London: MacGibbon and Kee.

Cook, M. L., and S. T. Miller. (1998). *Mystery, Detective, and Espionage Fiction: A Checklist of Fiction in U.S. Pulp Magazines, 1915–1974*. New York: Garland.

Cook, V. (2004). *Why Can't Anybody Spell?* New York: Touchstone.

Coupland, D. (2010). *Marshall McLuhan: You Know Nothing of My Work!* New York: Atlas.

Cronenberg, D. (1992). *Cronenberg on Cronenberg*. London: Faber and Faber.

Crothers, L. (2006). *Globalization and American Popular Culture*. Lanham, MD: Rowman & Littlefield.

Crystal, D. (2006). *Language and the Internet*. 2nd ed. Cambridge: Cambridge University Press.

Crystal, D. (2008). *txtng: the gr8 db8*. Oxford: Oxford University Press.

Cullen, R. (2007). *The Little Hiptionary*. White Plains, NY: Peter Pauper Press.

D'Ammassa, D. (2008). *Encyclopedia of Adventure Fiction*. New York: Facts on File.

Danesi, M. (2010). *Geeks, Goths, and Gangstas: Youth Culture and the Evolution of Modern Society*. Toronto: Canadian Scholars' Press.

Darby, D., and W. Shelby. (2005). *Hip Hop and Philosophy: Rhyme 2 Reason*. Chicago: Open Court.

Debbie, N. (2007). *Pornography*. Toronto: Groundwork Books.

Deleuze, G. (1968). *Difference and Repetition*. New York: Columbia University Press.

Derrida, J. (1976). *Of Grammatology*. Trans. Gayatri Chakravorty Spivak. Baltimore: Johns Hopkins Press.

Derrida, J. (1978). *Writing and Difference*. Chicago: University of Chicago Press.

Derry, C. (1988). *The Suspense Thriller: Films in the Shadow of Alfred Hitchcock*. Jefferson, NC: McFarland.

Deuze, M. (2010. *Media Life*. Cambridge: Polity Press.

Dovey, J. (2000). *Freakshow: First Person Media and Factual Television*. London: Pluto.

Duncan, B. (1988). *Mass Media and Popular Culture*. Toronto: Harcourt, Brace, Jovanovich.

Durkheim, É. (1912). *The Elementary Forms of Religious Life*. New York: Collier.

Dyer, G. (1982). *Advertising as Communication*. London: Routledge.

Eagleton, T. (1987). *Saints and Scholars*. London: Verso.

Eco, U. (1979). *The Role of the Reader: Explorations in the Semiotics of Texts*. Bloomington: Indiana University Press.

Edwards, D. (2011). *I'm Feeling Lucky: The Confessions of Google Employee Number 59*. Boston: Houghton Mifflin Harcourt.

Ehrenreich, B. (1990). *The Worst Years of Our Lives*. New York: Pantheon.

Ehrenreich, B. (2006). *Dancing in the Streets: A History of Collective Joy*. New York: Henry Holt.

Eisenstein, E. L. (1979). *The Printing Press as an Agent of Change: Communications and Cultural Transformations in Early-Modern Europe*. Cambridge: Cambridge University Press.

Ekman, P. (1985). *Telling Lies*. New York: Norton.

Ellis, J. (1992). *Visible Fictions: Cinema, Television, Video*. London: Routledge.

Ellis, M. (2000). *Slanguage: A Cool, Fresh, Phat, and Shagadelic Guide to All Kinds of Slang*. New York: Hyperion.

Essany, M. (2008). *Reality Check: The Business and Art of Producing Reality TV*. Oxford: Elsevier.

Ewen, S. (1988). *All Consuming Images*. New York: Basic.

Fedorak, S. A. (2009). *Pop Culture: The Culture of Everyday Life.* Toronto: University of Toronto Press.

Fine, G. A. (1983). *Shared Fantasy: Role-Playing Games as Social Worlds.* Chicago: University of Chicago Press.

Fingeroth, D. (2004). *Superman on the Couch: What Superheroes Really Tell Us about Ourselves and Our Society.* New York: Continuum.

Fishwick, M. W. (1999). *Popular Culture: Cavespace to Cyberspace.* New York: The Haworth Press.

Fishwick, M. W. (2002). *Popular Culture in a New Age.* New York: The Haworth Press.

Fiske, J. (1987). *Television Culture.* London: Methuen.

Forman, M., and M. A. Neal. (2004). *That's the Joint: The Hip-Hop Studies Reader.* Routledge: New York and London.

Foucault, M. (1972). *The Archeology of Knowledge.* Trans. A. M. Sheridan Smith. New York: Pantheon.

Frank, T. (1997). *The Conquest of Cool: Business Culture, Counterculture, and the Rise of Hip Consumerism.* Chicago: University of Chicago Press.

Frankel, A. (2004). *Word Craft: The Art of Turning Little Words into Big Business.* New York: Three Rivers Press.

Franklin, B. (1996). *The Autobiography of Benjamin Franklin (1706-1757).* New York: Dover.

Frederic J. (1991). *Postmodernism, or, The Cultural Logic of Late Capitalism.* Durham, NC: Duke University Press.

Frith, S. (1983). *Sound Effects: Youth, Leisure and the Politics of Rock.* London: Constable.

Fuchs, C. (2008). *Internet and Society: Social Theory in the Information Age.* London: Routledge.

Gauntlet, D. (2007). *Creative Explorations: New Approaches to Identities and Audiences.* London: Routledge.

Gauvreau Judge, M. (2000). *If It Ain't Got That Swing: The Rebirth of Grown-Up Culture.* New York: Spence.

Gedalof, A. J., J. Boulter, J. Faflak, and C. McFarlane, eds. (2005). *Cultural Subjects: A Popular Culture Reader.* Toronto: Nelson.

Gelder, K. (2007). *Subcultures: Cultural Histories and Social Practice.* London: Routledge.

Genosko, G. (1999). *McLuhan and Baudrillard.* London: Routledge.

George, N. (1998). *Hip-Hop America.* New York: Viking.

Gerbner, G., and L. Gross. (1976). Living with Television: The Violence Profile. *Journal of Communication* 26: 172–99.

Gibson, W. (1984). *Neuromancer.* London: Grafton.

Gilroy, P. (1990). *Their Ain't No Black in the Union Jack.* Chicago: University of Chicago Press.

Gleick, J. (2011). *The Information: A History, a Theory, a Flood.* New York: Pantheon.

Godard, J.-L. (1992). *Projections.* London: Faber and Faber.

Goodlad, L. M. E., and M. Bibby, eds. (2007). *Goth: Undead Subculture.* Durham, NC: Duke University Press.

Goodwin, A. (1992). *Dancing in the Distraction Factory: Music Television and Popular Culture.* Minneapolis: University of Minnesota Press.

Gough-Yates, A. (2003). *Understanding Women's Magazines.* London: Routledge.

Green, M. B. (1991). *Seven Types of Adventure Tale: An Etiology of a Major Genre.* University Park: Pennsylvania State University Press.

Greenwald, T. (1992). *Rock & Roll.* New York: Friedman.

Grossberg, L. (1992). *We Gotta Get Out of This Place: Popular Conservatism and Postmodern Culture.* London: Routledge.

Grossberg, L., C. Nelson, and P. Treichler, eds. (1991). *Cultural Studies.* London: Routledge.

Guertin, C. (2013). "Convergence." In *Encyclopedia of Media and Communication*, edited by M. Danesi, 201–2. Toronto: University of Toronto Press.

Hall, S. (1973). *Encoding and Decoding in the Television Discourse.* London: The Seminar Press.

Hall, S., ed. (1977). *Cultural Representations and Signifying Practice.* London: Open University Press.

Hall, S. (1978). *Policing the Crisis: Mugging, the State and Law and Order.* Houndsmills, Basingstoke, UK: Palgrave Macmillan.

Hall, S., and P. Whannel. (1964). *The Popular Arts.* London: Hutchinson.

Haraway, D. (1989). *Primate Visions: Gender, Race, and Nature in the World of Modern Science.* London: Routledge.

Haraway, D. (1991). *Simians, Cyborgs and Women: The Reinvention of Nature.* London: Routledge.

Harkin, J. (2009). *Lost in Cyburbia: How Life on the Net Has Created a Life of Its Own.* Toronto: Knopf.

Hebdige, D. (1979). *Subculture: The Meaning of Style.* London: Routledge.

Hedges, C. (2009). *Empire of Illusion: The End of Literacy and the Triumph of Spectacle.* New York: Knopf.

Heins, M. (2001). *Not in Front of the Children: Indecency, Censorship and the Innocence of Youth.* New York: Hill and Wang.

Helprin, M. (2009). *Digital Barbarism: A Writer's Manifesto.* New York: Harper Collins.

Henderson, J. L. (1964). "Ancient Myths and Modern Man." In *Man and His Symbols*, edited by C. G. Jung, 95–156. New York: Dell.

Herman, A., and T. Swiss, eds. (2000). *The World Wide Web and Contemporary Cultural Theory.* London: Routledge.

Herman, E. S., and N. Chomsky. (1988). *Manufacturing Consent: The Political Economy of the Mass Media.* New York: Pantheon.

Hermes, J. (2005). *Re-reading Popular Culture*. London: Blackwell.

Hesmondhalgh, D. (2005). "Producing Celebrity." In *Understanding Media: Inside Celebrity*, edited by Jessica Evans and David Hesmondhalgh, 97–134. Maidenhead, UK: Open University Press.

Heyer, P. (2005). *The Medium and the Magician: Orson Welles, the Radio Years, 1934–1952*. Lanham, MD: Rowman & Littlefield.

Hill, A. (2005). *Reality TV: Audiences and Popular Factual Television*. New York: Routledge.

Hinds, H. E., M. F. Motz, and A. M. S. Nelson, eds. (2006). *Popular Culture Theory and Methodology*. Madison: University of Wisconsin Press.

Hoffman, D. L., and T. P. Novak. (1996). "Marketing in Hypermedia Computer-Mediated Environments: Conceptual Foundations." *Journal of Marketing* 60: 50–68.

Holquist, M. (1990). *Dialogism: Bakhtin and His World*. London: Routledge.

Hong, S. (2001). *Wireless: From Marconi's Black-Box to the Audion*. Cambridge, MA: MIT Press.

Hoppenstand, G., ed. (2007). *The Greenwood Encyclopedia of World Popular Culture*. Westport, CT: Greenwood Publishing.

Huff, R. M. (2006). *Reality Television*. Westport, CT: Praeger.

Indick, W. (2006). *Psycho Thrillers: Cinematic Explorations of the Mysteries of the Mind*. Jefferson, NC: McFarland.

Inness, S. (1999). *Tough Girls: Women Warriors and Wonder Women in Popular Culture*. Philadelphia: University of Pennsylvania Press.

Irwin, W., M. T. Conrad, and A. J. Skoble, eds. (2001). *The Simpsons and Philosophy*. Chicago: Open Court.

Jackson, J. A. (1998). *American Bandstand: Dick Clark and the Making of a Rock 'n' Roll Empire*. Oxford: Oxford University Press.

James, C. (1983). *Glued to the Box*. London: Jonathan Cape.

Jameson, F. (1991). *Postmodernism, or, The Cultural Logic of Late Capitalism*. Durham: Duke University Press.

Jenkins, H. (2001). "Convergence? I Diverge." *Technology Review* (June). http://www.technologyreview.com/business/12434/.

Jenkins, H. (2006). *Convergence Culture: Where Old and New Media Collide*. New York: New York University Press.

Jensen, K. B. (2010). *Media Convergence: The Three Degrees of Network, Mass, and Interpersonal Communication*. London: Routledge.

Johnson, S. (2005). *Everything Bad Is Good for You: How Today's Popular Culture Is Actually Making Us Smarter*. New York: Riverside.

Jones, D. (2002). *Horror: A Thematic History in Fiction and Film*. London: Arnold.

Jung, C. G. (1983). *The Essential Jung*. Princeton, NJ: Princeton University Press.

Kane, M. (2008). *Game Boys: Professional Videogaming's Rise from the Basement to the Big Time*. London: Penguin.

Katz, E., J. G. Blumler, and M. Gurevitch. (1974). "Utilization of Mass Communication by the Individual." In *The Uses of Mass Communications: Current Perspectives on Gratifications Research*, edited by Jay G. Blumler and Elihu Katz, 19–32. London: Sage.

Katz, E., M. Gurevitch, and H. Haas. (1973). "On the Use of Mass Media for Important Things." *American Sociological Review* 38 (April 1973): 164–81.

Katz, E., and T. Liebes. (1993). *The Export of Meaning: Cross-Cultural Readings of "Dallas."* Cambridge: Polity.

Kendrick, W. (1987). *The Secret Museum: Pornography in Modern Culture.* Berkeley: University of California Press.

Keren, M. (2006). *Blogosphere: The New Political Arena.* Lanham, MD: Rowman & Littlefield.

Key, W. B. (1972). *Subliminal Seduction.* New York: Signet.

Keyes, C. L. (2002). *Rap Music and Street Consciousness.* Urbana: University of Illinois Press.

Kiesling, S. F. (2004). "You've Come a Long Way, Dude: A History." *American Speech* 69: 321–27.

Kilpatrick, N. (2004). *The Goth Bible.* New York: St. Martin's.

King, G. (2000). *Spectacular Narratives: Hollywood in the Age of the Blockbuster.* London: I.B. Tauris.

Kirkpatrick, D. (2010). *The Facebook Effect: The Inside Story of the Company That Is Connecting the World.* New York: Simon and Schuster.

Klaehu, J., ed. (2007). *Inside the World of Comic Books.* Montreal: Black Rose.

Klein, N. (2000). *No Logo: Taking Aim at the Brand Bullies.* Toronto: Knopf.

Klein, R. (1993). *Cigarettes Are Sublime.* Durham, NC: Duke University Press.

Kornberger, M. (2010). *Brand Society: How Brands Transform Management and Lifestyle.* Cambridge: Cambridge University Press.

Kristeva, J. (1969). *Séméiotiké: Recherches pour un sémanalyse.* Paris: Seuil.

Kundera, M. (1984). *The Unbearable Lightness of Being.* New York: Harper Perennial.

Kundera, M. (1991). *Immortality.* New York: Harper Perennial.

Kutner, L., and C. K. Olson. (2009). *Grand Theft Childhood: The Surprising Truth about Violent Video Games.* New York: Simon and Schuster.

Lahue, K. C. (1969). *Continued Next Week: A History of the Moving Picture Serial.* Norman: University of Oklahoma Press.

Lanier, J. (2010). *You Are Not a Gadget: A Manifesto.* New York: Knopf.

Laroche, P. (2007). *On Words: Insight into How our Words Work and Don't.* Oak Park, IL: Marion Street Press.

Lasn, K. (2000). *Culture Jam: The Uncooling of America.* New York: Morrow.

Lazarsfeld, P., et al. (1948). *The People's Choice.* New York: Columbia University Press.

Lear, J. (2011). *Insight by Surprise: A Case for Irony.* Cambridge, MA: Harvard University Press.

Lee, Joan H. (2011). *What Does texting Do 2 Language?* Calgary: University of Calgary Master's Thesis.

Leiss, W., S. Kline, S. Jhally, and J. Botterill. (2005). *Social Communication in Advertising: Consumption in the Mediated Marketplace.* London: Routledge.

Leland, J. (2004). *Hip: The History.* New York: HarperCollins.

Lenhart, A. (2011). "More and More Teens on Cell Phones." *Pew Internet and American Life Project.* Accessed September 1, 2011. http://pewresearch.org/pubs/1315/teens-use-of-cell-phones.

Leroy, M. (1997). *Some Girls Do: Why Women Do and Don't Make the First Move.* London: HarperCollins.

Lévi-Strauss, C. (1962). *La pensée sauvage.* Paris: Plon.

Lévi-Strauss, C. (1978). *Myth and Meaning: Cracking the Code of Culture.* Toronto: University of Toronto Press.

Levine, E. (2007). *Wallowing in Sex: The New Sexual Culture of 1970s American Television.* Durham, NC: Duke University Press.

Lieberman, A., and P. Esgate. (2014). *The Definitive Guide to Entertainment Marketing.* 2nd ed. Upper Saddle River, NJ: Pearson.

Light, A., ed. (1999). *The Vibe History of Hip-Hop.* New York: Three Rivers Press.

Lippmann, W. (1922). *Public Opinion.* New York: Macmillan.

Liu, Y., and L. J. Shrum. (2002). "What Is Interactivity and Is It Always Such a Good Thing? Implications of Definition, Person, and Situation for the Influence of Interactivity on Advertising Effectiveness." *Journal of Advertising* 31: 53–64.

Lopiano-Misdom, J., and J. De Luca. (1997). *Street Trends: How Today's Alternative Youth Cultures Are Creating Tomorrow's Mainstream Markets.* New York: Harper Business.

Lough, J. (2002). "The Analysis of Popular Culture." In *The Media Book*, edited by C. Newbold, O. Boyd-Barrett, and H. Van Den Bulck. London: Arnold.

Lyotard, J.-F. (1984). *The Postmodern Condition: A Report on Knowledge.* Minneapolis: University of Minnesota Press.

MacDonald, I. (1995). *Revolution in the Head: The Beatles' Records and the Sixties.* London: Pimlico.

Marcus, G. (1976). *Mystery Train.* New York: Dutton.

Marcus, G. (1991). *Dead Elvis: A Chronicle of a Cultural Obsession.* New York: Anchor Books.

Marcuse, H. (1964). *One-Dimensional Man.* Boston: Beacon Press.

Marks, C., and R. Tannenbaum. (2010). *I Want My MTV: The Uncensored Story of the Music Video Revolution.* New York: Dutton.

Marshall, P. D. (1997). *Celebrity and Power: Fame in Contemporary Culture.* Minneapolis: University of Minnesota Press.

Marwick, A. E. (2013). *Status Update: Celebrity, Publicity, and Branding in the Social Media Age.* New Haven, CT: Yale University Press.

McCombs, M. E., and D. L. Shaw. (1972). "The Agenda-Setting Function of Mass Media." *Public Opinion Quarterly* 36: 176–87.

McCombs, M. E., and D. L. Shaw. (1993). "The Evolution of Agenda-Setting Research: Twenty-Five Years in the Marketplace of Ideas." *Journal of Communication* 43: 58–67.

McCracken, S. (1998). *Pulp: Reading Popular Fiction*. Manchester, UK: Manchester University Press.

McKinney, D. (2004). *Magic Circles: The Beatles in Dream and History*. Cambridge, MA: Harvard University Press.

McLelland, B. (2006). *Slayers and Their Vampires: A Cultural History of Killing the Dead*. Ann Arbor: University of Michigan Press.

McLuhan, M. (1951). *The Mechanical Bride: Folklore of Industrial Man*. New York: Vanguard.

McLuhan, M. (1962). *The Gutenberg Galaxy*. Toronto: University of Toronto Press.

McLuhan, M. (1964). *Understanding Media: The Extensions of Man*. London: Routledge and Kegan Paul.

McMorran, W. (2006). *From Quixote to Caractacus: Influence, Intertextuality, and Chitty Chitty Bang*. Hoboken, NJ: Blackwell Publishers.

McQuail, D. (2000). *Mass Communication Theory: An Introduction*. London: Sage.

Meehan, E. R. (2005). *Why TV Is Not Our Fault: Television Programming, Viewers, and Who's Really in Control*. Lanham, MD: Rowman & Littlefield.

Meikle, G., and Young, S. (2012). *Media Convergence: Networked Digital Media in Everyday Life*. New York: Palgrave Macmillan.

Miller, D. L. (2014). *Supreme City: How Jazz Age Manhattan Gave Birth to Modern America*. New York: Simon & Schuster.

Miller, J. (1999). *Flowers in the Dustbin: The Rise of Rock and Roll, 1947–1977*. New York: Simon and Schuster.

Mills, B. (2005). *Television Sitcom*. London: British Film Institute.

Milner, M. (2004). *Freaks, Geeks, and Cool Kids: American Teenagers, Schools, and the Culture of Consumption*. London: Routledge.

Montgomery, K. C. (2007). *Generation Digital: Politics, Commerce, and Childhood in the Age of the Internet*. Cambridge, MA: MIT Press.

Moores, S. (1993). *Interpreting Audiences: The Ethnography of Media Consumption*. London: Sage.

Muggleton, D. (2002). *Inside Subculture: The Postmodern Meaning of Style*. New York: Oxford University Press.

Munson, W. (1993). *All Talk: The Talkshow in Media Culture*. Philadelphia: Temple University Press.

Murray, S., and L. Ouellette, eds. (2004). *Reality TV: Remaking Television Culture*. New York: New York University Press.

Nathan, D. (2007). *Pornography*. Toronto: Groundwork Books.

Neer, R. (2001). *FM: The Rise and Fall of Rock Radio*. New York: Villard.

Newcomb, H. (2000). *Television: The Critical View*. New York: Oxford University Press.

Newman, K. (1990). *Wild West Movies*. New York: Bloomsbury.

Noll, M. (2006). *The Evolution of Media*. Lanham, MD: Rowman & Littlefield.

O'Brien, S., and I. Szeman. (2004). *Popular Culture: A User's Guide*. Toronto: Thomson.

Otto, B. K. (2007). *Fools Are Everywhere: The Court Jester around the World*. Chicago: University of Chicago Press.

Owram, D. (1996). *Born at the Right Time: A History of the Baby Boom Generation*. Toronto: University of Toronto Press.

Packard, V. (1957). *The Hidden Persuaders*. New York: McKay.

Padel, R. (2000). *I'm a Man: Sex, Gods and Rock 'n' Roll*. London: Faber and Faber.

Paglia, C. (1992). *Sex, Art, and American Culture*. New York: Random House.

Palmer, J. (1978). *Thrillers: Genesis and Structure of a Popular Genre*. London: Arnold.

Palmer, R. (1995). *Rock & Roll: An Unruly History*. New York: Harmony Books.

Panati, C. (1984). *Browser's Book of Beginnings*. Boston: Houghton Mifflin.

Parissien, S. (2014). *The Life of the Automobile*. New York: St. Martin's.

Peiss, K. (1998). *Hope in a Jar: The Making of America's Beauty Culture*. New York: Metropolitan Books.

Peril, L. (2006). *Bluestockings, Sex Kittens, and Coeds, Then and Now*. New York: W. W. Norton.

Perkins, W. E. (1996). *Droppin' Science: Critical Essays on Rap Music and Hip Hop Culture*. Philadelphia: Temple University Press.

Perlmutter, D. D. (2009). *Blogwars*. Oxford: Oxford University Press.

Phoca, S., and R. Wright. (1999). *Introducing Postfeminism*. Cambridge: Icon Books.

Pinsky, Mark I. (2004). *The Gospel According to Disney: Faith, Trust, and Pixie Dust*. Louisville, KY: Westminster John Knox Press.

Pollock, B. (1993). *Hipper Than Our Kids: A Rock & Roll Journal of the Baby Boom Generation*. New York: Schirmer.

Potter, R. A. (1995). *Spectacular Vernaculars: Hip-Hop and the Politics of Postmodernism*. Albany: State University of New York Press.

Pough, G. D. (2004). *Check It While I Wreck It: Black Womanhood, Hip Hop Culture and the Public Sphere*. Boston: Northeastern University Press.

Propp, V. J. (1928). *Morphology of the Folktale*. Austin: University of Texas Press.

Queenan, J. (2000). *Balsamic Dreams: A Short but Self-Important History of the Baby Boomer Generation*. New York: Henry Holt.

Reynolds, R. (1992). *Super Heroes: A Modern Mythology*. Jackson: University of Mississippi Press.

Reynolds, S. (1999). *Generation Ecstasy: Into the World of Techno and Rave Culture*. London: Routledge.

Reynolds, S. (2010). *Retromania: Pop Culture's Addiction to Its Own Past*. New York: Faber and Faber.

Reynolds, S., and J. Press. (1995). *The Sex Revolts: Gender, Rebellion, and Rock 'n' Roll*. Cambridge, MA: Harvard University Press.

Ringmar, E. (2007). *A Blogger's Manifesto: Free Speech and Censorship in the Age of the Internet*. London: Anthem Press.

Robinson, F. M., and L. Davidson. (2007). *Pulp Culture: The Art of Fiction Magazines*. Portland: Collectors Press.

Robinson, L. S. (2004). *Wonderwomen: Feminisms and Superheroes.* London: Routledge.

Rodman, G. B. (1996). *Elvis after Elvis: The Posthumous Career of a Living Legend.* London: Routledge.

Rodzvilla, J., ed. (2009). *We've Got Blog: How Weblogs Are Changing Our Culture.* New York: Basic Books.

Rowe, D. (2011). *Global Media Sport: Flows, Forms and Futures.* London: Bloomsbury.

Rubin, M. (1999). *Thrillers.* Cambridge: Cambridge University Press.

Sarracino, C., and K. M. Scott. (2008). *The Porning of America: The Rise of Porn Culture, What It Means, and Where We Go from Here.* Boston: Beacon.

Saussure, F. (1916). *Cours de linguistique générale.* Paris: Payot.

Savan, L. (2005). *Slam Dunks and No-Brainers: Language in Your Life, the Media, Business, Politics, and, Like, Whatever.* New York: Knopf.

Sax, D. (2014). *The Tastemakers: Why We're Crazy for Cupcakes but Fed Up with Fondue.* New York: Public Affairs.

Scott, L. M. (2005). *Fresh Lipstick: Redressing Fashion and Feminism.* New York: Palgrave Macmillan.

Sebba, M. (2007). *Spelling and Society: The Culture and Politics of Orthography around the World.* Cambridge: Cambridge University Press.

Server, L. (1993). *Danger Is My Business: An Illustrated History of the Fabulous Pulp Magazines.* San Francisco: Chronicle Books.

Shaffer, P. (1993). *Amadeus.* London: Penguin.

Shifman, L. (2013). *Memes in Digital Culture.* Cambridge, MA: MIT Press.

Siegel, C. (2005). *Goth's Dark Empire.* Bloomington: Indiana University Press.

Sklar, R. (1994). *Movie-Made America: A Cultural History of American Movies.* New York: Vintage.

Slevin, J. (2000). *The Internet and Society.* London: Polity.

Smith, C. (2007). *One for the Girls! The Pleasures and Practices of Reading Women's Porn.* Chicago: University of Chicago Press.

South, J. B., and J. M. Held, eds. (2006). *Questions Are Forever: James Bond and Philosophy.* Chicago and Lasalle: Open Court.

Staiger, J. (2005). *Media Reception Studies.* New York: New York University Press.

Storey, J. (2003). *Inventing Popular Culture.* London: Blackwell.

Strangelove, M. (2010). *Watching YouTube: Extraordinary Videos by Ordinary People.* Toronto: University of Toronto Press.

Strausbaugh, J. (2001). *Rock Till You Drop.* London: Verso.

Stringer, J., ed. (2003). *Movie Blockbusters.* London: Routledge.

Szatmary, D. (1996). *A Time to Rock: A Social History of Rock 'n' Roll.* New York: Schirmer Books.

Tancer, B. (2008). *Click.* New York: Hyperion.

Taylor, T. L. (2006). *Play between Worlds: Exploring Online Culture.* Cambridge, MA: MIT Press.

Thompson, J. B. (2010). *Merchants of Culture: The Publishing Business in the Twenty-First Century*. New York: Polity.

Todorov, T. (1973). *The Fantastic: A Structural Approach to a Literary Genre*. Cleveland, OH: Press of Case Western Reserve University.

Turner, G. (1992). *British Cultural Studies*. London: Routledge.

Turner, G. (2004). *Understanding Celebrity*. London: Sage Publications.

Twinn, F. (2007). *The Miscellany of Sex: Tantalizing Travels through Love, Lust and Libido*. London: Capella.

Twitchell, J. B. (2000). *Twenty Ads That Shook the World*. New York: Crown.

Van Dijk, J. (1999). *The Network Society*. London: Sage.

Van Zoonen, L. (1994). *Feminist Media Studies*. London: Sage.

Vander Veer, E. A. (2008). *Facebook: The Missing Manual*. New York: Pogue.

Veblen, T. ([1899] 1994). *The Theory of the Leisure Class*. New York: Penguin Classics.

Vice, S. (1997). *Introducing Bakhtin*. Manchester, UK: Manchester University Press.

Vidal, G. (1974). *Homage to Daniel Shays: Collected Essays 1952–1972*. New York: Random House.

Wachal, R. S. (2002). Taboo or not Taboo: That Is the Question. *American Speech* 77: 195–206.

Walker, J. (2001). *Rebels on the Air: An Alternative History of Radio in America*. New York: New York University Press.

Weaver, D. H. (2007). Thoughts on Agenda Setting, Framing, and Priming. *Journal of Communication* 57 (2007): 142–47.

Webster, F. (2006). *Theories of the Information Society*. London: Routledge.

Welles, O. (1956). Cited in the *New York Herald Tribune*, October 12, 1956.

Whiteley, S. (1992). *The Space between the Notes: Rock and the Counterculture*. London: Routledge.

Whiteley, S., ed. (1997). *Sexing the Groove: Popular Music and Gender*. London: Routledge.

Wicke, P. (1987). *Rock Music: Culture, Aesthetics and Sociology*. Cambridge: Cambridge University Press.

Williams, R. (1982). *The Sociology of Culture*. New York: Schocken.

Willis, D. C. (1997). *Horror and Science Fiction Films*. Lanham, MD: Scarecrow Press.

Willis, P. E. (1978). *Profane Culture*. London: Routledge and Kegan Paul.

Wise, R. (2000). *Multimedia: A Critical Introduction*. London: Routledge.

Wright, A. (2007). *Gothic Fiction*. New York: Palgrave Macmillan.

Wright, B. W. (2001). *Comic Book Nation: The Transformation of Youth Culture in America*. Baltimore: Johns Hopkins University Press.

Wright, W. (1975). *Six-Guns and Society*. Berkeley: University of California Press.

ONLINE RESOURCES

Academy of Motion Picture Arts and Sciences: www.oscars.org
Ad Council: www.adcouncil.org
Ad Forum: www.adforum.com
Adbusters: www.adbusters.org
Advertising Age: www.adage.com/datacenter.cms
Advertising History: www.scriptorium.lib.duke.edu/hartman
All Music Guide: www.allmusic.com
Center for Democracy and Technology: www.cdt.org
Classic Television: www.classic-tv.com
Critical Communication Theory: www.theory.org.uk
Hollywood Movies: www.hollywood.com
Images (Journal of Media Criticism): www.imagesjournal.com
International Federation of Journalists: www.ifj.org
Internet Movie Database: www.us.imdb.com
Internet Radio: www.radio-locator.com
Internet Society: www.isoc.org/internet
Journal of Popular Culture: www.blackwellpublishing.com
Magazine Publishers of America: www.magazine.org
Marshall McLuhan Studies: www.mcluhan.utoronto.ca
Media History: www.mediahistory.umn.edu
Media Literacy: www.mediaed.org, www.acmecoalition.org
Movieweb: www.movieweb.com
Netlingo: www.NetLingo.com
Netlore: www.urbanlegends.about.com
Pop Culture Sites: www.popcultures.com, www.urbandictionary.com
Popular Culture Association: www.h-net.org/~pcaaca
Product Placement: www.productplacement.co.nz

Radio History: www.radiohistory.org
Recording Industry Association of America: www.riaa.com
Rock and Roll Hall of Fame: www.rockhall.com
Sundance Film Festival: www.sundance.org
Ultimate TV: www.ultimatetv.com
Web Journal of Mass Communication Research: www.scripps.ohiou.edu/wjmcr/index.htm
Web Radio: www.radio-directory.com

INDEX

ABOUT THE AUTHOR

Marcel Danesi is professor of anthropology, semiotics, and communication theory at the University of Toronto.